Treasure of Ambedkar Series 09

THE BUDDHA
AND
HIS DHAMMA

Treasure of Ambedkar Series 09

THE BUDDHA AND HIS DHAMMA

Dr B.R. Ambedkar

KALPAZ

Treasure of Ambedkar Series 09

THE BUDDHA AND HIS DHAMMA

ISBN: 978-93-5128-268-6

First Published 1957
Reprint **2017**, in India by
Kalpaz Publications
C-30, Satyawati Nagar,
Delhi – 110052
E-mail: kalpaz@hotmail.com
Ph.: 9212142040

Printed at: G. Print Process, Delhi

Contents

Campaign of Conversion

What the Buddha Taught

Religion and Dhamma

The Sangh

He and His Contemporaries

The Wanderer's Last Journey

The Man who was Siddharth Gautama

INTRODUCTION

INDICATIONS of a growth in the volume of interest in Buddhism are noticeable in some sections of the Indian people. Along with it there is naturally a growing demand for a clear and consistent statement of the life and teachings of the Buddha.

Anyone who is not a Buddhist finds it extremely difficult to present the life and teachings of the Buddha in a manner which would make it a consistent whole. Depending on the Nikayas, not only the presentation of a consistent story of the life of the Buddha becomes a difficult thing and the presentation of some parts of his teachings becomes much more so. Indeed it would not be an exaggeration to say that of all the founders of religions in the world the presentation of the life and teachings of the founder of Buddhism presents a problem which is quite puzzling if not baffling. Is it not necessary that these problems should be solved and the path for the understanding of Buddhism be made clear? Is it not time that those who are Buddhists should take up these problems at least for general discussion and throw what light they can on these problems?

With a view to raise a discussion on these problems I propose to set them out here. The first problem relates to the main event in the life of the Buddha, namely, Parivraja. Why did the Buddha take Parivraja? The traditional answer is that he took Parivraja because he saw a dead person, a sick person and an old person. This answer is absurd on the face of it. The Buddha took Parivraja at the age of 29. If he took Parivraja as a result of these three sights, how is it he did not see these three sights earlier? These are common events occurring by hundreds and the Buddha could not have failed to come across them earlier. It is impossible to accept the traditional explanation that this was the first time he saw them. The explanation is not plausible and does not appeal to reason. But if this is not the answer to the question, what is the real answer?

The second problem is created by the four Aryan Truths. Do they form part of the original teachings of the Buddha? This formula cuts at the root of Buddhism. If life is sorrow, death is sorrow and rebirth is sorrow, then there is an end of everything. Neither religion nor philosophy can help a man to achieve happiness in the world. If there is no escape from sorrow, then what can religion do, what can Buddha do to relieve man from such sorrow which is ever there in birth itself? The four Aryan Truths are a great stumbling block in the way of non-Buddhists accepting the gospel of Buddhism. For the four Aryan Truths deny hope to man. The four Aryan Truths make the gospel of the Buddha a gospel of pessimism. Do they form part of the original gospel or are they a later accretion by the monks?

The third problem relates to the doctrines of soul, of karma and rebirth. The Buddha denied the existence of the soul. But he is also said to have affirmed the doctrine of karma and rebirth. At once a question arises. If there is no soul, how can there be karma? If there is no soul, how can there be rebirth? These are baffling questions. In what sense did the Buddha use the words karma and rebirth? Did he use them in a different sense than the sense in which they were used by the Brahmins of his day? If so, in what sense? Did he use them in the same sense in which the Brahmins used them? If so, is there not a terrible contradiction between the denial of the soul and the affirmation of karma and rebirth? This contradiction needs to be resolved.

The fourth problem relates to the Bhikkhu. What was the object of the Buddha in creating the Bhikkhu? Was the object to create a perfect man? Or was his object to create a social servant devoting his life to service of the people and being their friend, guide and philosopher? This is a very real question. On it depends the future of Buddhism. If the Bhikkhu is only a perfect man he is of no use to the propagation of Buddhism because though a perfect man he is a selfish man. If, on the other hand, he is a social servant he may prove to be the hope of Buddhism. This question must be decided not so much in the interest of doctrinal consistency but in the interest of the future of Buddhism.

If I may say so, the pages of the journal of the Mahabodhi Society make, to me at any rate, dull reading. This is not because the material presented is not interesting and instructive. The dullness is due to the fact that it seems to fall upon a passive set of readers. After reading an article, one likes to know what the reader of the journal has to say about it. But the reader never gives out his reaction. This silence on the part of the reader is a great discouragement to the writer. I hope my questions will excite the readers to come and make their contribution to their solution.

PROLOGUE

"FROM time to time men find themselves forced to reconsider current and inherited beliefs and ideas, to gain some harmony between present and past experience, and to reach a position which shall satisfy the demands of feeling and reflexion and give confidence for facing the future. If, at the present day, religion, as a subject of critical or scientific inquiry, of both practical and theoretical significance has attracted increasing attention, this can be ascribed to (*a*) the rapid progress of scientific knowledge and thought ; (*b*) the deeper intellectual interest in the subject ; (*c*) the widespread tendencies in all parts of the world to reform or reconstruct religion, or even to replace it by some body of thought, more 'rational' and 'scientific' or less 'superstitious' ; and (*d*) the effect of social, political, and international events of a sort which, in the past, have both influenced and been influenced by religion. Whenever the ethical or moral value of activities or conditions is questioned, the value of religion is involved ; and all deep-stirring experiences invariably compel a reconsideration of the most fundamental ideas, whether they are explicitly religious or not. Ultimately there arise problems of justice, human destiny, God, and the universe ; and these in turn involve problems of the relation between 'religious' and other ideas, the validity of ordinary knowledge, and practicable conceptions of 'experience' and 'reality.'

—From "Encyclopædia of Religion and Ethics," Vol. X, p. 669.

BOOK I

Siddharth Gautama—How a Bodhisatta became the Buddha

Part I—From Birth to Parivraja

Part II—Renunciation for Ever

Part III—In Search of New Light

Part IV—Enlightenment and the Vision of a New Way

Part V—The Buddha and His Predecessors

Part VI—The Buddha and His Contemporaries

Part VII—Comparison and Contrast

PART I

From Birth to Parivraja

§ *1. His Kula*

1. Going back to the sixth century B.C., Northern India did not form a single Sovereign State.

2. The country was divided into many States, some large, some small. Of these some were monarchical and some non-monarchical. I

3. The monarchical States were altogether sixteen in number. 1 They were known by the name of Anga, Magadha, Kasi, Kosala, Vriji, Malla, Chedi, Vatsa, Kuru, Panchala, Matsya, Saursena, Asmaka, Avanti, Gandhara and Kambhoja.

4. The non-monarchical States were those of the Sakyas of Kapilvatsu, the Mallas of Pava and Kushinara, the Lichhavis of Vaisali, the Videhas of Mithila, the Koliyas of Ramagam, the Bulis of Allakapa, the Kalingas of Resaputta, the Mauriyas of Pipphalvana and the Bhaggas with their capital on Sumsumara Hill.

5. The monarchical States were known as Janapada and the non-monarchical as Sangh or Gana.

6. Not much is known about the nature of the polity of the Sakyas of Kapilvatsu, whether it was republican or oligarchic.

7. This much, however, is definitely known, that there were many ruling families in the Republic of the Sakyas and that they ruled in turns.

8. The head of the ruling family was known as Raja.

9. At the time of the birth of Siddharth Gautama it was the turn of Suddhodana to be the Raja.

10. The Sakya State was situated in the north-east corner of India. It was an independent State. But at a later stage the King of Kosala had succeeded in establishing his paramountcy over it.

11. The result of this paramountcy was that the Sakya State could not exercise certain sovereign powers without the sanction of the King of Kosala.

12. Of the kingdoms then in existence, Kosala was a powerful kingdom. So was the kingdom of Magadha. Pasanedi, King of Kosala and Bimbisara, King of Magadha, were the contemporaries of
I Siddharth Gautama.

2

§ 2. *His Ancestry*

1. The capital of the Sakyas was the city called Kapilavatsu, perhaps after the name of the great Rationalist Kapila.

2. There lived in Kapilavatsu a Sakya by name Jaya Sena. Sinahu was his son. Sinahu was married to Kaccana. Sinahu had five sons, Suddhodana, Dhotodana, Sakkodana and Amitodana. Besides five sons, Sinahu had two daughters, Amita and Pamita.

3. The Gotra of the family was Aditya.

4. Suddhodana was married to Mahamaya. Her father's name was Anjana and mother's Sulakshana. Anjana was a Koliya and was residing in the village called Devadaha.

5. Suddhodana was a man of great military prowess. When Suddhodana had shown his martial powers he was allowed to take a second wife and he chose Mahaprajapati. She was the elder sister of Mahamaya.

6. Suddhodana was a wealthy person. The lands he held were very extensive and the retinue under him was very large. He employed, it is said, one thousand ploughs to till the land he owned.

7. He lived quite a luxurious life and had many palaces.

§ 3. *His Birth*

1. To Suddhodana was born Siddharth Gautama and this was the manner of Gautama's birth.

2. It was a custom among the Sakyas to observe an annual midsummer festival which fell in the month of Ashad. It was celebrated by all the Sakyas

throughout the State and also by the members of the ruling family.

3. It was the usual practice to celebrate the festival for seven days.

4. On one occasion Mahamaya decided to observe the festival with gaiety, with splendour, with flowers, with perfume, but without drinking intoxicants.

5. On the seventh day she rose early, bathed in scented water, bestowed a gift of 4,00,000 pieces of money as alms, adorned herself with all precious ornaments, ate choicest food, took upon herself the fast-day vows, and entered the splendidly adorned royal bedchamber to sleep.

6. That night Suddhodana and Mahamaya came together and Mahamaya conceived. Lying on the royal bed she fell asleep. While asleep she had a dream.

7. In her dreams she saw that the four world-guardians raised her as she was sleeping on her bed and carried her to the tableland of the Himalayas, placed her under a great sal tree and stood on one side.

8. The wives of the four world-guardians then approached and took her to the lake Mansarovar.

9. They bathed her, robed her in a dress, anointed her with perfumes and decked her with flowers in a manner fit to meet some divinity.

10. Then a Bodhisatta, by name Sumedha, appeared before her saying, " I have decided to take my last and final birth on this earth, will you consent to be my mother ? " She said, " Yes, with great pleasure." At this moment Mahamaya awoke.

11. Next morning Mahamaya told her dream to Suddhodana. Not knowing how to interpret the dream, Suddhodana summoned eight Brahmins who were most famous in divination.

12. They were Rama, Dhaga, Lakkana, Manti, Yanna, Suyama, Subhoga and Sudatta and prepared for them a befitting reception.

13. He caused the ground to be strewn with festive flowers and prepared high seats for them.

14. He filled the bowls of the Brahmins with

gold and silver and fed them on cooked ghee, honey, sugar and excellent rice and milk. He also gave them other gifts such as new clothes and tawny cows.

15. When the Brahmins were propitiated, Sud-
I dhodana related to them the dream Mahamaya had, and said, "Tell me what it means."

4 16. The Brahmins said : "Be not anxious. You will have a son, and if he leads a householder's life he will become a universal monarch, and if he leaves his home and goes forth into a homeless state, and becomes a sanyasi, he will become a Buddha, a dispeller of illusions in the world."

17. Bearing the Bodhisatta in her womb like oil in a vessel for ten lunar months, Mahamaya, as her time of delivery was coming nearer, desired to go to her parents' home for delivery. Addressing her husband, she said : "I wish to go to Devadaha, the city of my father."

18. "Thou knowest that thy wishes will be done," replied Suddhodana. Having seated her in a golden palanquin borne by couriers, he sent her forth with a great retinue to her father's house.

19. Mahamaya, on her way to Devadaha, had to pass through a pleasure-grove of sal trees and other trees, flowering and non-flowering. It was known as the Lumbini Grove.

20. As the palanquin was passing through it, the whole Lumbini Grove seemed like the heavenly Cittalata grove or like a banqueting pavilion adorned for a mighty king.

21. From the roots to the tips of the branches the trees were loaded with fruits, flowers and numberless bees of the fine colours, uttering curious sounds, and flocks of various kinds of birds, singing sweet melodies.

22. Witnessing the scene, there arose a desire in the heart of Mahamaya for halting and sporting therein for a while. Accordingly she told the couriers to take her in the sal-grove and wait there.

23. Mahamaya alighted from her palanquin and walked up to the foot of a royal sal tree. A pleasant wind, not too strong, was blowing and the

boughs of the trees were heaving up and down and Mahamaya felt like catching one of them.

24. Luckily one of the boughs heaved down sufficiently low to enable her to catch it. So she rose on her toes and caught the bough. Immediately she was lifted up by its upward movement and being shaken, she felt the pangs of childbirth. While holding the branch of the sal tree she was delivered of a son in a standing position.

25. The child was born in the year 563 B.C. on the Vaishakha Paurnima day.

26. Suddhodana and Mahamaya were married for a long time. But they had no issue. Ultimately when a son was born to them his birth was celebrated with great rejoicing, with great pomp and ceremony by Suddhodana and his family and also by the Sakyas.

27. At the time of the birth of the child it was the turn of Suddhodana to be the ruler of Kapilavatsu and as such was in the enjoyment of the title of Raja. Naturally the boy was called Prince.

§ 4. *Visit by Asita*

1. At the moment when the child was born there dwelt on the Himalayas a great sage named Asita.

2. Asita heard that the gods over the space of the sky were shouting the word "Buddha" and making it resound. He beheld them waving their garments and coursing hither and thither in delight. He thought, what if I were to go and find out the land in which he was born?

3. Surveying with his divine eyes the whole of the Jambudvipa, Asita saw that a boy was born in the house of Suddhodana shining with all brilliance and that it was over his birth that the gods were excited.

4. So the great sage Asita with his nephew Nardatta rose up and came to the abode of Raja Suddhodana and stood at the door of his palace.

5. Now Asita, the sage, saw that at the door of Suddhodana's palace many hundred thousand beings

had assembled. So he approached the door-keeper and said, " Go, man, inform the Raja that a sage is standing at the door."

6. Then the door-keeper approached Suddhodana
I and with clasped hands said, " Know, O Raja, that
6 an aged sage, old and advanced in years, stands at the
door, and says that he desires to see you."

7. The king prepared a seat for Asita and said to the door-keeper, " Let the sage enter." So coming out of the palace the door-keeper said to Asita : " Please go in."

8. Now Asita approached King Suddhodana and, standing in front of him, said, " Victory, Victory, O Raja, may you live long, and rule thy kingdom righteously."

9. Then Suddhodana in reverence to Asita fell at his feet and offered him the seat ; and seeing him seated in comfort, Suddhodana said, " I do not remember to have seen thee before this, O Sage! With what purpose hast thou come hither? What is the cause? "

10. Thereupon Asita said to Suddhodana, " A son is born to thee, O Raja! Desiring to see him, have I come."

11. Suddhodana said, " The boy is asleep, O Sage! Will you wait for a while? " The sage said, " Not long, O King, do such great beings sleep. Such good beings are by nature wakeful."

12. Then did the child out of compassion for Asita, the great sage, make a sign of awaking.

13. Seeing that the child had become awake, Suddhodana took the boy firmly in both hands and brought him into the presence of the sage.

14. Asita observing the child, beheld that it was endowed with the thirty-two marks of a great man and adorned with the eighty minor marks, his body surpassing that of Sakra, Brahma, and his aura surpassing them a hundred thousand-fold, breathed forth this solemn utterance, " Marvellous, verily, is this person that has appeared in the world," and rising from his seat clasped his hands, fell at his feet, made a

rightwise circuit round and taking the child in his own hand stood in contemplation.

15. Asita knew the old well-known prophecy
that anyone endowed with the thirty-two marks of a
great man, as Gautama was, has two careers open I
to him, and no third. "If he becomes a householder,
he will become a universal monarch. But if he goes 7
forth from the home to a homeless life, he will become
a fully enlightened Buddha."

16. Asita was sure that the child would not remain a householder.

17. And looking at the child he wept, and shedding tears, sighed deeply.

18. Suddhodana beheld Asita shedding tears, and sighing deeply.

19. Beholding him thus weeping, the hair of his body rose, and in distress Suddhodana said to Asita, "Why, O Sage, dost thou weep and shed tears, and sigh so deeply? Surely, there is no misfortune in store for the child."

20. At this Asita said to the Raja, "O King, I weep not for the sake of the child. There will be no misfortune for him. But I weep for myself."

21. "And why?" asked Suddhodana. Asita replied, "I am old, aged, advanced in years, and this boy will without doubt become a Buddha and attain supreme and complete enlightenment and having done so, will turn the supreme wheel of the Doctrine that has not been turned before him by any other being in the world; for the weal and happiness of the world will he teach his Doctrine."

22. "The religious life, the Doctrine, that he will proclaim will be good in the beginning, good in the middle, good in the end, complete in the letter and the spirit, whole and pure."

23. "Just as an Oudumbara flower at some time and place arises in the world, even so at some time and place, after countless cycles, revered Buddhas arise in the world. So also, O Raja! this boy will without doubt obtain supreme, complete enlightenment, and having done so will take countless beings across the

ocean of sorrow and misery to a state of happiness."

24. "But I shall not see that Buddha. Hence, O Raja, I weep and in sadness I sigh deeply, for I shall not be able to reverence him."

25. The king thereafter offered to the great sage Asita and Nardatta, his nephew, suitable food, and having given him robes made a rightwise circuit round him.

26. Thereupon Asita said to Nardatta, his nephew, "When thou shalt hear, Nardatta, that the child has become a Buddha, then go and take refuge in his teachings. This shall be for thy weal and welfare and happiness." So saying Asita took leave of the Raja and departed for his hermitage.

§ 5. *Death of Mahamaya*

1. On the fifth day the ceremony of name-giving took place. The name chosen for the child was Siddharth. His clan name was Gautama. Popularly, therefore, he came to be called Siddharth Gautama.

2. In the midst of rejoicing over the birth and the naming of the child Mahamaya suddenly fell ill and her illness became very serious.

3. Realising that her end was near she called Suddhodana and Prajapati to her bedside and said : "I am sure that the prophecy made by Asita about my son will come true. My regret is that I will not live to see it fulfilled."

4. "My child will soon be a motherless child. But I am not worried in the least as to whether after me my child will be carefully nursed, properly looked after and brought up in a manner befitting his future."

5. "To you Prajapati, I entrust my child, I have no doubt that you will be to him more than his mother."

6. "Now do not be sorry. Permit me to die. God's call has come and His messengers are waiting to take me." So saying, Mahamaya breathed her last. Both Suddhodana and Prajapati were greatly grieved and wept bitterly.

7. Siddharth was only seven days old when his

mother died.

8. Siddharth had a younger brother by name Nanda. He was the son of Suddhodana born to Mahaprajapati.

9. He had also several cousins, Mahanama and Anuruddha, sons of his uncle Suklodan, Ananda, son of his uncle Amitodan, and Devadatta, son of his aunt Amita. Mahanama was older than Siddharth and Ananda was younger.

10. Siddharth grew up in their company.

§ 6. *Childhood and Education*

1. When Siddharth was able to walk and speak the elders of the Sakyas assembled and asked Suddhodana that the boy should be taken to the temple of the village goddess Abhya.

2. Suddhodana agreed and asked Mahaprajapati to dress the boy.

3. While she was doing so the child Siddharth, with a most sweet voice, asked his aunt where he was being taken. On learning that he was being taken to the temple he smiled. But he went, conforming to the custom of the Sakyas.

4. At the age of eight Siddharth started his education.

5. Those very eight Brahmins whom Suddhodana had invited to interpret Mahamaya's dream and who had predicted his future were his first teachers.

6. After they had taught him what they knew Suddhodana sent for Sabbamitta of distinguished descent and of high lineage in the land of Uddikka, a philologist and grammarian, well read in the Vedas, Vedangas and Upanishads. Having poured out water of dedication from a golden vase, Suddhodana handed over the boy to his charge, to be taught. He was his second teacher.

7. Under him Gautama mastered all the philosophic systems prevalent in his day.

8. Besides this he had learned the science of concentration and meditation from one Bhardawaj, a

disciple of Alara Kalam, who had his ashram at Kapilavatsu.

§ 7. *Early Traits*

I

1. Whenever he went to his father's farm and
10 found no work he repaired to a quiet place, and practised meditation.

2. While everything for the cultivation of the mind was provided, his education in the military science befitting a Kshatriya was not neglected.

3. For Suddhodana was anxious not to make the mistake of having cultivated the mind of his son at the cost of his manliness.

4. Siddharth was of kindly disposition. He did not like exploitation of man by man.

5. Once he went to his father's farm with some of his friends and saw the labourers ploughing the land, raising bunds, cutting trees, etc., dressed in scanty clothes under a hot burning sun.

6. He was greatly moved by the sight.

7. He said to his friends, can it be right that one man should exploit another ? How can it be right that the labourer should toil and the master should live on the fruits of his labour ?

8. His friends did not know what to say. For they believed in the old philosophy of life that the worker was born to serve and that in serving his master he was only fulfilling his destiny.

9. The Sakyas used to celebrate a festival called Vapramangal. It was a rustic festival performed on the day of sowing. On this day custom had made it obligatory on every Sakya to do ploughing personally.

10. Siddharth always observed the custom and did engage himself in ploughing.

11. Though a man of learning, he did not despise manual labour.

12. He belonged to a warrior class and had been taught archery and the use of weapons. But he did not like causing unnecessary injury.

13. He refused to join hunting parties. His

friends used to say : " Are you afraid of tigers ? " He used to retort by saying, " I know you are not going to kill tigers, you are going to kill harmless animals such as deer and rabbits."

14. " If not for hunting, come to witness how I
accurate is the aim of your friends," they said. Even
such invitations Siddharth refused, saying ; " I do 11
not like to see the killing of innocent animals."

15. Prajapati Gautami was deeply worried over this attitude of Siddharth.

16. She used to argue with him saying : " You have forgotten that you are a Kshatriya and fighting is your duty. The art of fighting can be learned only through hunting for only by hunting can you learn how to aim accurately. Hunting is a training ground for the warrior class."

17. Siddharth often used to ask Gautami : " But, mother, why should a Kshatriya fight ? And Gautami used to reply : " Because it is his duty."

18. Siddharth was never satisfied by her answer. He used to ask Gautami : " Tell me, how can it be the duty of man to kill man ? " Gautami argued, " Such an attitude is good for an ascetic. But Kshatriyas must fight. If they don't, who will protect the kingdom ? "

19. " But mother ! If all Kshatriyas loved one another, would they not be able to protect their kingdom without resort to killing ? " Gautami had to leave him to his own opinion.

20. He tried to induce his companions to join him in practising meditation. He taught them the proper pose. He taught them to fix their mind on a subject. He advised them to select such thoughts as " May I be happy, may my relations be happy, may all living animals be happy."

21. But his friends did not take the matter seriously. They laughed at him.

22. On closing their eyes they could not concentrate on their subject of meditation. Instead, some saw before their eyes deer for shooting or sweets for eating.

23. His father and his mother did not like his partiality for meditation. They thought it was so contrary to the life of a Kshatriya.

24. Siddharth believed that meditation on right
I subjects led to development of the spirit of universal
love. He justified himself by saying : "When we
12 think of living things, we begin with distinction and
discrimination. We separate friends from enemies, we separate animals we rear from human beings. We love friends and domesticated animals and we hate enemies and wild animals."

25. "This dividing line we must overcome and this we can do when we in our contemplation rise above the limitations of practical life." Such was his reasoning.

26. His childhood was marked by the presence of supreme sense of compassion.

27. Once he went to his father's farm. During recess he was resting under a tree enjoying the peace and beauty of nature. While so seated a bird fell from the sky just in front of him.

28. The bird had been shot at by an arrow which had pierced its body and was fluttering about in great agony.

29. Siddharth rushed to the help of the bird. He removed the arrow, dressed its wound and gave it water to drink. He picked up the bird, came to the place where he was seated and wrapped up the bird in his upper garment and held it next to his chest to give it warmth.

30. Siddharth was wondering who could have shot this innocent bird. Before long there came his cousin Devadatta armed with all the implements of shooting. He told Siddharth that he had shot a bird flying in the sky, the bird was wounded but it flew some distance and fell somewhere there, and asked him if he had seen it.

31. Siddharth replied in the affirmative and showed him the bird which had by that time completely recovered.

32. Devadatta demanded that the bird be handed

over to him. This Siddharth refused to do. A sharp argument ensued between the two.

33. Devadatta argued that he was the owner of the bird because by the rules of the game, he who kills a game becomes the owner of the game.

34. Siddharth denied the validity of the rule. He argued that it is only he who protects that has the right to claim ownership. How can he who wants to kill be the owner?

35. Neither party would yield. The matter was referred to arbitration. The arbitrator upheld the point of view of Siddharth Gautama.

36. Devadatta became his permanent enemy. But Gautama's spirit of compassion was so great that he preferred to save the life of an innocent bird to securing the goodwill of his cousin.

37. Such were the traits of character found in the early life of Siddharth Gautama.

§ 8. *Marriage*

1. There was a Sakya by name Dandapani. Yeshodhara was his daughter. She was well known for her beauty and for her 'sila.'

2. Yeshodhara had reached her sixteenth year and Dandapani was thinking about her marriage.

3. According to custom Dandapani sent invitations to young men of all the neighbouring countries for the Swayamvar of his daughter.

4. An invitation was also sent to Siddharth Gautama.

5. Siddharth Gautama had completed his sixteenth year. His parents also were equally anxious to get him married.

6. They asked him to go to the Swayamvar and offer his hand to Yeshodhara. He agreed to follow his parents' wishes.

7. From amongst the young men Yeshodhara's choice fell on Siddharth Gautama.

8. Dandapani was not very happy. He felt doubtful about the success of the marriage.

9. Siddharth, he felt, was addicted to the company of saints and sages. He preferred loneliness. How could he be a successful householder?

10. Yeshodhara, who was determined to marry none but Siddharth, asked her father whether to be in the company of saints and sages was a crime. She did not think it was.

11. Knowing her daughter's determination to marry no one but Siddharth Gautama, the mother of Yeshodhara told Dandapani that he must consent. Dandapani did.

12. The rivals of Gautama were not only disappointed but felt that they were insulted.

13. They wanted that in fairness to them Yeshodhara should have applied some test for her selection. But she did not.

14. For the time being they kept quiet, believing that Dandapani would not allow Yeshodhara to choose Siddharth Gautama so that their purpose would be served.

15. But when Dandapani failed, they made bold and demanded that a test of skill in archery be prescribed. Dandapani had to agree.

16. At first Siddharth was not prepared for this. But Channa, his charioteer, pointed out to him what disgrace his refusal would bring upon his father, upon his family and upon Yeshodhara.

17. Siddharth Gautama was greatly impressed by this argument and agreed to take part in the contest.

18. The contest began. Each candidate showed his skill in turn.

19. Gautama's turn came last. But his was the highest marksmanship.

20. Thereafter the marriage took place. Both Suddhodana and Dandapani were happy. So was Yeshodhara and Mahaprajapati.

21. After a long term of married life Yeshodhara gave birth to a son. He was named Rahula.

§ 9. *Father's Plans to Save His Son*

1. While the king was happy to see his son married and thus enter the life of a householder the prophecy of the sage Asita continued to haunt him.

2. To prevent the prophecy from coming true, he thought of getting him engrossed in the pleasures and carnal joys of life.

3. With this object in view Suddhodana built three luxurious palaces for his son to live in, one for summer, one for the rainy season and one for winter, furnished with all the requirements and excitements for a full amorous life.

4. Each palace was surrounded by an extensive garden beautifully laid out with all kinds of trees and flowers.

5. In consultation with his family priest Udayin, he thought of providing a harem for the prince with very beautiful inmates.

6. Suddhodana then told Udayin to advise the girls how to go about the business of winning over the prince to the pleasures of life.

7. Having collected the inmates of the harem, Udayin first advised them how they should win over the prince.

8. Addressing them he said : " Ye are all skilled in all the graceful arts, ye are proficient in understanding the language of amorous sentiments, ye are possessed of beauty and gracefulness, ye are thorough masters in your own styles.

9. " With these graces of yours, ye are able to move even sages who have lost all their desires, and to ensnare even the gods, who are charmed by heavenly nymphs.

10. " By your skill in expressing the heart's feelings, by your coquetry, your grace, and your perfect beauty ye are able to enrapture even women, how much more easily men.

11. " Thus, skilled as ye are, each set in your own proper sphere, it should not be beyond your reach to captivate and capture the prince and hold

him in your bondage.

12. "Any timid action on your part would be fit for new brides whose eyes are closed through shame.

13. "What though this hero be, great by his exalted glory, yet 'great is the might of woman.' Let this be your firm resolve.

14. "In olden time a great seer, hard to be conquered even by gods, was spurned by a harlot, the beauty of Kasi, planting her feet upon him.

15. "And the great seer Visvamitra, though plunged in a profound penance, was carried captive for ten years in the forests by the nymph Ghritaki.

16. "Many such seers as these have women brought to naught, how much more then a delicate prince in the first flower of his age?

17. "This being so, boldly put forth your efforts that the posterity of the king's family may not be turned away from him.

18. "Ordinary women captivate simple men; but they are truly women, who subdue the nature of high and hard."

§ *10. The Failure of the Women to Win the Prince*

1. Having heard these words of Udayin, the women strung to the heart, rose even above themselves for the conquest of the prince.

2. But even with their brows, their glances, their coquetries, their smiles, their delicate movements, the girls of the harem did not feel sure of themselves.

3. But they soon regained their confidence through the command of the family priest and the gentle temperament of the prince, and through the power of intoxication and of love.

4. The women then set upon their task and made the prince wander in the woods like an elephant in the forests of Himavat, accompanied by a herd of females.

5. Attended by women, he shone in that pleasant grove, as the sun surrounded by Apsaras in his royal garden.

6. There, some of them urged by passion, pressed him with their full, firm bosoms in gentle collisions.

7. Others violently embraced him after pretending to stumble, then leaning on him with their shoulders drooping down, and with their gentle creeper-like arms.

8. Others with their mouths smelling of spirituous liquor, their lower lips red like copper, whispered in his ear, "Let my secret be heard."

9. Others, all wet with unguents, as if giving him a command, clasped his hand eagerly and said, "Perform thy rites of adoration here."

10. Another with her blue garments continually slipping down in pretended intoxication, stood conspicuous with her tongue visible like the night with its lightning lashing.

11. Others with their golden ones tinkling, wandered about here and there, showing him their bodies veiled with thin cloth.

12. Others leaned, holding a mango bough in hand, displaying their bosoms like golden jars.

13. Some, coming from a lotus bed, carrying lotuses and with eyes like lotuses, stood like the lotus goddess Padma, by the side of that lotus-faced prince.

14. Another sang a sweet song easily understood and with the proper gesticulations, rousing him, self-subdued though he was, by her glance, as saying, "O how thou art deluded!"

15. Another, having armed herself with her bright face, with its brow drawn to its full, imitated his action, as playing the hero.

16. Another, with beautiful, full bosoms, and having her earrings waving in the wind, laughed loudly at him, as if saying, "Catch me, sir, if you can!"

17. Some, as he was going away, bound him with strings of garlands, others punished him with words like an elephant-driver's hook, gentle yet reproachful.

18. Another, wishing to argue with him, seizing a mango spray, asked, all bewildered with passion, "This flower, whose is it?"

19. Another, assuming a gait and attitude like

that of a man, said to him, " You who are conquered by a woman, go and conquer this earth ! "

20. Then another with rolling eyes, smelling a
blue lotus, thus addressed the prince with words
I slightly indistinct in her excitement :

21. " See, my lord, this mango covered with its
18 honey-scented flowers, where the bird *kokila* sings,
as if imprisoned in a golden cage.

22. " Come and see this *Asoka* tree, which augments lovers' sorrows, where the bees make a noise as if they were scorched by fire.

23. " Come and see this *Tilaka* tree, embraced by a slender mango branch, like a man in a white garment by a woman decked with yellow ungents.

24. " Behold the *kurubaka* in flower, bright like fresh resin-juice, which bends down as if it felt reproached by the colour of women's nails.

25. " Come and see this young *Asoka*, covered all over with new shoots, which stands as if it were ashamed at the beauty of our hands.

26. " See this lake surrounded by the *Sinduvara* shrubs growing on its banks, like a fair woman reclining, clad in fine white cloth.

27. " See the imperial power of females, yonder *Ruddygoose* in the water, goes behind, his mate following her like a slave.

28. " Come and listen to the notes of the intoxicated *Cuckoo* as he sings, while another *cuckoo* sings as if consenting wholly without care.

29. " Would that thine was the intoxication of the birds which the spring produces, and not the thought of a thinking man, ever pondering how wise he is ! "

30. Thus these young women, their souls carried away by love, assailed the prince with all kinds of stratagems.

31. But although thus attacked, he, having his sense guarded by self-control, neither rejoiced nor smiled.

32. Having seen them in their real condition, the Prince pondered with an undisturbed and steadfast mind.

33. " What is it that these women lack that they perceive not that youth is fickle? For old age will destroy whatever beauty has."

34. This round of blandishment went on for months and years with no results. I

§ *11. The Prime Minister's Admonition to the Prince* 19

1. Udayin realized that the girls had failed and that the Prince had shown no interest in them.

2. Udayin, well skilled in the rules of policy, thought of talking to the prince.

3. Meeting the prince all alone, Udayin said: " Since I was appointed by the king as a fitting friend for thee, therefore, I wish to speak to thee in the friendliness of my heart." So began Udayin.

4. " To hinder from what is disadvantageous, to urge to do what is advantageous and not to forsake in misfortune, these are the three marks of a friend.

5. " If I, after having promised my friendship, were not to heed when thou turnest away from the great end of man, there would be no friendship in me.

6. " It is right to woo a woman even by guile, this is useful both for getting rid of shame and for one's own enjoyment.

7. " Reverential behaviour and compliance with her wishes are what bind a woman's heart; good qualities truly are a cause of love, and women love respect.

8. " Wilt thou not then, O large-eyed prince, even if thy heart is unwilling, seek to please them with a courtesy worthy of this beauty of thine?

9. " Courtesy is the balm of women, courtesy is the best ornament; beauty without courtesy is like a grove without flowers.

10. " But of what use is courtesy by itself? Let it be assisted by the heart's feelings; surely, when worldly objects so hard to attain are in the grasp, thou wilt not despise them.

11. " Knowing that pleasure was the best of

objects, even the god Purandara (Indra) wooed in olden times Ahalya, the wife of the saint Gautama.

12. "So too Agastya wooed Rohini, the wife of Soma ; and therefore, as Sruti saith, a like thing
I befell Lopamudra.

13. "The great ascetic Brihaspati begot
20 Bharadvaja on Mamata the daughter of the Maruta, the wife of Autathya.

14. "The Moon, the best of offerers, begat Buda of divine nature on the spouse of Vrihaspati as she was offering a libation.

15. "So too in old times Parasara, overpowered by passion on the banks of the Yamuna, lay with the maiden Kali who was the daughter of the son of Varuna.

16. "The sage Vasishtha through lust begot a son Kapinglada on Akshmala, a despised low-caste woman.

17. "And the seer-king Yayat, even when the vigour of his prime was gone, sported in the Kaitrartha forest with the Apsara Visvaki.

18. "And the Kaurava king Pandu, though he knew that intercourse with his wife would end in death, yet overcome by the beauty and good qualities of Madri, yielded to the pleasures of love.

19. "Great heroes such as these, pursued even contemptible desires for the sake of pleasure, how much more so when they are praiseworthy of their kind ?

20. "And yet thou, a young man, possessed of strength and beauty, despisest enjoyments which rightly belong to thee and to which the whole world is devoted."

§ 12. *The Prince's Reply to the Prime Minister*

1. Having heard these specious words of his, well-supported by sacred tradition, the prince made reply, in a voice like the thundering of a cloud :

2. "This speech manifesting affection is well-befitting in thee ; but I will convince thee as to where

thou wrongly judgest me.

3. "I do not despise worldly objects, I know that all mankind is bound up therein. But remembering that the world is transitory, my mind cannot find pleasure in them.

4. "Yet even though this beauty of women were to remain perpetual, still delight in the pleasures of desires would not be worthy of the wise man.

5. "And as for what thou sayest as to even those great men having become victims to desire, do not be led away by them ; for destruction was also their lot.

6. "Real greatness is not to be found there, where there is destruction, or where there is attachment to earthly objects, or a want of self-control.

7. "And when thou sayest, 'Let one deal with women by guile,' I know about guile, even if it be accompanied with courtesy.

8. "That compliance too with a woman's wishes pleases me not, if truthfulness be not there ; if there be not a union with one's whole soul and nature, then 'out upon it' say I.

9. "A soul overpowered by passion, believing in falsehood, carried away by attachment and blind to the faults of its objects, what is there in it worth being deceived ?

10. "And if the victims of passion do deceive one another, are not men unfit for women to look at and women for men ?

11. "Since then these things are so, thou surely wouldst not lead me astray into ignoble pleasures."

12. Udayin felt silenced by the firm and strong resolve of the prince and reported the matter to his father.

13. Suddhodana, when he heard how his son's mind turned away from all objects of sense, could not sleep all that night. Like an elephant with an arrow in his heart, he was full of pain.

14. He and his ministers spent much of their time in consultation hoping to find some means to draw Siddharth to the pleasures of carnal life and thus

to dissuade him from the likely turn which he may give to his life. But they found no other means besides those they had tried.

15. And the seraglio of women wearing their
I garlands and ornaments in vain, with their graceful
arts and endearments all fruitless, concealing their love
 deep in their hearts, was disbanded.

§ *13. Initiation into the Sakya Sangh*

1. The Sakyas had their Sangh. Every Sakya youth above twenty had to be initiated into the Sangh and be a member of the Sangh.

2. Siddharth Gautama had reached the age of twenty. It was time for him to be initiated into the Sangh and become a member thereof.

3. The Sakyas had a meeting-house which they called Sansthagar. It was situated in Kapilavatsu. The session of the Sangh was also held in the Sansthagar.

4. With the object of getting Siddharth initiated into the Sangh, Suddhodana asked the Purohit of the Sakyas to convene a meeting of the Sangh.

5. Accordingly the Sangh met at Kapilavatsu in the Sansthagar of the Sakyas.

6. At the meeting of the Sangh, the Purohit proposed that Siddharth be enrolled as a member of the Sangh.

7. The Senapati of the Sakyas then rose in his seat and addressed the Sangh as follows : " Siddharth Gautama, born in the family of Suddhodana of the Sakya clan, desires to be a member of the Sangh. He is twenty years of age and is in every way fit to be a member of the Sangh. I, therefore, move that he be made a member of the Sakya Sangh. Pray, those who are against the motion speak."

8. No one spoke against it. "A second time do I ask those who are against the motion to speak," said the Senapati.

9. No one rose to speak against the motion. Again the Senapati said : "A third time do I ask those who are against the motion to speak."

10. Even for the third time no one spoke against it.

11. It was the rule of procedure among the Sakyas that there could be no debate without a motion and no motion could be declared carried unless it was passed three times.

12. The motion of the Senapati having been carried three times without opposition, Siddharth was declared to have been duly admitted as a member of the Sakya Sangh.

13. Thereafter the Purohit of the Sakyas stood up and asked Siddharth to rise in his place.

14. Addressing Siddharth, he said : " Do you realize that the Sangh has honoured you by making you a member of it ? " " I do, sir, " replied Siddharth.

15. " Do you know the obligation of membership of the Sangh ? " " I am sorry, sir, I do not. But I shall be happy to know them, sir," said Siddharth.

16. " I shall first tell you what your duties as a member of the Sangh are " said the Purohit and he then related them one by one : " (1) You must safeguard the interests of the Sakyas by your body, mind and money. (2) You must not absent yourself from the meetings of the Sangh. (3) You must without fear or favour expose any fault you may notice in the conduct of a Sakya. (4) You must not be angry if you are accused of an offence but confess if you are guilty or state if you are innocent."

17. Proceeding, the Purohit said : " I shall next tell you what will disqualify you for membership of the Sangh : (1) You cannot remain a member of the Sangh if you commit rape. (2) You cannot remain a member of the Sangh if you commit murder. (3) You cannot remain a member of the Sangh if you commit theft. (4) You cannot remain a member of the Sangh if you are guilty of giving false evidence."

18. " I am grateful to you, sir," said Siddharth, " for telling me the rules of discipline of the Sakya Sangh. I assure you I will do my best to follow them in letter and in spirit."

§ 14. *Conflict with the Sangh*

1. Eight years had passed by since Siddharth was made a member of the Sakya Sangh.

I 2. He was a very devoted and steadfast member of the Sangh. He took the same interest in the affairs
24 of the Sangh as he did in his own. His conduct as a member of the Sangh was exemplary and he had endeared himself to all.

3. In the eighth year of his membership, an event occurred which resulted in a tragedy for the family of Suddhodana and a crisis in the life of Siddharth.

4. This is the origin of the tragedy.

5. Bordering on the State of the Sakyas was the State of the Koliyas. The two kingdoms were divided by the river Rohini.

6. The waters of the Rohini were used by both the Sakyas and the Koliyas for irrigating their fields. Every season there used to be disputes between them as to who should take the water of the Rohini first and how much. These disputes resulted in quarrels and sometimes in affrays.

7. In the year when Siddharth was twenty-eight, there was a major clash over the waters between the servants of the Sakyas and the servants of the Koliyas. Both sides suffered injuries.

8. Coming to know of this, the Sakyas and the Koliyas felt that the issue must be settled once for all by war.

9. The Senapati of the Sakyas, therefore, called a session of the Sakya Sangh to consider the question of declaring war on the Koliyas.

10. Addressing the members of the Sangh, the Senapati said : " Our people have been attacked by the Koliyas and they had to retreat. Such acts of aggression by the Koliyas have taken place more than once. We have tolerated them so far. But this cannot go on. It must be stopped and the only way to stop it is to declare war against the Koliyas. I propose that the Sangh do declare war on the Koliyas. Those who wish to oppose may speak."

11. Siddharth Gautama rose in his seat and said : "I oppose this resolution. War does not solve any question. Waging war will not serve our purpose. It will sow the seeds of another war. The slayer gets a slayer in his turn ; the conqueror gets one who conquers him ; a man who despoils is despoiled in his turn."

12. Siddharth Gautama continued : "I feel that the Sangh should not be in haste to declare war on the Koliyas. Careful investigation should be made to ascertain who is the guilty party. I hear that our men have also been aggressors. If this be true, then it is obvious that we too are not free from blame."

13. The Senapati replied : "Yes, our men were the aggressors. But it must not be forgotten that it was our turn to take the water first."

14. Siddharth Gautama said : "This shows that we are not completely free from blame. I therefore propose that we elect two men from us and the Koliyas should be asked to elect two from them and the four should elect a fifth person and these should settle the dispute."

15. The amendment moved by Siddharth Gautama was duly seconded. But the Senapati opposed the amendment, saying : "I am sure that this menace of the Koliyas will not end unless they are severely punished."

16. The resolution and the amendment had therefore to be put to vote. The amendment moved by Siddharth Gautama was put first. It was declared lost by an overwhelming majority.

17. The Senapati next put his own resolution to vote. Siddharth Gautama again stood up to oppose it. "I beg the Sangh," he said, "not to accept the resolution. The Sakyas and the Koliyas are close relations. It is unwise that they should destroy each other."

18. The Senapati encountered the plea urged by Siddharth Gautama. He stressed that in war the Kshatriyas cannot make a distinction between relations and strangers. They must fight even against brothers

for the sake of their kingdom.

19. Performing sacrifices is the duty of the Brahmins, fighting is the duty of the Kshatriyas, trading is the duty of the Vaishas and service is the duty
I of the Shudras. There is merit in each class performing its duty. Such is the injunction of our Shastras.

26 20. Siddharth replied : "Dharma, as I understand it, consists in recognising that enmity does not disappear by enmity. It can be conquered by love only."

21. The Senapati, getting impatient, said : "It is unnecessary to enter upon this philosophical disquisition. The point is that Siddharth is opposed to my resolution. Let us ascertain what the Sangh has to say about it by putting it to vote."

22. Accordingly the Senapati put his resolution to vote. It was declared carried by an overwhelming majority.

§ *15. Offer of Exile*

1. Next day the Senapati called another meeting of the Sakya Sangh to have his plan of mobilisation considered by the Sangh.

2. When the Sangh met, he proposed that he be permitted to proclaim an order calling to arms for the war against the Koliyas every Sakya between the ages of 20 and 50.

3. The meeting was attended by both sides—those who at the previous meeting of the Sangh had voted in favour of a declaration of war as well as those who had voted against it.

4. For those who had voted in favour there was no difficulty in accepting the proposal of the Senapati. It was a natural consequence of their earlier decision.

5. But the minority who had voted against it had a problem to face. Their problem was—to submit or not to submit to the decision of the majority.

6. The minority was determined not to submit to the majority. That is the reason why they had

decided to be present at the meeting. Unfortunately, none of them had the courage to say so openly. Perhaps they knew the consequences of opposing the majority.

7. Seeing that his supporters were silent, Siddharth stood up, and addressing the Sangh, said : " Friends ! You may do what you like. You have a majority on your side, but I am sorry to say I shall oppose your decision in favour of mobilisation. I shall not join your army and I shall not take part in the war."

8. The Senapati, replying to Siddharth Gautama, said : " Do remember the vows you had taken when you were admitted to the membership of the Sangh. If you break any of them you will expose yourself to public shame."

9. Siddharth replied : "Yes, I have pledged myself to safeguard the best interests of the Sakyas by my body, mind and money. But I do not think that this war is in the best interests of the Sakyas. What is public shame to me before the best interests of the Sakyas ? "

10. Siddharth proceeded to caution the Sangh by reminding it of how the Sakyas have become the vassals of the King of Kosala by reason of their quarrels with the Koliyas. "It is not difficult to imagine," he said, " that this war will give him a greater handle to further reduce the freedom of the Sakyas."

11. The Senapati grew angry and addressing Siddharth, said : " Your eloquence will not help you. You must obey the majority decision of the Sangh. You are perhaps counting upon the fact that the Sangh has no power to order an offender to be hanged or to exile him without the sanction of the king of the Kosalas and that the king of the Kosalas will not give permission if either of the two sentences was passed against you by the Sangh."

12. " But remember the Sangh has other ways of punishing you. The Sangh can declare a social boycott against your family and the Sangh can confiscate your family lands. For this the Sangh does not have to

obtain the permission of the king of the Kosalas."

13. Siddharth realised the consequences that would follow if he continued his opposition to the Sangh in its plan of war against the Koliyas. He had three alternatives to consider—to join the forces and participate in the war ; to consent to being hanged or exiled ; and to allow the members of his family to be condemned to a social boycott and confiscation of property.

14. He was firm in not accepting the first. As to the third he felt it was unthinkable. Under the circumstances he felt that the second alternative was the best.

15. Accordingly, Siddharth spoke to the Sangh. "Please do not punish my family. Do not put them in distress by subjecting them to a social boycott. Do not make them destitute by confiscating their land which is their only means of livelihood. They are innocent. I am the guilty person. Let me alone suffer for my wrong. Sentence me to death or exile, whichever you like. I will willingly accept it and I promise I shall not appeal to the king of the Kosalas."

§ *16. Parivraja-the Way Out*

1. The Senapati said : "It is difficult to accept your suggestion. For even if you voluntarily agreed to undergo the sentence of death or exile, the matter is sure to become known to the king of the Kosalas and he is sure to conclude that it is the Sangh which has inflicted this punishment and take action against the Sangh."

2. "If this is the difficulty I can easily suggest a way out," said Siddharth Gautama. "I can become a Parivrajaka and leave this country. It is a kind of an exile."

3. The Senapati thought this was a good solution. But he had still some doubt about Siddharth being able to give effect to it.

4. So the Senapati asked Siddharth : "How can you become a Parivrajaka unless you obtain the consent

of your parents and your wife?"

5. Siddharth assured him that he would do his best to obtain their permission. "I promise," he said, "to leave this country immediately whether I obtain their consent or not."

6. The Sangh felt that the proposal made by Siddharth was the best way out and they agreed to it.

7. After finishing the business before the meeting, the Sangh was about to rise when a young Sakya got up in his place and said: "Give me a hearing, I have something important to say."

8. Being granted permission to speak, he said: "I have no doubt that Siddharth Gautama will keep his promise and leave the country immediately. There is, however, one question over which I do not feel very happy.

9. "Now that Siddharth will soon be out of sight, does the Sangh propose to give immediate effect to its declaration of war against the Koliyas?

10. "I want the Sangh to give further consideration to this question. In any event, the king of the Kosalas is bound to come to know of the exile of Siddharth Gautama. If the Sakyas declare a war against the Koliyas immediately, the king of Kosalas will understand that Siddharth left only because he was opposed to war against the Koliyas. This will not go well with us.

11. "I, therefore, propose that we should also allow an interval to pass between the exile of Siddharth Gautama and the actual commencement of hostilities so as not to allow the King of Kosala to establish any connection between the two."

12. The Sangh realised that this was a very important proposal. And as a matter of expediency, the Sangh agreed to accept it.

13. Thus ended the tragic session of the Sakya Sangh and the minority which was opposed to the war but who had not the courage to say so, heaved a sigh of relief that it was able to overcome a situation full of calamitous consequences.

§ 17. *Parting Words*

1. The news of what happened at the meeting of the Sakya Sangh had travelled to the Raja's palace long before the return of Siddharth Gautama.

I 2. For on reaching home he found his parents
30 weeping and plunged in great grief.

3. Suddhodana said : " We were talking about the evils of war. But I never thought that you would go to such lengths."

4. Siddharth replied, " I too did not think things would take such a turn. I was hoping that I would be able to win over the Sakyas to the cause of peace by my argument.

5. " Unfortunately, our military officers had so worked up the feelings of the men that my argument failed to have any effect on them.

6. " But I hope you realise how I have saved the situation from becoming worse. I have not given up the cause of truth and justice and whatever the punishment for my standing for truth and justice, I have succeeded in making its infliction personal to me."

7. Suddhodana was not satisfied with this. "You have not considered what is to happen to us." " But that is the reason why I undertook to become a Parivrajaka," replied Siddharth. " Consider the consequences if the Sakyas had ordered the confiscation of your lands."

8. " But without you what is the use of these lands to us ? " cried Suddhodana. Why should not the whole family leave the country of the Sakyas and go into exile along with you ? "

9. Prajapati Gautami, who was weeping, joined Suddhodana in argument, saying : " I agree. How can you go alone leaving us here like this ? "

10. Siddharth said : " Mother, have you not always claimed to be the mother of a Kshatriya ? Is that not so ? You must then be brave. This grief is unbecoming of you. What would you have done if I had gone to the battle-field and died ? Would you have grieved like this ? "

11. " No," replied Gautami. " That would have been befitting a Kshatriya. But you are now going into the jungle far away from people, living in the company of wild beasts. How can we stay here in peace? I say you should take us along with you." I

12. " How can I take you all with me? Nanda is
only a child. Rahul my son is just born. Can you 31
come leaving them here?" He asked Gautami.

13. Gautami was not satisfied. She urged: " It is possible for us all to leave the country of the Sakyas and go to the country of the Kosalas under the protection of their king."

14. " But mother! What would the Sakyas say?" asked Siddharth. " Would they not regard it as treason? Besides, I pledged that I will do nothing either by word or by deed to let the king of the Kosalas know the true cause of my Parivraja.

15. " It is true that I may have to live alone in the jungle. But which is better? To live in the jungle or to be a party to the killing of the Koliyas!"

16. " But why this impatience?" asked Suddhodana. " The Sakyas Sangh has decided to postpone the date of the hostilities for some time.

17. " Perhaps the hostilities may not be started at all. Why not postpone your Parivraja? May be, it would be possible to obtain the permission of the Sangh for you to stay among the Sakyas."

18. This idea was repellent to Siddharth. " It is because I promised to take Parivraja that the Sangh decided to postpone the commencement of hostilities against the Koliyas.

19. " It is possible that after I take Parivraja the Sangh may be persuaded to withdraw their declaration of war. All this depends upon my first taking Parivraja.

20. " I have made a promise and I must carry it out. The consequences of any breach of promise may be very grave both to us and to the cause of peace.

21. " Mother, do not now stand in my way. Give me your permission and your blessings. What is happening is for the best."

22. Gautami and Suddhodana kept silent.

23. Then Siddharth went to the apartment of Yeshodhara. Seeing her, he stood silent, not knowing what to say and how to say it. She broke the silence by saying : "I have heard all that has happened at the meeting of the Sangh at Kapilavatsu."

24. He asked her :—"Yeshodhara, tell me what you think of my decision to take Parivraja ?"

25. He expected she would collapse. Nothing of the kind happened.

26. With full control over her emotions, she replied : "What else could I have done if I were in your position ? I certainly would not have been a party to a war on the Koliyas.

27. "Your decision is the right decision. You have my consent and my support. I too would have taken Parivraja with you. If I do not, it is only because I have Rahula to look after.

28. "I wish it had not come to this. But we must be bold and brave and face the situation. Do not be anxious about your parents and your son. I will look after them till there is life in me.

29. "All I wish is that now that you are becoming a Parivrajaka leaving behind all who are near and dear to you, you will find a new way of life which would result in the happiness of mankind."

30. Siddharth Gautama was greatly impressed. He realised as never before what a brave, courageous and noble-minded woman Yeshodhara was, and how fortunate he was in having her as his wife and how fate had put them asunder. He asked her to bring Rahula. He cast his fatherly look on him and left.

§ *18. Leaving His Home*

1. Siddharth thought of taking Parivraja at the hands of Bharadwaja who had his Ashram at Kapilavatsu. Accordingly he rose the next day and started for the Ashram on his favourite horse Kanthaka with his servant Channa walking along.

2. As he came near the Ashram, men and women

came out and thronged the gates to meet him as a newly arrived bridegroom.

3. And when they came up to him, their eyes wide open in wonder, they performed their due homage with hands folded like a lotus calyx.

4. Then they stood surrounding him, their minds overpowered by passion, as if they were drinking him in with their eyes motionless and blossoming wide with love.

5. Some of the women verily thought that he was Kama incarnate, decorated as he was with his brilliant signs as with connate ornaments.

6. Others thought from his gentleness and his majesty that it was the moon with its ambrosial beams as it were visibly come down to the earth.

7. Others, smitten by his beauty, yawned as if to swallow him, and fixing their eyes on each other, softly sighed.

8. Thus the women only looked upon him, simply gazing with their eyes. They spoke not, nor did they smile. They surrounded him and stood aghast thinking of his decision to take Parivraja.

9. With great difficulty he extricated himself from the crowd and entered the gates of the Ashram.

10. Siddharth did not like Suddhodana and Prajapati Gautami to be present to witness his Parivraja. For he knew that they would break down under the weight of grief. But they had already reached the Ashram without letting him know.

11. As he entered the compound of the Ashram he saw in the crowd his father and mother.

12. Seeing his parents he first went to them and asked for their blessing. They were so choked with emotion that they could hardly say a word. They wept and wept, held him fast and bathed him with their tears.

13. Channa had tied Kanthaka to a tree in the Ashram and was standing. Seeing Suddhodana and Prajapati in tears he too was overcome with emotion and was weeping.

14. Separating himself with great difficulty from

his parents, Siddharth went to the place where Channa was standing. He gave him his dress and his ornaments to take back home.

15. Then he had his head shaved, as was required for a Parivrajaka. His cousin Mahanama had brought the clothes appropriate for a Parivrajaka and a begging bowl. Siddharth wore them.

16. Having thus prepared himself to enter the life of a Parivrajaka, Siddharth approached Bharadwaja to confer on him Parivraja.

17. Bharadwaja with the help of his disciples performed the necessary ceremonies and declared Siddharth Gautama to have become a Parivrajaka.

18. Remembering that he had given a double pledge to the Sakya Sangh to take Parivraja and to leave the Sakya kingdom without undue delay, Siddharth Gautama immediately on the completion of the Parivraja ceremony started on his journey.

19. The crowd which had collected in the Ashram was unusually large. That was because the circumstances leading to Gautama's Parivraja were so extraordinary. As the prince stepped out of the Ashram the crowd also followed him.

20. He left Kapilavatsu and proceeded in the direction of the river Anoma. Looking back he saw the crowd still following him.

21. He stopped and addressed them, saying : "Brothers and sisters, there is no use your following me. I have failed to settle the dispute between the Sakyas and the Koliyas. But if you create public opinion in favour of settlement you might succeed. Be, therefore, so good as to return." Hearing his appeal, the crowd started going back.

22. Suddhodana and Gautami also returned to the palace.

23. Gautami was unable to bear the sight of the robes and the ornaments discarded by Siddharth. She had them thrown into a lotus pool.

24. Siddharth Gautama was only twenty-nine when he underwent Parivraja (Renunciation).

25. People admired him and sighed for him,

saying : " Here was a Sakya blessed with high lineage, noble parentage, possessed of considerable riches, in the bloom of youthful vigour, accomplished in mind and body, brought up in luxury, who fought his kinsmen for the sake of maintaining peace on earth and goodwill towards men.

26. " Here was a Sakya youth who when outvoted by his kinsmen refused to submit but preferred to undergo voluntary punishment which involved the exchange of riches for poverty, comfort for alms, home for homelessness. And so he goes with none in the world to care for him and with nothing in the world which he could claim as his own.

27. " His was an act of supreme sacrifice willingly made. His is a brave and a courageous act. There is no parallel to it in the history of the world. He deserves to be called a Sakya Muni or Sakya Sinha."

28. How true were the words of Kisa Gotami, a Sakya maiden. When referring to Siddharth Gautama, she said : " Blessed indeed is the mother, blessed indeed is the father, who has such a son. Blessed indeed is the wife who has such a husband."

§ *19. The Prince and the Servant*

1. Channa too should have gone back home with Kanthaka. But he refused to go. He insisted on seeing the Prince off with Kanthaka at least to the banks of the river Anoma and so insistent was Channa that the Gautama had to yield to his wishes.

2. At last they reached the banks of the river Anoma.

3. Then turning to Channa he said : " Good friend, thy devotion to me has been proved by thy thus following me. I am wholly won in heart by thee, ye who have such a love for your master.

4. " I am pleased with your noble feelings towards me, even though I am powerless of conferring any reward.

5. " Who would not be favourably disposed to one who stands to him as bringing him reward ? But

even one's own people commonly become mere strangers in a reverse of fortune.

6. "A son is brought up for the sake of the family, the father is honoured by the son for the sake
I of his own future support ; the world shows kindness for the sake of hope ; there is no such thing as
36 unselfishness without a motive.

7. "Thou art the only exception. Take now this horse and return.

8. "The king, with his loving confidence, still unshaken, must be enjoined to stay his grief.

9. "Tell him, I have left him—with no thirst for heaven, with no lack of love, nor feeling of anger.

10. "He should not think of mourning for me who am thus gone forth from my home ; union, however long it may last, in time will come to an end.

11. "Since separation is certain, how shall there not be repeated severings from one's kindred?

12. "At a man's death there are doubtless heirs to his wealth but heirs to his merit are hard to find on the earth or exist not at all.

13. "The king, my father, requires to be looked after. The king may say, 'He is gone at a wrong time.' But there is no wrong time for duty.

14. "Do thou address the king, O friend, with these and suchlike words ; and do thou use thy efforts so that he may not even remember me.

15. "Yes, do thou repeat to my mother my utter unworthiness to deserve her affection. She is a noble person, too noble for words."

16. Having heard these words, Channa, overwhelmed with grief, made reply with folded hands, his voice choked by emotion :

17. "Seeing that ye are causing affliction to thy kindred, my mind, O my Lord, sinks down like an elephant in a river of mud.

18. "To whom would not such a determination as this of thine, cause tears, even if his heart were of iron—how much more if it were throbbing with love?

19. "Where is gone this delicacy of limb, fit to lie only in a palace, and where is the ground of the

ascetic forest, covered with the shoots of rough Kusa grass?

20. "How could I, O Prince, by mine own will,—knowing this thy decision,—carry back the horse to the sorrow of Kapilavatsu?

21. "Surely thou will not abandon that fond old king, so devoted to his son, as a heretic might the true religion?

22. "And her, thy second mother, worn with the care of bringing thee up,—thou will not surely forget her, as an ingrate does a benefit?

23. "Thou wilt not surely abandon thy wife endowed with all virtues, illustrious for her family, devoted to her husband and with a young son.

24. "Thou wilt not abandon the young son of Yeshodhara, worthy of all praise, thou the best of the cherishers of religion and fame, as a dissolute spendthrift his choicest glory?

25. "Or even if thy mind be resolved to abandon thy kindred and thy kingdom, thou will not, O Master, abandon me,—thy feet are my only refuge.

26. "I cannot go to the city with my soul thus burning, leaving thee behind in the forest.

27. "What will the king say to me, returning to the city without thee, or what shall I say to thy wife by way of telling them good news?

28. "As for what thou sayest, 'thou must repeat my unworthiness to the king' who could think or believe it?" continued Channa. "Even if I ventured to speak it with a heart ashamed and a tongue cleaving to my mouth, he may not appreciate it.

29. "Him who is always compassionate and who never fails to feel pity, it ill befits to abandon one who loves; turn back and have mercy on me."

30. Having heard these words of Channa overcome with sorrow, Siddharth Gautama with the utmost gentleness answered:

31. "Abandon this distress Channa, regarding thy separation from me,—change is inevitable in corporeal beings who are subject to different births.

32. "Even if I through affection were not to

abandon my kindred, death would still make us helplessly abandon one another.

33. "She, my mother, by whom I was born
in the womb with great thirst and pains,—where am
I I now with regard to her, and where is she with regard
to me?

38 34. "As birds go to their roosting-tree and then depart, so the meeting of beings inevitably ends in separation.

35. "As clouds, having come together, depart asunder again, such I consider the meeting and parting of living things.

36. "And since this world goes away, each one deceiving the other,—it is not right to think anything thine own in a time of union which is a dread.

37. "Therefore, since it is so, grieve not, my good friend, but go ; or if thy love lingers, then go and afterwards return.

38. "Say without reproaching me, to the people of Kapilavatsu, 'Let your love for him be given up, and hear his resolve.'"

39. Having heard this conversation between the master and the servant, Kanthaka, the noblest steed, licked his feet with his tongue and dropped hot tears.

40. With his hand whose fingers were untied with a membrane and which was marked with the auspicious svastika, and with its middle part curved, Gautama stroked him and addressed him like a friend:

41. "Shed not tears, Kanthaka, bear with it, thy labours will soon have its fruit."

42. Then Channa, knowing that the time for the parting of the ways had come, forthwith paid honour to the sylvan dress of Gautama.

43. Then Gautama, having bidden good-bye to Kanthaka and Channa, went on his way.

44. While his master, thus regardless of his kingdom, was going to the ascetic-wood in mean garments, the groom, tossing up his arms, wailed bitterly and fell on the ground.

45. Having looked back again he wept aloud, and embraced the horse Kanthaka with his arms;

and then, hopeless and repeatedly lamenting, started on his return journey.

46. On the way, sometimes he pondered, sometimes he lamented, sometimes he stumbled and sometimes he fell, and so going along, wretched through his devoted attachment, he performed all kinds of actions on the road knowing not what he was doing.

§ 20. *The Return of Channa*

1. Then Channa in deep distress, when his master thus went into the forest, made every effort on the road to dissolve his load of sorrow.

2. His heart was so heavy that the road which he used to traverse in one night with Kanthaka, that same road he now took eight days to travel, pondering over his lord's absence.

3. The horse Kanthaka, though he still went on bravely, fagged and had lost all spirit ; and decked though he was with ornaments, he in the absence of his master seemed to have lost all his beauty.

4. And turning round towards the direction in which his master went, he neighed repeatedly with a mournful sound ; and though pressed with hunger, he welcomed not, nor tasted any grass or water on the road, as before.

5. Slowly the two at long last reached Kapilavatsu which seemed empty when deserted by Gautama. They reached the city in body but not in soul.

6. Bright as it was with lotus-covered waters, adorned with trees full of flowers, the citizens had lost all their gladness.

7. When the two, their brightness gone and their eyes dim with tears, slowly entered the city, it seemed all bathed in gloom.

8. Having heard that they had returned with their limbs all relaxed, coming back without the pride of the Sakya race, the men of the city shed tears.

9. Full of wrath, the people followed Channa in the road, crying behind him with tears, " Where is the king's son, the glory of his race and his kingdom ? "

10. "This city bereft of him is a forest, and that forest which possesses him is a city; the city without him has no charms for us."

11. Next the women crowded to the rows of
I windows, crying to one another, "The prince has
returned"; but having seen that his horse had
40 an empty back, they closed the windows again and
wailed aloud.

§ *21. The Family in Mourning*

1. The members of the family of Suddhodana were anxiously awaiting the return of Channa in the hope that he might persuade Gautama to return home.

2. On entering the royal stable, Kanthaka uttered a loud sound, uttering his woe to the palace people.

3. Then the people, who were in the neighbourhood of the king's inner apartments, thought in their hearts, "Since the horse Kanthaka neighs, it must be that the prince has come."

4. And the women, who were fainting with sorrow, now in wild joy, with their eyes rolling to see the prince, rushed out of the palace full of hope. But they were disappointed. There was Kanthaka without the prince.

5. Gautami, abandoning all self-control, cried aloud—she fainted, and with a weeping face exclaimed:

6. "With his long arms and lion gait, his bull-like eye, and his beauty, bright like gold, his broad chest, and his voice deep as a drum or a cloud,—should such a hero as this dwell in a hermitage?

7. "This earth is indeed unworthy as regards that peerless doer of noble actions, for such a virtuous hero has gone away from us.

8. "Those two feet of his, tender with their beautiful web spread between the toes, with their ankles concealed and soft like a blue lotus,—how can they, bearing a wheel mark in the middle, walk on the hard ground of the skirts of the forest?

9. "That body, which deserves to sit or lie on the roof of a palace, honoured with costly garments,

aloes, and sandalwood, how will that manly body live in the woods, exposed to the attacks of the cold, the heat, and the rain?

10. "He who was proud of his family, goodness, strength, energy, sacred learning, beauty, and youth, who was ever ready to give, not ask, how will he go about begging alms from others?

11. "He who, lying on a spotless golden bed, was awakened during the night by the concert of musical instruments, how alas! will he, my ascetic, sleep today on the bare ground with only one rag of cloth interposed?"

12. Having heard this piteous lamentation, the women, embracing one another with their arms, rained tears from their eyes, as the shaken creepers drop honey from their flowers.

13. Then Yeshodhara, forgetting that she had permitted him to go, fell upon the ground in utter bewilderment.

14. "How has he abandoned me his lawful wife? He has left me widowed. He could have allowed his lawful wife to share his new life with him.

15. "I have no longing for the heaven, my one desire was that my beloved may never leave me either in this world or the next.

16. "Even if I am unworthy to look on my husband's face with its long eyes and bright smile, still is this poor Rahula never to roll about in his father's lap?

17. "Alas! the mind of that wise hero is terribly stern, gentle as his beauty seems, it is pitilessly cruel. Who can desert of his own accord such an infant son with his inarticulate talk, one who would charm even an enemy?

18. "My heart too is certainly most stern, yea, made of rock or fashioned even of iron, which does not break when its lord is gone to the forest, deserted by his royal glory like an orphan,—he so well worthy of happiness. But what can I do? My grief is too heavy for me to bear."

19. So fainting in her woe, Yeshodhara wept

and wept aloud—self-possessed though she was by nature, yet in her distress she had lost her fortitude.

20. Seeing Yeshodhara thus bewildered with her wild utterances of grief and fallen on the ground, all the women cried out, with their faces streaming with tears like large lotuses beaten by the rain.

21. Having heard of the arrival of both Channa and Kanthaka, and having learned of the fixed resolve of his son, Suddhodana fell struck down by sorrow.

22. Distracted by his grief for his son, being held up for a moment by his attendants, Suddhodana gazed on the horse with his eyes filled with tears, and then falling on the ground wailed aloud.

23. Then Suddhodana got up and entered his temple, offered prayers, performed auspicious rites and vowed certain sacrifices for the safe return of his son.

24. So Suddhodana, Gautami and Yeshodhara passed their days asking : "How long, O God, how long, before, shall we see him again ?"

PART II

Renunciation for ever

1. From Kapilavatsu to Rajagraha.
2. King Bimbisara and His Advice.
3. Gautama answers Bimbisara.
4. Reply by Gautama (concluded).
5. News of Peace.
6. The problem in a New Perspective.

§ 1. *From Kapilavatsu to Rajagraha*

1. Leaving Kapilavatsu, Siddharth Gautama thought of going to Rajagraha, the capital of the kingdom of Magadha. I

2. The reigning king was Bimbisara. It was a place which great philosophers and leaders of thought 45 had made their headquarters.

3. With this thought in mind he crossed the Ganges, fearing not her rapid flow.

4. On his way he halted at the hermitage of a Brahmin woman Saki, then at the hermitage of another Brahmin woman by name Padma and then at the hermitage of the Brahmin sage Raivata. All of them entertained him.

5. Having seen his personality and dignity and his splendid beauty, surpassing all other men, the people of that region were all astonished at him wearing the clothes of a sanyasi.

6. On seeing him, he who was going elsewhere stood still, and he who was standing there followed him on the way ; he who was walking gently and gravely ran quickly, and he who was sitting at once sprang up.

7. Some people reverenced him with their hands, others in worship saluted him with their heads, some addressed him with affectionate words ; not one went on without paying him homage.

8. Those who were wearing gay-coloured dresses were ashamed when they saw him, those who were talking on random subjects fell to silence ; no one indulged in an improper thought.

9. His eyebrows, his forehead, his mouth,—his body, his hand, his feet, or his gait,—whatever part of him anyone beheld, that at once rivetted his gaze.

10. After a long and arduous journey Gautama reached Rajagraha surrounded by five hills, well guarded and adorned with mountains, and supported and hallowed by auspicious and sacred places.

11. On reaching Rajagraha he selected a spot

at the foot of the Pandava hill and put up a small hut made of the leaves of trees for his sojourn.

12. Kapilavatsu by foot is nearly 400 miles distant from Rajagraha.

13. This long journey Siddharth Gautama did all on foot.

§ 2. *King Bimbisara and his Advice*

1. Next day he got up and started to go into the city with a begging bowl asking for alms. A vast crowd gathered round him.

2. Then Sreniya Bimbisara, the lord of the kingdom of the Magadhas, beheld from the outside of his palace the immense concourse of people, and asked the reason of it ; and thus did a courtier recount it to him :

3. " He who was thus foretold by the Brahmins, 'He will either attain supreme wisdom or be the emperor of the earth '—it is he, the son of the king of the Sakyas, who is now an ascetic. It is he at whom the people are gazing at."

4. The king, having heard this and perceiving its meaning in his mind, thus at once spoke to that courtier : " Let it be known whither he is going " ; and the courtier, receiving the command, followed the prince.

5. With fixed eyes, seeing only a yoke's length before him, with his voice hushed, and his walk slow and measured, he, the noblest of mendicants, went begging for alms, keeping his limbs and his wandering thoughts under control.

6. Having received such alms as were offered, he retired to a lonely corner of the mountain ; and having eaten it there, he ascended the Pandava hill.

7. In that wood, thickly filled with *lodhra* trees, having its thickness resonant with the notes of the peacocks, he, the sun of mankind, shone, wearing his red dress, like the morning sun above the eastern mountains.

8. That royal courtier having thus watched him there, related it all to the king : and the king when he

heard it, in his deep veneration, started himself to go thither with a modest retinue.

9. Like a mountain in stature, the king ascended the hill.

10. There he beheld Gautama, resplendent as he I
sat on his hams, with subdued senses, as if the mountain
was moving, and he himself was a peak thereof. 47

11. Him, distinguished by his beauty of form and perfect tranquillity, filled with astonishment and affectionate regard, the king of men approached.

12. Bimbisara having courteously drawn nigh to him, inquired as to the condition of his bodily humours ; and Gautama with equal gentleness assured the king of his health of mind and freedom from all ailments.

13. Then the king sat down on the clean surface of the rock, and being seated, he thus spoke, desiring to convey his state of mind :

14. " I have a strong friendship with thy family, come down by inheritance and well proved ; since from this, a desire to speak to thee, my son, has arisen in me, therefore, listen to my words of affection.

15. " When I consider thy race, beginning with the sun, thy fresh youth, and thy conspicuous beauty, I wonder whence comes this resolve of thine, so out of all harmony with the rest, set wholly on a mendicant's life, not on a kingdom?

16. " Thy limbs are worthy of red sandalwood perfumes,—they do not deserve the rough contact of red cloth, this hand of thine is fit to protect subjects, it deserves not to hold food given by another.

17. " If, therefore, gentle youth, thou desirest not thy paternal kingdom, then in thy generosity, accept forthwith one half of my kingdom.

18. " If thou actest thus, there will be no sorrow caused to thine own people, and by the mere lapse of time imperial power at last flies for refuge to the tranquil mind ; therefore, be pleased to do me this kindness. The prosperity of the good becomes very powerful, when aided by the good.

19. " But if from thy pride of race thou dost

not now feel confidence in me, then plunge with thy arrows into countless armies, and with me as thy ally seek to conquer thy foes.

20. "Choose thou, therefore, one of these ends.
I Pursue according to the rules of religious merit, wealth, and pleasure; pursue love and the rest, in reverse order.
48 These are the three objects in life; when men die they pass into dissolution as far as regards this world.

21. "Do thou, therefore, by pursuing the three objects of life, cause this personality of thine to bear its fruit; they say that when the attainment of religion, wealth and pleasure is complete in all its parts, then the end of man is complete.

22. "Do not thou let these two brawny arms lie useless which are worthy to draw the bow; they are well fitted to conquer the three worlds, much more the earth.

23. "I speak this to you out of affection,—not through love of dominion or through arrogance beholding this mendicant-dress of thine, I am filled with compassion and I shed tears.

24. "O, thou who desirest the mendicant's stage of life, enjoy pleasures now, in due time—ere old age comes on and overcomes this thy beauty, well worthy of thy illustrious race.

25. "The old man can obtain merit by religion; old age is helpless for the enjoyment of pleasures; therefore, they say that pleasures belong to the young man, wealth to the middle-aged, and religion to the old.

26. "Youth in this present world is the enemy of religion and wealth—since pleasures, however much we guard against them, are hard to hold, therefore, wherever pleasures are to be found, there thy youth seize them.

27. "Old age is prone to reflection, it is grave and intent on remaining quiet; it attains unimpassionedness with but little effort, unavoidably, and for very shame.

28. "Therefore, having passed through the deceptive period of youth, fickle, intent on external objects, heedless, impatient, not looking at the dis-

tance,—they take breath like men who have escaped safe through a forest.

29. " Let, therefore, this fickle time of youth first pass by, reckless and giddy,—our early years are
earmarked for pleasure, they cannot be kept from the I
power of the senses.

30. " Or, if religion is really thy one aim, then 49
offer sacrifices,—this is thy family's immemorial custom, climbing to highest heaven by sacrifices.

31. " With their arms pressed by golden bracelets, and their variegated diadems resplendent with the light of gems, royal sages have reached the same goal by sacrifice which great sages reached by self-mortification."

§ 3. *Gautama Answers Bimbisara*

1. Thus spoke the monarch of the Magadhas, who spoke well and strongly like Indra ; but having heard it, the prince did not falter. He was firm like a mountain.

2. Being thus addressed by the monarch of the Magadhas, Gautama, in a strong speech with a friendly face,—self-possessed, unchanged, thus made answer :

3. " What you have said is not to be called a strange thing for thee. O King ! born as thou art in the great family whose ensign is the lion, and lover as thou art of thy friends, that ye should adopt this line of approach towards him who stands as one of thy friends is only natural.

4. " Amongst the evil-minded, a friendship worthy of their family, ceases to continue and fades; it is only the good who keep increasing the old friendship of their ancestors by a new succession of friendly acts.

5. " But those men who act unchangingly towards their friends in reverses of fortune, I esteem in my heart as true friends. Who is not the friend of the prosperous man, in his times of abundance?

6. " So those who, having obtained riches in the world, employ them for the sake of their friends

and religions,—their wealth has real solidity, and when it perishes it produces no pain at the end.

7. "This thy suggestion concerning me, O King, is prompted by pure generosity and friendship; I
I will meet thee courteously with simple friendship; I would not utter aught else in my reply.

50 8. "I am not so afraid even of serpents nor of thunderbolts falling from heaven, nor of flames blown together by the wind, as I am afraid of these worldly objects.

9. "These transient pleasures,—the robbers of our happiness and our wealth, and which float empty and like illusions through the world,—infatuate man's minds even when they are only hoped for,—still more when they take up their abode in the soul.

10. "The victims of pleasure attain not to happiness even in the heaven of the gods, still less in the world of mortals; he who is athirst is never satisfied with pleasures, as the fire, the friend of the wind, with fuel.

11. "There is no calamity in the world like pleasures, people are devoted to them through delusion; when he once knows the truth and so fears evil, what wise man would of his own choice desire evil?

12. "When they have obtained all the earth girdled by the sea, kings wish to conquer the other side of the great ocean; mankind is never satiated with pleasures, as the ocean with the waters that fall into it.

13. "When it had rained a golden shower from heaven, and when he had conquered the continents and had even obtained the half of Sakra's throne, Mandhatri was still full of craving for worldly objects.

14. "Though he enjoyed the kingdom of the gods in heaven, when Indra had concealed himself through fear of Vritra, and though in his pride he had made the great Rishis bear his litter, Nahusha was not satisfied.

15. "Who would seek these enemies bearing the name of pleasures, by whom even those sages have been overcome, who were devoted to other pursuits, whose only clothes were rags, whose food roots, fruits,

and water and who wear their twisted locks as long as snakes?

16. "When they hear of the miseries of those who are intent on pleasure and are devoted to worldly pursuits it well befits the self-controlled to fling it away.

17. "Success in pleasure is to be considered a misery in the man of pleasure, for he becomes intoxicated when the pleasures of his desire are attained; through intoxication he does what should not be done, not what should be done; and being wounded thereby he falls into a miserable end.

18. "These pleasures which are gained and kept by toil, which after deceiving leave you and return whence they came,—these pleasures which are but borrowed for a time,—what man of self-control, if he is wise, would delight in them?

19. "What man of self-control could find satisfaction in these pleasures which are like a torch of hay,—which excite thirst when you seek them and when you grasp them?

20. "What man of self-control could find satisfaction in these pleasures which are like flesh that has been flung away, and which produces misery by their being held in common with kings?

21. "What man of self-control could find satisfaction in these pleasures, which, like the senses, are destructive, which bring calamity on every hand to those who abide in them?

22. "Those men of self-control who are bitten by them in their hearts, fall into ruin and attain not bliss—what man of self-control could find satisfaction in these pleasures, which are like an angry, cruel serpent?

23. "Even if they enjoy them men are not satisfied,—like dogs famishing with hunger over a bone,—what man of self-control could find satisfaction in these pleasures, which are like a skeleton composed of dry bones?

24. "He whose intellect is blinded with pleasures, the wretch, who is the miserable slave of hope for the

sake of pleasures, well deserves the pain of death even in the world of living.

25. "Deer are lured to their destruction by songs, insects for the sake of the brightness fly into the fire,
I the fish greedy for the flesh swallows the iron hook,—therefore, worldly pleasures produce misery as their
52 end.

26. "As for the common opinion, 'pleasures are enjoyment,' none of them when examined are worthy of being enjoyed; fine garments and the rest are only the accessories of things,—they are to be regarded as merely the remedies for pain.

27. "Water is desired for allaying thirst; food in the same way for removing hunger; a house for keeping off the wind, the heat of the sun, and the rain; and dress for keeping off the cold and to cover one's nakedness.

28. "So too a bed is for removing drowsiness; a carriage for remedying the fatigue of a journey; a seat for alleviating the pain of standing; so bathing as a means for washing, health, and strength.

29. "External objects therefore are to human beings means for remedying pain—not in themselves sources of enjoyment; what wise man would allow that he enjoys those delights which are only used as remedial?

30. "He who, when burned with the heat of bilious fever, maintains that cold appliances are an enjoyment, when he is only engaged in alleviating pain,—he indeed might give the name of enjoyment to pleasures.

31. "Since variableness is found in all pleasures, I cannot apply to them the name of enjoyment; the very conditions which mark pleasure, bring also in their turn pain.

32. "Heavy garments and fragrant aloe-wood are pleasant in the cold, but an annoyance in the heat; and the moonbeams and sandalwood are pleasant in the heat, but a pain in the cold.

33. "Since the well-known opposite pairs, such as gain and loss and the rest, are inseparably connected

with everything in this world,—therefore, no man is invariably happy on the earth nor invariably wretched.

34. "When I see how the nature of pleasure and pain are mixed, I consider royalty and slavery as the same; a king does not always smile, nor is a slave always in pain.

35. "Since to be a king involves a wider range of responsibility, therefore, the sorrows of a king are great; for a king is like a peg,—he endures trouble for the sake of the world.

36. "A king is unfortunate, if he places his trust in his royalty which is apt to desert and loves crooked turns; and, on the other hand, if he does not trust in it, then what can be the happiness of a timid king?

37. "And since after even conquering the whole earth, one city only can serve as a dwelling place and even there only one house can be inhabited, is not royalty mere labour for others?

38. "And even in royalty nothing more than one pair of garments is all he needs, and just enough food to keep off hunger; so only one bed, and only one seat is all that a king needs; other distinctions are only for pride.

39. "And if all these fruits are desired for the sake of satisfaction, I can be satisfied without a kingdom; and if a man is once satisfied in this world, are not all distinctions unnecessary?

40. "He then who has attained the auspicious road to happiness is not to be deceived in regard to pleasures. Remembering thy professed friendship, I ask, tell me again and again, are the pleasures worth anything?

41. "I have not left home through anger, nor because my diadem has been dashed down by an enemy's arrow; nor have I set my desires on loftier objects, that I thus refuse thy proposal.

42. "Only he who, having once let go a malignant incensed serpent, or a blazing hay-torch all on fire, would strive again to seize it, would ever seek pleasures

again after having once abandoned them.

43. "Only he who, though seeing would envy the blind, though free, the bound, though wealthy, the destitute, though sound in his reason, the maniac—
I only he, I say, would envy one who is devoted to wordly objects.

54 44. "He who lives on alms, my good friend, is not to be pitied. He has here the best happiness, perfect calm, and hereafter all sorrows are for him abolished.

45. "But he is to be pitied who is overpowered by craving though in the midst of great wealth,—who attains not the happiness of calm here, while pain has to be experienced hereafter.

46. "What thou hast spoken to me is well worthy of thy character, thy mode of life, and thy family; and to carry out my resolve is also befitting my character, my mode of life, and my family."

§ 4. *Reply by Gautama* (concluded)

1. "I have been wounded by the strife of the world, and I have come out longing to obtain peace; I would not accept any empire in the third heaven, for saving me from all the ills of the earth how much less amongst men?

2. "But as for what thou hast said to me, O King, that the universal pursuit of the three objects is the supreme end of man,—and thou saidst that what I regard as the desirable is misery,—thy three objects are perishable and also unsatisfying.

3. "And as for what thou saidst, 'wait till old age comes, for youth is ever subject to change';—this want of decision is itself uncertain; for age too can be irresolute and youth can be firm.

4. "But since Fate is so well skilled in its art as to draw the world in all its various ages into its power,—how shall the wise man, who desires tranquillity, wait for old age, when he knows not when the time of death will be?

5. "When death stands ready like a hunter,

with old age as his weapon, and diseases scattered about as his arrows, smiting down living creatures who fly like deer to the forest of destiny, what desire can there be in anyone for length of life?

6. "It well befits the youthful son or the old man or the child so to act with all promptitude that they may choose the path of the religious man whose soul is all mercy.

7. "And as for what thou saidst, 'be diligent in sacrifices for religion, such as are worthy of thy race and bring a glorious fruit,'—honour to such sacrifices! I desire not that fruit which is sought by causing pain to others!

8. "To kill a helpless victim through a wish for future reward,—it would be unseemly action for a merciful, good-hearted man, even if the reward of the sacrifice were eternal.

9. "And even if true religion did not consist in quite another rule of conduct, by self-restraint, moral practice and a total absence of passion,—still it would not be seemly to follow the rule of sacrifice, where the highest reward is described as attained only by slaughter.

10. "Even that happiness which comes to a man, while he stays in this world, through the injury of another, is hateful to the wise compassionate heart; how much more if it be something beyond our sight in another life?

11. "I am not to be lured into a course of action for future reward,—my mind does not delight, O King, in future births; these actions are uncertain and wavering in their direction, like plants beaten by the rain from a cloud."

12. The king himself, folding his hands, replied, "Thou art obtaining thy desire without hindrance; when thou hast at last accomplished all that thou hast to do, thou shalt show hereafter thy favour towards me."

13. Having received a firm promise from Gautama to visit him again, the monarch, taking his courtiers with him, returned to the palace.

§ 5. *News of Peace*

1. While Gautama was staying in Rajagraha
there came five other Parivrajakas who also put up a
hut by the side of the hut which Gautama had erected
I for himself.

56 2. These five Parivrajakas were Kundinya,
Ashvajit, Kasyapa, Mahanam and Bhaduka.

3. They too were struck by Gautama's appearance and wondered what could have led him to take Parivraja.

4. They questioned him over the issue in the same way as did King Bimbisara.

5. When he explained to them the circumstances which led him to take Parivraja, they said, " We have heard of it. But do you know what has happened since you left ? " they asked.

6. Siddharth said, " No. " Then they told him that after he left Kapilavatsu there was a great agitation among the Sakyas against going to war with the Koliyas.

7. There were demonstrations and processions by men and women, boys and girls, carrying flags with such slogans as, " Koliyas are our brothers," " It is wrong for a brother to fight against brother. "Think of the exile of Siddharth Gautama," etc.

8. The result of the agitation was that the Sakya Sangh had to call a meeting and reconsider the question. This time the majority was for compromise with the Koliyas.

9. The Sangh decided to select five Sakyas to act as their envoys and negotiate peace with the Koliyas.

10. When the Koliyas heard of this they were very glad. They too selected five Koliyas to deal with the envoys of the Sakyas.

11. The envoys on the two sides met and agreed to appoint a permanent Council of Arbitration with authority to settle every dispute regarding the sharing of the waters of the river Rohini and both sides to abide by its decision. Thus the threatened war had ended in peace.

12. After informing Gautama of what had happened at Kapilavatsu, the Parivrajakas said, "There is now no need for you to continue to be a Parivrajaka. Why don't you go home and join your family ? "

13. Siddharth said : " I am happy to have this good news. It is a triumph for me. But I will not go back to my home. I must not. I must continue to be a Parivrajaka."

14. Gautama asked the five Parivrajakas, what their programme was. They replied, " We have decided to do *tapasya*. Why don't you join us ? " Siddharth said, " By and by ; I must examine other ways first."

15. The five Parivrajakas then left.

§ 6. *The Problem in a New Perspective*

1. The news brought by the five Parivrajakas that the Koliyas and Sakyas had made peace, made Gautama very uneasy.

2. Left alone, he began to reflect on his own position and to make sure if any reason was left for him to continue his Parivraja.

3. He had left his people for what ?, he asked himself.

4. He had left his home because he was opposed to war. " Now that the war is over is there any problem left to me ? Does my problem end because war has ended ? "

5. On a deep reflection he thought not.

6. " The problem of war is essentially a problem of conflict. It is only a part of a larger problem.

7. " This conflict is going on not only between kings and nations but between nobles and Brahmins, between householders, between mother and son, between son and mother, between father and son, between sister and brother, between companion and companion.

8. " The conflict between nations is occasional. But the conflict between classes is constant and

perpetual. It is this which is the root of all sorrow and suffering in the world.

9. "True, I left home on account of war. But I cannot go back home although the war between the Sakyas and Koliyas has ended. I see now that my problem has become wider. I have to find a solution for this problem of social conflict.

10. "How far do the old-established philosophies offer a solution of this problem?"

11. Can he accept any one of the social philosophies?

12. He was determined to examine everything for himself.

PART III

In Search of New Light

1. Halt at Brighu's Ashram.
2. Study of Sankhya.
3. Training in Samadhi Marga.
4. Trial of Asceticism.
5. Abandonment of Asceticism.

§ 1. *Halt at Brighu's Ashram*

1. With the desire to pursue other ways, Gautama left Rajagraha to meet Arada Kalam.

2. On his way he beheld the hermitage of Brighu I
and entered it out of curiosity.

3. The Brahmin inmates of the Ashram who had 61
gone outside for the sake of fuel, having just come back with their hands full of fuel, flowers, and kusa grass, pre-eminent as they were in penances, and proficient in wisdom, went just to see him, and went not to their cells.

4. Then he being duly honoured by those dwellers of the hermitage paid his homage to the Elders of the Ashram.

5. He, the wise one, longing for liberation, traversed that hermitage, filled with the holy company desirous of heaven,—gazing at their strange penances.

6. He, the gentle one, saw for the first time the different kinds of penances practised by the ascetics in that sacred grove.

7. Then the Brahmin Brighu, well-versed in the technique of penance, told Gautama all the various kinds of penances and the fruits thereof.

8. "Uncooked food, growing out of water, and roots and fruits,—this is the fare of the saints according to the sacred texts ; but the different alternatives of penance vary.

9. "Some live like the birds on gleaned corn, others graze on grass like the deer, others live on air like the snakes, as if turned into ant-hills.

10. "Others win their nourishment with great effort from stones, others eat corn ground with their own teeth ; some, having boiled for others, keep for themselves what may chance to be left.

11. "Others, with their tufts of matted hair continually wet with water, twice offer oblations to Agni with hymns ; others, plunging like fishes into the water, dwell there with their bodies scratched by tortoises.

12. "By such penances endured for a time,—by

the higher they attain heaven, by the lower the world of men, by the path of pain they eventually dwell in happiness,—pain, they say, is the root of merit."

13. On hearing this Gautama said : "Today is my first sight of such a hermitage and I do not understand this rule of penance.

14. "This is all I would say at the moment. This devotion of yours is for the sake of heaven—while my desire is that the ills of life on earth be probed and a solution found. Will you allow me to take your leave. I wish to learn the Sankhya Philosophy and train myself in the Samadhi marga, and see what help it can give me for the solution of my problem.

15. "There is sorrow to me when I reflect that I shall have to depart, leaving you who are thus engaged, you who are such a refuge and who have shown such excessive kindness to me,—just as there was when I had to leave my kindred behind.

16. "It is not, therefore, any dislike on my part or the wrong conduct of another, which makes me go away from this wood ; for ye are like great sages, standing fast in the religious duties which are in accordance with former sages.

17. "I wish to go to Muni Arada Kalam who is known to be the master of the subject."

18. Seeing his resolve Brighu, the chief of the hermitage, said : "Prince, brave indeed is thy purpose, who, young as thou art, having pondered thoroughly between heaven and liberation have made up your mind for liberation, ye are indeed brave !

19. "If what you have said is thy settled purpose go quickly to Vindhyakoshtha ; the Muni Arada lives there who has gained an insight into absolute bliss.

20. "From him thou wilt learn the path but as I foresee, this purpose of thine will go further, after having studied his theory."

21. Gautama thanked him, and having saluted the company of sages he departed ; the hermits also, having duly performed to him all the rites of courtesy, entered again into the ascetic grove.

§ 2. *Study of Sankhya*

1. Leaving the Ashram of Brighu, Gautama started to find the abode of Arada Kalam.

2. Arada Kalam was staying at Vaishali. Gautama went thither. On reaching Vaishali he went to his Ashram.

3. Approaching Arada Kalam, he said : "I wish to be initiated into your doctrine and discipline."

4. Thereupon Arada Kalam said : "You are welcome. Such is my doctrine that an intelligent man like you in no long time may of himself comprehend, realise and attain my teaching and abide by it.

5. "Verily thou art a worthy vessel to receive this highest training."

6. The prince, having heard these words of Arada, was filled with great pleasure and thus made reply.

7. "This extreme kindliness which thou showest to me, makes me, imperfect as I am, seem even already to have attained perfection.

8. "Will you, therefore, deign to tell me what your doctrine is ?"

9. Said Arada, "I am so much impelled by your noble nature, by your sincerity of character and by your resolution that I need not put you to any preliminary examination to test your worthiness.

10. "Listen, best of listeners, to our tenets."

11. He then expounded to Gautama the tenets of what was known as the Sankhya Philosophy.

12. At the conclusion of his discourse Arada Kalam said :

13. "These are, O Gautama, the tenets of our system. I have told them to you in a summary form."

14. Gautama was greatly pleased with the clear exposition given by Arada Kalam.

§ 3. *Training in Samadhi Marga*

1. At the time when Gautama was examining the various ways of finding a solution to his problem

he thought of getting himself acquainted with the Dhyana Marga (Concentration of the Mind).

2. There were *three* schools of the Dhyana Marga.

3. All of them had one thing in common,
I namely, that control of breathing was the means of achieving Dhyana.

64 4. One school followed a way of controlling breathing which is called *Anapanasati.*

5. Another school followed the way of control of breathing known as *Pranayama.* It divided the breathing process into three parts : (1) Breathing *in* (Puraka) ; (2) *holding* the breath (Kumbhaka) ; and (3) breathing *out* (Rechak). The third school was known as Samadhi School.

6. Arada Kalam was well known as the master of Dhyana Marga. Gautama felt that it might be well for him if he could get some training in the Dhyana Marga under Arada Kalam.

7. So he spoke to Arada Kalam and asked him if he would be so good as to give training in the Dhyana Marga.

8. Arada Kalam replied, " With great pleasure."

9. Arada Kalam taught him his technique of the Dhyana Marga. It consisted of seven stages.

10. Gautama practised the technique every day.

11. After acquiring complete mastery over it Gautama asked Arada Kalam if there was anything further to be learned.

12. Arada Kalam replied : " No friend, that is all that I have to teach." With this Gautama took leave of Arada Kalam.

13. Gautama had heard of another yogi, by name Uddaka Ramaputta, who was reputed to have devised a technique which enabled a Dhyani to go one stage higher than that devised by Arada Kalam.

14. Gautama thought of learning his technique and experiencing the highest stage of Samadhi. Accordingly he went to the Ashram of Uddaka Ramaputta and placed himself under his training.

15. Within a short time did Gautama master the technique of Uddaka's eighth stage. After having

perfected himself in the technique of Uddaka Ramaputta, Gautama asked him the same question which he had asked Arada Kalam : "Is there anything further to be learned ?"

16. And Uddaka Ramaputta gave the same I
reply. "No friend, there is nothing more that I can
teach you." 65

17. Arada Kalam and Uddaka Ramaputta were famous for their mastery of Dhyana Marga in the country of the Kosalas. But Gautama had heard that there were similar masters of Dhyana Marga in the country of the Magadhas. He thought he should have a training in their system also.

18. Gautama accordingly went to Magadha.

19. He found that their technique of Dhyana Marga, though based on control of breathing, was different from what was in vogue in the Kosala country.

20. The technique was not to breathe but to reach concentration by stopping breathing.

21. Gautama learned this technique. When he tried concentration by stopping breathing he found that piercing sounds used to come out of his ears, and his head appeared to him to be pierced as though by a sharp pointed knife.

22. It was a painful process. But Gautama did not fail to master it.

23. Such was his training in the Samadhi Marga.

§ 4. *Trial of Asceticism*

1. Gautama had given a trial to the Sankhya and Samadhi Marga. But he had left the Ashram of the Brighus without giving a trial to Asceticism.

2. He felt he should give it a trial and gain experience for himself so that he could speak authoritatively about it.

3. Accordingly Gautama went to the town of Gaya. From there he reconnoitred the surrounding country and fixed his habitation at Uruvela in the hermitage of Negari, the Royal Seer of Gaya, for practising asceticism. It was a lonely and solitary

place on the banks of the river Nairanjana for practising asceticism.

4. At Uruvela he found the five Parivrajakas whom he had met at Rajagraha and who had brought
I news of peace. They too were practising asceticism.

5. The mendicants saw him there and approached
66 him to take them with him. Gautama agreed.

6. Thereon they served him reverently, abiding as pupils under his orders, and were humble and compliant.

7. The austerities and self-mortification practised by Gautama were of the severest sort.

8. Sometimes he visited two but not more than seven houses a day and took at each only two but not more than seven morsels.

9. He lived on a single saucer of food a day, but not more than seven saucers.

10. Sometimes he had but one meal a day, or one every two days, and so on, upto once every seven days, or only once a fortnight, on a rigid scale of rationing.

11. As he advanced in the practice of asceticism his sole diet was herbs gathered green, or the grain of wild millets and paddy, or snippets hide, or water-plants, or the red powder round rice-grains within the husk or the discarded scum of rice on the boil, or the flour of oilseeds.

12. He lived on wild roots and fruit, or on windfalls only.

13. His raiment was of hemp or hempen mixture of cerements of rags from the dust-heap, of bark, of the black antelope's pelt either whole or split down the middle, of grass, of strips of bark or wood, hair of men or animals woven into a blanket, or of owl's wings.

14. He plucked out the hair of his head and the hair of his beard, never quitted the upright for the sitting posture, squatted and never rose up, moving only squatting.

15. After this wise, in diverse fashions, he lived to torment and to torture his body—to such a length in asceticism did he go.

16. To such a length in loathliness did he go that there became accumulated on his body the dirt and filth for years till it dropped off by itself.

17. He took up his abode in the awesome depths of the forest, depths so awesome that it was reputed that none but the senseless could venture without his hair standing on end.

18. When the cold season brought chill wintry nights, then it was that in the dark half of the months he dwelt by night in the open air and in the dark thicket by day.

19. But when there came the last broiling month of summer before the rains, he made his dwelling under the baking sun by day and in the stifling thicket by night.

20. In a charnel ground did he lay down with charred bones for pillow.

21. Thereafter Gautama lived on a single bean a day—on a single sesamum seed a day—or a single grain of rice a day.

22. When he was living on a single fruit a day, his body grew emaciated in the extreme.

23. If he sought to feel his belly, it was his backbone which he found in his grasp ; if he sought to feel his backbone he found himself grasping his belly, so closely did his belly cleave to his backbone and all because he ate so little.

§ 5. *Abandonment of Asceticism*

1. The austerities and mortification practised by Gautama were of the severest sort. They lasted for a long period of six years.

2. At the end of six years his body had become so weak that he was quite unable to move.

3. Yet he had seen no new light and was no nearer to the solution to the problem of misery in the world on which his mind was centred.

4. He reflected to himself : " This is not the way, even to passionlessness, nor to perfect knowledge, nor to liberation.

5. " Some undergo misery for the sake of this world, others meet toil for the sake of heaven ; all living beings wretched through hope and always missing their aim, fall certainly for the sake of happi-
I ness into misery.

6. " Has not something like this happened to me?

68 7. " It is not the effort itself which I blame,—which flinging aside the base pursues a high path of its own.

8. " What I ask is, 'Can the mortification of the body be called religion ?'

9. " Since it is only by the mind's authority that the body either acts or ceases to act, therefore, to control the thought is alone befitting—without thought the body is like a dog.

10. " If there was only the body to be considered, merit may be gained by purity of food, but then there is merit also in the doer. But of what good is it?

11. " New light cannot be attained by him who has lost his strength and is wearied with hunger, thirst and fatigue with his mind no longer self-possessed through fatigue.

12. " How could he who is not absolutely calm, reach the end which is to be attained by his mind?

13. " True calm and the self-possession of the mind is properly obtained by the constant satisfaction of the body's wants."

14. At this time there lived at Uruvela a house-holder by name Senani. Sujata was his daughter.

15. Sujata had uttered a wish to a Banyan Tree, and vowed a yearly offering to it if she should have a son.

16. The wish having been fulfilled, she sent her maid Punna to prepare the place for the offering.

17. Punna finding Gautama sitting beneath the Banyan Tree, thought he was the god of the tree who had come down.

18. Sujata came and offered Gautama the food prepared by her in a golden bowl.

19. He took the bowl to the river bank, bathed

at a ford or a bathing place called Suppatitthita and ate the food.

20. Thus ended his trial of asceticism.

21. The five ascetics who were with Gautama
became angry with him for having given up the life I
of austerity and self-mortification and in disgust 69
left him.

PART IV

Enlightenment and the Vision of a New Way

1. Meditation for New Light.
2. Enlightenment.
3. The Discovery of a New Dhamma.
4. Gautama who was a Bodhisatta after Sammabodhi becomes a Buddha.

§ 1. Meditation for New Light

1. Having refreshed himself with food Gautama sat thinking over his past experiences. He realised that all paths had failed. I

2. The failure was so complete that it could have led anyone into a state of frustration. He was, of course, 73
sorry. But frustration as such did not touch him.

3. He was always hopeful of finding a way. So much so that on the night of the day on which he partook of the food sent by Sujata, Gautama had five dreams and when he awoke he interpreted his dreams to mean that he was sure to attain enlightenment.

4. He had also tried to forecast his future. This he did by throwing the bowl of food, Sujata's maid brought, into the river Nairanja, saying : "If I am to have enlightenment let the bowl ascend the stream; if not let it go down." The vessel, indeed, began to float against the current and at last sank near the abode of Kala, a Naga king.

5. Fortified with hope and determination he left Uruvela and towards evening went along the wide road to Gaya. There he saw a Banyan Tree. He thought of sitting under it in meditation in the hope of a new light dawning upon him and enabling him to find a way which would solve his problem.

6. After trying each of the four directions he chose the East which is always chosen by all the great sages for the removal of all defilements.

7. Gautama sat down cross-legged and upright under the Banyan Tree. Determined to achieve enlightenment, he said to himself, "Skin, sinew and bone may dry up as they will, my flesh and blood may dry in my body, but without attaining complete enlightenment I will not leave this seat."

8. Then Kala, the king of the Nagas, whose majesty was like the lord of elephants, and his wife Suvarnaprabhasa, having been awakened by the vision of Gautama sitting under the Banyan Tree, uttered this in praise of him being sure that he was destined to attain perfect knowledge.

9. " Inasmuch as the earth, pressed down by thy feet, O Sage, resounds repeatedly, and inasmuch as thy splendour shines forth like the sun, thou shalt assuredly reap the desired fruit.

I 10. " Inasmuch as flocks of birds fluttering in
the sky offer thee reverential salutation, O Lotus-eyed
74 One ; and inasmuch as gentle breezes blow in the sky,
thou shalt certainly attain thy object."

11. As he sat down for meditation a crowd of evil thoughts and evil passions—mythologically called the children of Mara (Kama), which is another name for evil passions, entered his mind.

12. Gautama was greatly frightened lest they should overpower him and defeat his purpose.

13. He knew that in this battle with evil passions many Rishis and Brahmins had succumbed.

14. So he summoned all the courage he had and said to Mara, " Faith is found in me, and heroism and wisdom. How can ye evil passions defeat me? The streams even of rivers may this wind dry up. Ye would be unable to dry up my resolutions, when I am so intent." Better to me is death in battle than that I should be defeated in life.

15. The evil passions entered the mind of Gautama as a crow goes after a stone that looks like a hump of fat, thinking surely, " here I shall find a tender morsel, here perchance is something sweet."

16. And finding no sweetness there, the crow departs thence. So like a crow attacking a rock, the evil passions left Gautama in disgust.

§ 2. *Enlightenment*

1. To feed himself during the period of meditation Gautama had collected enough food to last him for forty days.

2. Having routed the evil thoughts that disturbed his mind Gautama refreshed himself with food and gained strength. He thus prepared himself for meditation with the aim of obtaining enlightenment.

3. It took Gautama four weeks of meditation

to obtain enlightenment. He reached final enlightenment in four stages.

4. In the first stage he called forth reason and investigation. His seclusion helped him to attain it easily.

5. In the second stage he added concentration.

6. In the third stage he brought to his aid equanimity and mindfulness.

7. In the fourth and final stage he added purity to equanimity and equanimity to mindfulness.

8. Thus with mind concentrated, purified, spotless, with defilement gone, supple, dexterous, firm, impassionate, not forgetting what he is after, Gautama concentrated himself on the problem of finding an answer to the question which had troubled him.

9. On the night of the last day of the fourth week light dawned upon him. He realised that there were two problems. The first problem was that there was suffering in the world and the second problem was how to remove this suffering and make mankind happy.

10. So in the end, after meditation for four weeks, darkness was dispelled, light arose, ignorance was dispelled and knowledge arose. He saw a new way.

§ 3. *The Discovery of a New Dhamma*

1. Gautama when he sat in meditation for getting new light was greatly in the grip of the Sankhya Philosophy.

2. That suffering and unhappiness in the world he thought was an incontrovertible fact.

3. Gautama was, however, interested in knowing how to do away with suffering. This problem the Sankhya Philosophy did not deal with.

4. It is, therefore, on this problem—how to remove suffering and unhappiness—that he concentrated his mind.

5. Naturally, the first question he asked himself was—" What are the causes of suffering and unhappiness which an individual undergoes ? "

6. His second question was—" How to remove unhappiness ? "

7. To both these questions he got a right answer which is called '*Samma Bodhi*' (Right Enlightenment).

I 8. It is because of this that the Banyan Tree
76 has come to be known as the Bodhi Tree.

§ 4. *Gautama who was a Bodhisatta After Sammabodhi Becomes a Buddha*

1. Before enlightenment Gautama was only a Bodhisatta. It is after reaching enlightenment that he became a Buddha.

2. Who and what is a Bodhisatta ?

3. A Bodhisatta is a person who is seeking to be a Buddha.

4. How does a Bodhisatta become a Buddha ?

5. A Bodhisatta must be a Bodhisatta for ten lives in succession. What must a Bodhisatta do in order to qualify himself to become a Buddha ?

6. In his first life he acquires Mudita (joy). The Bodhisatta having blown off his impurities, as the smith blows the dross from silver, reflects that man who has been reckless and becomes sober brightens up the world like the moon freed from clouds. Joy springs up in him realising this, and he is fervent in his desire to benefit all beings.

7. In his second life he acquires Vimala (Purity). The Bodhisatta has now removed all thoughts of lust ; he is kind ; he is kind to all ; he neither flatters the vices of men nor disparages their virtues.

8. In his third life he acquires Prabhakari (Brightness). The intellect of the Bodhisatta now becomes as bright as a mirror. He fully knows and grasps the truths of Anatta and Anicca. His only wish is for the highest wisdom, and for this he is ready to sacrifice anything.

9. In his fourth life he acquires Arcishmati (Intelligence of Fire). The Bodhisatta in this life fixes his mind on the Eightfold Path, the Four Contempla-

tions, the Fourfold Contest, the Fourfold Will Power, the Fivefold Morality.

10. In his fifth life he acquires Sudurjaya (Difficult to Conquer). He fully understands the connection of the relative and the absolute.

11. In his sixth life he becomes Abhimukhi. In this stage the Bodhisatta is now prepared fully to grasp the evolution of things, its cause, the Twelve Nidanas ; and this knowledge, called Abhimukhi, awakens the most profound compassion in his heart for all beings blinded by Avidya.

12. In his seventh life the Bodhisatta becomes a Durangama (going far off). The Bodhisatta is now beyond time and space ; he is one with Infinity, but he still retains nama-rupa out of his great compassion for all beings. He is secluded from others, in that the lusts of the world no more cling to him than water to a lotus leaf. He quenches desires in his fellow beings, practices charity, patience, tactfulness, energy, calmness, intelligence and the highest wisdom.

13. While in this life he knows the Dharma, but presents it in ways understood by the people, he knows he must be tactful and patient. Whatever men do to him he bears with equanimity, for he knows that it is through ignorance they misunderstand his motives. At the same time he never slackens his energy to benefit all beings, nor does he withdraw his mind from wisdom, therefore misfortune can never turn him from the righteous path.

14. In his eighth life he becomes Acala. In the stage of Acala, or 'immovable,' all strivings on the part of the Bodhisatta cease. He follows good spontaneously ; whatever he will do he will succeed in.

15. In his ninth life he becomes Sadhumati. This is the stage or condition of one who has vanquished and penetrated all dharmas or systems, all quarters, and does not enter time.

16. In his tenth life he becomes Dharmamegha. The Bodhisatta attains the infinite divine eye of a Buddha.

17. The Bodhisatta acquires these ten powers

which are necessary for him when he becomes a Buddha.

18. The Bodhisatta must not only acquire these ten powers as he evolves from stage to stage but he must also practice to perfection the ten Paramitas.

I 19. One Paramita is to be the end of one life. Specialisation in the Paramitas must go stage by stage.
78 One Paramita in one life and not a little of one and a little of the other.

20. It is only when he is doubly equipped that a Bodhisatta becomes qualified for becoming a Buddha. The Buddha is a culminating point in the life of a Bodhisatta.

21. The theory of the Jatakas or the birth stages of a Bodhisatta appears analogous to the Brahmanic theory of Avataras, i.e., the theory of incarnations of God.

22. The Jataka theory is based upon the Buddha having the highest degree of purity as the essence of his being.

23. The Avatar theory does not require that the God should be pure in his making. All that the Brahmanic theory of Avatar says is that God saves his followers by taking different forms although the God may be very impure and immoral in his conduct.

24. The theory that to be a Bodhisatta for ten lives as a condition precedent for becoming a Buddha has no parallel anywhere. No other religion calls upon its founder to answer such a test.

PART V

The Buddha and His Predecessors

1. The Buddha and the Vedic Rishis.
2. Kapila—The Philosopher.
3. The Bramhanas.
4. The Upanishads and their Teachings.

§ 1. *The Buddha and the Vedic Rishis*

1. The Vedas are a collection of *Mantras*, i.e., hymns or chants. The reciters of these hymns are called Rishis. I

2. The Mantras are mere invocations to deities such as *Indra*, *Varuna*, *Agni*, *Soma*, *Isana*, *Prajapati*, 81
Bramha, *Mahiddhi*, *Yama* and others.

3. The invocations are mere prayers for help against enemies, for gift of wealth, for accepting the offerings of food, flesh and wine from the devotee.

4. There is not much philosophy in the Vedas. But there were some Vedic sages who had entered into speculations of a philosophical nature.

5. These Vedic sages were : (1) Aghamarsana; (2) Prajapati Parmesthin; (3) Brahmanaspati, otherwise known as Brihaspati; (4) Anila; (5) Dirghatamas; (6) Narayan; (7) Hiranyagarbha; and (8) Visvakarman.

6. The main problems of these Vedic philosophers were : How did the world originate ? In what manner were individual things created ? Why have they their unity and existence ? Who created, and who ordained ? From what did the world spring up and to what again will it return ?

7. *Aghamarsana* said that the world was created out of Tapas (heat). Tapas was the creative principle from which eternal law and truth were born. From these were produced the night (tamas). Tamas produced water and from water originated time. Time gave birth to the sun and the moon, the heaven and the earth, the firmament and light and ordained the days and nights.

8. *Brahmanaspati* postulated the genesis of being from non-being. By the term non-existence, he denoted apparently the infinite. The existent originally sprang up from the non-existent. The non-existent (asat, nonens) was the permanent foundation of all that is existent (sat, ens) and of all that is possible and yet non-existent (asat).

9. *Prajapati Parmesthin* started with the problem: "Did being come out of non-being?" His view was that this was an irrelevant question. For him water was the original substance of that which exists. For
I him the original matter—water—came neither under the definition of being nor under that of non-being.

82 10. *Paramesthin* did not draw any distinction between matter and motive power. According to him water transformed itself into particular things by some inherent principle to which he gave the name Kama, Cosmic Desire.

11. *Anila* was another Vedic Philosopher. To him the principal element was air (vayu). It possesses the inherent capacity for movement. It is endowed with the generating principle.

12. *Dirghtamas* maintained that all living beings rest and depend ultimately on the sun. The sun held up and propelled by its inherent force went backward and forward.

13. The sun is composed of a grey coloured substance and so are lightning and fire.

14. The sun, lightning and fire formed the germ of water. Water forms the germ of plants. Such were the views of *Dirghatamas.*

15. According to *Narayana*, Purusha (God) is the first cause of the universe. It is from Purusha that the sun, the moon, the earth, water, fire, air, mid-air, the sky, the regions, the seasons, the creatures of the air, all animals, all classes of men, and all human institutions, had originated.

16. *Hiranyagarbha.* From doctrinal point of view he stood midway between *Parmeshthin* and *Narayan.* Hiranyagarbha means the golden germ. It was the great power of the universe, from which all other powers and existences, divine and earthly, were derived.

17. *Hiranyagarbha* means fire. It is fire that constituted the solar essence, the generating principle of the universe.

18. From the point of view of *Vishvakarman* it was quite inadequate and unsatisfactory to hold that water was the primitive substance of all that is, and

then to derive from it this world as a whole by giving it an inherent power of movement. If water be the primitive substance which is endowed with the inherent principle of change, we have yet to account for that from which water derived its being, and derived the motive power, the generating principle, the elemental forces, the laws and all the rest.

19. *Vishvakarman* held the view that it was God which was the motive power. God is first and God is last. He is earlier than the visible universe ; he had existed before all cosmic forces came into being. He is the sole God who created and ordained this universe. God is one, and the only one. He is the unborn one (aja) in whom all the existing things abide. He is the one who is mighty in mind and supreme in power. He is the maker—the disposer. As father he generated us, and as disposer he knows the fate of all that is.

20. The Buddha did not regard all the Vedic Sages as worthy of reverence. He regarded just ten Vedic Rishis as the most ancient and as the real authors of the Mantras.

21. But in the Mantras he saw nothing that was morally elevating.

22. In his view the Vedas were as worthless as a desert.

23. The Buddha, therefore, discarded the Mantras as a source from which to learn or to borrow.

24. Similarly, the Buddha did not find anything in the philosophy of the Vedic Rishis. They were groping to reach the truth. But they had not reached it.

25. Their theories were mere speculations not based on logic nor on facts. Their contributions to philosophy created no social values.

26. He therefore rejected the philosophy of the Vedic Rishis as useless.

§ 2. *Kapila — The Philosopher*

1. Among the ancient philosophers of India the most pre-eminent was Kapila.

2. His philosophical approach was unique, and as philosopher he stood in a class by himself. His philosophy was known as the Sankhya Philosophy.

I 3. The tenets of his philosophy were of a startling nature.

84 4. Truth must be supported by proof. This is the first tenet of the Sankhya system. There is no truth without proof.

5. For purposes of proving the truth Kapila allowed only two means of proof—(1) perception and (2) inference.

6. By perception is meant mental apprehension of a present object.

7. Inference is threefold : (1) from cause to effect, as from the presence of clouds to rain ; (2) from effect to cause, as from the swelling of the streams in the valleys to rain in the hills, and (3) by analogy, as when we infer from the fact that a man alters his place when he moves that the stars must also move, since they appear in different places.

8. His next tenet related to causality—creation and its cause.

9. Kapila denied the theory that there was a being who created the universe. In his view a created thing really exists beforehand in its cause just as the clay serves to form a pot, or the threads go to form a piece of cloth.

10. This is the first ground on which Kapila rejected the theory that the universe was created by a being.

11. But there are other grounds which he advanced in support of his point of view.

12. The non-existent cannot be the subject of an activity : There is no new creation. The product is really nothing else than the material of which it is composed : the product exists before its coming into being in the shape of its material of which it is composed. Only a definite product can be produced from such material ; and only a specific material can yield a specific result.

13. What then is the source of the empirical universe?

14. Kapila said the empirical universe consists of things evolved (Vyakta) and things that are not evolved (Avyakta).

15. Individual things (Vyakta Vastu) cannot be the source of unevolved things (Avyakta Vastu).

16. Individual things are all limited in magnitude and this is incompatible with the nature of the source of the universe.

17. All individual things are analogous, one to another and, therefore, no one can be regarded as the final source of the other. Moreover, as they all come into being from a source, they cannot constitute that source.

18. Further, argued Kapila, an effect must differ from its cause, though it must consist of the cause. That being so, the universe cannot itself be the final cause. It must be the product of some ultimate cause.

19. When asked why the unevolved cannot be perceived, why does it not show movement which would make it perceivable, Kapila replied :

20. "It may be due to various causes. It may be that its fine nature makes it imperceptible, just as other things of whose existence there is no doubt, cannot be perceived ; or because of their too great a distance or proximity ; or through the intervention of a third object, or through admixture with similar matter ; or through the presence of some more powerful sensation, or the blindness or other defect of the senses or the mind of the observer."

21. When asked : "What then is the source of the universe? What makes the difference between the evolved and unevolved part of the universe?

22. Kapila's reply was : 'Things that have evolved have a cause and the things that have not evolved have also a cause. But the source of both is uncaused and independent.'

23. "The things that have evolved are many in number and limited in space and name. The source is one, eternal and all-pervasive. The things evolved

have activities and parts : the source is imminent in all, but has neither activities nor parts."

24. Kapila argued that the process of development of the unevolved is through the activities of three constituents of which it is made up, Sattva, Rajas and Tamas. These are called three Gunas.

25. The first of the constituents, or factors, corresponds to what we call as light in nature, which reveals, which causes pleasure to men ; the second is that impels and moves, what produces activity ; the third is what is heavy and puts under restraint, what produces the state of indifference or inactivity.

26. The three constituents act essentially in close relation, they overpower and support one another and intermingle with one another. They are like the constituents of a lamp, the flame, the oil and wick.

27. When the three Gunas are in perfect balance, none overpowering the other, the universe appears static (Achetan) and ceases to evolve.

28. When the three Gunas are not in balance, one overpowers the other, the universe becomes dynamic (sachetan) and evolution begins.

29. Asked why the Gunas become unbalanced, the answer which Kapila gave was this disturbance in the balance of the three Gunas was due to the presence of Dukha (suffering).

30. Such were the tenets of Kapila's philosophy.

31. Of all the philosophers the Buddha was greatly impressed by the doctrines of Kapila.

32. He was the only philosopher whose teachings appeared to the Buddha to be based on logic and facts.

33. But he did not accept everything which Kapila taught. Only three things did the Buddha accept from Kapila.

34. He accepted that reality must rest on proof. Thinking must be based on rationalism.

35. He accepted that there was no logical or factual basis for the presumption that God exists or that he created the universe.

36. He accepted that there was Dukha (suffering) in the world.

37. The rest of Kapila's teachings he just bypassed as being irrelevant for his purpose.

§ 3. *The Bramhanas* I

1. Next to the Vedas are the religious books known as the Bramhanas. Both were held as sacred books. Indeed the Bramhanas are a part of the Vedas. The two went together and were called by a common name Sruti. 87

2. There were four theses on which the Bramhanic Philosophy rested.

3. The first thesis was that the Vedas are not only sacred but that they are infallible and they are not to be questioned.

4. The second thesis of the Bramhanic Philosophy was that salvation of the soul—that is escape from transmigration—can be had only by the due performance of Vedic sacrifices and observances of religious rites and ceremonies and the offering of gifts to Brahmins.

5. The Brahmins had not only a theory of an ideal religion as contained in the Vedas but they also had a theory for an ideal society.

6. The pattern of this ideal society they named *Chaturvarna.* It is imbedded in the Vedas and as the Vedas are infallible and as their authority cannot be questioned so also Chaturvarna as a pattern of society was binding and unquestionable.

7. This pattern of society was based upon certain rules.

8. The first rule was that society should be divided into four classes: (1) Brahmins; (2) Kshatriyas; (3) Vaishyas; and (4) Shudras.

9. The second rule was that there cannot be social equality among these four classes. They must be bound together by the rule of graded inequality.

10. The Brahmins to be at the top, the Kshatriyas to be kept below the Brahmins but above the Vaishyas, the Vaishyas to be below the Kshatriyas but above the Shudras and the Shudras to be the lowest of all.

11. These four classes were not to be equal to one another in the matter of rights and privileges. The rule of graded inequality governed the question of rights and privileges.

I 12. The Brahmin had all the rights and privileges which he wished to claim. But a Kshatriya
88 could not claim the rights and privileges which a Brahmin could. He had more rights and privileges than a Vaishya could claim. The Vaishya had more rights and privileges than a Shudra. But he could not claim the rights and privileges which a Kshatriya could. And the Shudra was not entitled to any right, much less any privilege. His privilege was to subsist without offending the three superior classes.

13. The third rule of Chaturvarna related to the division of occupations. The occupation of the Brahmin was learning and teaching and the performance of religious observances. The occupations of the Kshatriya was fighting. Trade was assigned to the Vaishyas. The occupations of the Shudras was service of the three superior classes. These occupations assigned to different classes were exclusive. One class could not trespass upon the occupation of the other.

14. The fourth rule of Chaturvarna related to the right to education. The pattern of Chaturvarna gave the right to education to the first three classes, the Brahmins, Kshatriyas and Vaishyas. The Shudras were denied the right to education. This rule of Chaturvarna did not deny the right to education to the Shudras only. It denied the right to education to all women including those belonging to the class of Brahmins, Kshatriyas and Vaishyas.

15. There was a fifth rule. According to it, man's life was divided into four stages. The first stage was called *Bramhacharya ;* the second stage was called *Grahastashram ;* the third stage was called *Vanaprasta* and the fourth stage was called *Sannyasa.*

16. The object of the first stage was study and education. The object of the second stage was to live a married life. The object of the third stage was

to familiarise a man with the life of a hermit, i.e., severing family ties, but without deserting his home. The object of the fourth stage was to enable a man to go in search of God and seek union with him.

17. The benefits of these stages were open only to the male members of the three superior classes. The first stage was not open to the Shudras and women. Equally the last stage was not open to the Shudras and women.

18. Such was the divine pattern of an ideal society called Chaturvarna. The Brahmins had idealised the rule and had realised the ideal without leaving any cracks or loopholes.

19. The fourth thesis of Brahmanic Philosophy was the doctrine of Karma. It was part of the thesis of transmigration of the soul. The Karma of the Brahmins was an answer to the question: "Where did the soul land on transmigration with his new body on new birth?" The answer of the Brahmanic Philosophy was that it depended on a man's deeds in his past life. In other words, it depended on his Karma.

20. The Buddha was strongly opposed to the first tenet of Brahmanism. He repudiated their thesis that the Vedas are infallible and their authority could never be questioned.

21. In his opinion, nothing was infallible and nothing could be final. Everything must be open to re-examination and reconsideration whenever grounds for re-examination and reconsideration arise.

22. Man must know the truth and real truth. To him freedom of thought was the most essential thing. And he was sure that freedom of thought was the only way to the discovery of truth.

23. Infallibility of the Vedas meant complete denial of freedom of thought.

24. For these reasons this thesis of the Brahmanic Philosophy was most obnoxious to him.

25. He was equally an opponent of the second thesis of the Brahmanic Philosophy. The Buddha did admit that there was any virtue in a sacrifice. But

he made a distinction between true sacrifice and false sacrifice.

26. Sacrifice in the sense of self-denial for the good of others he called true sacrifice. Sacrifice in the sense of killing an animal as an offering to God for personal benefit he regarded as a false sacrifice.

27. The Brahmanic sacrifices were mostly sacrifices of animals to please their gods. He condemned them as false sacrifices. He would not allow them even though they be performed with the object of getting salvation for the soul.

28. The opponents of sacrifices used to ridicule the Brahmins by saying : " If one can go to heaven by sacrificing an animal why should not one sacrifice one's own father. That would be a quicker way of going to heaven."

29. The Buddha wholeheartedly agreed with this view.

30. The theory of *Chaturvarna* was as repugnant to the Buddha as the theory of sacrifices was repulsive to him.

31. The organization of society set up by Brahmanism in the name of *Chaturvarna* did not appear to him a natural organization. Its class composition was compulsory and arbitrary. It was a society made to order. He preferred an open society and a free society.

32. The *Chaturvarna* of the Brahmins was a fixed order never to be changed. Once a Brahmin always a Brahmin. Once a Kshatriya always a Kshatriya, once a Vaishya always a Vaishya and once a Shudra always a Shudra. Society was based on status conferred upon an individual by the accident of his birth. Vice, however heinous, was no ground for degrading a man from his status, and virtue, however great, had no value to raise him above it. There was no room for worth nor for growth.

33. Inequality exists in every society. But it was different with Brahmanism. The inequality preached by Brahmins was its official doctrine. It was not a mere growth. Brahmanism did not believe in equality. In fact, it was opposed to equality.

34. Brahmanism was not content with inequality. The soul of Brahmanism lay in graded inequality.

35. Far from producing harmony, graded inequality, the Buddha thought, might produce in society an ascending scale of hatred and a descending scale of contempt, and might be a source of perpetual conflict.

36. The occupations of the four classes were also fixed. There was no freedom of choice. Besides, they were fixed not in accordance with skill but in accordance with birth.

37. On a careful review of the rules of *Chaturvarna* the Buddha had no difficulty in coming to the conclusion that the philosophic foundations on which the social order was reared by Brahmanism were wrong if not selfish.

38. It was clear to him that it did not serve the interests of all, much less did it advance the welfare of all. Indeed, it was deliberately designed to make many serve the interests of the few. In it man was made to serve a class of self-styled supermen.

39. It was calculated to suppress and exploit the weak and to keep them in a state of complete subjugation.

40. The law of Karma as formulated by the Brahmins, thought the Buddha, was calculated to sap the spirit of revolt completely. No one was responsible for the suffering of man except he himself. Revolt could not alter the state of suffering ; for suffering was fixed by his past Karma as his lot in this life.

41. The Shudras and women—the two classes whose humanity was most mutilated by Brahmanism, had no power to rebel against the system.

42. They were denied the right to knowledge with the result that by reason of their enforced ignorance they could not realize what had made their condition so degraded. They could not know that Brahmanism had robbed them completely of the significance of their life. Instead of rebelling against Brahmanism they had become the devotees and upholders of Brahmanism.

43. The right to bear arms is the ultimate means of achieving freedom which a human being has.

But the Shudras were denied the right to bear arms.

44. Under Brahmanism the Shudras were left as helpless victims of a conspiracy of selfish Brahmanism, powerful and deadly Kshatriyas and wealthy Vaishyas.

45. Could it be amended? Knowing that it was a divinely ordained social order, he knew that it could not be. It could only be ended.

46. For these reasons the Buddha rejected Brahmanism as being opposed to the true way of life.

§ 4. *The Upanishads and Their Teachings*

1. The Upanishads constituted another piece of literature. It is not part of the Vedas. It is uncanonical.

2. All the same they did form a part of religious literature.

3. The number of the Upanishads is quite large. Some important, some quite unimportant.

4. Some of them were ranged against the Vedic theologians, the Brahmin priests.

5. All of them agreed in viewing Vedic study as a study of nescience or ignorance (avidya).

6. They were all agreed in their estimate of the four Vedas and the Vedic science as the lower knowledge.

7. They were all agreed in questioning the divine origin of the Vedas.

8. They were all agreed in denying the efficacy attributed to sacrifices, to the funeral oblations, and the gifts to the priests which are the fundamentals of the Brahmanic philosophy.

9. This, however, was not the main topic with which the Upanishads were concerned. Their discussions centred round Brahman and Atman.

10. Brahman was the all-pervading principle which binds the universe and that salvation lay in the Atman realizing that it is Brahman.

11. The main thesis of the Upanishads was that

Brahmana was a reality and that *Atmana* was the same as *Brahmana*. The *Atmana* did not realize that it was *Brahman* because of the *Upadhis* in which it was entangled.

12. The question was: Is Brahmana a reality? The acceptance of the Upanishadic thesis depended upon the answer to this question.

13. The Buddha could find no proof in support of the thesis that *Brahmana* was a reality. He, therefore, rejected the thesis of the Upanishads.

14. It is not that questions on this issue were not put to the authors of the Upanishads. They were :

15. Such questions were put to no less a person than Yajnavalkya, a great *seer* who plays so important a part in the Brahadarnyka Upanishad.

16. He was asked : "What is Brahmana? What is Atmana?" All that Yajnavalkya could say : "Neti! Neti! I know not! I know not!"

17. "How can anything be a reality about which no one knows anything," asked the Buddha. He had, therefore, no difficulty in rejecting the Upanishadic thesis as being based on pure imagination.

PART VI

The Buddha and His Contemporaries

1. His Contemporaries.
2. His attitude to His Contemporaries.

§ 1. His Contemporaries

1. At the time when Gautama took Parivraja
there was a great intellectual ferment in the country.
Besides the Brahmanic Philosophy there were as many I
as sixty-two different schools of philosophy, all opposed
to the Brahmanic Philosophy. Of them at least six 97
were worthy of attention.

2. Of these schools of philosophy there was one headed by *Purana Kassappa*. His doctrine was known as *Akriyavada*. He maintained that the soul was not affected in any way by *Karma*. One may do, or one may get things done. One may do injury or one may get someone to kill. One may commit theft or dacoity or one may get theft or dacoity committed, one may commit adultery or one may get adultery committed, one may tell a lie or one may get a lie told. Nothing affects the soul. An act, however licentious, does not affect the soul with sin. An act, however good, does not bring merit to the soul. Nothing has any *Kriya* (result) on the soul. When a person dies, all the elements of which he is made join in their originals. Nothing survives after death, neither body nor soul.

3. Another school of thought was known as *Niyativada*. Its chief propounder was *Makhali Ghosal*. His doctrine was a kind of fatalism or determinism. He taught that no one can do anything or undo anything. Things happen. No one can make them happen. No one can remove unhappiness, increase it or diminish it. One must undergo one's share of the experiences of the world.

4. The third school was known as *Ucchedavada*. Its chief propounder was *Ajit Kesakambal*. His doctrine was a kind of *Annihilism*. He taught that there was nothing in *Yajna, Haom ;* there is no such thing as the fruits or effects of deeds to be enjoyed or suffered by the soul. There is neither heaven nor hell. Man is made up of certain elements of unhappiness in the world. The soul cannot escape it. Whatever sorrow

or unhappiness there was in the world the soul cannot escape. This sorrow or unhappiness will come to an end automatically. The soul must undergo rebirth during eighty-four lakhs of cycles of Mahakalpas. Then only the sorrow and unhappiness of the soul will end, not before nor by any other means.

5. The fourth school was known as *Annyonyavad.* The head of this school was *Pakudha Kacchyana.* He preached that there are seven elements which go to make up a being, namely, Prathvi, Apa, Tej, Vayu, Sukha, Dukha and the Soul. Each is independent of the other ; one does not affect the other. They are self-existent and they are eternal. Nothing can destroy them. If any one chops off the head of man he does not kill him. All that happens is that the weapon has entered the seven elements.

6. *Sanjaya Belaputta* had his own school of philosophy. It was known as *Vikshepavada*, a kind of scepticism. He argued, "if anyone asked me is there heaven, if I feel there was I would say yes. But if I feel there was no heaven I would say no. If I am asked whether human beings are created, whether man has to suffer the fruits of his action whether good or bad, and whether the soul lives after death, I say nay to all these because I don't think they exist. This is how Sanjaya Belaputta summed up his doctrine.

7. The sixth school of philosophy was known as *Chaturyamsamvarvad.* The head of this school who was alive at the time when Gautama was searching for light was *Mahavir*, who was also called *Nigantha Nathaputta.* Mahavir taught that the soul had to undergo rebirth because of the bad karmas done in the past life and in the present life. One must therefore get over the bad, he suggested, by *tapascharya.* For preventing the doing of bad karmas in this life Mahavira prescribed the observance of chaturyama dharma, i.e., observance of four rules : (1) not to kill ; (2) not to steal ; (3) not to tell a lie ; and (4) not to have property and to observe celibacy.

§ 2. *His Attitude to His Contemporaries*

1. The Buddha did not accept the teachings of the new philosophers.

2. His rejection of their teaching was not without reasons. He said that : I

3. If the doctrines of *Purana Kassyappa* or 99
Pakudha Kacchyana were true then one can do any evil or any harm ; one may even go to the length of killing another without involving any social responsibility or social consequences.

4. If the doctrine of *Makhali Ghosal* is true then man becomes the slave of destiny. He cannot liberate himself.

5. If the doctrine of *Ajit Kesakambal* is true then all that man has to do is to eat, drink and make merry.

6. If the doctrine of *Sanjaya Belaputta* was true then man must float about and live without a positive philosophy of life.

7. If the doctrine of *Nigantha Nathaputta* was true then man's life must be subjected to Asceticism and Tapascharya, a complete subjugation and uprooting of man's instincts and desires.

8. Thus, none of the paths of life suggested by the philosophers appealed to the Buddha. He thought they were the thoughts of men who had become hopeless, helpless and reckless. He therefore decided to seek light elsewhere.

PART VII

Comparison and Contrast

1. What HE Rejected.
2. What HE Modified.
3. What HE Accepted.

§ 1. *What HE Rejected*

1. This survey of the philosophical and religious thought shows that at the time when the Buddha formulated his Sasana, certain ideas had a firm grip on the mind of the people. They were : I

(i) Belief in the infallibility of the Vedas ; 103

(ii) Belief in Moksha or Salvation of the soul, i.e., its ceasing to be born again ;

(iii) Belief in the efficacy of rites, ceremonies and sacrifices as means of obtaining moksha ;

(iv) Belief in Chaturvarna as the ideal for social organization ;

(v) Belief in Iswara as the creator of and in Brahmana as the principle underlying the universe.

(vi) Belief in Atmana, or the soul.

(vii) Belief in *Sansara*, (wandering together), i.e., transmigration of the soul.

(viii) Belief in Karma, i.e., the determination of man's position in present life by deeds done by him in his past life.

2. In formulating the principles of his Sasana the Buddha dealt with this old stock of ideas in his own way.

3. The following are the ideas which he rejected :

(i) He condemned indulging in speculation as to the whence, whither and what am I ?

(ii) He discarded heresies about the soul and refrained from identifying it with either the body, sensations, volitions and consciousness.

(iii) He discarded all the Nihilistic views which were promulgated by certain religious teachers.

(iv) He condemned such views as were held by heretics.

(v) He discarded the theory that the cosmic progress had a known beginning.

(vi) He repudiated the theory that a God created man or that he came out of the body of some Bramha.

(vii) The existence of the soul he either ignored or denied.

§ 2. *What HE Modified*

I

104 (i) He accepted the great grand law of cause and effect with its corollaries.

(ii) He repudiated the fatalistic view of life and other equally foolish view that a God predestined as to what should happen for man and the world.

(iii) He discarded the theory that all deeds committed in some former birth have the potency to produce suffering, making present activity impotent. He denied the fatalistic view of Karma. He replaced the view of Karma by a much more scientific view of Karma. He put new wine in old bottle.

(iv) Transmigration (sansara) was replaced by the doctrine of re-birth.

(v) He replaced the doctrine of moksha or salvation of the soul by the doctrine of Nibbana.

5. The Buddha Sasana is thus an original piece. The little in it which is old is either modified or restated.

§ 3. *What HE Accepted*

1. The first distinguishing feature of his teachings lay in the recognition of the mind as the centre of everything.

2. Mind precedes things, dominates them, creates them. If mind is comprehended all things are comprehended.

3. Mind is the leader of all its faculties. Mind is the chief of all its faculties. The very mind is made up of those faculties.

4. The first thing to attend to is the culture of the mind.

5. The second distinguishing feature of his

teachings is that mind is the fount of all the good and evil that arises within and befalls us from without.

6. Whatsoever there is of evil, connected with evil, belonging to evil—that issues from the mind. Whatsoever there is of good, connected with good, belonging to good—all issues from mind.

7. If one speaks or acts with a pounded mind then affliction follows him as the wheels of the cart follow the feet of the bullocks who pull the cart. The cleaning of the mind is, therefore, the essence of religion.

8. The third distinguishing feature of his teachings is the avoidance of all sinful acts.

9. The fourth distinguishing feature of his teaching is that real religion lies not in the books of religion but in the observance of the tenets of the religion.

10. Can anyone say that the Buddha's religion was not his own creation?

BOOK II

Campaign of Conversion

PART I

Buddha and His Vishad Yoga

1. To preach or not to preach.
2. Proclamation of good news by Bramha Sahampati.
3. Two types of conversion.

§ 1. *To Preach or Not to Preach*

1. After having attained enlightenment and after having formulated his way, doubt arose in the mind of the Buddha. Should he go forth and preach his doctrine or should he continue to devote himself to II
his own personal perfection. III

2. He said to himself: "True, I have gained a new doctrine. But it is too difficult for the common man to accept it and follow it. It is too subtle even for the wise.

3. "It is hard for mankind to liberate itself from the entanglement of God and Soul. It is hard for mankind to give up its belief in rites and ceremonies. It is hard for mankind to give up its belief in Karma.

4. "It is hard for mankind to give up its belief in the immortality of the Soul and accept my doctrine that the Soul as an independent entity does not exist and does not survive after death.

5. "Mankind is intent on its selfishness and takes delight and pleasure in it. It is hard for mankind to accept my doctrine of righteousness overriding selfishness.

6. "If I were to teach my doctrine, and others did not understand it or understanding it did not accept or accepting it did not follow it, it would be weariness to others and a vexation to me.

7. "Why not remain a sanyasi away from the world and use my gospel to perfect my own self?" He asked himself. "At least I can do good to myself."

8. Thus as he reflected, his mind turned to inaction, not to teaching of the gospel.

9. Then Brahma Sahampati knowing what was passing in the mind of the Buddha thought, "Verily the world is being destroyed, verily the world is going to destruction, if the Tathagata, the fully enlightened, turns to inaction and not to teaching his doctrine."

10. Filled with anxiety Brahma Sahampati left

the Brahma world and appeared before the Buddha. And arranging his upper robe on one shoulder he bent down and with clasped hands said : "Thou art no longer Siddharth Gautama. Thou art Buddha. Thou art the Blessed One who is blessed with the fullest enlightenment. Thou art the Tathagatha. How canst thou refuse to enlighten the world ? How canst thou refuse to save erring humanity ?

11. "There are beings full of impurity that are falling away through not hearing the doctrine.

12. "As the Lord knows," proceeded Brahma Sahampati, "Among the Magadhas arose in ancient times, doctrine impure, with many blemishes devised.

13. "Will not the Lord open for them the door of his immortal doctrine ?

14. "As one upon a rocky mountain standing, beholdeth all the people round about him even thus, O thou, with wisdom distilled, ascending all, behold, look down, thou griefless one, upon those plunged in their griefs.

15. "Rise up, O hero, victor in battle, O caravan-leader, free from the debt of birth, go to the world and not turn away from it.

16. "May the Lord in his compassion design to teach his gospel to men and to *gods*."

17. "O Brahma, Eminent and Excellent among men, if I did not give public utterance to my gospel, it is because I perceived vexation," was the reply of the Buddha.

18. Knowing that there was so much unhappiness in the world the Buddha realized that it was wrong for him to sit as a sanyasi with folded arms and allow things to remain as they were.

19. Asceticism he found to be useless. It was vain to attempt to escape from the world. There is no escape from the world even for an ascetic. He realized that what is necessary is not escape from the world. What is necessary is to change the world and to make it better.

20. He realized that he left the world because there was so much conflict resulting in misery and

unhappiness and for which he knew no remedy. If he can banish misery and unhappiness from the world by the propagation of his doctrine, it was his duty to return to the world and serve it and not sit silent as the personification of inactive impassivity.

21. The Buddha therefore agreed to the request of Brahma Sahampati and decided to preach his doctrine to the world.

§ 2. *Proclamation of Good News by Brahma Sahampati*

1. Then, Brahma Sahampati, thinking, "I have been instrumental in persuading the Buddha to agree to preach his doctrine to the masses," felt extremely happy. He saluted the Buddha, went round him passing to the right, took a look and departed.

2. On his way back he kept on proclaiming to the world: "Rejoice at the glad tidings. The Buddha, our Lord, has found the root of all evil and unhappiness in the world. He knows the way out.

3. "The Buddha will bring comfort to the weary and sorrow-laden. He will give peace to those stricken by war. He will give courage to those who are broken in heart. He will give to those who are suppressed and oppressed, faith and hope.

4. "Ye that suffer from the tribulations of life, ye that have to struggle and endure, ye that yearn for justice, rejoice at the glad tidings.

5. "Heal your wounds, ye that are wounded. Eat your fill, ye that are hungry. Rest, ye that are weary, and quench your thirst, ye that are thirsty. Seek the light, ye that are in darkness. Be of good cheer, ye that are forlorn.

6. "In his doctrine there is love to create a longing to own those who are disowned or unowned: to the degraded there is the ennoblement ever present to raise them: to the disinherited and the down-trodden there is equality blazing forth their path to advancement.

7. " His doctrine is the doctrine of righteousness and his aim is to establish the kingdom of righteousness on earth.

8. " His doctrine is the truth, the whole truth,
II and nothing but the truth.

9. " Blessed is the Buddha for his is the path of
114 reason and his is the way of emancipation from superstition. Blessed is the Buddha who teaches the middle way. Blessed is the Buddha who teaches the law of righteousness. Blessed is the Buddha who teaches the peace of Nibbana. Blessed is the Buddha who preaches love, kindness and fellowship to help fellow beings to obtain salvation."

§ 3. *Two Types of Conversion*

1. In the Buddha's scheme of things conversion has two meanings.
2. Conversion to the Order of Bhikkus called Sangh.
3. Secondly, it means conversion of a householder as an Upasaka or lay follower of the Buddha's Dhamma.
4. Except on four points there is no difference in the way of life of the Bhikku and the Upasaka.
5. An Upasaka remains a householder. A Bhikku becomes a homeless wanderer.
6. Both the Upasakas and the Bhikkus must observe in their life certain rules.
7. Here again to the Bhikku they are vows the breach of which ends in punishment. To the Upasaka they are precepts. They must be observed to the best of his ability.
8. An Upasaka can have property. A Bhikku cannot have.
9. To become an Upasaka there is no ceremony.
10. To become a Bhikku he must undergo a ceremony called Upasampada.
11. The Buddha converted those who came to him according to their wish either as Bhikku or as Upasaka.

12. An Upasaka could become a Bhikku whenever he felt like it.

13. And a Bhikku had to cease to be a Bhikku when he committed a breach of the major vows or whenever he wished to give up his membership of the Order.

14. It must not be understood that the Buddha converted only those whose names occur in the following pages.

15. The instances are chosen only to show that he did not observe any distinction as to caste or sex in admitting persons to his Sangh or preaching his Dhamma.

PART II

The Conversion of the Parivrajakas

1. Arrival at Sarnath.
2. The Buddha's First Sermon.
3. The Buddha's First Sermon (continued).
4. The Buddha's First Sermon (continued).
5. The Buddha's First Sermon (continued).
6. The Buddha's First Sermon (concluded).
7. The Response of the Parivrajakas.

§ 1. *Arrival at Sarnath*

1. Having decided to preach his doctrine the Buddha asked himself " to whom shall I first teach the doctrine ? " The thought of Alara Kalam whom II
the Buddha adored as the learned, wise, intelligent and of little impurity ; " What if I first teach him the 119
doctrine ? " But he was told that Alara Kalam was dead.

2. Then thought he of preaching it to Uddaka Ramputta. But he too was dead.

3. Then he thought of the five old companions of his who were with him at Niranjana when he was practising austerities and who had left him in anger on his abandonment of austerities.

4. " They did much for me, attended me and looked after me, what if I first teach the doctrine to them ? " said he to himself.

5. He asked for their whereabouts. Having learnt that they were dwelling at Sarnath in the deer park of Isipatana, he left in search of them.

6. The five, seeing him coming, decided among themselves not to welcome him. Said one of them, " This, friends, is the ascetic Gautama coming, who has abandoned austerities and has turned to life of abundance and luxury. He has committed a sin. We must not therefore greet him, nor rise in respect, nor take his bowl and robe. We will only set apart a seat for him. If he wishes, he may sit down." And they all agreed.

7. But when the Buddha approached, the five Parivrajakas were not able to abide by their decision, so greatly impressed were they by his personality that they all rose in their seats. One took his bowl, one took his robe, and one prepared a seat, and one brought water to wash his feet.

8. It was really a great welcome to an unwelcome guest.

9. Thus those who intended to scoff remained to pray.

§ 2. *The Buddha's First Sermon*

1. After exchange of greetings the five Parivrajakas asked the Buddha whether he still believed in asceticism. The Buddha replied in the negative.

2. He said there were two extremes, a life of pleasure and a life of self-mortification.

3. One says let us eat and drink, for tomorrow we die. The other says, kill all *vasanas* (desires) because they bring rebirth. He rejected both as unbecoming to man.

4. He was a believer in the Madhyama Marga (Majjhima Patipada), the middle path, which is neither the path of pleasure nor the path of self-mortification.

5. " Answer me this," he said to the Parivrajakas, " So long as your self remains active and continues to lust after either worldly or heavenly pleasures, is not all mortification vain ? " And they answered, " It is as thou sayest."

6. " How can ye be free from self by leading a wretched life of self-mortification if ye do not thereby succeed in quenching the fires of lust ? " And they replied, " It is as thou sayest."

7. " Only when the self in ye has been conquered that ye are free from lust ; ye will then not desire worldly pleasures, and the satisfaction of your natural wants will not defile ye. Let ye eat and drink according to the needs of your body.

8. " Sensuality of all kinds is enervating. The sensual man is a slave of his passion. All pleasure-seeking is degrading and vulgar. But I say unto you that to satisfy the needs of life is not an evil : to keep the body in good health is a duty, or otherwise you shall not be able to keep your mind strong and clear and have the lamp of wisdom burning.

9. " Know ye, O Parivrajakas, that there are these two extremes which man ought not to follow—the habitual indulgence on the one hand, of those things whose attraction depends upon the passions, and especially of sensuality—a low and pagan way of seeking

satisfaction, unworthy, unprofitable and the habitual practice thereof, and on the other hand, of asceticism or self-mortification, which is painful, unworthy and unprofitable.

10. "There is a middle path which avoids both these extremes. Know ye, that, this is the path which I preach."

11. The five Parivrajakas listened to him with attention. Not knowing what to say in reply to the Buddha's middle path, they asked him what he was doing after they had left him. Then the Buddha told them how he left for Gaya, how he sat in contemplation under the Banyan Tree and how after four weeks of contemplation he obtained enlightenment as a result of which he was able to discover a new path of life.

12. On hearing this, the Parivrajakas became extremely impatient to know what the path was and requested the Buddha to expound it to them.

13. The Buddha agreed.

14. He began by saying that his path which is his Dhamma (religion) had nothing to do with God and Soul. His Dhamma had nothing to do with life after death. Nor has his Dhamma any concern with rituals and ceremonies.

15. The centre of his Dhamma is man and the relation of man to man in his life on earth.

16. This he said was his first postulate.

17. His second postulate was that men are living in sorrow, in misery and poverty. The world is full of suffering and that how to remove this suffering from the world is the only purpose of Dhamma. Nothing else is Dhamma.

18. The recognition of the existence of suffering and to show the way to remove suffering is the foundation and basis of his Dhamma.

19. This can be the only foundation and justification for Dhamma. A religion which fails to recognise this is no religion at all.

20. "Verily, Parivrajakas! whatsoever recluses or Brahmins (i.e., preachers of religion) understand not, as it really is, that the misery in the world and the

escape therefrom, is the main problem of Dhamma, such recluses and Brahmins in my opinion are not to be regarded as recluses and Brahmins ; nor have those worthies come to know fully of themselves what in this very life is the real meaning of Dhamma."

21. The Parivrajakas then asked him : " If the foundation of your Dhamma is the recognition of the existence of suffering and the removal of suffering, tell us how does your Dhamma remove suffering !"

22. The Buddha then told them that according to his Dhamma if every person followed (1) the Path of Purity ; (2) the Path of Righteousness ; and (3) the Path of Virtue, it would bring about the end of all suffering.

23. And he added that he had discovered such a Dhamma.

§ 3. *The Buddha's First Sermon*—(contd.)

The Path of Purity

1. The Parivrajakas then asked the Buddha to explain to them his Dhamma.

2. And the Buddha was pleased to do so.

3. He addressed them first on the Path of Purity.

4. " The Path of Purity," he told the Parivrajakas, " teaches that a person who wishes to be good must recognize some principles as principles of life.

5. "According to my Path of Purity the principles of life recognised by it are : Not to injure or kill : Not to steal or appropriate to oneself anything which belongs to another : Not to speak untruth : Not to indulge in lust : Not to indulge in intoxicating drinks.

6. "The recognition of these principles, I say, is most essential for every man. For every man must have a standard by which to judge whatever he does. And these principles according to my teachings constitute the standard.

7. "There are everywhere people who are *patit* (fallen). But there are two classes of the *patit* : the *patit* who has a standard and a *patit* who has no standard.

8. "The *patit* who has no standard does not know that he has fallen. Consequently he always remains fallen. On the other hand, a *patit* who has a standard tries to rise from his fallen state. Why? The answer is because he knows that he has fallen.

9. "This is the difference between having a standard and having no standard for regulating a man's life. What matters is not so much the fall of the man but the absence of any standard.

10. "You may ask, ye Parivrajakas! Why are these principles worthy of recognition as a standard of life.

11. "The answer to this question you will find for yourselves, if you ask: "Are these principles good for the individual?" also if you ask: "Do they promote social good?"

12. "If your answers to these questions are in the affirmative then it follows that the principles of my Path of Purity are worthy of recognition as forming a true standard of life."

§ 4. *The Buddha's First Sermon*—(contd.)

Ashtanga Marga or the Path of Righteousness

1. The Buddha next addressed the Parivrajakas on the Ashtangamarga. He said that there are eight constituents in the Ashtangamarga.

2. He began his discourse with the exposition of *Samma Ditti* (Right Views), the first and foremost element in the *Ashtangmarga.*

3. "To realize the importance of *Samma Ditti,*" the Buddha said to the Parivrajakas:

4. "O, ye, Parivrajakas, you must realize that the world is a dungeon and man is a prisoner in the dungeon.

5. "This dungeon is full of darkness. So dark is it that scarce anything at all can rightly be seen by the prisoner. The prisoner cannot see that he is a prisoner.

6. "Indeed, man has not only become blind by living too long in the darkness, but he very much

doubts if any such strange thing as light is said to be, can ever exist at all.

7. " Mind is the only instrument through which light can come to man.

8. " But the mind of these dungeon-dwellers is by no means a perfect instrument for the purpose.

9. " It lets through only a little light, just enough to show to those with sight that there is such a thing as darkness.

10. " Thus defective in its nature, such understanding as this is.

11. " But know, ye, Parivrajakas! the case of the prisoner is not as hopeless as it appears.

12. " For there is in man a thing called will. When the appropriate motives arise the will can be awakened and set in motion.

13. " With the coming of just enough light to see in what directions to guide the motions of the will, man may so guide them that they shall lead to liberty.

14. " Thus though man is bound, yet he may be free ; he may at any moment begin to take the first steps that will ultimately bring him to freedom.

15. " This is because it is possible to train the mind in whatever directions one chooses. It is mind that makes us to be prisoners in the house of life, and it is mind that keeps us so.

16. " But what mind has done, that mind can undo. If it has brought man to thraldom, it can also, when rightly directed, bring him to liberty.

17. " This is what *Samma Ditti* can do."

18. " What is the end of *Samma Ditti*? " asked the Parivrajakas. " The end of *Samma Ditti*," replied the Buddha, " is the destruction of Avijja (Nescience). It is opposed to Miccha Ditti.

19. " And Avijja means the failure to understand the noble truths, of the existence of suffering and the removal of suffering.

20. " *Samma Ditti* requires giving up of belief in the efficacy of rites and ceremonies, to have disbelief in the sanctity of the Shastras.

21. "*Samma Ditti* requires the abandonment of superstition and supernaturalism.

22. "*Samma Ditti* requires the abandonment of all doctrines which are mere speculations without any basis in fact or experience.

23. "*Samma Ditti* requires free mind and free thought.

24. "Every man has aims, aspirations and ambitions. *Samma Sankappo* teaches that such aims, aspirations and ambitions shall be noble and praiseworthy and not ignoble and unworthy.

25. "*Samma Vacca* (Right Speech) teaches: (1) that one should speak only that which is true; (2) that one should not speak what is false; (3) that one should not speak evil of others; (4) that one should refrain from slander; (5) that one should not use angry and abusive language towards any fellow man; (6) that one should speak kindly and courteously to all; (7) that one should not indulge in pointless, foolish talk, but let his speech be sensible and to the purpose.

26. "The observance of Right Speech, as I have explained, is not to be the result of fear or favour. It is not to have the slightest reference to what any superior being may think of his action or to any loss which Right Speech may involve.

27. "The norm for Right Speech is not the order of the superior or the personal benefit to the individual.

28. "*Samma Kamanto* teaches right behaviour. It teaches that every action should be founded on respect for the feelings and rights of others.

29. "What is the norm for *Samma Kamanto?* The norm is that course of conduct which is most in harmony with the fundamental laws of existence.

30. "When his actions are in harmony with these laws they may be taken to be in accord with *Samma Kamanto*.

31. "Every individual has to earn his livelihood. But there are ways and ways of earning one's livelihood. Some are bad; some are good. Bad ways are those

which cause injury or injustice to others. Good ways are those by which the individual earns his livelihood without causing injury or injustice to others. This is *Samma Ajivo.*

II 32. "*Samma Vyayamo* (Right Endeavour) is
126 primary endeavour to remove Avijja ; to reach the door that leads out of this painful prison house, to swing it open.

33. "Right endeavour has four purposes.

34. "One is to prevent states of mind which are in conflict with the Ashtangamarga.

35. "Second is to suppress such states of mind which may already have arisen.

36. "Third is to bring into existence states of mind which will help a man to fulfil the requirements of the Ashtangamarga.

37. "Fourth is to promote the further growth and increase of such states of mind as already may have arisen.

38. "*Samma Satti* calls for mindfulness and thoughtfulness. It means constant wakefulness of the mind. Watch and ward by the mind over the evil passions is another name for *Samma Satti.*

39. "There are, ye Parivrajakas, five fetters or hindrances which come in the way of a person trying to achieve *Samma Ditti, Samma Sankappo, Samma Vacca, Samma Kamanto, Samma Ajeevo, Samma Vyayamo* and *Samma Satti.*

40. "These five hindrances are covetousness, ill-will, sloth and torpor, doubt and indecision. It is, therefore, necessary to overcome these hindrances which are really fetters and the means to overcome them is through *Samadhi.* But know ye Parivrajakas, *Samma Samadhi* is not the same as *Samadhi.* It is quite different.

41. "*Samadhi* is mere concentration. No doubt it leads to Dhyanic states which are self-induced, holding the five hindrances in suspense.

42. "But these Dhyana states are temporary. Consequently the suspension of the hindrances is also temporary. What is necessary is a permanent turn

to the mind. Such a permanent turn can be achieved only by *Samma Samadhi.*

43. " Mere *Samadhi* is negative inasmuch as it leads to temporary suspension of the hindrances. In
it there is no training to the mind. *Samma Samadhi* II
is positive. It trains the mind to concentrate and to
think of some *Kusala Kamma* (Good Deeds and 127
Thoughts) during concentration and thereby eliminate the tendency of the mind to be drawn towards *Akusala Kamma* (Bad Deeds and Bad Thoughts) arising from the hindrances.

44. " *Samma Samadhi* gives a habit to the mind to think of good and always to think of good. *Samma Samadhi* gives the mind the necessary motive power to do good."

§ 5. *The Buddha's First Sermon*—(contd.)

The Path of Virtue

1. The Buddha then explained to the Parivrajakas the Path of Virtue.

2. He told them that the path of virtue meant the observance of the virtues called : (1) *Sila ;* (2) *Dana ;* (3) *Uppekha ;* (4) *Nekkhama ;* (5) *Virya ;* (6) *Khanti ;* (7) *Succa ;* (8) *Adhithana ;* (9) *Karuna ;* and (10) *Maitri.*

3. The Parivrajakas asked the Buddha to tell them what these virtues meant.

4. The Buddha then proceeded to satisfy their desire.

5. " *Sila* is moral temperament, the disposition not to do evil and the disposition to do good ; to be ashamed of doing wrong. To avoid to do evil for fear of punishment is *Sila. Sila* means fear of doing wrong.

6. " *Nekkhama* is renunciation of the pleasures of the world.

7. " *Dana* means the giving of one's possessions, blood and limbs and even one's life, for the good of others without expecting anything in return.

8. " *Virya* is right endeavour. It is doing with

all your might whatever you have undertaken to do with never a thought of turning back, whatever you have undertaken to do.

9. "*Khanti* is forbearance. Not to meet hatred by hatred is the essence of it. For hatred is not appeased by hatred. It is appeased only by forbearance.

10. "*Succa* is truth. A person must never tell a lie. His speech must be truth and nothing but truth.

11. "*Adhithana* is resolute determination to reach the goal.

12. "*Karuna* is loving kindness to human beings.

13. "*Maitri* is extending fellow feeling to all beings, not only to one who is a friend but also to one who is a foe : not only to man but to all living beings.

14. "*Upekka* is detachment as distinguished from indifference. It is a state of mind where there is neither like nor dislike. Remaining unmoved by the result and yet engaged in the pursuit of it.

15. "These virtues one must practice to his utmost capacity. That is why they are called Paramitas (States of Perfection).

§ 6. *The Buddha's First Sermon*—(concld.)

1. Having explained His Dhamma and what it involved, the Buddha then asked the Parivrajakas:

2. "Is not personal purity the foundation of good in the world ?" And they answered, "It is as thou sayest."

3. And he continued : "Is not personal purity undermined by covetousness, passion, ignorance, the destruction of life, theft, adultery and lying ? Is it not necessary for personal purity to build up sufficient strength of character so that these evils should be kept under control ? How can a man be the instrument of good if he has no personal purity in him ?" And they replied, "It is as thou sayest."

4. "Again why do men not mind enslaving or dominating others ? Why do men not mind making the lives of others unhappy ? Is it not because men are

not righteous in their conduct towards one another?" And they answered in the affirmative.

5. "Will not the practice of the Ashtanga Marga, the path of right views, right aims, right speech, right livelihood, right means, right mindfulness, right perseverance, and right contemplation, in short, the Path of Righteousness, if followed by every one, remove all injustice and inhumanity that man does to man?" And they said, "Yes."

6. Turning to the path of virtue, he asked, "Is not Dana necessary to remove the suffering of the needy and the poor and to promote general good? Is not Karuna necessary to be drawn to the relief of poverty and suffering wherever it exists? Is not Nekkamma necessary to selfless work? Is not Uppekka necessary for sustained endeavour even though there is no personal gain?

7. "Is not love for man necessary?" And they said "Yes."

8. "I go further and say, "Love is not enough; what is required is Maitri." It is wider than love. It means fellowship not merely with human beings but with all living beings. It is not confined to human beings. Is not such Maitri necessary? What else can give to all living beings the same happiness which one seeks for one's own self, to keep the mind impartial, open to all, with affection for every one and hatred for none?"

9. They all said "Yes."

10. "The practice of these virtues must, however, be accompanied by Prajna, *i.e.*, intelligence.

11. "Is not Prajna necessary?" The Parivrajakas gave no answer. To force them to answer his question the Buddha went on to say that the qualities of a good man are: "do no evil, think nothing that is evil, get his livelihood in no evil way and say nothing that is evil or is likely to hurt anyone." And they said, "Yes, so it is."

12. "But is doing good deeds blindly to be welcomed?" asked the Buddha "I say, 'no.' This is not enough," said the Buddha to the Pariv-

rajakas. " If it was enough," said the Buddha to the Parivrajakas, " then a tiny babe could be proclaimed to be always doing good. For as yet, the babe does not know what a body means, much less will it do evil with its body beyond kicking about : it does not know what speech is, much less will it say anything evil beyond crying ; it does not know what thought is, beyond crying with delight ; it does not know what livelihood is, much less will it get its living in an evil way, beyond sucking its mother.

13. " The Path of Virtue must, therefore, be subject to test of Prajna which is another name for understanding and intelligence.

14. " There is also another reason why Prajna-paramita is so important and so necessary. There must be Dana. But without Prajna, Dana may have a demoralizing effect. There must be Karuna. But without Prajna, Karuna may end in supporting evil. Every act of Paramita must be tested by Prajna Paramita which is another name for wisdom.

15. " I premise that there must be knowledge and consciousness of what wrong conduct is, how it arises ; similarly, there must also be knowledge and consciousness of what is right conduct and wrong conduct. Without such knowledge there cannot be real goodness though the act may be good. That is why I say Prajna is a necessary virtue."

16. The Buddha then concluded his sermon by addressing the following admonition to the Parivrajakas.

17. " You are likely to call my Dhamma pessimistic because it calls the attention of mankind to the existence of suffering. I tell you such a view of my Dhamma would be wrong.

18. " No doubt my Dhamma recognizes the existence of suffering but forget not that it also lays equal stress on the removal of suffering.

19. " My Dhamma has in it both hope and purpose.

20. " Its purpose is to remove Avijja, by which I mean ignorance of the existence of suffering.

21. " There is hope in it because it shows the way to put an end to human suffering.

22. " Do you agree with this or not ? " And the Parivrajakas said , "Yes, we do."

II

§ 7. *The Response of the Parivrajakas*

131

1. The five Parivrajakas at once realized that this was really a new Dhamma. They were so struck by this new approach to the problems of life that they were unanimous in saying : " Never in the history of the world has any founder of religion taught that the recognition of human suffering was the real basis of religion.

2. " Never in the history of the world has any founder of religion taught that the removal of this misery is the real purpose of it !

3. " Never in the history of the world had a scheme of salvation been put forth, so simple in its nature, so free from supernatural and superhuman agency, so independent of, even so antagonistic to, the belief in a soul, to the belief in God and to the belief in life after death !

4. " Never in the history of the world had a scheme of religion been put forth which had nothing to do with revelation and whose commands are born of the examination of the social needs of man and which are not the orders of a God !

5. " Never in the history of the world has salvation been conceived as the blessing of happiness to be attained by man in this life and on this earth by righteousness born out of his own efforts ! "

6. These were the sentiments which the Parivrajakas uttered after they had heard the Buddha's Sermon on his new Dhamma.

7. They felt that in him they had found a reformer, full of the most earnest moral purpose and trained in all the intellectual culture of his time, who had the originality and the courage to put forth deliberately and with a knowledge of opposing views, the doctrine of a salvation to be found here, in this life,

in inward change of heart to be brought about by the practice of self-culture and self-control.

8. Their reverence for him became so unbounded that they at once surrendered to him and requested him
II to accept them as his disciples.

9. The Buddha admitted them into his order by
132 uttering the formula "Ehi Bhikkave" (come in Bhikkus). They were known as the Panchavargiya Bhikkus.

PART III

Conversion of the High and the Holy

1. Conversion of Yashas.
2. Conversion of the Kassyapas.
3. Conversion of Sariputta and Moggallana.
4. Conversion of Bimbisara.
5. Conversion of Anathapindika.
6. Conversion of Pasenjit.
7. Conversion of Jeevaka.
8. Conversion of Ratthapala.

§ 1. Conversion of Yashas

1. There lived in the town of Benares a noble-
man's son called Yashas. He was young in years and
very attractive in appearance. He was beloved of his II
parents. He lived in abounding wealth. He had a
big retinue and a large harem and passed his time in 135
nothing but dancing, drinking and carnal pleasures.

2. As time past, a feeling of disgust came over him. How could he escape from this orgy? Was there any better way of life than the way he was leading? Not knowing what to do, he decided to leave his father's house.

3. One night he left his father's house and was wandering about; He happened to wend his way towards Isipathana.

4. Feeling tired he sat down and as he was seated he said to himself in loud tones: 'Where am I, what is the way? Alas! What distress; alas! What danger!'

5. This happened on the night of the same day on which the Blessed One preached his first sermon to the Panchavargiya Bhikkus at Isipathana. Just when Yashas was approaching Isipathana, the Blessed One who was staying at Isipathana, having arisen at dawn, was walking up and down in the open air. And the Blessed One saw Yashas, the noble youth coming from after giving utterance to his feelings.

6. And the Blessed One having heard his cry of distress, said: "There is no distress, there is no danger. Come, I will show you the way," and the Blessed Lord preached his gospel to Yashas.

7. And Yashas, when he heard it, became glad and joyful; and he put off his gilt slippers, and went and sat down near the Blessed One and respectedly saluted him.

8. Yashas hearing the Buddha's words, requested the Blessed One to take him as his disciple.

9. Then he bade him come and asked him to be a Bhikku to which Yashas agreed.

10. The parents of Yashas were in great distress

on finding that their son had disappeared. The father started in search. Yashas's father passed by the same spot where the Lord and Yashas in the Bhikku's garb were seated, and in passing, he asked the Blessed One : " Pray, have you seen Yashas, my son ? "

11. The Lord replied : " Come in, Sir, you will find your son." He went in and sat near his son but he knew him not.

12. The Lord explained to him how Yashas met him and how on hearing him he became a Bhikku. The father then recognized his son and was happy his son had chosen the right path.

13. " My son, Yashas," said the father, " your mother is absorbed in lamentations and grief. Return home and restore your mother to life."

14. Then Yashas looked at the Blessed One, and the Blessed One said to Yashas's father, " Is that your wish that Yashas should return to the world and enjoy the pleasures of a worldly life as he did before ? "

15. And Yasha's father replied : " If Yashas, my son, finds it a gain to stay with you, let him stay." Yashas preferred to remain a Bhikku.

16. Before departing Yashas's father said : " May the Blessed One, O Lord, consent to take his meal at my home with the members of my family."

17. The Blessed One, having donned his robes, took his alms bowl and went with Yashas to the house of his father.

18. When they arrived there, they met the mother and also the former wife of Yashas. After the meal the Blessed One preached to the members of the family his doctrine. They became very happy and promised to take refuge in it.

19. Now there were four friends of Yashas belonging to the wealthy family of Benares. Their names were Vimala, Subahu, Punyajit and Gavampati.

20. When Yashas's friends learned that Yashas had taken refuge in the Buddha and his Dhamma they felt that what is good for Yashas must be good for them.

21. So they went to Yashas and asked him to

approach the Buddha on their behalf to receive them as his disciples.

22. Yashas agreed and he went to the Buddha, saying : " May the Blessed One preach the Dhamma to these four friends of mine." The Lord agreed and Yashas's friends took refuge in the Dhamma.

§ 2. *Conversion of the Kassyapas*

1. There lived in Benaras a family known as the Kassyapa family. There were three sons in the family. They were very highly educated and carried on a rigorous religious life.

2. After some time the eldest son thought of taking up Sannyasa. Accordingly he left his home, took Sannyasa and went in the direction of Uruvella where he established his Ashram.

3. His two younger brothers followed him and they too became Sannyasis.

4. They were all Agnihotris or worshippers of fire. They were called Jatilas because they kept long hair.

5. The three brothers were known as Uruvella Kassyapa, Nadi Kassyapa (Kassyapa of the River, i.e., the Niranjana), and Gaya Kassyapa (of the village Gaya).

6. Of these the Uruvella Kassyapa had a following of five hundred Jatilas ; Nadi Kassyapa had three hundred Jatilas as his disciples and Gaya Kassyapa had two hundred Jatilas. Of these the chief was Uruvella Kassyapa.

7. The fame of Uruvella Kassyapa had spread far and wide. He was known to have obtained Mukti (Salvation) while alive. People from far-away places came to his Ashram which was located on the banks of the river Falgu.

8. The Blessed Lord having come to know of the name and fame of Uruvella Kassyapa, thought of preaching his gospel to him and if possible to convert him to his Dhamma.

9. Having come to know of his whereabouts the Blessed Lord went to Uruvella.

10. The Blessed One met him and wanting to have an opportunity to instruct him and convert him, said: "If it is not disagreeable to you, Kassyapa, let me dwell one night in your Ashram."

11. "I am not agreeable to this," said Kassyapa. "There is a savage Naga king called Muchalinda who rules over this place. He is possessed of dreadful powers. He is the deadly enemy of all ascetics performing fire worship. He pays nocturnal visits to their Ashrams and does them great harm. I fear he may do you the same harm as he does to me."

12. Kassyapa did not know that the Nagas had become the friends and followers of the Blessed One. But the Blessed One knew it.

13. So the Blessed One pressed for his request, saying : "He is not likely to do any harm to me : pray, Kassyapa, allow me a place in your fire room, for one night."

14. Kassyapa continued to raise many difficulties and the Blessed One continued to press his request.

15. Then Kassyapa said : "My mind desires no controversy, only I have my fears and apprehensions, but follow your own good pleasure."

16. The Blessed Lord forthwith stepped into the fire grove and took his seat.

17. The Naga king Muchalinda came into the room at his usual time. But instead of finding Kassyapa he found the Blessed One seated in his place.

18. Muchalinda, seeing the Lord seated, his face glowing with peace and serenity, felt as though he was in the presence of a great divinity, and bending his head, began to worship.

19. That night Kassyapa's sleep was very much disturbed by the thought of what might have happened to his guest. So he got up with great misgivings fearing that his guest might have been burnt up.

20. Then Kassyapa and his followers at morning light came one and all to have a look. Far from seeing

the Lord injured by Muchalinda, they found Muchalinda worshipping the Lord.

21. Beholding the scene, Kassyapa felt that he was witnessing a great miracle.

22. Struck by this miracle Kassyapa requested the Blessed Lord to stay near him and make an Ashram, and promised to look after him.

23. The Blessed Lord agreed to stay on.

24. The two, however, had different motives. Kassyapa's motive was to obtain protection against Muchalinda Naga. The Blessed Lord thought that one day Kassyapa will give him opportunity to propound his gospel.

25. But Kassyapa showed no such inclination. He thought that the Blessed Lord was only a miracle maker and nothing more.

26. One day the Blessed Lord thought of himself taking the initiative and asked Kassyapa, "Are you an Arhant?

27. "If you are not an Arhant, what good is this Agnihotra going to do to you?"

28. Kassyapa said: "I do not know what is to be an Arhant? Will you explain it to me?"

29. The Lord then told Kassyapa, "An Arhant is one who has conquered all the passions which disturb a man from pursuing the eight-fold Path. Agnihotra cannot cleanse a man of his sins."

30. Kassyapa was a proud person. But he did feel the force of the Blessed Lord's argument. Making his mind pliant and yielding, until at length prepared to be a vehicle of the true law, he confessed that his poor wisdom could not compare with the wisdom of the world-honoured One.

31. And so, convinced at last, humbly submitting, Uruvella Kassyapa accepted the doctrine of the Lord and became his follower.

32. Following their master, the followers of Kassyapa, virtuously submissive, in turn received the teaching of the law. Kassyapa and all his followers were thus entirely converted.

33. Uruvella Kassyapa, then, lifting his goods and

all his sacrificial vessels, threw them together into the river, which floated down upon the surface of the current.

34. Nadi and Gaya, who dwelt down the stream,
II seeing these articles of clothing (and the rest) floating
along the stream disorderly, said, "These are the
140 belongings of our brother ; why has he thrown them
away ? Some great change has happened," and were
deeply pained and restless. The two, each with five
hundred followers, went up the stream to seek their
brother.

35. On seeing him and all his followers now dressed as hermits, strange thoughts engaged their minds and they inquired into the reasons. Uruvella Kassyapa told them the story of his conversion to the Buddha's Dhamma.

36. "Our brother having submitted thus, we too should also follow him," they said.

37. They conveyed their wishes to their eldest brother. Then the two brothers, with all their band of followers, were brought to hear the Lord's discourse on the comparison of a fire sacrifice with his own gospel.

38. In his discourse to the two brothers the Blessed Lord said : "The dark smoke of ignorance arises, whilst confused thoughts, like wood drilled into wood, create the fire.

39. "Lust, anger, delusion, these are as fire produced, and these enflame and burn all other things which cause grief and sorrow in the world.

40. "If once this way is found and lust, anger and delusion consumed, then with it is born sight, knowledge and pure conduct.

41. "So when the heart of a man has once conceived distaste for sin, this distaste removes covetous desire, covetous desire extinguished, there is recluse."

42. The great Rishis listening to him, lost all regard for fire worship and wished to be the disciples of the Buddha.

43. The conversion of the Kassyapas was a great

triumph for the Blessed Lord. For they had a very strong hold on the imagination of the people.

§ 3. *Conversion of Sariputta and Moggallana* II

1. While the Blessed Lord was in Rajagraha there 141
resided a well-known person by name Sanjaya with a great retinue of Parivrajakas numbering about two hundred and fifty as his disciples.

2. Among his disciples were Sariputta and Moggallana—two young Brahmins.

3. Sariputta and Moggallana were not satisfied with the teachings of Sanjaya and were in search of something better.

4. Now one day the venerable Assaji, one of the Panchvargiya Bhikkus, in the forenoon, having put on his under-robes, and having taken his alms bowl and outer robe, entered the city of Rajagraha for alms.

5. Sariputta was observing the dignified deportment of Assaji and was struck by it. On seeing the venerable Assaji, Sariputta thought, "Indeed this person is one of those monks who are the worthy ones in the world. What if I were to approach this monk and to ask him : 'In whose name, friend, have you retired from the world? Who is your teacher? Whose Dhamma do you profess?'"

6. Now Sariputta thought : "This is not the time to ask this monk ; he has entered the inner yard of a house for alms. What if I were to follow this monk step by step, according to the course recognized by those who want something?"

7. And the venerable Assaji, having finished his alms pilgrimage through Rajagraha, went back with the food he had received. Then Sariputta went to the place where the venerable Assaji was ; having approached him, he exchanged greetings and with complaisant words, he stood at his side.

8. Standing at his side the wandering ascetic Sariputta said to the venerable Assaji : "Your countenance, friend, is serene ; your complexion is

pure and bright. In whose name, friend, have you retired from the world? Who is your teacher? Whose Dhamma do you profess?"

9. Assaji replied : "There is, friend, the great recluse of the Sakya's clan ; in this Blessed One's name, have I retired from the world ; this Blessed One is my teacher, and it is the Dhamma of this Blessed One that I follow."

10. "And what, venerable Sir, is the doctrine which your teacher holds? And what does he preach to you?"

11. "I am only a young disciple, friend ; I have but recently received ordination ; and I have newly adopted this Dhamma and discipline. I cannot explain to you the Dhamma in detail ; but I will tell you in short what it means."

12. Then Sariputta, the wandering ascetic, said to the venerable Assaji : "So be it, friend, tell me as much or as little as you like, but tell me the meaning, I want just meaning. Why make so much of the letter?"

13. Then the venerable Assaji explained to Sariputta the substance of the teachings of the Buddha and Sariputta was completely satisfied.

14. Sariputta and Moggallana, though not brothers, were bound together as though they were brothers. They had given their word to each other. He who first attains the truth shall tell the same to the other one. That was their mutual engagement.

15. Accordingly Sariputta went to the place where Moggallana was. Seeing him, he said to Sariputta : "Your countenance, friend, is serene ; your complexion is pure and bright. Have you then really reached the truth?"

16. "Yes, friend, I have come to know the truth." "And how, friend, have you done so?" Then Sariputta told him what happened between him and Assaji.

17. Then Moggallana said to Sariputta, "Let us go, friend, and join the Blessed One ; that he, the Blessed One, may be our teacher."

18. Sariputta replied : "It is on our account,

friend, that these two hundred and fifty wandering Parivrajakas live here, and it is we whom they regard ; let us first tell them before taking leave of them ; they will do what they think fit."

19. Then Sariputta and Moggallana went to the place where they were ; having approached them they said to them, " Friends, we are going to join the Blessed One ; he, the Blessed One, is our teacher."

20. They replied : " It is on your account, Sirs, that we live here, and it is you whom we regard ; if you, Sirs, will lead the holy life under the great Samana, we all will do the same."

21. Then Sariputta and Moggallana went to the place where Sanjaya was ; having approached him, they said : " Friend, we go to join the Blessed One ; he, the Blessed One, is our teacher."

22. Sanjaya replied : " Nay, friends, do not go ; we will all three look after this company."

23. And a second and third time Sariputta and Moggallana said this and Sanjaya answered as before.

24. Then Sariputta and Moggallana took with them two hundred and fifty wandering ascetics and went to the Veluvana in Rajagraha where the Blessed One was staying.

25. And the Blessed One saw them—Sariputta and Moggallana, coming from afar : on seeing them he thus addressed the monks : " There, monks, arrive two companions," pointing towards Sariputta and Moggallana, " these will be my chief pair of disciples, and auspicious pair."

26. When they had arrived at the bamboo grove, they went to the place where the Blessed One was ; having approached him, they prostrated themselves, with their heads at the feet of the Blessed One, and said to the Blessed One : " Lord, let us receive ordination from the Blessed One."

27. The Blessed One then uttered the usual formula indicating admission, " Ehi Bhikku " (Come Monks), and Sariputta and Moggallana and the two hundred Jatilas became the disciples of the Buddha."

§ 4. *Conversion of King Bimbisara*

1. Rajagraha was the capital of Seniya Bimbisara; King of Magadha.

II 2. Having heard of the conversions of this large number of Jatilas, everyone in the city had begun to talk
144 about the Blessed One.

3. Thus King Bimbisara came to know of his arrival in the city.

4. " To have converted the most orthodox and the most obstinate Jatilas was no mean task." " Truly so," said King Bimbisara to himself, " he must be the Blessed, holy, absolute Buddha, proficient in knowledge and conduct, the way-farer, who understands the world, the highest one, who guides men, the teacher of gods and men. He must be teaching the truth, which he understood himself.

5. " He must be preaching that Dhamma which is lovely in the beginning, lovely in the middle, lovely at the end, in the spirit and in the letter ; he must be proclaiming the consummate perfect, pure and holy life. It is good to obtain the sight of a man like him."

6. So King Bimbisara, surrounded by twelve myriads of Magadha Brahmins and householders, went to the place where the Blessed One was. Having approached him and respectfully saluted the Blessed One, he sat down near him. And of those twelve myriads of Magadha Brahmins and householders, some also respectfully saluted the Blessed One and sat down near him ; some exchanged greetings with the Blessed One, and having done so they sat down near him with complaisant words ; some bent their clasped hands towards the Blessed One and sat down near him ; some made known their name and family name before the Blessed One and sat down near him ; some sat down near him silently.

7. Now those twelve myriads of Magadha Brahmins and householders saw Uruvella Kassyapa among the monks who came with the Blessed Lord. They thought : " How now is this? Does the great

Samana follow the holy life under Uruvella Kassyapa, or does Uruvella Kassyapa follow the holy life under the great Samana ?"

8. And the Blessed One, who understood in his mind the reflection which had arisen in the minds of II
those twelve myriads of Magadha Brahmins and house-
holders, addressed the venerable Uruvella Kassyapa : 145
"What hast thou seen, O dweller of Uruvella, that thou who art called the great one hast forsaken the fire worship ? How is it thou hast forsaken the fire sacrifice ?"

9. Kassyapa replied : "It is sights and sounds, and also tastes, and women of sense desire that the sacrifices promise ; because I understood that these things are impure that I took no more delight in sacrifices and offerings."

10. "But if you don't mind, tell us what made you think so ?"

11. Then the venerable Uruvella Kassyapa rose from his seat, adjusted his upper robe so as to cover one shoulder, prostrated himself, inclining his head to the feet of the Blessed One, and said to the Blessed One: "My teacher is the Blessed One, I am his pupil." Then those twelve myriads of Magadha Brahmins and householders understood : "Uruvella Kassyapa follows the holy life under the great Samana."

12. And the Blessed One, who understood in his mind the reflection that had arisen in the minds of those twelve myriads of Magadha Brahmins and householders, preached to them his Dhamma. Just as a clean cloth free from black specks properly takes the dye, thus eleven myriads of those Magadha Brahmins and householders with Bimbisara at their head, while sitting there, obtained the pure and spotless dye of the Dhamma. One myriad announced their having become lay followers.

13. Then the Magadha king, Seniya Bimbisara, having witnessed the scene, having understood the Dhamma, having penetrated the Dhamma, having overcome uncertainty, having dispelled all doubts,

having gained full knowledge, said to the Blessed One : " In former days, Lord, when I was a prince, I entertained five aspirations ; these are now fulfilled.

14. " In former days, Lord, to me when I was a
II prince, came this thought : 'O that I might be
inaugurated king !' That was my first aspiration,
146 Lord ; that is now fulfilled. 'And might then a holy
one, a fully Enlightened One, come over into my kingdom !' This was my second aspiration, Lord ; that is now fulfilled. 'And might I minister to that Blessed One !' That was my third aspiration, Lord ; that is now fulfilled. 'And might he, the Blessed One, preach the Dhamma to me !' This was my fourth aspiration, Lord ; and that is now fulfilled. 'And might I understand the Dhamma of that Blessed One !' This was my fifth aspiration, Lord ; this is now fulfilled. These were my five aspirations, Lord, which I entertained in former days when I was a prince.

15. " Wonderful, Lord ! Wonderful, just as if one should set up, what had been overturned, or should reveal what had been hidden, or should point out the way to one who had lost his way, or should bring a lamp into the darkness, in order that those who had eyes might see things, thus has the Blessed One preached the Dhamma in many ways. I take refuge, Lord, in that Blessed One, and in the Dhamma, and in the fraternity of Bhikkus (monks). May the Blessed One receive me from this day forth, while my life lasts, as a lay disciple who has taken refuge in him."

§ 5. *Conversion of Anathapindika*

1. Sudatta was a resident of Shravasti, the capital of the kingdom of Kosala. It was ruled by King Pasenjit. Sudatta was treasurer of the king. From his bounties to the poor, Sudatta was known as Anathapindika.

2. When the Lord was at Rajagraha, Anathapindika happened to visit the place on some private business of his own. He was stopping with his sister

who was married to the guild master of Rajagraha.

3. When he arrived he found the guild master preparing a meal for the Lord and his monks on so great a scale that he thought that a wedding was in progress or that the king had been invited.

4. On learning the truth he became very eager to visit the Lord and he set out in the very night to meet the Blessed One.

5. And the Blessed One saw at once the sterling quality of Anathapindika's heart and greeted him with words of comfort. After taking his seat Anathapindika expressed a desire to hear a discourse on some religious subject.

6. The Blessed Lord responding to his wishes raised the question, " Who is it that shapes our lives ? Is it Ishavara, a personal creator ? If Ishavara be the maker, all living things should have silently to submit to their maker's power. They would be like vessels formed by the potter's hand. If the world had been made by Ishavara there should be no such thing as sorrow, or calamity, or sin ; for both pure and impure deeds must come from him. If not, there would be another cause beside him, and he would not be the self-existent one. Thus, you see, the thought of Ishavara is overthrown.

7. " Again, it is said that the Absolute cannot be a cause. All things around us come from a cause as the plant comes from the seed; how can the Absolute be the cause of all things alike ? If it pervades them, then certainly it does not make them.

8. " Again, it is said that self is the maker. But if self is the maker, why did he not make things pleasing? The cases of sorrow and joy are real and objective. How can they have been made by self ?

9. " Again, if you adopt the argument, there is no maker, or fate in such as it is, and there is no causation, what use would there be in shaping our lives and adjusting means to an end ?

10. " Therefore, we argue that all things that exist are not without cause. However, neither Ishavara, nor the Absolute, nor the self, nor causeless chance, is

the maker, but our deeds produce results both good and evil.

11. "The whole world is under the law of causation, and the causes that act are not un-mental,
II for the gold of which the cup is made is gold throughout.

12. "Let us, then, surrender the heresies of
148 worshipping Ishavara and praying to him; let us not lose ourselves in vain speculations of profitless subtleties; let us surrender self and all selfishness, and as all things are fixed by causation, let us practise good so that good may result from our actions."

13. And Anathapindika said: "I see the truth of what the Blessed One has said and I wish to open my whole mind. Having listened to my words let the Lord advise me what I should do.

14. "My life is full of work, and having acquired great wealth, I am surrounded with cares. Yet do I enjoy my work, and I apply myself to it with all diligence. Many people are in my employ and depend upon the success of my enterprises.

15. "Now, I have heard your disciples praise the bliss of the hermit and denounce the unrest of the world. 'The Blessed One,' they say, 'has given up his kingdom and his inheritance, and has found the path of righteousness, thus setting an example to all the world how to attain Nirvana.'

16. "My heart yearns to do what is right and to be a blessing unto my fellow-beings. Let me then ask you, must I give up my wealth, my home, and my business enterprises, and, like you, go into homelessness in order to attain the bliss of a religious life?"

17. And the Blessed Lord replied: "The bliss of a religious life is attainable by every one who walks in the noble eight-fold path. He that cleaves to wealth, had better cast it away than allow his heart to be poisoned by it; but he who does not cleave to wealth, and possessing riches, uses them rightly, will be a blessing unto his fellow-beings.

18. "I say unto thee, remain in thy station of life and apply thyself with diligence to thy enterprises. It is not life and wealth and power that enslave men,

but the cleaving to life and wealth and power.

19. " The Bhikku who retires from the world in order to lead a life of leisure will have no gain. For a life of indolence is an abomination, and lack of energy is to be despised.

20. "The Dhamma of the Tathagata does not require a man to go into homelessness or to resign the world unless he feels called upon to do so ; what the Dhamma of the Tathagata requires is for every man to free himself from the illusion of self, to cleanse his heart, to give up his thirst for pleasure, and lead a life of righteousness.

21. " And whatever men do, whether they remain in the world as artisans, merchants, and officers of the king, or retire from the world and devote themselves to a life of religious meditation, let them put their whole heart into their task ; let them be diligent and energetic, and, if they are like the lotus, which, though it grows in the water, yet remains untouched by the water, if they struggle in life without cherishing envy or hatred, if they live in the world a life not of self but a life of truth, then surely joy, peace, and bliss will dwell in their minds."

22. Anathapindika perceived that this was the most excellent system of truth, simple and of wisdom-born.

23. Thus firmly settled in the true doctrine he slowly bent in worship at the feet of the Blessed One and with closed hands made his request.

§ 6. *Conversion of King Pasenjit*

1. Then King Pasenjit, hearing that the Lord had come, went in his royal equippage to the Jetavana Vihara. Saluting him with clasped hands, he said :

2. " Blessed is my unworthy and obscure kingdom that it has met with so great a fortune. For how can calamities and dangers befall it in the presence of Lord of the World, the Dharma Raja, the King of Truth.

3. " Now that I have seen your sacred features, let me partake of the refreshing waters of your teachings.

4. " Worldly profit is fleeting and perishable,
II but religious profit is eternal and inexhaustible.
A worldly man, though a king, is full of trouble,
150 but even a common man who is holy has peace
of mind."

5. Knowing the tendency of the king's heart, weighed down by avarice and love of pleasure, the Blessed One seized the opportunity and said :

6. " Even those who, have been born in low degree, when they see a virtuous man, feel reverence for him, how much more must an independent king, who by his previous conditions of life has acquired much merit, feel ?

7. " And now as I briefly expound the law, let the Maharaja listen and weigh my words, and hold fast to what I say.

8. " Our good or evil deeds follow us continually like shadows.

9. " That which is most needed is a loving heart !

10. " Regard your people as we do an only son. Do not oppress them, do not destroy them ; keep in due check every member of your body, forsake unrighteous doctrines and walk in the straight path ; do not exalt yourself by trampling down others. Give comfort and befriend the sufferer.

11. " Neither ponder much on kingly dignity, nor listen to the smooth words of flatterers.

12. " There is no profit in vexing oneself by austerities, but meditate on Dhamma and weigh the righteous law.

13. " We are enclosed on all sides by the rocks of sorrow and ill and only by considering the true law can we escape from this sorrow-filled mountain.

14. " What profit, then, in practising inequity ?

15. " All who are wise spurn the pleasures of the body. They loathe lust and seek to promote their spiritual existence.

16. " When a tree is burning with fierce flames,

how can the birds congregate therein? Truth cannot dwell where passion lives. Without a knowledge of this, the learned man, though he may be praised as a sage, is ignorant.

17. " On him who has this knowledge true wisdom dawns. To acquire this wisdom is the one aim needed. To neglect it implies the failure of life.

18. " The teachings of all schools should centre here, for without it there is no reason.

19. " This truth is not for the hermit alone; it concerns every human being, priest and layman alike. There is no distinction between the monk who has taken the vows, and the man of the world living with his family. There are hermits who fall into perdition, and there are humble householders who mount to the rank of rishis.

20. " The tide of lust is a danger common to all; it carries away the world. He who is involved in its eddies finds no escape. But wisdom is the handy boat, reflection is the rudder. The slogan of religion calls you to the rescue of your self from the assaults of Mara, the enemy.

21. " Since it is impossible to escape the result of our deeds, let us practise good works.

22. " Let us inspect our thoughts that we do no evil, for as we sow so shall we reap.

23. " There are ways from light into darkness and from darkness into light. There are ways, also, from gloom into deeper darkness, and from the dawn into brighter light. The wise man will use the light as he has to receive more light. He will constantly advance to the knowledge of the truth.

24. " Exhibit true superiority by virtuous conduct and the exercise of reason; meditate deeply on the vanity of earthly things, and understand the fickleness of life.

25. " Elevate the mind, and seek sincere faith with firm purpose; transgress not the rules of kingly conduct, and let your happiness depend, not upon external things but upon your own mind. Thus you will lay up a good name for distant ages.

26. The king listened with reverence and remembered all the words of the Blessed One in his heart and promised to become his lay disciple.

II § 7. *Conversion of Jeevaka*

152 1. Jeevaka was the son of Salvati, a courtesan of Rajagraha.

2. Immediately after birth the child, being illegitimate, was placed in a basket and thrown on a dust-heap.

3. A large number of people were standing by the dust-heap watching the child. Abhaya, the Rajakumara, happened to pass by the site. He questioned the people who said : " It is alive."

4. For this reason the child was called Jeevaka. Abhaya adopted him and brought him up.

5. When Jeevaka grew in age he learned how he was saved and was charged with the intense desire to qualify himself to save others.

6. He therefore went to the University of Takashila without the knowledge and permission of Abhaya and studied medicine for seven years.

7. Returning to Rajagraha he set up his practice as a doctor and within a very short time acquired a great name and fame in the profession.

8. His first patient was the wife of a sethi of Saketa and for curing her he received sixteen thousand kahapanas, a man-servant, a maid-servant and a coach with a horse.

9. Knowing his eminence, Abhaya gave him residence in his own establishment.

10. At Rajagraha he cured Bimbisara of a troublesome fistula and is said to have received as reward all the ornaments of Bimbisara's five hundred wives.

11. Other noteworthy cures of Jeevaka included that of the sethi of Rajagraha on whom he performed the operation of trepanning and of the son of the sethi of Benares who was suffering from chronic intestinal trouble due to misplacement.

12. Jeevaka was appointed physician to the king and the king's women.

13. But Jeevaka was greatly attached to the Blessed Lord. Consequently he also acted as a physician to him and the Sangh.

14. He became a disciple of the Lord. The Blessed Lord did not make him a Bhikku as he wanted him to remain free to tend to the sick and the wounded.

15. When Bimbisara died Jeevaka continued to serve his son Ajatsatru and was mainly instrumental in bringing him to the Lord after his crime of parricide.

§ 8. *The Conversion of Ratthapala*

1. Once when the Lord was on an alms pilgrimage in the Kuru country with a great company of almsmen, he stayed at Thullakotthita, which was a township of the Kurus.

2. They came to know of it and went to him to pay their respects.

3. When they were seated, the Lord instructed them with a discourse on the Doctrine. Having received their instruction from the Lord, the Brahmin heads of houses of Thullakotthita gratefully thanked him, rose up and departed with deep obeisance.

4. Seated among them was a young man named Ratthapala, a scion of a leading family of the place, to whom this thought came : " So far as I understand, the Doctrine which the Lord has preached is no easy matter for one who lives in a home to lead the higher life in all its fullness, purity, and perfection.

5. " What if I were to cut off hair and beard, don the yellow robes and go forth from home to homelessness as a pilgrim !"

6. When the Brahmins had not been gone long, then Ratthapala came up and, after salutations, told the Lord the thought which had come to him, and asked to be admitted to, and confirmed in, the confraternity under him.

7. " Have you your parents' consent to this step, Ratthapala ? ' asked the Lord.

8. " No, Sir."

9. " I do not admit those who have not their parents' consent."

10. " That consent, Sir, I will take steps to
II obtain," said the young man, who rising up and taking
a reverential leave of the Lord, went off to his parents,
154 told them his thoughts and asked their consent to his
becoming a Bhikku.

11. The parents made answer as follows : " Dear Ratthapala, you are our only son, very dear to us and beloved ; you live in comfort and have been brought up in comfort, with no experience at all of discomfort. Go away ; eat, drink, enjoy yourself, and do good works in all happiness. We refuse our consent.

12. " Your death would leave us desolate, with no pleasure left in life ; why, while we have you still, should we consent to your going forth from home to homelessness as a Bhikku".

13. A second and yet a third time did Ratthapala repeat his request, only to be met by the same refusal from his parents.

14. Failing thus to get his parents' consent, the young man flung himself down on the bare ground, declaring that he would either die there or become a Bhikku.

15. His parents entreated him to get up while repeating their objections to his becoming a Bhikku, but the young man said not a word. A second and a third time they entreated him but still he said not a word.

16. So the parents sought out Ratthapala's companions to whom they told all this and besought them to urge, as from themselves, what his parents had said to him.

17. Thrice his companions appealed to him, but still he said not a word. So his companions came to the parents with this report : " There on the bare ground he lies, declaring that he will either die there or become a Bhikku. If you refuse your consent, he will never get up alive. But, if you give your consent, you will see him when he has become a Bhikku. Should

he not like being a Bhikku, what alternative will he have! Why, only to come back here. Do give your consent!" they urged.

18. "Yes, we consent; but when he is a Bhikku, he must come and see us."

19. Off now went his companions to Ratthapala, and they told him that his parents had given their consent, but that when he was a Bhikku he was to come and see them.

20. Thereupon the young man arose and, when he had regained his strength, betook himself to the Lord, and after salutations seated himself on one side, saying: "I have got my parents' consent to my becoming a Bhikku; I ask the Lord to admit me."

21. Admission and confirmation were granted him under the Lord; and a fortnight afterwards the Lord, having stayed at Thullakotthita as long as he wanted, proceeded on his alms pilgrimage towards Sravasti, where he took up his abode in Jeta's grove in Anathapindika's pleasance.

22. Dwelling alone and aloof, strenuous, ardent and purged of self, the reverend Ratthapala was not long before he won the prize in quest of which young men go forth from home to homelessness as Bhikkus, that prize of prizes which crowns the highest life.

23. Then, he went to the Lord and, seated on one side after salutations, said that with the Lord's permission, he wished to go and see his parents.

24. Scanning with his own heart the thoughts of Ratthapala's heart, and recognizing thereby that he was incapable of abandoning his training and reverting to the lower life of a layman, the Lord bade him go when he would.

25. Hereupon, rising up and taking his leave of the Lord with deep reverence, Ratthapala, after duly putting away his bedding, set out, with his robe and bowl, on an alms pilgrimage to Thullakotthita where he took up his abode in the deer-park of the Kuru king.

26. Early next morning, duly robed and bowl in hand, he went into the town for alms, and there as he

passed from house to house on his undiscriminating round, he came to his father's house.

27. Indoors, in the hall within the middle door, his father was having his hair combed and, seeing
II Ratthapala coming in the distance, he said : "It was these shavelings of recluses who made Bhikku of my
156 only dear and beloved son."

28. So at his own father's house Ratthapala was given nothing, not even a refusal; all he got was abuse.

29. At this moment a slave-girl of the family was about to throw away the previous day's stale rice; and to her Ratthapala said: "If, sister, that is to be thrown away, put it in my bowl here."

30. As the girl was doing so, she recognized his hands and feet and voice, and going straight to her mistress, cried out: "Do you know, madam, the young master is back."

31. "If what you say is true, you are a slave no longer," said the mother, who hurried off to tell her husband that she heard their son was back.

32. Ratthapala was eating that stale rice under the hedge when his father arrived, exclaiming; "Can it be, my dear son, that you are eating stale rice? Should you not have come to your own house ?"

33. Said Ratthapala, "What house of our own, householder, can we have who are homeless, having gone forth from home to homelessness ? I did come to your house, where I was given nothing not even a refusal ; all I got was abuse."

34. 'Come, my son; let us go indoors.' 'Not so, householder; I have finished my eating for today.' said Ratthapala.

35. 'Well then, my son promise to take your meal here tomorrow.'

36. By his silence the reverend Ratthapala gave consent.

37. Then the father went indoors,—where first he ordered great heaps of gold and bullion to be piled up under a covering of mats and then he told his daughters-in-law, who had been the reverend

Ratthapala's wives aforetime, to deck themselves out in all the finery their husband liked to see them in.

38. When night had passed, the father, having ordered an excellent meal to be got ready in his house,
told his son when it was ready. Early that forenoon, II
the reverend Ratthapala, duly robed and bowl in 157
hand, came and took the seat set for him.

39. Hereupon, ordering the heap of treasure to be unveiled, the father said: 'This is your mother's fortune, that is your father's and that came from your grand-father. You have the wherewithal both to enjoy yourself and to do good works.

40. 'Come, my son ; abandon your training; revert to the lower life of the layman; enjoy your substance and do good works.'

41. 'If you will take my advice, householder, you will cart away all this heaped-up treasure and sink it in the middle of the Ganges. And why? Because thence you will only derive sorrow and lamentation, ills, pain of mind, pain of body and tribulation.'

42. Clinging to his feet, the reverend Ratthapala's whilom wives asked like what were the nymphs divine for whose sake he was leading the higher life.

43. "For the sake of no nymphs at all, sisters," said he.

44. At hearing themselves called sisters, the ladies all fainted and fell to the ground.

45. Said Ratthapala to his father: "If food is to be given, householder, give it; trouble me not."

46. "The food is ready, my son ; begin," said the father as he served that excellent meal without stint till his son had his fill.

47. After taking food he departed to the deer-park of the Kuru king, where he sat down under a tree during the noontide heat.

48. Now the king had given directions to his huntsman to tidy up the park against his coming to see it ; and the obedient huntsman was engaged on his task when he saw Ratthapala seated under a tree during the noontide heat, and reported to the king that the park was in order but that under a tree there

was seated Ratthapala, the young gentleman of whom His Majesty had often heard tell.

49. "Never mind about the park today," said the king; "I will pay a call on His Reverence."
II Ordering, therefore, all the repast which had been
158 prepared to be made ready, he mounted a chariot and
drove forth in procession in royal state out of the city to see Ratthapala.

50. Riding as far as the ground was passable for his chariot and proceeding thence on foot with his princely train, the king came at last upon the reverend Ratthapala, whom, after exchange of courteous greetings, the king—still standing—invited to be seated on a clump of flowers.

51. "Nay, sire; sit you there, I have got a seat."

52. Seating himself on the seat indicated to him, the king said: "There are four kinds of losses, Ratthapala, which impel men to cut off hair and beard, don the yellow robes, and go forth from home to homelessness—namely, (i) old age, (ii) failing health, (iii) impoverishment, and (iv) death of kinsfolk.

53. "Take a man who, being aged and old, far advanced in life, stricken in years, and at the close of life, recognizes his position, and realizes the difficulty either of acquiring new wealth or of doing well with what he has got; so he decides to take to homelessness. This is known as the loss which old age entails. But here are you in the prime of youth and early manhood, with a wealth of coal-black hair untouched by grey, and in all the beauty of your prime;—not yours is the loss old age entails. What have you known or seen or heard to make you take to homelessness?

54. "Or take a man who, being in ill-health or pain, or gravely ill, recognizes his position and realizes the difficulty either of acquiring new wealth or doing well with what he has already; so he decides to take to homelessness. This is known as the loss which failing health entails. But here are you neither ill nor ailing, with a good digestion maintained by humours neither too hot nor too cold; not yours is the loss which failing health entails. What have you

known or seen or heard to make you take to homelessness ?

55. " Or take a man who, after being rich and wealthy and of great substance, and after gradually losing it, recognizes his position and realizes the difficulty either of acquiring new wealth or of doing well with what he has got ; so he decides to become a pilgrim. This is known as the loss which kinsfolk's death entails. But here are you with a host of friends and relations ; not yours is the loss which kinsfolk's death entails. What have you known or seen or heard to make you take to homelessness ? "

56. " I have gone, forth," replied Ratthapala, " sire, from home to homelessness because I have known, seen, and heard the following four propositions enunciated by the All-Enlightened Lord who knows and sees :

" (i) The world is in continual flux and change.

" (ii) The world has no protector or preserver.

"(iii) We own nothing ; we must leave everything behind.

"(iv) The world lacks and hankers, being enslaved to craving."

57. " It is wonderful, it is marvellous," said the king, " how right in this the Lord was ! "

PART IV

Call from Home

1. Suddhodana and the Last Look.
2. Meeting Yeshodhara and Rahula.
3. Reception by the Sakyas.
4. Last attempt to make Him a Householder.
5. The Buddha's answer.
6. The Minister's reply.
7. The Buddha's Determination.

§ *1. Suddhodana and the Last Look*

1. After the conversion of Sariputta and Moggallana the Lord stayed in Rajagraha for two months.

2. Having heard that the Lord was residing at Rajagraha, Suddhodana, his father, sent word to him saying : " I wish to see my son before I die. Others have had the benefit of his doctrine, but not his father nor his relatives."

3. The man with whom the message was sent was Kaludayin, the son of one of the courtiers of Suddhodana.

4. And the messenger on arrival said : " O, world-honoured Tathagata, your father looks for your coming, as the lily longs for the rising of the sun."

5. The Blessed One consented to the request of his father and set out on the journey to his father's house accompanied by a large number of his disciples.

6. The Lord journeyed by slow stages. But Kaludayin went ahead of him to inform Suddodhana that the Blessed One was coming and was on his way.

7. Soon the tidings spread in the Sakya country. " Prince Siddharth, who wandered forth from home into homelessness to obtain enlightenment, having attained his purpose, is coming home to Kapilavatsu." This was on the lips of every one.

8. Suddhodana and Mahaprajapati went out with their relatives and ministers to meet their son. When they saw their son from afar, they were struck with his beauty and dignity and his lustre and they rejoiced in their heart, but they could find no words to utter.

9. This indeed was their son ; these were the features of Siddharth ! How near was the great Samana to their heart and yet what a distance lay between them ! That noble muni was no longer Siddharth their son ; he was now the Buddha, the Blessed One, the Holy One, Lord of Truth and Teacher of Mankind !

10. Suddhodana, considering the religious dignity of their son, descended from the chariot and having saluted him first, said : " It is now seven years since

we saw you. How we have longed for this moment."

11. Then the Buddha took a seat opposite his father, and the king eagerly gazed at his son. He longed to call him by his name but he dared not.
II "Siddharth," he exclaimed silently in his heart, "Siddharth, come back to your old father and be his
164 son again." But seeing the determination of his son, he suppressed his sentiments. Desolation overcame him and Mahaprajapati.

12. Thus the father sat face to face with his son, rejoicing in his sadness and sad in his rejoicing. Well may he be proud of his son, but his pride broke down at the idea that his great son would never be his heir.

13. "I would offer thee my kingdom," said the king, "but if I did, thou wouldst account it but as ashes."

14. And the Lord said: "I know that the king's heart is full of love and that for his son's sake he feels deep grief. But let the ties of love that bind you to the son whom you lost, embrace with equal kindness all your fellow-beings, and you will receive in his place a greater one than your son Siddharth; you will receive one who is the teacher of truth, the preacher of righteousness, and the bringer of peace and of Nirvana will enter into your heart."

15. Suddhodana trembled with joy when he heard the melodious words of his son, the Buddha, and clasping his hands, exclaimed with tears in his eyes: "Wonderful is the change! The overwhelming sorrow has passed away. At first my sorrowing heart was heavy but now I reap the fruit of your great renunciation. It was right that moved by your mighty sympathy, you should reject the pleasures of power and achieve your noble purpose in religious devotion. Having found the path you can now preach your Dhamma to all that yearn for deliverance."

16. Suddhodana returned to his house while the Buddha remained in the grove with his companions.

17. The next morning the Blessed Lord took his bowl and set out to beg for his food in Kapilavatsu.

18. And the news spread: "Siddharth is going

from house to house to receive alms in the city where he used to ride in a chariot attended by his retinue. His robe is like a red clod and he holds in his hand an earthen bowl."

19. On hearing the strange rumour, Suddhodana went forth in great haste and exclaimed : "Why do you disgrace me thus? Do you not know that I can easily supply you and your Bhikkus with food?"

20. And the Lord replied: "It is the custom of my Order."

21. "But how can this be? You are not one of them that ever begged for food."

22. "Yes, father," rejoined the Lord, "You and your race may claim descent from kings; my descent is from the Buddhas of old. They begged their food, and always lived on alms."

23. Suddhodana made no reply, and the Blessed One continued: "It is customary, when one has found a hidden treasure, for him to make an offering of the most precious jewel to his father. Suffer me, therefore, to offer you this treasure of mine which is the Dhamma."

24. And the Blessed Lord told his father: "If you free yourself from dreams, if you open your mind to truth, if you be energetic, if you practise righteousness, you will find eternal bliss."

25. Suddhodana heard the words in silence and replied: "My son! What thou sayst will I endeavour to fulfil."

§ 2. *Meeting Yeshodhara and Rahula*

1. Then Suddhodana conducted the Blessed Lord into his house and all the members of the family greeted him with great reverence.

2. But Yeshodhara, the mother of Rahula, did not make her appearance. Suddhodana sent for Yeshodhara, but she replied: "Surely, if I am deserving of any regard, Siddhartha will come and see me."

3. The Blessed One, having greeted all his

relatives and friends, asked: "Where is Yeshodhara?" and on being informed that she had refused to come, he rose straightaway and went to her apartment.

4. "I am free," the Blessed One said to his disciples Sariputta and Moggallana whom he had bidden to accompany him into Yeshodhara's chamber; "But Yeshodhara, however, is not as yet free. Not having seen me for a long time, she is exceedingly sorrowful. Unless her grief be allowed to run its course her heart will cleave. Should she touch the Tathagata, the Holy One, you must not prevent her."

5. Yeshodhara sat in her room in deep reflection. When the Blessed One entered, she was, from the abundance of her affection, like an overflowing vessel, unable to contain herself.

6. Forgetting that the man whom she loved was Buddha, the Lord of the World, the Preacher of Truth, she held him by his feet and wept bitterly.

7. Remembering, however, that Suddhodana was present, she felt ashamed and rose up, sitting herself reverently at a little distance.

8. Suddhodana apologized for Yeshodhara, saying: "This arises from her deep affection, and is more than a temporary emotion. During the seven years that she has lost her husband, when she heard that Siddharth had shaved his head, she did likewise; when she heard that he had left off the use of perfumes and ornaments she also refused their use. Like her husband she has eaten at appointed times from an earthen bowl only.

9. "If this is more than a temporary emotion it is not for want of courage."

10. And the Blessed One spoke to Yeshodhara telling of her great merits and the great courage she showed when he took Parivraja. Her purity, her gentleness, her devotion had been invaluable to him as a Bodhisattva when he aspired to the highest aim of mankind to attain enlightenment. This, then, was her karma, and it was the result of great merits.

11. Her grief had been unspeakable, and the glory that surrounded her spiritual inheritance increased

by her noble attitude during her life and had made her a unique person.

12. Then Yeshodhara dressed Rahula, now seven years old, in all the splendour of a prince and said to him :

13. "This holy man, whose appearance is so glorious that he looks like the Great Brahma, is your father. He possesses great mines of wealth which I have not yet seen. Go to him and entreat him to put you in the possession thereof for the son ought to inherit the property of the father."

14. Rahula replied : "Who is my father. I know of no father but Suddhodana."

15. Yeshodhara took the boy in her arms and from the window she pointed out to the Lord, who happened to be near, partaking of food among the Bhikkus, informing him that he was his father and not Suddhodana.

16. Rahula then went to him and looking up in his face, said without fear and with much affection:

17. "Aren't thou my father !" And standing near by him, he added: "O Samana, even your shadow is full of bliss !" The Blessed One remained silent.

18. When the Tathagata had finished his repast, he gave blessings and went away from the palace, but Rahula followed and asked him for his inheritance.

19. No one prevented the boy, nor did the Blessed One himself.

20. Then the Blessed One turned to Sariputta, saying: "My son asks for his inheritance. I cannot give him perishable treasures that will bring cares and sorrows, but I can give him the inheritance of a holy life, which is a treasure that will not perish."

21. Addressing Rahula with earnestness, the Blessed One said : "Gold and silver and jewels have I none. But if you are willing to receive spiritual treasures, and are strong to carry them and to keep them, I have plenty. My spiritual treasure is the path of righteousness. Do you desire to be admitted to the brotherhood of those who devote their life to the

culture of the mind seeking for the highest bliss attainable?"

22. And Rahula replied with firmness: "I do."

23. When Suddhodana heard that Rahula had joined the brotherhood of the Bhikkus he was greatly grieved.

§ 3. *Reception by the Sakyas*

1. On his return to the country of the Sakyas the Lord found his countrymen divided into two camps. One in favour and the other against him.

2. This recalled to his mind the old clash of opinion that took place in the Sakya Sangh when the issue of war between the Sakyas and Koliyas was fought and in which he had played so prominent a part.

3. Those against him refused even now to do obeisance to him and to recognize his greatness. Those for him had already decided to dedicate a son per household to form a retinue for him. These now decided to enter the Order and set out with the Lord on his return to Rajagraha.

4. Among the families which had decided to dedicate a son there was the family of Amitodana.

5. Amitodana had two sons. One was Anuruddha, who had been very delicately nurtured, and the other Mahanama.

6. And Mahanama went to Anuruddha, saying: "Either do you renounce the world, or I will do so." And Anuruddha replied, "I am delicate. It is impossible for me to go forth from the household life into the homeless state. You do so."

7. "But come now, dear Anuruddha, I will tell you what is incident to the household life. First, you have to get your fields ploughed. When that is done, you have to get them sown. When that is done, you have to get the water led down over them. When that is done, you have to get the water led off again. When that is done, you have to get the seeds pulled up. When that is done, you have to get the crop reaped.

When that is done, you have to get the crop carried away. When that is done, you have to get it arranged into bundles. When that is done, you have to get it trodden out. When that is done, you have to get the straw picked out. When that is done you have to get the chaff removed. When that is done, you have to get it winnowed. When that is done, you have to get the harvest garnered. When that is done, you have to do just the same next year, and the same all over again the year after that.

8. "The work is never over ; one sees not the end of one's labour. O, when shall our work be over ? When shall we see the end of our labours ? When shall we, still possessing and retaining the pleasures of our five senses, yet dwell at rest ? Yes, the work, dear Anuruddha, is never over ; no end appears to our labours."

9. "Then do you take thought for the household duties. I will go forth from the household life into the houseless state," said Anuruddha.

10. And Anuruddha, the Sakyan, went to his mother, and said to her. "I want, mother, to go forth from the household life into the houseless state. Grant me thy permission to do so."

11. And when he had thus spoken, his mother replied to Anuruddha, the Sakyan, saying : "You two, dear Anuruddha, are my two sons, near and dear to me, in whom I find no evil. Through death I shall some day, against my will, be separated from you but how can I be willing, whilst you are still alive, that you should go forth from the household life into the houseless state ?"

12. And a second time Anuruddha made the same request, and received the same reply. And a third time Anuruddha made the same request to his mother.

13. Now at that time Bhaddiya, the Sakyan Raja, held rule over the Sakyans ; and he was a friend of Anuruddha. And the mother of Anuruddha, thinking that that being so, the raja would not be able to renounce the world, said to her son: "Dear Anuruddha,

if Bhaddiya the Sakyan raja will renounce the world, you also may go forth with him."

14. Then Anuruddha went to Bhaddiya and said to him : "My renunciation of the world, dear friend,
II is being obstructed by you."

15. "Then let that obstruction, dear friend, be
170 removed. I am with you. Renounce the world according to your wish."

16. "Come, dear friend, let us both renounce the world together!"

17. "I am not capable, dear friend, of giving up the household life. Whatsoever else you can ask of me, that will I do. Do you go forth alone," said Bhaddiya.

18. "Mother, dear friend, has told me that if you do so, I may. And you have even now declared, 'If your renunciation be obstructed by me, then let that obstruction be removed. Even with you will I renounce the world according to your wish.' Come then, dear friend, let us both renounce the world."

19. And Bhaddiya, the Sakyan raja said to Anuruddha, "Wait, my friend, for seven years. At the end of seven years we will renounce the world together."

20. "Seven years are too long, dear friend. I am not able to wait for seven years."

21. Bhaddiya reduced the offer to six years and so on down to one year, to seven months and so on down to one month, and a fortnight. To each offer Anuruddha replied, "Too long a time to wait."

22. Then the raja says : "Wait, my friend, for seven days, whilst I hand over the kingdom to my sons and my brothers."

23. "Seven days is not too long. I will wait thus far," was the reply.

24. So Bhaddiya the Sakyan raja and Anuruddha and Ananda and Bhagu and Kimbila and Devadatta—just as they had so often previously gone out to the pleasure-ground with fourfold array—even so did they now go out with fourfold array, and Upali, the barber, went with them, making seven in all.

25. And when they had gone some distance they sent their retinue back and crossed over into the neighbouring district, and took off their fine things and wrapped them in their robes, and made a bundle of them, and said to Upali the barber : " Do you now, good Upali, turn back to Kapilavatsu. These things will be sufficient for you to live upon. We will go and join the Blessed One." And so they went ahead.

26. They went on and Upali parted company for the purpose of going back home.

§ 4. *Last attempt to make Him a Householder*

1. Suddhodana wept bitterly at the thought of his son going away never to be seen again.

2. Then Suddhodana spoke to his counsellor and his family priest and asked them if they could go and persuade his son to stay back and join the family.

3. The family priest accompanied by the counsellor, in obedience to the wishes of the king, went and overtook him on the way.

4. They paid him honour as was fitting, and having obtained his permission, sat down near him.

5. The family priest addressed the Lord as he sat at the foot of the tree.

6. " O prince, consider for a moment the feelings of the king with his eyes raining tears with the arrow of thy separation plunged into his heart. He has asked you to come back home. It is then only that he can die peacefully.

7. " I know that thy resolve is fixed upon religion, and I am convinced that this purpose of thine is unchanging ; but I am consumed with a flame of anguish like fire at thy going into this homeless state.

8. " Come, thou who lovest duty,—abandon this purpose for the sake of duty.

9. " Enjoy for a while the sovereignty of the earth, —thou shalt go to the forest at the time provided by the sastras,—do not show disregard for thy unhappy

kindred. Compassion for all creatures is the true religion.

10. "Religion is not wrought out only in the forests, the salvation of ascetics can be accomplished even in a city ; thought and effort are the true means ; the forest and the badge are only a coward's signs.

11. "The king of the Sakyas is drowned in a deep sea of sorrow, full of waves of trouble, springing from thee ; do thou therefore deliver him who is helpless and protectorless like an ox drowning in the sea.

12. "Consider also the queen, who brought thee up, who has not yet gone to the region inhabited by Agastya—wilt thou not take some heed of her, who ceaselessly grieves like a cow that has lost her calf?

13. "Surely thou wilt succour thy wife by the sight of thee, who now mourns as a widow yet with her lord still alive,—like a swan separated from her mate or a female elephant deserted in the forest by her companion."

14. The Lord having heard the words of the family priest, reflected for a moment, knowing all the virtues of the virtuous, and then thus uttered his gentle reply :

§ 5. *The Buddha's Answer*

1. "I well know the paternal tenderness of the king, especially that which he has displayed towards me ; yet knowing this as I do, still alarmed at the ill and sorrow which pervades the world, I am inevitably forced to leave my kindred.

2. "Who would not wish to see his dear kindred, if but this separation from beloved ones did not exist? But since even after it has been once, separation will still come again, it is for this that I abandon my father, however loving.

3. "I do not however approve that thou shouldst think the king's grief as caused by me, when in the midst of his dream-like unions, he is afflicted by thoughts of separations in the future.

4. "Thus let thy thoughts settle into certainty,

having seen the multiform in its various developments; neither a son nor kindred is the cause of sorrow,—this sorrow is caused only by ignorance.

5. " Since parting is inevitably fixed in the course of time for all beings, just as for travellers who have joined company on a road,—what wise man would cherish sorrow, when he loses his kindred, even though he loves them?

6. " Leaving his kindred in another world, he departs hither, and having stolen away from them here, he goes forth once more ; having gone thither, he goes elsewhere also,—such is the lot of mankind,—what consideration can the liberated have for them?

7. " Since from the moment of leaving the womb death is a characteristic adjunct, why, in thy affection for thy son, hast thou called my departure to the forest ill-timed?

8. " There may be an 'ill time' in one's attaining a worldly object,—time indeed is described as inseparably connected with all things; time drags the world into all its various times ; but all time suits a bliss which is really worthy of praise.

9. " That the king should wish to surrender to me his kingdom,—this is a noble thought, well worthy of a father ; but it would be as improper for me to accept it, as for a sick man through greed to accept unwholesome food.

10. " How can it be right for the wise to enter royalty, the home of illusion, where are found anxiety, passion, and weariness ; and the violation of all right through another's service?

11. " The golden palace seems to me to be on fire ; the daintiest viands seem mixed with poison ; infested with crocodiles is the tranquil lotus-bed."

§ 6. *The Minister's Reply*

1. Having heard the Buddha's discourse, well suitable to his virtues and knowledge, freed from all desires, full of sound reasons, and weighty,—the counsellor thus made answer :

2. "This resolve of thine is an excellent counsel, not unfit in itself but only unfit at the present time: it could not be thy duty, loving duty as thou dost, to leave thy father in his old age to sorrow.

II 3. "Surely thy mind is not very penetrating, or it
174 is ill-skilled in examining duty, wealth, and pleasure,—
when for the sake of an unseen result thou departest
disregarding a visible end.

4. "Again some say that there is another birth,—others with confident assertion say that there is not, since then the matter is all in doubt, it is right to enjoy the good fortune which comes into thy hand.

5. "If there is any activity hereafter, we will enjoy ourselves in it as may offer; or if there is no activity beyond this life, then there is an assured liberation to all the world without any effort.

6. "Some say there is a future life, but they do not allow the possibility of liberation; as fire is hot by nature, and water liquid, so they hold that there is a special nature in our power of action.

7. "Some maintain that all things arise from inherent properties,—both good and evil and existence and non-existence: and since all this world thus arises spontaneously, therefore also all effort of ours is vain.

8. "Since the action of the senses is fixed, and so too the agreeableness or the disagreeableness of outward objects,—then for that which is united to old age and pains, what effort can avail to alter it? Does it not all arise spontaneously?

9. "The fire becomes quenched by water, and fire causes water to evaporate; and different elements, united in a body, producing unity, bear up the world.

10. "That the nature of the embryo in the womb is produced as composed of hands, feet, belly, back, and head, and that it is also united with the soul,—the wise declare that all this comes of itself spontaneously.

11. "Who causes the sharpness of the thorn? Or the various natures of beasts and birds? All this has arisen spontaneously; there is no acting from desire, how then can there be such a thing as will?

12. "Others say that creation comes from Isvara,

—what need then is there of the effort of the conscious soul? That which is the cause of the action of the world, is also determined as the cause of its ceasing to act.

13. " Some say that the coming into being and the destruction of being are alike caused by the soul, but they say that coming into being arises without effort, while the attainment of liberation is by effort.

14. " A man discharges his debt to his ancestors by begetting offspring, to the saints by sacred lore, to the gods by sacrifices ; he is born with these three debts upon him,—whoever has liberation (from these), he indeed has liberation.

15. " Thus by this series of rules the wise promise liberation to him who uses effort ; but however ready for effort with all their energy, those who seek liberation will find weariness.

16. " Therefore, gentle youth, if thou hast a love for liberation, follow rightly the prescribed rule ; thus wilt thou thyself attain to it, and the king's grief will come to an end.

17. " And as for thy meditations on the evils of life ending in thy return from the forest to thy home,—let not the thought of this trouble thee, my son,—those in old time also have returned from the forests to their houses." He mentioned Ambarish Drumakesha, Rama and others.

§ 7. *The Buddha's Determination*

1. Then having heard the affectionate and loyal words of the minister, who was as the eye of the king,—firm in his resolve, the king's son made his answer, with nothing omitted or displaced, neither tedious nor hasty:

2. " This doubt whether anything exists or not, is not to be solved for me by another's words ; having determined the truth by asceticism or quietism, I will myself grasp whatever is the truth concerning it.

3. " It is not for me to accept a theory which depends on the unknown and is all controverted, and

which involves a hundred prepossessions ; what wise man would go by another's belief ? Mankind is like the blind directed in darkness by the blind.

4. " But even though I cannot discern the truth,
II yet still, if good and evil are doubted, let one's mind
be set on the good ; even a toil in vain is to be chosen
176 by him whose soul is good.

5. " But having seen that this ' sacred tradition ' is uncertain, know that that only is right which has been uttered by the trustworthy ; and know that trustworthiness means the absence of faults ; he who is without faults will not utter an untruth.

6. " And as for what thou saidst to me in regard to my returning home, the examples you give are no authority,—for in determining duty, how canst thou quote as authorities those who have broken their vows ?

7. " Even the sun therefore may fall to the earth, even the mountain Himavat may lose its firmness ; but never could I return to my home as a man of the world, with my senses only alert for external objects.

8. " I would enter the blazing fire, but not my house with my purpose unfulfilled." Rising up in accordance with his resolve full of disinterestedness, he went his way.

9. Then the minister and the Brahmin, both full of tears, having heard his firm determination, and having followed him awhile with despondent looks, and overcome with sorrow, slowly returned to Kapilavatsu.

10. Through their love for the prince and their devotion to the king they returned, and often stopped looking back, they could neither behold him on the road nor yet lose the sight of him,—shining in his own splendour and beyond the reach of all others, like the sun.

11. Having failed to persuade him to return home, the minister and the priest went back with faltering steps, saying to each other, " How shall we approach the king and see him, who is longing for his dear son ?"

PART V

Campaign for Conversion resumed

1. Conversion of Rustic Brahmins.
2. Conversion of the Brahmins of Uttaravati.

§ 1. *Conversion of Rustic Brahmins*

1. At the back of the Gridhrakutta mountains, near Rajagriha, there was a village, of some seventy or so families, all of them Brahmins.

2. The Buddha, wishing to convert these people, II
came to the place and sat down under a tree. 179

3. The people seeing the dignity of his presence, and the glorious appearance of his body, flocked round him, on which he asked the Brahmins how long they had dwelt in the mountain there, and what their occupation was.

4. To this they replied: " We have dwelt here during thirty generations past, and our occupation is to tend cattle."

5. On asking further as to their religious belief they said : " We pay homage and sacrifice to the sun and the moon, the rain (water), and fire, according to the several seasons.

6. " If one of us dies, we assemble and pray that he may be born in the heaven of Brahma, and so escape further transmigrations."

7. The Buddha replied: "This is not a safe way, not by it can you benefit. The true way is to follow me, become true ascetics, and practise complete self-composure with a view to obtain Nirvana "; and then he added these lines :

8. " They who consider truth as that which is untrue, and regard that which is untrue as truth, this is but to adopt heretical opinions, and can never lead to true advantage.

9. " But to know as truth that which is true, and to regard as false that which is false, this is perfect rectitude, and this shall bring true profit.

10. " Everywhere in the world there is death—there is no escape from it.

11. " To consider this as the condition of all states of being that there is nothing born but must die, and, therefore, to desire to escape birth and death, this is to exercise one's self in Religious Truth."

12. The seventy Brahmins hearing these words,

desired at once to become Shamans ; and on being welcomed by Buddha, their hair fell off, and they presented the appearance of true disciples.

13. Then they all set out to return to the Vihara,
II and on the road certain thoughts about their wives and families troubled them whilst at the same time a
180 heavy downpour of rain prevented their advance.

14. There were some ten houses on the roadside, in which they sought shelter; but on entering one of them it was soon perceived that through the roof the rain found its way, and there was but little protection from the rain.

15. On this the Buddha added these lines, and said, " As when a house-roof is not properly secured, then the rain finds a way through it and drops within, so when the thoughts are not carefully controlled, the desires (sexual desires) will soon bore through all our good resolutions.

16. "But as when a roof is well stopped then the water cannot leak through, so by controlling one's thoughts, and acting with reflection, no such desires can arise or disturb us."

17. The seventy Brahmins, on hearing these lines, although convinced that their desires were reprehensible, yet were not wholly free from doubt, nevertheless they went forward.

18. As they advanced they saw some scented wrapping on the ground, and Buddha took the opportunity of calling their attention to it ; and after this, seeing some fish-gut also lying about, he directed their notice to its ill odour and then added these lines and said :

19. "He who consorts with the low and the base, contracts the same character as he who handles a foul substance; he goes from worse to worse, and utterly without reason, he perfects himself in wickedness.

20. " But the wise man (consorting with the wise) contracts the same character, even as the scent of a sweet odour adheres to him who handles it; advancing in wisdom, practising virtue, he goes on to perfection, and is satisfied."

21. The seventy Brahmins, hearing these verses, convinced that their desire to return home and enjoy personal indulgence was the evil taint that adhered to them, cast off such thoughts, and, going forward, came to the Vihara, and finally obtained the condition of Arahtas.

§ 2. *Conversion of the Brahmins of Uttaravati*

1. Once the Buddha was residing in the Jetavana, at Shravasti, and preaching his doctrine for the benefit of men and gods, there were in a country to the eastward, called Uttaravati, a company of 500 Brahmins.

2. They had agreed to go together to the residence of a Nirgrantha ascetic on the banks of the Ganges, who, by polluting himself with dirt, etc., aspired to the condition of a Rishi.

3. On their way they were overtaken in the desert with thirst. Seeing a tree, and hoping to find some human habitation near, they hastened to it, but when they arrived there they found no sign of life.

4. On this they raised their voices in lamentation. Suddenly from the tree they heard the voice of the resident Spirit, who asked them why they lamented so, and on hearing the reason, supplied them to the full with drink and meat.

5. The Brahmins, ready to start onward, asked the Spirit what had been his previous history, that he was thus born.

6. On which he explained that having gone to the assembly of priests in Shravasti when Sudatta had bestowed the garden on the Buddha, he had remained all night listening to the law Dhamma and having filled his drinking cup with water as he went, had bestowed it in charity among the priests.

7. On his return next morning, his wife in anger asked him what annoyance he had received that he should stay away all night. On which he replied that he was not annoyed, but he had been to

listen to the Buddha preaching at the Jetavana.

8. On this his wife began roundly to abuse the Buddha, and said, "This Gotama is but a mad preacher, who deceives the people," and so on.

II 9. "On this" he said, "I resented not her
statements, but rather submitted to them and so
182 when I came to die I was born as a spirit, but on account of my pusillanimity I was confined to this tree," and then he recited these verses.

10. "Sacrifices and such services are sources of misery, day and night, a continual burden and anxiety.

11. "To escape sorrow, and destroy the elements of the body, a man should attend to the Law (of Buddha), and arrive at deliverance from all worldly Rules of Religion (World Rishis)."

12. The Brahmins having heard these words, resolved themselves to go to Shravasti, to the place where the Buddha was, and having explained the object of their visit, the world-honoured said to them :

13. "Although a man goes naked with tangled hair, or though he clothes himself with a few leaves or garment of bark, though he covers himself with dirt and sleeps on the stones, what use is this in getting rid of impure thoughts?

14. "But he who neither contends or kills, or destroys by fire, who desires not to get the victory, who is moved by goodwill towards all the world, there is no ground in such a case for ill-will or hate.

15. "To sacrifice to spirits in order to find peace (merit), or, after this life expecting reward, his happiness, is not one quarter of that man's who pays homage to the good.

16. "He who is ever intent on good conduct and due reverence to others, who always venerates old age, four happy consequences increasingly attend that man—beauty and strength, and life and peace."

17. On hearing this from her husband the wife became reconciled.

PART VI

Conversion of the Low and the Lowly

1. Conversion of Upali, the Barber.
2. Conversion of Sunita, the Sweeper.
3. Conversion of Sopaka and Suppiya, the Untouchables.
4. Conversion of Sumangala and other Low Castes.
5. Conversion of Suprabuddha, the Leper.

§ 1. *Conversion of Upali, the Barber*

1. While going back Upali, the barber thought: "The Sakyans are a fierce people. If I go back with these ornaments they will kill me thinking that I have killed my companions and run away with their ornaments. Why should I not go the way these young men of the Sakya clan have gone?"

2. "Why indeed should I not?" asked Upali to himself. And he let down the bundle of ornaments from his back, and hung it on a tree, saying: "Let him who finds it take it as a gift," and returned to follow the Sakya youths.

3. And the Sakyans saw him coming from afar, and on seeing, they said to him: "What have you come back for, good Upali?"

4. Then he told them what he felt and they replied: "Thou hast done well, good Upali, in that thou didst not return; for the Sakyans are fierce, and they might have killed thee."

5. And they took Upali the barber with them to the place where the Blessed One was. And on arriving there, they bowed down before the Blessed One and took their seats on one side. And so seated they said to the Blessed One :

6. "We Sakyans, Lord, are haughty. And this Upali, the barber, has long been an attendant, Lord, upon us. May the Blessed One admit him to the Order before us, so that we may render him respect and reverence, and bow down with outstretched hands before him as our senior and thus shall the Sakyan pride be humbled in us !"

7. Then the Blessed One received first Upali, the barber, and afterwards those young men of the Sakya clan, into the ranks of the Order.

§ 2. *Conversion of Sunita, the Sweeper*

1. There lived in Rajagraha a scavenger by name Sunita. He earned his living as a road sweeper, sweeping away the rubbish thrown by the householders

on the roadside. His was a low and hereditary occupation.

2. One day in the early hours of the dawn the Blessed One rose, dressed himself and walked into
II Rajagraha for alms followed by a large number of Bhikkus.

186 3. Now Sunita was cleaning the street, collecting scraps, rubbish, and so on into heaps and filling therewith the basket which he carried on a yoke.

4. And when he saw the Master and his train approaching, his heart was filled with joy and awe.

5. Finding no place to hide in on the road, he placed his yoke in a bend in the wall and stood as if stuck to the wall, saluting the Lord with clasped hands.

6. Then the Lord when he had come near, spoke to him in voice divinely sweet, saying: "Sunita! What to you is this wretched mode of living? Can you endure to leave home and come into the Order?"

7. And Sunita, experiencing the rapture of one who has been sprinkled with Ambrosia, said: "If even such as the Exalted One may in this life take Orders, why should I not? May the Exalted One suffer me to come forth."

8. Then the Master said: "Come Bhikku!" And Sunita by that word received sanction and ordination and was invested with bowl and robes.

9. The Master leading him to the Vihar taught him the Dhamma and the Discipline and said, "By the discipline of holy life, restraint and mastery of self, a man becomes holy."

10. When asked how Sunita became so great, the Buddha said, "As on a rubbish-heap on highway cast a lily may grow, fragrant and sweet, so among rubbish-creatures, worldlings blind by insight shines the very Buddha's child."

§ 3. *Conversion of Sopaka and Suppiya, the Untouchables*

1. Sopaka was a pariah of Shravasti. In her travail at his birth his mother fell into a long deep

swoon, so that her husband and kinsfolk said " She is dead !" And they bore her to the cemetery and prepared to cremate her body.

2. But on account of the storm of wind and rain the fire would not burn. So they went away leaving Sopaka's mother on the funeral pyre.

3. Sopaka's mother was not then dead. She died afterwards. Before her death she gave birth to a child.

4. The child was adopted by the watchman of the cemetery and was brought up by him along with his own child Suppiya. The child was known by the name of the community Sopaka to which its mother belonged.

5. The Blessed Lord one day happened to pass by the cemetery. Sopaka, seeing the Lord, approached him. After saluting the Lord he asked his permission to join him as his disciple.

6. Sopaka was then only seven years old. So the Lord asked him to obtain his father's consent.

7. Sopaka went and fetched his father. The father saluted the Lord and requested him to admit his son to the Order.

8. Notwithstanding that he belonged to the pariah community the Lord admitted him to the Order and instructed him in the doctrine and discipline.

9. Sopaka later became a Thera.

10. Suppiya and Sopaka had grown together from childhood and Sopaka having been adopted and brought up by Suppiya's father, Suppiya learned the Lord's doctrine and discipline from his companion, Sopaka, and requested Sopaka to admit him to the Order, although Sopaka belonged to a community which was lower in rank than the community to which Suppiya belonged.

11. Sopaka agreed and Suppiya, a member who belonged to the despised community whose occupation was to perform the duties of watchmen in the cemetery, became a Bhikku.

§ 4. *Conversion of Sumangala and other Low Castes*

1. Sumangala was a peasant of Shravasti. He earned his living by work in the fields, working with a little sickle, plough and spade.

II · 188 2. Channa was a native of Kapilavatsu and was a slave in the house of Suddhodana.

3. Dhanniya was a resident of Rajagraha. He was a potter.

4. Kappata-Kura was a native of Shravasti. The only way he knew of, to support himself, was to go about, clad in rags, pan in hand, seeking for rice-grains. Hence he became known as Kappata-Kura—"Rags and-rice." When grown up, he maintained himself by selling grass.

5. All of them sought from the Buddha permission to become Bhikkus and enter the Order. The Buddha without hesitation and without caring for their low birth or their previous condition, admitted them into the Order.

§ 5. *Conversion of Supprabuddha, the Leper*

1. Once the Exalted One was staying near Rajagraha, in the bamboo grove, at the squirrels' feeding-ground.

2. Now there lived in Rajagraha at that time a certain man, who was a leper, named Supprabuddha, a poor, wretched, miserable creature.

3. And it happened at that time that the Exalted One was sitting there in the midst of a great multitude, teaching the Dhamma.

4. And Supprabuddha, the leper, saw from afar the multitude gathered together, and at the sight he thought, " Without a doubt an alms-giving of food, both hard and soft, is toward yonder. Suppose I draw near to yonder crowd, I might get there something to eat, food soft or hard."

5. So Supprabuddha, the leper, drew near that crowd, and he beheld the Exalted One sitting there amid

a great crowd, preaching the Norm. So, seeing the Exalted One he thought : " No. There is no alms-giving here of food. It is Gotama the Samana preaching the Dhamma in the assembly. Suppose I were
to listen to his teaching." II

6. So he sat down at one side, thinking, " I too
will listen to the teaching." 189

7. Now the Exalted One, reading with His thought the thoughts of that whole gathering, said to Himself, " Who, I wonder, of these present, is able to grasp the Truth ? " Then He saw Supprabuddha, the leper, sitting in the crowd : and at the sight of him He knew, " This one can grasp the Truth."

8. So for the sake of Supprabuddha, the leper, the Master preached a sermon, dealing in due order with these topics. On alms-giving, on the holy life, and on the heaven-world : and He pointed out the meanness and vileness of sensual desires and the profit of freedom from the asavas.

9. Now when the Exalted One saw that the heart of Supprabuddha, the leper, was softened, pliant, set free, elated, and full of faith, then He set forth to him the Dhamma most excellent of the Buddha, to wit, suffering, the cause of suffering, the ceasing of suffering, and the path.

10. Then, just as a white cloth, free from stains, is ready to receive the dye, even so in Supprabuddha, the leper, as he sat there in that very place, arose the pure stainless insight of the Truth, the knowledge that whatsoever hath a beginning, that also must have an end. And Supprabuddha, the leper, saw the Truth, reached the Truth, perceived the truth, plunged into the Truth, crossed beyond doubting, was freed from all questionings, won confidence, and needing nothing further, being established in the Master's teaching, sprang up from his seat and drew near to Him, and there he sat down at one side.

11. So seated he said to the Exalted One, " Excellent, O Lord Excellent, O, Lord, just as if, Lord, one should lift up the fallen, discover the hidden,

point out the way to one bewildered, show a light in
the gloom, saying, 'Now they who have eyes to see can
see shapes,' even so in diverse ways has the Exalted
One expounded the truth. I, even I, Lord, do go for
II refuge to the Exalted One, to the Norm and to the
Order of Brethren. May the Exalted One accept me
190 as His follower, as one who from this time forth even
to life's end has gone to refuge in Him."

12. Thereupon Supprabuddha, the leper, being taught, established, roused, and made happy by the Exalted One's pious talk, praised and welcomed His words, gave thanks and rose up from his seat, saluted the Exalted One by the right, and went away.

13. Unfortunately it came to pass that a young calf flung the leper Supprabuddha down and gored him to death.

PART VII

Conversion of Women

1. Conversion of Mahaprajapati Gotami, Yeshodhara and her Companions.
2. Conversion of Prakrati, a Chandalika.

§ *1. Conversion of Mahaprajapati Gotami and Yeshodhara and her Companions*

1. When the Blessed One had been on a visit to II
his father's home the desire to join the Sangh was as
keen among the Sakya women as it was among the 193
Sakya men.

2. The leader of such women was no other than Mahaprajapati Gotami.

3. Now at the time when the Blessed One was staying among the Sakyas in the Nigrodharama, Mahaprajapati Gotami went to him and said: "It would be well, Lord, if women were allowed to become Parivrajakas and enter the Sangh under the doctrine and discipline proclaimed by the Tathagata!"

4. "Enough, O Gotami! Let not such a thought come into your mind." And a second and a third time did Mahaprajapati make the same request in the same words, and a second and a third time did she receive the same reply.

5. Then Mahaprajapati Gotami, sad and sorrowful, bowed down before the Blessed One, and went away weeping and in tears.

6. After the Blessed One had left Nigrodharama for his wanderings, Mahaprajapati and the Sakya women sat together to give further consideration to their request for admission to the Sangh and the refusal of the Lord to grant such a request.

7. The Sakya women refused to take the Lord's refusal as final. They decided to go further to assume the garb of a Parivrajaka and present the Lord with a *fait accompli.*

8. Accordingly Mahaprajapati Gotami cut off her hair and put on orange-coloured robes and set out with a number of women of the Sakya clan, on her journey to meet the Lord who was at that time staying in Vesali in the Mahavana in the Kutagara Hall.

9. In due course Mahaprajapati Gotami with her companions arrived at Vesali and with swollen feet and covered with dust came to the Kutogara Hall.

10. Again she made the same request to the Blessed Lord which she had made when he was staying at Nigrodharama and he refused it again.

11. On receiving his refusal a second time
II Mahaprajapati withdrew and was standing outside the entrance of the hall not knowing what to do. While
194 she was so standing Ananda on his way to the hall saw her and recognized her.

12. He then asked Mahaprajapati, " Why standest thou there, outside the porch, with swollen feet, covered with dust, and sorrowful, weeping and in tears ?" " Inasmuch, O Ananda, as the Lord, the Blessed One, does not permit women to renounce their homes and enter the homeless state under the doctrine and discipline proclaimed by the Tathagata," said Mahaprajapati.

13. Then did the Venerable Ananda go up to the place where the Blessed One was, and bowed down before the Blessed One, and take his seat on one side. And, so sitting, the Venerable Ananda said to the Blessed One : " Behold, Lord, Mahaprajapati Gotami is standing outside under the entrance porch, with swollen feet covered with dust, sad and sorrowful, weeping and in tears, inasmuch as the Blessed One does not permit women to renounce their homes and enter the homeless state under the doctrine and discipline proclaimed by the Blessed One. It were well, Lord, if women were to have permission granted to them to do as she desires.

14. " Has not Mahaprajapati proved herself of great service to the Blessed One, when as aunt and nurse she nourished him and gave him milk, and on the death of his mother suckled the Blessed One at her own breast; it were, therefore, well, Lord that women should have permission to go forth from the household life and enter the homeless state, under the doctrine and discipline proclaimed by the Tathagata."

15. " Enough Ananda! Let it not, please, that women should be allowed to do so." A second time and a third time did Ananda make the same request, in the same words, and received the same reply.

16. Then the Venerable Ananda asked the Blessed One : " What can be the ground, Lord, for your refusal to allow women to take Parivraja.

17. " The Lord knows that the Brahmins hold that the Shudras and women cannot reach moksha (Salvation) because they are unclean and inferior. They do therefore not allow Shudras and women to take Parivraja. Does the Blessed One hold the same view as the Brahmins ?

18. Has not the Blessed One allowed the Shudras to take Parivraja and join the Sangh in the same way he has done to the Brahmins ? What is the ground, Lord, for treating women differently ?

19. Does the Blessed One hold that women are not capable of reaching Nibbana under the doctrine and discipline proclaimed by the Blessed One ?"

20. The Blessed One replied : " Ananda ! Do not misunderstand me. I hold that women are as much capable as men in the matter of reaching Nibbana. Ananda ! do not misunderstand me, I am not an upholder of the doctrine of sex inequality. My rejection of Mahaprajapati's request is not based on sex inequality. It is based on practical grounds."

21. " I am happy, Lord, to know the real reason. But must the Lord refuse her request because of practical difficulties ? Would not such an act bring the Dhamma into discredit and make it open to the charge of upholding sex inequality ? Could not the Lord devise some rules to get over such practical difficulties by which the Lord is worried ?"

22. " Well, Ananda, I grant if Mahaprajapati insists that women must be allowed to take Parivraja under the doctrine and discipline proclaimed by me. But it shall be subject to eight conditions. Let Mahaprajapati Gotami take upon herself the responsibility of enforcing the Eight Chief Rules. That will be her initiation."

23. Then the Venerable Ananda, when he learnt from the Blessed One these Eight Chief Rules, went to Mahaprajapati Gotami and told her all that the Blessed One had said.

24. "Just, Ananda, as a man or a woman, when young and of tender years, accustomed to adorn himself, would, when he had bathed his head, receive with both hands a garland of lotus flowers, or of
II jasmine flowers or of stimutaka flowers, and place it on the top of his head ; even so do I, Ananda, take
196 upon me these Eight Chief Rules, never to be transgressed during my lifelong," said Mahaprajapati to Ananda.

25. Then the Venerable Ananda returned to the Blessed One, and bowed down before him, and took his seat, on one side. And, so sitting, the Venerable Ananda said to the Blessed One: "Mahaprajapati Gotami, Lord, has taken upon herself the responsibility for the enforcement of the Eight Chief Rules, she may therefore be regarded as having received the Upasampada initiation," (entry into the Sangha).

26. Now Mahaprajapati received ordination, and 500 Sakya ladies who had come with her were also ordained at the same time. Thus ordained great Prajapati came before the Master, and saluting him, stood on one side and the Blessed One taught her the Dhamma, the doctrine and the discipline.

27. The other five hundred Bhikkhunis were instructed by Nandaka, one of the disciples of the Blessed One.

28. Among the Sakya women who became Bhikkhunis along with Mahaprajapati was Yeshodhara. After her initiation she came to be known as Bhadda Kaccana.

§ 2. *Conversion of Prakrati, a Chandalika*

1. Once the Blessed Lord was living in Shravasti in the Jetavana Arama of Anathpindika.

2. It so happened that Ananda, his disciple, had gone into the city to beg for alms. After eating his food Ananda was going to the river for drinking water.

3. He saw a girl on the river bank filling her pot. Ananda asked her to give him some water.

4. The girl, whose name was Prakrati, refused, saying she was a Chandalika.

5. Ananda said, "I am concerned with water. I am not concerned with your caste." The girl then gave him some water from her pot.

6. Thereafter Ananda left for Jetavana. The girl followed him and saw where he was staying and found that his name was Ananda and that he was a follower of the Buddha.

7. On returning home she told her mother Matangi what had happened and falling on the ground started weeping.

8. The mother asked for the cause of her weeping. The girl told the whole story, and said, "If you wish to marry me I can only marry Ananda. I will not marry anybody else."

9. The mother started on an inquiry. On return she told the girl that such a marriage was impossible for Ananda was under a vow of celibacy.

10. On hearing this news the girl was filled with extreme sorrow and gave up food. She was not prepared to take things as though it was a decree of fate. So she said: "Mother, you know the art of sorcery, don't you? Why don't you employ it to achieve our purpose?" The mother said, "I will see what can be done."

11. Matangi invited Ananda to her house for a meal. The girl became very happy. Matangi then told Ananda that her daughter was very anxious to marry him. Ananda replied, "I am vowed to be celibate and therefore I cannot marry any woman."

12. "If you do not marry my daughter, she will commit suicide, so attached she is to you," Matangi told Ananda. "But I cannot help," replied Ananda.

13. Matangi went inside and told her daughter that Ananda refused to marry her.

14. The girl cried: "Mother, where is your sorcery?" The mother said, "My sorcery cannot win against the Tathagata."

15. The girl shouted and said, " Close the door and do not allow him to go out. I shall see that he becomes my husband this very night."

16. The mother did what the girl wanted her to do. As night fell the mother brought in the room a bed. The girl, dressed in her best, stepped in. But Ananda remained unmoved.

17. The mother at last used her sorcery. As a result a fire broke out in the room. The mother then held Ananda by his clothes and said, " If you will not agree to marry my daughter, I will throw you in this fire." However, Ananda did not yield, and the mother and the daughter feeling helpless, left him free.

18. Ananda on his return told the Blessed Lord all that had happened.

19. On the second day the girl came to Jetavana in search of Ananda. Ananda was going out for alms. Ananda saw her and wanted to avoid her. But the girl followed him wherever he went.

20. When Ananda returned to Jetavana he found the girl waiting at the door of his Vihar.

21. Ananda told the Blessed One how the girl was pursuing him. The Blessed One sent for her.

22. When the girl appeared before him the Blessed One asked her why she was pursuing Ananda. The girl replied that she was intent on marrying him " I have heard he is unmarried and I am also unmarried."

23. The Bhagavan said, " Ananda is a Bhikku and he has no hair on his head. If you can get yourself clean shaven I shall see what could be done."

24. The girl replied, " I am prepared for it." The Bhagavan said, "You must get your mother's permission for undergoing tonsure."

25. The girl returned to her mother and said, " Mother ! I have achieved what you failed to achieve. The Bhagavan has promised to get me married to Ananda if I undergo tonsure."

26. The mother grew angry and said, " You must not do that. You are my daughter and you must keep hair. Why are you so eager to marry a Shramana

like Ananda. I can get you married to a better man."

27. She replied, "I will either die or marry Ananda. There is no third alternative for me."

28. The Mother said, "Why are you insulting me?" The girl said, "If you love me you must let me do as I wish."

29. The mother withdrew her objection and the girl underwent tonsure.

30. Then the girl presented herself before the Blessed Lord saying, "I have tonsured my head as directed by you."

31. The Blessed Lord then asked her, "What do you want? What part of his body you cherish?" The girl said, "I am in love with his nose, I am in love with his mouth, I am in love with his ears, I am in love with his voice, I am in love with his eyes and I am in love with his gait."

32. The Blessed Lord then said to the girl, "Do you know that the eyes are the home of tears, the nose is the home of dirt, the mouth is the home of spit, the ear is the home of dirt and the body is the container of dung and urine."

33. "When men and women come together they procreate children. But where there is birth there is death also; where there is death there is sorrow also. My dear girl, what are you going to get by marrying Ananda. I do not know."

34. The girl began to cogitate and agreed that there was no purpose in her marriage with Ananda on which she was so intent and she told the Blessed Lord accordingly.

35. After saluting the Blessed Lord the girl said: "Owing to ignorance I was going in pursuit of Ananda. My mind is now enlightened. I am like a sailor whose ship after a mishap has reached the other bank. I am like an unprotected aged person who has found protection. I am like the blind who has got new sight. The Blessed Lord by his wise words of advice has awakened me from my sleep."

36. "Blessed art thou, Prakrati, for though you are a Chandalika you will be a model for noblemen

and noblewomen. You are of low caste, but Brahmins will learn a lesson from you. Swerve not from the path of justice and righteousness and you will outshine the royal glory of queens on the throne."

II 37. The marriage having failed, the only course for her was to join the Bhikkhuni Sangh.

200 38. Having expressed her wish she was admitted into it, though she belonged to the lowest class.

PART VIII

Conversion of the Fallen and the Criminals

1. Conversion of a Vagabond.
2. Conversion of Angulimala, the Robber.
3. Conversion of Other Criminals.
4. Risk of Conversion.

§ *1. Conversion of a Vagabond*

1. There was in olden times a certain disorderly person living in Rajagraha, who neither reverenced his parents nor paid respect to his superiors, but always had resort to sacrifice and worship of the sun and moon and fire when he went wrong, hoping thereby to get merit, and feel happy in himself.

2. But notwithstanding all his bodily exercises, in worship and offerings, he found no peace, even after three years' incessant perseverance.

3. He at length resolved to go to Shravasti to inquire of the Buddha. Arrived there, and seeing the glory of his person, he fell down at his feet, and said how he was pleased.

4. Then the Lord explained the folly of animal sacrifice, and the uselessness of all such exercises where the heart was untouched, and where there was no final reverence or dutiful behaviour to those to whom it belonged ; and in conclusion recited certain gathas, which resplendent with glory, lit up the place and all the surrounding country with the brightness of his presence.

5. On this, the villagers, and especially the parents of the children, came near to worship him.

6. On seeing the parents, and hearing their account of the children, Buddha smiled, and recited these gathas.

7. " The great man is entirely free from covetous desire; he dwells in a place of light himself enlightened. Although perchance he meets with sorrow, he rejoices; without consternation, he exhibits his wisdom.

8. " The wise man (bhadra) concerns himself with no worldly business ; he desires neither wealth, children, or possessions (land), always carefully observing the precepts, and walking in the way of supreme wisdom, he hankers not after strange doctrine (or wealth or honour).

9. " The wise man, knowing the character of instability, as a tree in the midst of sand (uses every effort) to change his friend whose mind is unfixed, and to bring him back from impurity to virtue (purity)."

§ 2. *Conversion of Angulimala, the Robber*

1. There was, in the realm of Pasenadi, king of
II Kosala, a robber named Angulimala, a ruffian whose
hands were red with blood, who was always killing and
204 wounding, and showed no mercy to any living creature. Because of him, what had been villages were villages no more, what had been townships were townships no more, and what had been countryside was countryside no more.

2. From every human being whom he slew, he took a finger to make for himself a necklace, and so got his name of " Necklace of Fingers."

3. Once when the Lord was staying in Shravasti in Jeta's grove he had heard of the ravages committed by the robber Angulimala. The Blessed Lord decided to convert him into a righteous man. So one day after taking his meal and after putting away his bedding and then, with robes and bowl, set out on his journey to find the robber Angulimala.

4. Seeing him journeying thither, neatherds, goatherds, ploughmen and wayfarers called out: " Don't go that way, recluse ! It will take you to the robber Angulimala.

5. " Why, even when, ten, twenty, thirty, or forty people band themselves together to travel this road, the whole company falls into the robber's hands !" But, without a word, the Lord held on to his way.

6. A second time, and yet a third time those near there and the rest repeated their warning ; but still, without a word, the Lord went his way.

7. From some way off the robber saw the Lord coming and marvelled exceedingly that, where even companies of ten to fifty travellers dare not come his way, this solitary recluse should be seen to be forcing his way alone; and the robber was minded to slay ' this recluse.' So, armed with sword and buckler and with his bow and quiver, the robber followed up the Lord's trail.

8. The Lord, while he himself was proceeding at

his wonted pace, the robber, for all his efforts, could not catch him up.

9. Thought the robber: "This is a wonderful and marvellous thing. Heretofore, I could always overtake an elephant, or horse, or carriage, or deer, when going full speed; and yet here am I unable, despite all my efforts, to overtake this recluse while he proceeds at his wonted pace." So he stopped and shouted to the Lord to stop.

10. When the two met the Lord said: "I have stopped, Angulimala, for your sake. Will you stop following your career of an evil doer? I have been pursuing you in order to win you over, to cover you to the path of righteousness. The good in you is not yet dead. If you will only give it a chance it will transform you."

11. Angulimala felt overcome by the words of the Blessed One, saying, "At last this sage has tracked me down."

12. "And now that thy hallowed words ask me to renounce evil deeds forever, I am prepared to give myself a trial," replied Angulimala.

13. Angulimala threw into a deep abyss the string of his victims' fingers which he wore round his neck and fell at the Master's feet and craved admission to the Brotherhood.

14. The Lord, the guide of gods and men, said: "Almsman, follow me"; and almsman since that summons Angulimala did become.

15. With Angulimala as his almsman in attendance, the Lord now proceeded on his way to the pleasance in Shravasti. At this very time the portals of King Pasenadi's inner palace were beset by a huge crowd loudly shouting that in the realm he had conquered there was a robber named Angulimala, a ruffian who was committing ravages and was killing and wounding innocent people and who took pride in wearing a necklace made of fingers of victims whom he slew. "Suppress him, sire," they cried. Pasenadi promised to run him down to earth. But he failed.

16. One morning King Pasenadi went to the

pleasance to see the Lord. The Blessed Lord inquired: "What is the matter, sire? Is there trouble with Seniya Bimbisara of Magadha, or with Licchavis of Vesali or with any other hostile power?"

II 17. "No trouble at all of that sort, sir. In my
realms there is a robber named Angulimala who is
206 infesting my territories and harassing my subjects. I
want to suppress him but I have failed."

18. "If now, sire, you were to see Angulimala with his hair and beard off, in the yellow robes, as a pilgrim who kills not, steals not, lies not, eats but one meal a day, and leads the higher life in virtue and goodness,—what would you do to him?"

19. "Sir, I would salute him, or rise to meet him or would invite him to be seated or invite him to accept robes and other requisites, or I would extend to him the defence, protection and safeguards which are his due. But how could the shadow of such virtue ever extend to one so wicked and depraved?"

20. At that moment the Reverend Angulimala was seated quite close to the Lord, who stretching forth his right arm, said: "This, sire, is Angulimala!"

21. At this the king in his alarm became dumbfounded, with every hair of his body standing erect. Seeing this, the Lord said, "Fear not, sire; fear not; there is no cause for fear here."

22. So the king's fears and alarm abated; and across to the reverend Angulimala he went, saying: "Is your reverence indeed Angulimala?" "Yes, sire."

23. "What sire, was your father's family, and your mother's?" "My father was a Gagga, sire, and my mother a Mantani."

24. "Be of good cheer, Gagga Mantani-putta; I will take care to supply you with all requisites."

25. Now at the time the Reverend Angulimala having pledged to be resident in the wilds, subsisting on alms, and wearing clothes from the dust heap not exceeding three in number, he declined the king's offer on the ground that he had already got his full three robes.

26. Then the king went across to the Lord and

after salutations seated himself to the one side, saying; "It is wonderful, sir, it is marvellous, what a tamer of the untamed the Lord is, how he quells the unquelled, and how he calms the uncalmed ! Here is one whom I could not subdue with cudgel and sword; but without either cudgel or sword the Lord has subdued him! And now, sir, I must be going, for I have much to do and attend to."

27. "When Your Majesty pleases." Then, rising from his seat, the king saluted the Lord with deep reverence and withdrew.

28. One day when, duly robed and bowl in hand, Angulimala had gone into Shravasti for alms, he was hit by a clod flung by one man, by a club flung by a second and by a potsherd flung by a third, so that it was with a broken head streaming with blood, with his bowl smashed, and with his cloak in tatters, that he presented himself before the Lord. Seeing him drawing near, the Lord said to Angulimala: "Endure it all, endure it all."

29. Thus did Angulimala the robber become a righteous man by accepting the teachings of the Buddha.

30. Expressing the joy of the bliss of deliverance he said: "Who shows zeal, where zeal was none, who with virtue clokes his past, who in youth to Buddha cleaves, he, like the moon, floods earth with light.

31. "Let my foes hear this gospel, embrace this creed and follow wisdom's sons who cleave to it. Let my foes hear in season, love's message which is meek forbearance—and conform their lives to it.

32. "As 'Finger Necklace,' I, bandit, lived and whirled downstream, till He brought me to land. As 'Finger Necklace,' I was steeped in blood; saved now am I."

§ 3. *Conversion of Other Criminals*

1. There was to the south of Rajagraha a great mountain, distant from the city about 200 li.

2. Through this mountain there was a pass,

deep and lonely, through which the road to South India lay.

3. Five hundred robbers had taken up their abode in this defile, who used to murder and rob all
II travellers that passed that way.

4. The king had vainly sent his forces to capture
208 them, but they always escaped.

5. The Buddha, residing in the neighbourhood, and considering the case of these men, that they understood not the nature of their conduct, and that although he had come into the world to teach them, yet their eyes had not seen him, nor their ears heard the tidings of his law, he resolved to go to them.

6. Consequently he transformed himself into a man richly dighted, on a well-caparisoned steed, with his sword and bow, with bags of silver and gold on his saddle-bow, and precious stones studding his horse's bravery.

7. On entering the defile loud neighed his steed. On hearing the sound the 500 robbers started up, and spying the traveller, exclaimed, " Never have we had such a prospect of booty; let us be up, and capture him !"

8. So they proceeded to surround the traveller, with a view to prevent his escape; but on seeing him they fell on the ground.

9. On their falling to the ground, they exclaimed, " What God is this ?" " What God is this ?"

10. On this the traveller began to explain that such hurts and pains as they give and receive were trivial compared with the pain caused by the sorrow that rules the world, and the wounds of unbelief and doubt, and that nought but the wisdom resulting from earnest attention (hearing) to the Scriptures could heal such wounds; and then he added these words and said :

11. " There is no painful wound so bad as sorrow—no piercing arrow so sharp as folly. Nothing can remedy these but an earnest attention to religious instruction. From this the blind receive sight, the deluded are enlightened.

12. "Men are guided and led by this, as eyes, given to them without eyes.

13. "This, then, is able to dispel unbelief, to remove sorrow, to impart joy; the highest wisdom is the lot of those who "hear." II

14. "This is the title of him who has acquired the greatest merit (most to be revered)." 209

15. On hearing this the robbers repented of their evil lives, and the arrows, of themselves, left their bodies, and their wounds were healed.

16. They then became disciples, and obtained rest and peace.

§ 4. *Risk of Conversion*

1. In olden times, Buddha was residing in a country about 500 li from Rajagraha, full of mountains. In these mountains there lived a certain clan of about 122 persons, who occupied themselves in hunting, and fed themselves on the flesh of the animals they killed.

2. (Buddha goes to the place and converts the women, who were left alone during the day, whilst their husbands were hunting, and then adds these lines.)

3. "He who is humane does not kill (or, it is humane not to kill); he is ever able to preserve (his own ?) life.

4. "This principle (chu) is imperishable; whoever observes it, no calamity shall betide that man.

5. "Politeness, indifference to wordly things, hurting no one, without place for annoyance—this is the character of the Brahma Heaven (or of Brahma Deva).

6. "Ever exercising love towards the infirm; pure, according to the teaching of Buddha; knowing when sufficient has been had; knowing when to stop,—this is to escape (the recurrence of) birth and death."

The women, having heard these words, were converted, and on the men's return, although they wished at first to kill Buddha, they were restrained by their wives ; and, listening to these words of love, they also were converted.

7. And then he added these lines.

8. " There are eleven advantages which attend
II the man who practices mercifulness, and is tender to
210 all that lives.

9. "His body is always in health (happy); he is blessed with peaceful sleep, and when engaged in study he is also composed."

10. " He has no evil dreams, he is protected by Heaven (Devas) and loved by man ; he is unmolested by poisonous things, and escapes the violence of war; he is unharmed by fire or water.

11. " He is successful wherever he lives, and when dead goes to the Heaven of Brahma. These are the eleven."

12. Having uttered these words, both men and women were admitted into the company of his disciples, and obtained rest.

BOOK III

What the Buddha Taught

Part I — His Place in His Dhamma.

Part II — Different Views of the Buddha's Dhamma.

Part III — What is Dhamma.

Part IV — What is Not Dhamma.

Part V — What is Saddhamma.

PART I

His Place in His Dhamma

1. The Buddha claimed no place for Himself in His Own Dhamma.

2. The Buddha did not promise to give salvation. He said He was Marga Data (Way Finder) and not Moksha Data (Giver of Salvation).

3. The Buddha did not claim any Divinity for Himself or for His Dhamma. It was discovered by man for man. It was not a Revelation.

§ 1. *The Buddha claimed no place for Himself in His own Dhamma*

1. Christ claimed to be the Prophet of Christianity.

2. He further claimed that he was the Son of God.

3. Christ also laid down the condition that there III
was no salvation for a person unless he accepted
that Christ was the Son of God. 215

4. Thus Christ secured a place for Himself by making the salvation of the Christian depend upon his acceptance of Christ as the Prophet and Son of God.

5. Mohammad, the Prophet of Islam, claimed that he was a Prophet sent by God.

6. He further claimed that no one could get salvation unless he accepted two other conditions.

7. A seeker of salvation in Islam must accept that Mohammad is the Prophet of God.

8. A seeker after salvation in Islam must further accept that he is the last prophet.

9. Salvation in Islam is thus ensured only to those who accept these two conditions.

10. Mohammad thus secured a place for Himself by making the salvation of the Muslim depend upon his acknowledgment of Mohammad as the Prophet of God.

11. No such condition was ever made by the Buddha.

12. He claimed that he was no more than the natural son of Suddhodana and Mahamaya.

13. He carved for himself no place in his religion by laying down any such conditions regarding himself for salvation as Jesus and Mahommad did.

14. That is the reason why we are left to know so little about himself even though abundant material was available.

15. As is known, the first Buddhist congregation

was held soon after the death of the Buddha at Rajagraha.

16. Kassyappa presided over the congregation. Anand, Upali and many others who belonged to
III Kapilavatsu and who wandered with him wherever he went and were with him till his death were
216 present.

17. But what did Kassyappa the President do?

18. He asked Anand to repeat the Dhamma and put the question to the congregation, "Is this right?" They answered in the affirmative. And Kassyappa then closed the question.

19. Thereafter he asked Upali to repeat the Vinaya and put the question to the congregation, "Is this right?" They answered in the affirmative. Kassyappa then closed the question.

20. Kassyappa then should have put the third question to someone present in the congregation to record some important incidents in the life of the Buddha.

21. But Kassyappa did not. These were the only two questions with which he thought the Sangh was concerned.

22. If Kassyappa had collected the record of the Buddha's life we would have had today a full-fledged biography of the Buddha.

23. Why did it not strike Kassyappa to collect the record about the Buddha's life?

24. It could not be indifference. The only answer one can give is that the Buddha had carved no niche for himself in his religion.

25. The Buddha and his religion were quite apart.

26. Another illustration of the Buddha keeping himself out of his religion is to be found in his refusal to appoint a successor.

27. Twice or thrice the Buddha was requested by his followers to appoint a successor.

28. Every time the Buddha refused.

29. His answer was, "The Dhamma must be its own successor.

30. "Principle must live by itself, and not by the authority of man.

31. "If principle needs the authority of man it is no principle.

32. "If every time it becomes necessary to invoke the name of the founder to enforce the authority of Dhamma then it is no Dhamma."

33. Such was the view he took of his own position regarding his Dhamma.

§ 2. The Buddha did not promise to give Salvation. He said He was Marga Data (Way Finder) and not Moksha Data (Giver of Salvation)

1. Most religions are described as revelations. But the Buddha's religion is not a revelation.

2. A revealed religion is so called because it is a message of God to His creatures to worship their maker (i.e., God) and to save their souls.

3. Often the message is sent through a chosen individual who is called a prophet to whom the message is revealed and who reveals it to the people. It is then called Religion.

4. The obligation of the prophet is to ensure salvation to the faithful.

5. Salvation of the faithful means the saving of their souls, from being sent to hell provided they obey God's commands and recognize the prophet as his messenger.

6. The Buddha never claimed that he was a prophet or a messenger of God. He repudiated any such description.

7. A more important point than this is that his religion is a discovery. As such it must be sharply distinguished from a religion which is called Revelation.

8. His religion is a discovery in the sense that it is the result of inquiry and investigation into the conditions of human life on earth and understanding of the working of human instincts with which man is

born, the moulding of his instincts and dispositions which man has formed as a result of history and tradition and which are working to his detriment.

9. All prophets have promised salvation. The Buddha is the one teacher who did not make any such promise. He made a sharp distinction between a *moksha data* and a *marga data*, one who gives salvation and one who only shows the way.

10. He was only a *marga data*. Salvation must be sought by each for himself by his own effort.

11. He made this very clear to the Brahmin Moggallana in the following Sutta.

12. "Once the Exalted One was staying at Shravasti, in the East Park, at the storeyed house of Migara's mother.

13. "Then, the Brahmin Moggallana, the accountant, came to the Exalted One and gave him friendly greeting and after the exchange of courtesies sat down at one side. So seated, the Brahmin Moggallana, the accountant, said this to the Exalted One :

14. "'Just as, Master Gautama, one gets a gradual view of this storeyed house, a progress, a graduated path, and so on right up to the last step of the stairs, just so is the progressive training of us Brahmins : that is to say, in our course of study in the Vedas.'

15. "'Just as in a course of archery, Gautama, with us the Brahmins, the training, the progress, the approach is step by step ; for instance, in counting.'

16. "' When we take a private pupil we make him count thus: 'One one, twice two, thrice three, four times four, and so on up to a hundred.' Now is it possible, Master Gautama, for you to point to a similar progressive training on the part of your followers in your Dhamma.'

17. "'It is so, Brahmin. Take the case, Brahmin, of a clever horse-trainer. He takes a thoroughbred in hand, gives him his first lesson with bit and bridle, and then proceeds to the further course.'

18. "'Just so, Brahmin, the Tathagata takes in hand a man who is to be trained and gives him his

first lesson, thus : 'Come thou, brother ! Be virtuous. Abide, constrained by the restraint of the obligation.'

19. "'Become versed in the practice of right behaviour ; seeing danger in trifling faults, do you undertake the training and be a pupil in the moralities.' III

20. "'As soon as he has mastered all that, the
Tathagata gives him his second lesson, thus : 'Come 219
thou brother ! Seeing an object with the eye, be not charmed by its general appearance or its details.'

21. "'Persist in the restraint of that dejection that comes from craving, caused by the sense of sight uncontrolled, these ill states, which would overwhelm one like a flood. Guard the sense of sight, win control over the sense of sight.'

22. "'And so do with the other organs of sense. When you hear a sound with the ear, or smell a scent with the nose, taste a taste with the tongue, or with body touch things tangible, and when with mind you are conscious of a thing, be not charmed with its general appearance or its details.'

23. "'As soon as he has mastered all that, the Tathagata gives him a further lesson, thus : 'Come thou, brother ! Be moderate in eating ; earnest and heedful do you take your food, not for sport not for indulgence, not for adding personal charm or comeliness to body, but do it for body's stabilising, for its support, for protection from harm, and for keeping up the practice of the righteous life, with this thought ; 'I check my former feeling. To no new feeling will I give rise, that maintenance and comfort may be mine.'

24. "'Then, Brahmin, when he has won restraint in food, the Tathagata gives him a further lesson thus : 'Come thou, brother ! Abide given to watchfulness. By day, when walking or sitting, cleanse your heart from things that may hinder you. By night spend the first watch walking up and down or sitting and do likewise. By night in the second watch, lie down on the right side in the posture of a lion, and placing one foot upon the other, mindful and self-possessed, set your thoughts on the idea of exertion. Then in the

third watch of the night rise up, and walking up and down, or sitting, cleanse the heart of things that may hinder.'

25. "'Then, Brahmin, when the brother is
III devoted to watchfulness, the Tathagata gives him a
further lesson, thus : 'Come thou, brother ! Be
220 possessed of mindfulness and self-control. In going
forth or going back, have yourself under control. In looking forward or looking back, in bending or relaxing, in wearing robes or carrying robe and bowl, in eating, chewing, tasting, in easing yourself, in going, standing, sitting, lying, sleeping or waking, in speaking or keeping silence have yourself under control.'

26. "'Then Brahmin, when he is possessed of self-control, the Tathagata gives him a further lesson thus : 'Come thou, brother ! Seek out a secluded lodging, a forest or root of a tree, a mountain or a cave or a mountain grotto, a charnel field, a forest retreat, the open air, a heap of straw.' And he does so. And when he has eaten his food he sits down cross-legged, and keeping his body straight up, he proceeds to practise the four ecstacies.'

27. "'Now, Brahmin, for all brothers who are pupils, who have not yet attained mastery of mind, who abide aspiring, for such is the manner of my training.'

28. "'But as to those brethren who are arhants, who have destroyed the asavas, who have lived the life, done their task, laid down the burden, won their own salvation, utterly destroyed the fetters of becoming, and are released by the perfect insight, for such as those these things are conducive to ease in the present life and to mindful self-control as well.'

29. "When this was said, the Brahmin Moggallana, the accountant, said to the Exalted One :

30. "'But tell me, Master Gautama. Do the disciples of the worthy Gautama,—do all of them win the absolute perfection which is Nibbana : or do some fail thus to attain ?'

31. "Some of my disciples, Brahmin, thus advised and trained by me, do so attain. Others do not."

32. " But what is the reason. Master Gautama ? What is the cause, Master Gautama ? Here we have Nibbana. Here we have the Path to Nibbana. Here we have the worthy Gautama as instructor. What is the reason, I say, why some disciples thus advised and III
trained do attain, while others do not attain ? "

33. " That, Brahmin, is a question that I will 221
answer. But first do you answer me this, so far as you think fit. Now how say you, Brahmin—Are you well skilled in the road to Rajagraha ?"

34. " I am, master, ' Skilled indeed am I in the road to Rajagraha ! '

35. " Well, thus instructed, thus advised, he takes the wrong road, and off he goes with his face set to the west.

36. " Then a second man comes up with the same request and you give him the same instructions. He follows your advice and comes safe to Rajagraha.

37. " ' That is my business ? '

38. " ' What do I in the matter, Brahmin ? The Tathagata is one who only shows the way. ' "

39. Here is a full statement that he does not promise salvation. He only shows the way.

40. Besides what is salvation ?

41. With Mohammad and Jesus salvation means saving the soul from being sent to hell by the intercession of the Prophet.

42. With Buddha salvation means Nibbana and Nibbana means control of passions.

43. What promise of salvation can there be in such a Dhamma ?

§ 3. *The Buddha did not Claim any Divinity for himself or for his Dhamma. It was discovered by man for man. It was not a Revelation*

1. Every founder of religion has either claimed divinity for himself or for his teachings.

2. Moses, although he did not claim for himself

any divine origin, did claim divine origin for his teachings. He told his followers that if they wished to reach the land of milk and honey they must accept the teachings because they were the teachings of Jehovah the God.

3. Jesus claimed divinity for himself. He claimed that he was the Son of God. Naturally His teachings acquired a divine origin.

4. Krishna said that he was God himself and the Gita was his own word.

5. The Buddha made no such claim either for himself or his Sasana.

6. He claimed that he was one of the many human beings and his message to the people was the message of man to man.

7. He never claimed infallibility for his message.

8. The only claim he made was that his message was the only true way to salvation as he understood it.

9. It was based on universal human experience of life in the world.

10. He said that it was open to anyone to question it, test it and find what truth it contained.

11. No founder has so fully thrown open his religion to such a challenge.

PART II

Different views of the Buddha's Dhamma

1. What others have understood Him to have Taught.
2. The Buddha's Own Classification.

§ 1. *What others have understood Him to have Taught*

1. " What are the teachings of the Buddha ?"

2. This is a question on which no two followers of the Buddha or the students of Buddhism agree. III

3. To some Samadhi is his principal teaching. 225

4. To some it is Vippassana (a kind of Pranayam).

5. To some Buddhism is esoteric. To others it is exoteric.

6. To some it is a system of barren metaphysics.

7. To some it is sheer mysticism.

8. To some it is a selfish abstraction from the world.

9. To some it is a systematic repression of every impulse and emotion of the heart.

10. Many other views regarding Buddhism could be collected.

11. This divergence of views is astonishing.

12. Some of these views are those of men who have a fancy for certain things. Such are those who regard that the essence of Buddhism lies in Samadhi or Vippassana, or Esoterism.

13. The other views are the results of the fact that the majority of the writers on Buddhism are students of ancient Indian history. Their study of Buddhism is incidental and occasional.

14. Some of them are not students of Buddhism.

15. They are not even students of anthropology, the subject matter which deals with the origin and growth of religion.

16. The question that arises is—" Did the Buddha have no Social Message ? "

17. When pressed for an answer, students of Buddhism refer to the two points. They say—

18. " The Buddha taught Ahimsa."

19. " The Buddha taught peace ! "

20. Asked—" Did the Buddha give any other Social Message ? "

21. " Did the Buddha teach justice ? "

22. " Did the Buddha teach love ? "

23. "Did the Buddha teach liberty?"

24. "Did the Buddha teach equality?"

25. "Did the Buddha teach fraternity?"

26. "Could the Buddha answer Karl Marx?"

27. These questions are hardly ever raised in discussing the Buddha's Dhamma.

28. My answer is that the Buddha has a Social Message. He answers all these questions. But they have been buried by modern authors.

§ 2. *The Buddha's Own Classification*

1. The Buddha adopted a different classification of Dhamma.

2. The first category he called Dhamma.

3. He created a new category called Not-Dhamma (Adhamma) though it went by the name of Dhamma.

4. He created a third category which he called Saddhamma.

5. The third category was another name for Philosophy of Dhamma.

6. To understand His Dhamma one must understand all the three—Dhamma, Adhamma and Saddhamma.

PART III

What is Dhamma ?

1. To Maintain Purity of Life is Dhamma.
2. To Reach Perfection in Life is Dhamma.
3. To Live in Nibbana is Dhamma.
4. To Give up Craving is Dhamma.
5. To believe that all compound things are impermanent is Dhamma.
6. To believe that Karma is the instrument of Moral Order is Dhamma.

§ 1. *To Maintain Purity of Life is Dhamma*

1. "There are these three forms of purity... And of what sort is purity of body ? III

2. "Herein a certain one abstains from taking life, from stealing, from sinful living. This is called 229 'purity of body.'

3. "And of what sort is purity of speech ?

4. "Herein a certain one abstains from falsehood . . .

5. "And of what sort is purity of mind ?

6. "Herein a monk, if he have some personal sensual desire, is aware : 'There is in me sensual desire.' If there be none he is likewise aware of it. Also he is aware of how the arising of sensual desire not yet arisen comes about, and how it is abandoned when it has arisen, and how in the future there is no such arising.

7. "If he have some personal malevolence, he is aware ; 'There is within me malevolence.' Also he is aware of the arising . . . and the abandoning thereof, and of how in future there is no recurrence thereof.

8. "If he have some personal sloth-and-torpor . . . excitement and flurry . . . if he have some personal doubt-and-wavering, he is aware of the fact. Also of how (each of these) arises, is abandoned and recurs not again in future. This is called 'purity of mind.'

9. "He who is pure in body, speech, and mind,
"Sinless and clean and blessed with purity,—
"'Sin-washer' is the name men give to him."

(ii)

1. "There are three forms of purity . . . Purity of body, purity of speech, purity of mind."

2. "And of what sort is purity of body ?"

3. "Herein a certain one abstains from taking life, from stealing from wrong practice in sensual lusts. This is called 'purity of body'."

4. "And of what sort is purity of speech?"

5. "Herein a certain one abstains from falsehood . . . from idle babble. This is called 'purity of speech.'"

III 6. "And of what sort is purity of mind?"

7. "Herein a certain one is not covetous or
230 malevolent of heart and has right view. This is
called 'purity of mind.' These are the three forms
of purity."

(iii)

1. There are these five weaknesses, which are a source of weakness to training. What five?

2. Taking life; taking what is not given; lustful, evil practices; lying; and indulging in spirituous liquors, which cause idleness.

3. These are the five causes which lead to failure.

4. When these five sources of weakness to training are put away, four arisings of mindfulness should be made to become.

5. Herein a monk abides contemplating the body as body, strenuous, mindful and self-possessed, having overcome both the hankering and discontent common in the world.

6. He abides contemplating the feelings as feelings . . .

7. He abides contemplating the mind as mind . . .

8. He abides contemplating ideas as ideas, strenuous, mindful and self-possessed, having overcome both the hankering and discontent common in the world.

9. When these five sources of weakness to training are put away, these four arisings of mindfulness should be made to become.

(iv)

1. There are these three failures. Failure in morals, failure in mind, failure in view.

2. And of what sort is failure in morals? A certain one takes life, steals, is a wrong-doer in sensual desires, a liar, a slanderer, of bitter speech, an idle babbler. This is called "failure in morals."

3. And of what sort is failure in mind?

4. A certain one is covetous and malevolent of heart. This is called "failure in mind."

5. And of what sort is failure in view?

6. Herein a certain one holds the depraved, III
the perverse view that there is no (virtue in) almsgiving,
in sacrifice, in offerings: that there is no fruit, no 231
result of good and evil deeds: that this world is not, that there is no world beyond: that there is no mother, no father, no beings of spontaneous birth: that in the world are no recluses and Brahmins who have won the summit, who have won perfection, who of themselves by their own intuitional powers have realized the world beyond and can proclaim it. This, monks, is called "failure in view."

7. Monks, it is due to failure in morals, failure in mind and in view that beings, when body breaks up after death, are reborn in the Waste, the Way of Woe, in the Downfall, in Purgatory. Such are the three failures.

8. Monks, there are these three successes. What three? Success in morals, success in mind, success in view.

9. Now of what sort is success in morals?

10. A certain one abstains from taking life and the rest . . . from bitter speech and idle babbling. This is called "success in morals."

11. And of what sort is success in mind?

12. Herein a certain one is not covetous or malevolent of heart. This is called "success in mind."

13. And of what sort is success in view?

14. Herein a certain one has right view: he holds with certainty that there is (virtue in) almsgiving, in sacrifice, in offerings: that there is fruit and result of good and evil deeds: that this world is, that there is a world beyond: that mother, father and beings of spontaneous birth do exist: that in the world there are recluses and Brahmins who have realized the world beyond and can proclaim it. This, monks, is called "success in view."

15. It is owing to success in these three things

that beings, when body breaks up after death, are reborn in the Happy Lot, in the Heaven World. Such, monks, are the three successes.

III

232

§ 2. *To Reach Perfection in Life is Dhamma*

1. There are these three perfections.

2. Perfection in body, speech and mind.

3. And of what sort is perfection in mind?

4. By the destruction of the asavas, realizing in this very life himself, knowing it thoroughly—the heart's release, the release by insight which is free from the asavas, having attained it abides therein. This is called "perfection in mind." These are the three bodily perfections.

5. There are other perfections. The Buddha explained them to Subhuti.

6. SUBHUTI : What is a Bodhisattva's perfection of giving?

7. THE LORD : Here a Bodhisattva, his thoughts associated with the knowledge of all modes, gives gifts, i.e., inward or outward things, and, having made them common to all beings, he dedicates them to supreme enlightenment ; and also others he instigates thereto. But there is nowhere an apprehension of anything.

8. SUBHUTI : What is a Bodhisattva's perfection of morality?

9. THE LORD : He himself lives under the obligation of the ten ways of wholesome acting, and also others he instigates thereto.

10. SUBHUTI : What is a Bodhisattva's perfection of patience?

11. THE LORD : He himself becomes one who has achieved patience, and others also he instigates to patience.

12. SUBHUTI : What is a Bodhisattva's perfection of vigour?

13. THE LORD : He dwells persistently in the five perfections, and also others he instigates to do likewise.

14. SUBHUTI : What is the Bodhisattva's perfection of concentration (or meditation)?

15. THE LORD : He himself, through skill in means, enters into the trances, yet he is not reborn in the corresponding heavens of form as he could ; and others also he instigates to do likewise.

16. SUBHUTI : What is a Bodhisattva's perfection of wisdom?

17. THE LORD : He does not settle down in any dharma, he contemplates the essential original nature of all dharmas ; and others also he instigates to the contemplation of all dharmas.

18. It is Dhamma to cultivate these perfections.

§ 3. *To Live in Nibbana is Dhamma*

1. "Nothing can give real happiness as Nibbana." So said the Buddha.

2. Of all the doctrines taught by the Buddha the doctrine of Nibbana is the most central one.

3. What is Nibbana? Nibbana as taught by the Buddha has a totally different meaning and content than what has been given to it by his predecessors.

4. By Nibbana they meant the salvation of the soul.

5. Thus there were four ways in which Nibbana was conceived of : (1) Laukik (material, eat, drink and be merry type) ; (2) Yogic ; (3) Brahmanic and (4) Upanishadic.

6. There was one common feature of the Brahmanic and Upanishadic conceptions of Nibbana. They involved the recognition of a soul as an independent entity—a theory which the Buddha had denied. The Buddha had therefore no difficulty in rejecting the Brahmanic and Upanishadic teaching of Nibbana.

7. The Laukik conception of Nibbana was too materialistic to appeal to the Buddha. It meant nothing but the satisfaction of man's animal appetites. There was nothing spiritual in it.

8. To accept such a conception of Nibbana the

Buddha felt was a gross wrong that can be done to a human being.

9. For the satisfaction of appetites can result
only in creating more appetites. Such a way of
III life could bring no happiness, he thought. On the
contrary, such happiness was sure to bring more
234 unhappiness.

10. The Yogic conception of Nibbana was a purely temporary state. The happiness it brought was negative. It involved disassociation from the world. It avoided pain but gave no happiness. Whatever happiness it may be said to bring lasted as long as the yoga lasted. It was not permanent. It was temporary.

11. The Buddha's conception of Nibbana is quite different from that of his predecessors.

12. There are three ideas which underlie his conception of Nibbana.

13. Of these the happiness of a sentient being as distinct from the salvation of the soul is one.

14. The second idea is the happiness of the sentient being in *Samsara* while he is alive. But the idea of a soul and the salvation of the soul after death are absolutely foreign to the Buddha's conception of Nibbana.

15. The third idea which underlies his conception of Nibbana is the exercise of control over the flames of the passions which are always on fire.

16. That the passions are like burning fire was the text of a sermon which the Buddha delivered to the Bhikkus when he was staying in Gaya. This is what he said :

17. " All things, O Bhikkus, are on fire. And what, O Priests, are all these things which are on fire ?

18. " The eye, O Bhikkus, is on fire ; forms are on fire ; eye-consciousness is on fire ; impressions received by the eye are on fire ; and whatever sensation, pleasant, unpleasant, or indifferent, originates in dependence on impression received by the type, that also is on fire."

19. " And with what are these on fire ?"

20. " With the fire of passion say I, with the fire of hatred, with the fire of infatuation ; with birth, old age, death, sorrow, lamentation, misery, grief and despair are they on fire."

21. " The ear is on fire ; sounds are on fire ; the nose is on fire ; odours are on fire ; the tongue is on fire ; tastes are on fire ; the body is on fire ; ideas are on fire ; and whatever sensation, pleasant, unpleasant, or indifferent, originates in dependence on impression received by the mind, that also is on fire.

22. " And with what are these on fire ? "

23. " With the fire of passion, say I ; with the fire of hatred ; with the fire of infatuation ; with birth ; old age, death, sorrow, lamentation, misery, grief, and despair are they on fire."

24. " Perceiving this, O Bhikkus, the learned and noble conceives an aversion. And in conceiving this aversion, he becomes divested of passion, and by the absence of passion he becomes free, and when he is free he becomes aware that he is free."

25. How can Nibbana give happiness ? That is the next question which calls for explanation.

26. The common notion is that man is unhappy because he is in want. But this is not always true. Man is unhappy even though he is in the midst of plenty.

27. Unhappiness is the result of greed, and greed is the bane of life of those who have as well as of those who have not.

28. This the Buddha has made clear in a sermon delivered to the Bhikkus in which he said.

29. " Excited by greed (lobha), brothers, furious with anger (dosa), blinded by delusion (moha), with mind overwhelmed, with mind enslaved, men reflect upon their own misfortune, men reflect upon the misfortune of others, men experience mental suffering and anguish.

30. If, however, greed, anger and delusion are done away, men reflect neither upon their own misfortune nor on mental suffering and anguish.

31. Thus, brothers, is Nibbana visible in this

life and not merely in the future ; inviting, attractive, accessible to the wise disciple."

32. Herein lies the explanation of what consumes man and makes him unhappy. By using this analogy of burning fire to the working of human passions the Buddha has given the most forceful explanation for the unhappiness of man.

33. What makes man unhappy is his falling a prey to his passions. These passions are called fetters which prevent a man from reaching the state of Nibbana. The moment he is free from the sway of his passions, i.e., he learns to achieve Nibbana, man's way to happiness is open to him.

34. These passions, according to the Buddha's analysis, fall under three groups.

35. First : that which refers to all degrees of craving or attachment—such as lust, infatuation and greed (lobha).

36. Second: that which refers to all degrees of antipathy—hatred, anger, vexation or repugnance (dosa).

37. Third: that which refers to all degrees of ignorance—delusion, dullness and stupidity (moha or avidya).

38. The first and second fires relate to the emotions and over the whole scale of one's attitudes and feelings towards other beings, while the third fire relates to all ideas that are in any way removed from the truth.

39. There are certain misunderstandings about the Buddha's doctrine of Nibbana.

40. The word Nibbana etymologically means outblowing, extinguishing.

41. Taking hold of this root meaning of the word, critics have tried to make nonsense of the doctrine of Nibbana.

42. They hold that Nibbana means extinction of all human passions which is equivalent to death.

43. They have by this means tried to throw ridicule over the doctrine of Nibbana.

44. That such is not the meaning of Nibbana

is quite clear if one examines the language of the fire sermon.

45. The fire sermon does not say that life is burning and death is extinction. It says passions are on fire.

46. The fire sermon does not say that the passions must be extinguished completely. It says do not add fuel to the flame.

47. Secondly, critics have failed to make a distinction between Nibbana and Parinibbana.

48. As the Udana says: "Parinibbana occurs when the body becomes disintegrated, all perceptions become stopped, all sensations die away, the activities cease and consciousness goes away. Thus Parinibbana means complete extinction."

49. Nibbana can never have this meaning. Nibbana means enough control over passion so as to enable one to walk on the path of righteousness. It was not intended to mean anything more.

50. That Nibbana is another name for righteous life is made clear by the Buddha himself to Radha.

51. Once the venerable Radha came to the Exalted One. Having done so he saluted the Exalted One and sat down at one side. So seated the venerable Radha thus addressed the Exalted One: "Pray Lord, what for is Nibbana?"

52. "Nibbana means release from passion" replied the Lord.

53. "But Nibbana, Lord,—what is the aim of it?"

54. "Rooted in Nibbana, Radha, the righteous life is lived. Nibbana is its goal. Nibbana is its end."

55. That Nibbana does not mean extinction is also made clear by Sariputta in the following sermon:

56. "Once the Blessed Lord was staying at Shravasti in Anathpindika's Arama where Sariputta was also staying.

57. "The Lord, addressing the brethren, said: 'Almsmen, be ye partakers not of the world's goods but of my doctrine; in my compassion for you all I am anxious to ensure this.'

58. “ Thus spoke the Lord, who thereupon rose and passed to his own cell.

59. “[Sariputta remained behind and the brethren asked him to explain what is Nibbana.

III 60. “ Then Sariputta in reply to the brethren said : ‘ Brethren, know ye that greed is vile, and vile
238 is resentment.

61. “ ‘ To shed this greed and this resentment, there is the Middle Way which gives us eyes to see and makes us know, leading us on to peace, insight, enlightenment and Nibbana.

62. “ ‘ What is this Middle Way ? It is naught but the Noble Eightfold Path of right outlook, right aims, right speech, right action, right means of livelihood, right effort, right mindfulness, and right concentration; this, almsmen is the Middle Way.

63. “ ‘ Yes, sirs : anger is vile and malevolence is vile, envy and jealousy are vile, niggardliness and avarice are vile, hypocrisy and deceit and arrogance are vile, inflation is vile, and indolence is vile.

64. “ ‘ For the shedding of inflation and indolence there is the Middle Way—giving us eyes to see, making us know, and leading us on to peace, insight, enlightenment.

65. “ ‘ Nibbana which is naught but that Noble Eightfold Path.’ ”

66. Thus spoke the revered Sariputta—Glad at heart, the almsmen rejoiced at what he had said.

67. That the idea underlying Nibbana is that it is the path of righteousness. No one will mistake Nibbana for anything else.

68. Complete annihilation is one extreme and Parinibbana is another extreme. Nibbana is the Middle Way.

69. So understood all confusion about Nibbana will disappear.

§ 4. *To Give up Craving is Dhamma*

1. In the Dhammapada the Buddha says: “ There is no greater benefit than health and there is

nothing more valuable than the spirit of contentment."

2. This spirit of contentment is not to be understood to mean meekness or surrender to circumstances.

3. Because that would be quite contrary to the other teachings of the Buddha.

4. The Buddha has not said, "Blessed are they who are poor."

5. The Buddha has not said that the sufferer should not try to change his condition.

6. On the other hand, he has said that riches are welcome and instead of listless suffering he taught Virya which is energetic action.

7. What the Buddha meant when he said that contentment is the highest form of wealth is that man should not allow himself to be overpowered by greed which has no limits.

8. As the Bhikku Rathapala has said: "Rich men I see who, folly-led, never give, but still amass, athirst for pleasures new; the king whose conquests to the sea extend, for sway over empires overseas will pine, still craving, kings and subjects pass away; lacking, still lacking, they their bodies quit; never on earth can pleasures' measure be filled."

9. In the Maha-Nidan-Suttanta the Buddha has explained to Ananda the necessity of controlling greed. This is what he said.

10. "This it is, Ananda, that craving comes into being because of desire for gain, when desire for gain becomes a passion for possession when the spirit of possession gives rise to tenacity of possession it becomes avarice.

11. "Avarice or possession due to uncontrolled acquisitive instinct calls for watch and ward.

12. "Why is this craving or greed to be condemned? Because of this," said the Buddha to Ananda, "many a bad and wicked state of things arises—blows and wounds, strife, contradiction and retorts; quarrelling, slander and lies."

13. That this is the correct analysis of class struggle there can be no doubt.

14. That is why the Buddha insisted upon the control of greed and craving.

§ 5. *To believe that all compound things are impermanent is Dhamma*

1. This doctrine of impermanence has three aspects.

2. There is the impermanence of composite things.

3. There is the impermanence of the individual being.

4. There is the impermanence of the self nature of conditioned things.

5. The impermanence of composite things has been well explained by the great Buddhist philosopher Asanga.

6. "All things," says Asanga, "are produced by the combination of causes and conditions and have no independent noumenon of their own. When the combination is dissolved, their destruction ensures.

7. "The body of a living being consists of the combination of four great elements, viz., earth, water, fire and air, and when this combination is resolved into the four component elements, dissolution ensues.

8. "This is what is called the impermanence of a composite entity."

9. Impermanence of the living individual is best described by the formula—being is becoming.

10. In this sense a being of a past moment has lived, but does not live nor will he live. The being of a future moment will live but has not lived nor does he live ; the being of the present moment does live but has not lived and will not live.

11. In short, a human being is always changing, always growing. He is not the same at two different moments of his life.

12. The third phase of the doctrine of impermanence is somewhat difficult for a common man to follow.

13. To realize that every living being will die sometime or other is a very easy matter to understand.

14. But it is not quite so easy to understand how a human being can go on changing—becoming—while he is alive.

15. "How is this possible?" The Buddha's
answer was, "This is possible because all is imper- III
manent."

16. This later on gave rise to what is called 241
Sunnya Vad.

17. The Buddhist Sunnyata does not mean nihilism out and out. It only means the perpetual changes occurring at every moment in the phenomenal world.

18. Very few realize that it is on account of Sunnyata that everything becomes possible; without it nothing in the world would be possible. It is on the impermanence of the nature of all things that the possibility of all other things depends.

19. If things were not subject to continual change but were permanent and unchangeable, the evolution of all of life from one kind to the other and the development of living things would come to a dead stop.

20. If human beings died or changed but had continued always in the same state what would the result have been? The progress of the human race would have come to a dead halt.

21. Immense difficulty would have arisen if Sunnya is regarded as being void or empty.

22. But this is not so. Sunnya is like a point which has substance but neither breadth nor length.

23. All things are impermanent was the doctrine preached by the Buddha.

24. What is the moral of this doctrine of the Buddha? This is a much more important question.

25. The moral of this doctrine of impermanence is simple. Do not be attached to anything.

26. It is to cultivate detachment, detachment from property, from friends, etc., that he said "All these are impermanent."

§ 6. *To believe that Karma is the instrument of Moral Order is Dhamma*

1. There is an order in the physical world. This is proved by the following phenomenon.

2. There is a certain order in the movements and actions of the starry bodies.

3. There is a certain order by which seasons come and go in regular sequence.

4. There is a certain order by which seeds grow into trees and trees yield fruits and fruits give seeds.

5. In Buddhist terminology these are called Niyamas, laws which produce an orderly sequence such as Rutu Niyam, Bija Niyam.

6. Similarly is there a moral order in Human Society. How is it produced? How is it maintained?

7. Those who believe in the existence of God have no difficulty in answering the question. And their answer is easy.

8. Moral order, they say, is maintained by Divine Dispensation. God created the world and God is the Supreme Governor of the world. He is also the author of moral as well as of physical law.

9. Moral law, according to them, is for man's good because it ensues from Divine will. Man is bound to obey God who is his maker and it is obedience to God which maintains the moral order.

10. Such is the argument in support of the view that the moral order is maintained by Divine Dispensation.

11. The explanation is by no means satisfactory. For if the moral law has originated from God, and if God is the beginning and end of the moral order and if man cannot escape from obeying God, why is there so much moral disorder in the world?

12. What is the authority of the Divine Law? What is the hold of the Divine Law over the individual? These are pertinent questions. But to none of them is there any satisfactory answer from those who rely on Divine Dispensation as the basis for the moral order.

13. To overcome these difficulties the thesis has been somewhat modified.

14. It is said : no doubt creation took effect at the command of God. It is also true that the cosmos entered upon its life by his will and by his direction. It is also true that He imparted to the cosmos once for all the energy which served as the driving power of a stupendous mechanism.

15. But God leaves it to Nature to work itself out in obedience to the laws originally given by him.

16. So that if the moral order fails to work out as expected by God, the fault is of Nature and not of God.

17. Even this modification in the theory does not solve the difficulty. It only helps to exonerate God from his responsibility. For the question remains, why should God leave it to Nature to execute His laws ? What is the use of such an absentee God ?

18. The answer which the Buddha gave to the question,—" How is moral order maintained ? " is totally different.

19. His answer was simple. "It is the Kamma Niyam and not God which maintains the moral order in the universe." That was the Buddha's answer to the question.

20. The moral order of the universe may be good or it may be bad. But according to the Buddha the moral order rests on man and on nobody else.

21. Kamma means man's action and Vipaka is its effect. If the moral order is bad it is because man does Akusala (Bad) Kamma. If the moral order is good it is because man does Kusala (Good) Kamma.

22. The Buddha was not content with merely speaking of Kamma. He spoke of the law of Kamma which is another name for Kamma Niyam.

23. By speaking of the law of Kamma what the Buddha wanted to convey was that the effect of the deed was bound to follow the deed, as surely as night follows day. It was like a Niyam or rule.

24. No one could fail to benefit by the good effects of a Kusala Kamma and no one could escape the evil effects of Akusala Kamma.

25. Therefore, the Buddha's admonition was: Do Kusala Kamma so that humanity may benefit by a good moral order which a Kusala Kamma helps to sustain ; do not do Akusala Kamma for humanity will
III suffer from the bad moral order which an Akusala Kamma will bring about.

244 26. It may be that there is a time interval between the moment when the Kamma is done and the moment when the effect is felt. It is so, often enough.

27. From this point of view, Kamma is either (1) Ditthadamma Vedaniya Kamma (Immediately Effective Kamma) ; (2) Upapajjavedaniya Kamma (Remotely Effective Kamma); and (3) Aporapariya Vedaniya Kamma (Indefinitely Effective Kamma).

28. Kamma may also fall into the category of Ahosi Kamma, i.e., Kamma which is non-effective. This Ahosi Kamma comprises all such Kammas which are too weak to operate, or which are counteracted by a more Kamma, at the time when it should have worked.

29. But making allowance for all these considerations, it does not in any sense derogate from the claim made by the Buddha that the law of Kamma is inexorable.

30. The theory of the law of Kamma does not necessarily involve the conception that the effect of the Kamma recoils on the doer of it and there is nothing more to be thought about it. This is an error. Sometimes the action of one affects another instead of the doer. All the same it is the working of the law of Kamma because it either upholds or upsets the moral order.

31. Individuals come and individuals go. But the moral order of the universe remains and so also the law of Kamma which sustains it.

32. It is for this reason that in the religion of the Buddha, Morality has been given the place of God.

33. Thus the Buddha's answer to the question— "How the moral order in the universe is sustained?" is so simple and so irrefutable.

34. And yet its true meaning is scarcely grasped.

Often, almost always, it is either misunderstood or misstated or misinterpreted. Not many seem to be conscious that the law of Kamma was propounded by the Buddha as an answer to the question—" How the
moral order is maintained ?" III

35. That, however, is the purpose of Buddha's
Law of Kamma. 245

36. The Law of Kamma has to do only with the question of general moral order. It has nothing to do with the fortunes or misfortunes of an individual.

37. It is concerned with the maintenance of the moral order in the universe.

38. It is because of this that the law of Kamma is a part of Dhamma.

PART IV

What is Not—Dhamma

1. Belief in the Supernatural is Not—Dhamma.
2. Belief in Ishwara (God) is Not Essentially Part of Dhamma.
3. Dhamma Based on Union with Brahma is a False Dhamma.
4. Belief in Soul is Not—Dhamma.
5. Belief in Sacrifices is Not—Dhamma.
6. Belief Based on Speculation is Not—Dhamma.
7. Reading Books of Dhamma is Not—Dhamma.
8. Belief in the Infallibility of Books of Dhamma is Not—Dhamma.

§ 1. *Belief in the Supernatural is Not–Dhamma*

1. Whenever any phenomenon occurs, humanity
is always wanting to know how it has happened, what III
is the cause of it.

2. Sometimes cause and the effect are so 249
proximate and so close that it is not difficult to
account for the occurrence of the event.

3. But often-times the effect is so far away from the cause for the effect is not accountable. Apparently there appears to be no cause for it.

4. Then the question arises: How has this event occurred?

5. The commonest answer is that the occurrence of the event is due to some supernatural cause which is often called a miracle.

6. The Buddha's predecessors gave very different answers to this question.

7. Pakauda Katyana denied that there was a cause for every event. Events, he said, occurred independently.

8. Makhali Ghosal admitted that an event must have a cause. But he preached that the cause is not to be found in human agency but is to be sought in nature, necessity, inherent laws of things, predestination or the like.

9. The Buddha repelled these doctrines. He maintained that not only every event has a cause but the cause is the result of some human action or natural law.

10. His contention against the doctrine of Time, Nature, Necessity, etc., being the cause of the occurrence of an event, was this.

11. If Time, Nature, Necessity, etc., be the sole cause of the occurrence of an event, then who are we?

12. Is man merely a puppet in the hands of Time, Nature, Chance, Gods, Fate, Necessity?

13. What is the use of man's existence if he is not free? What is the use of man's intelligence if he continues to believe in supernatural causes?

14. If man is free, then every event must be the result of man's action or of an act of Nature. There cannot be any event which is supernatural in its origin.

III 15. It may be that man is not able to discover
the real cause of the occurrence of an event. But
250 if he has intelligence he is bound one day to
discover it.

16. In repudiating supernaturalism the Buddha had three objects.

17. His first object was to lead man to the path of rationalism.

18. His second object was to free man to go in search of truth.

19. His third object was to remove the most potent source of superstition, the result of which is to kill the spirit of inquiry.

20. This is called the law of Kamma or Causation.

21. This doctrine of Kamma and Causation is the most central doctrine in Buddhism. It preaches Rationalism and Buddhism is nothing if not rationalism.

22. That is why worship of the supernatural is Not—Dhamma.

§ 2. *Belief in Ishwara (God) is Not Essentially Part of Dhamma*

1. Who created the world is a common question. That the world was created by God is also a very common answer.

2. In the Brahmanic scheme this God is called by a variety of names—Prajapati, Ishwar, Brahma or Maha Brahma.

3. To the question who this God is and how He came into being there is no answer.

4. Those who believe in God describe Him as a being who is *omnipotent*, i.e., all-powerful, *Omnipresent*, i.e., he fills the whole universe, and *Omniscient*, i.e., he knows everything.

5. There are also certain moral qualities which are attributed to God. God is said to be good, God is said to be just and God is said to be all-loving.

6. The question is did the Blessed Lord accept God as the creator of the universe. III

7. The answer is, " No. " He did not.

8. There are various grounds why he rejected 251
the doctrine of the Existence of God.

9. Nobody has seen God. People only speak of God.

10. God is unknown and unseen.

11. Nobody can prove that God has created the world. The world has evolved and is not created.

12. What advantage can there be in believing in God ? It is unprofitable.

13. The Buddha said that a religion based on God is based on speculation.

14. A religion based on God is, therefore, not worth having.

15. It only ends in creating superstition.

16. The Buddha did not leave the question there. He discussed the question in its various aspects.

17. The grounds on which he rejected the doctrine were various.

18. He argued that the doctrine of the Existence of God is not based on truth.

19. This he made clear in his dialogue with the two Brahmins, Vasettha and Bhardvaja.

20. Now a dispute arose between them as to which was the true path of salvation and which false.

21. About the time the Blessed One was journeying through Kosala with a great company of the brethren he happened to halt at the Brahmin village called Manaskata and stayed in the mango grove on the bank of the river Akiravati.

22. Manaskata was the town in which Vasettha and Bhardvaja lived. Having heard that the Blessed Lord was staying in their town, they went to him and each one put forth his point of view.

23. Bhardvaja said : " The path of Tarukkha is the straight path, this is the direct way which makes

for salvation, and leads him, who acts according to it, into a state of union with Brahma."

24. Vasettha said : "Various Brahmins, O
Gotama, teach various paths. The Addhariya Brah-
III mins, the Tittiriya Brahmins, the Kanchoka Brah-
mins, the Bheehuvargiya Brahmins. They all lead
252 those who act according to them, into a state of union
with Brahma.

25. "Just as near a village or a town there are many and various paths yet they all meet together in the village—just in the same way all the various paths taught by the various Brahmins lead to union with Brahma."

26. "Do you say that they all lead aright, Vasettha?" asked the Buddha. "I say so, Gautama," replied Vasettha.

27. "But Vasettha, is there a single one of the Brahmins versed in the three Vedas who has ever seen Brahma face to face."

28. "No, indeed, Gautama."

29. "Is there a single one of the teachers of the Brahmanas versed in the three Vedas who has seen Brahma face to face ?"

30. "No, indeed, Gautama."

31. "Nobody has seen Brahma. There is no perceptual knowledge about Brahma." "So it is," said Vasettha. "How then can you believe that the assertion of the Brahmins that Brahma exists is based on truth ?

32. "Just, Vasettha, as when a string of blind men are clinging one to the other, neither can the foremost see nor can the middle one see nor can the hindmost see—just even so, methinks, Vasettha, is the talk of the Brahmins nothing but blind talk. The first sees not, the middle one sees not, nor can the latest one. The talk of these Brahmins turns out to be ridiculous, mere words, a vain and empty thing.

33. "Is this not a case, Vasettha, of a man falling in love with a woman whom he has not seen ?" "Yes, it is," replied Vasettha.

34. "Now what think you Vasettha ? If people

should ask you, 'Well! Good friend! This most beautiful woman in the land, whom you thus love and long for, who is she? Is she a noble lady, or a Brahmin woman, or of the trader class, or a Sudra?'

35. "With regard to the origin of Maha Brahma, the so-called creator," the Blessed Lord said, addressing Bhardvaja and Vasettha, "Friends, that being who was first born thinks thus: I am Brahma, the Great Brahma, the Vanquisher, the Unvanquished, the All-seeing, the Disposer, the Lord, the Maker, the Creator, the Chief, the Assignor, the Master of Myself, the father of all that are and are to be. By me are these beings created.

36. "This means that Brahma is the father of those that are and are to be.

37. "You say that the worshipful Brahma, the Vanquisher, the Unvanquished, Father of all that are and are to be, he by whom we were created, he is permanent, constant, eternal, unchanging, and he will remain so for ever and ever. Then why are we who are created by that Brahma, have come hither, all impermanent, transient, unstable, short-lived, destined to pass away?"

38. To this Vasettha had no answer.

39. His third argument had reference to the Omnipotence of God. "If God is Omnipotent and is also the efficient cause of creation, then because of this man cannot have any desire to do anything, nor can there be any necessity to do anything, nor can he have the will to do anything or to put forth any effort. Man must remain a passive creature with no part to play in the affairs of the world. If this is so, why did Brahma create man at all?"

40. To this also Vasettha had no answer.

41. His fourth argument was that if God is good then why do men become murderers, thieves, unchaste, liars, slanderers, abusive babblers, covetous, malicious and perverse? The cause of this must be Ishwara. Is this possible with the existence of God who is good?

42. His fifth argument was related to God being Omniscient, just and merciful.

43. "If there is a supreme creator who is just and merciful, why then does so much injustice prevail in the world ?" asked the Blessed Lord. "He who has eyes can see the sickening sight ; why does not Brahma set his creatures right ? If his power is so wide that no limits can restrain, why is his hand so rarely spread to bless ? Why are his creatures all condemned to suffering ? Why does he not give happiness to all ? " Why do fraud, lies and ignorance prevail ? Why does falsehood triumph over truth ? Why does truth and justice fail ? I count your Brahma as one of the most unjust, who made a world only to shelter wrong.

44. "If there exists some Lord all-powerful to fulfil in every creature, bliss or woe, and action, good or ill, then that Lord is stained with sin. Either man does not work his will or God is not just and good or God is blind."

45. His next argument against the doctrine of God was that the discussion of this question about the existence of God was unprofitable.

46. According to him the centre of religion lay not in the relation of man to God. It lay in the relation between man and man. The purpose of religion is to teach man how he should behave towards other men so that all may be happy.

47. There was also another reason why the Blessed Lord was against belief in the existence of God.

48. He was against religious rites, ceremonies, and observances. He was against them because they were the home of superstition and superstition was the enemy of *Samma Ditthi*, the most important element in his Ashtangmarg.

49. To the Blessed Lord belief in God was the most dangerous thing. For belief in God gave rise to belief in the efficacy of worship and prayer and the efficacy of worship and prayer gave rise to the office of the priest and the priest was the evil genius who

created all superstition and thereby destroyed the growth of *Samma Ditthi.*

50. Of these arguments against belief in the existence of God some were practical but the majority of them theological. The Blessed Lord knew that III
they were not fatal to the belief in the existence 255
of God.

51. It must not, however, be supposed that he had no argument which was fatal. There was one which he advanced which is beyond doubt fatal to belief in God. This is contained in his doctrine of *Patit Samutpad* which is described as the doctrine of Dependent Origination.

52. According to this doctrine, the question whether God exists or does not exist is not the main question. Nor is the question whether God created the universe the real question. The real question is how did the creator create the world. The justification for the belief in God is a conclusion which follows from our answer to the question how was the world created.

53. The important question is : Did God create something out of nothing or did he create something out of something ?

54. It is impossible to believe that something could have been created out of nothing.

55. If the so-called God has created something out of something, then that something out of which something new was created has been in existence before he created anything. God cannot therefore be called the Creator of that something which has existed before him.

56. If something has been created by somebody out of something before God created anything then God cannot be said to be the Creator or the first Cause.

57. Such was his last but incontrovertible argument against belief in the existence of God.

58. Being false in premises, belief in God as the creator of the universe is Not—Dhamma. It is only belief in falsehood.

§ 3. *Dhamma Based on Union with Brahma is a False Dhamma*

1. When the Buddha was preaching his religion
III there was current a doctrine called Vedantism.

2. The tenets of this doctrine are few and simple.

256 3. Behind the universe there is omnipresent a common principle of life called *Brahma* or *Brahman.*

4. This Brahma is a reality.

5. The Atman or the individual soul is the same as Brahma.

6. Man's liberation lies in making Atman to be one with Brahma. This is the second principle.

7. This unity with Brahma the Atman can achieve by realising that it is the same as Brahman.

8. And the way to make the Átman realize that it is the same as Brahman is to give up Sansara.

9. This doctrine is called *Vedantism.*

10. The Buddha had no respect for the doctrine. He regarded it as based on false premises and producing nothing of value and, therefore, not worth having.

11. This he made clear in his discussion with two Brahmins, Bharadvaj and Vasettha.

12. The Buddha argued that there must be proof before one can accept a thing to be a reality.

13. There are two modes of proof, perception and inference.

14. The Buddha asked, " Has anybody perceived Brahma ; have you seen Brahma ; have you spoken to Brahma ; have you smelt Brahma ? "

15. Vasettha said, " No.

16. " The other mode of proof is inadequate to prove the existence of Brahma."

17. " From what is Brahma the inference of ? " asked the Buddha. There again was no answer.

18. There are others who argue that a thing exists although it is invisible. So they say that Brahma exists although it is invisible.

19. In this bald statement it is an impossible position.

20. But for argument's sake let it be granted that a thing exists although it is invisible.

21. The best illustration of it is electricity. It exists although it is invisible.

22. This argument is not enough.

23. An invisible thing must show itself in some other form that is visible. Then alone it can be called real.

24. But if an invisible thing does not show itself in any visible form then it is not a reality.

25. We accept reality of electricity although it is invisible because of the results it produces.

26. Electricity produces light. From light we accept the reality of electricity although it is invisible.

27. What does this invisible Brahma produce? Does it produce any visible results?

28. The answer is in the negative.

29. Another illustration may be given. In law too it is common to adopt as a basic concept a fiction—a proposition, the existence of which is not proved but which is assumed to be true.

30. And we all accept such a legal fiction.

31. But why is such a legal fiction accepted?

32. The reason is that a legal fiction is accepted because it gives a fruitful and just result.

33. "Brahma is a fiction. What fruitful result does it give?"

34. Vasettha and Bharadvaj were silent.

35. To drive the argument home he turned to Vasettha and asked "Have you seen Brahma?"

36. "Is there a single one of the Brahmanas versed in three Vedas who has ever seen Brahma face to face?"

37. "No, indeed, Gautama."

38. "Is there a single one of the teachers of the Brahmanas versed in the three Vedas who have seen Brahma face to face?"

39. "No, indeed, Gautama."

40. "Is there, Vasettha, a single one of the Brahmanas upto the seventh generation who has seen Brahma face to face?"

41. " No, indeed, Gautama."

42. " Well then, Vasettha—did the ancient Rishis of the Brahmanas—did even they speak thus, saying : ' We know it, we have seen it, where Brahma is, whither Brahma is ? '

43. " Not so, Gautama."

44. The Buddha continued his questioning of the two Brahmin boys and said :

45. " Now what think you, Vasettha ? Does it not follow, this being so, that the talk of the Brahmanas about union with Brahma turns out to be foolish talk ?

46. " Just, Vasettha, as when a string of blind men are clinging one to the other, neither can the foremost see, nor can the middle one see, nor can the hindmost see—just even so, methinks, Vasettha, is the talk of the Brahmanas all but blind talk ? The first sees not, the middle one sees not, nor can the last one. The talk of these Brahmanas turns out to be ridiculous, mere words, a vain and empty thing.

47. " Just, Vasettha, as if a man should say, ' How I long for, how I love the most beautiful woman in this land.'

48. " And people should ask him, ' Well ! good friend ! This most beautiful woman in the land, whom you thus love and long for, do you know whether that beautiful woman is a noble lady or a Brahmin woman, or of the trader class, or a Sudra ? '

49. "But when so asked, he would answer : 'No.'

50. " And when people should ask him, ' Well ! good friend ! This most beautiful woman in all the land, whom you love and long for, do you know what the name of that most beautiful woman is, or what her family name, whether she be tall or short or of medium height, dark or brunette or golden in colour, or in what village or town or city she dwells ? ' But when so asked, he would answer : ' No. '

51. " Now what think you, Vasettha ? Would it not turn out that being so, that the talk of that man was foolish talk ? "

52. " In sooth, Gautama, that would be so, " said the two Brahmins.

53. So Brahma is not real and any religion based upon it is useless.

§ 4. *Belief in Soul is Not Dhamma*

1. The Buddha said that religion based on soul is based on speculation.
2. Nobody has seen the soul or has conversed with the soul.
3. The soul is unknown and unseen.
4. The thing that exists is not the soul but the mind. Mind is different from the soul.
5. Belief in soul He said is unprofitable.
6. A religion based on soul is therefore not worth having.
7. It only ends in creating superstition.
8. The Buddha did not leave the question there. He discussed it in all its aspects.
9. Belief in the existence of soul is as common as the belief in the existence of God.
10. Belief in the existence of soul was also a part of the Brahmanic Religion.
11. In the Brahmanic Religion the soul is called *Atma* or *Atman.*
12. In the Brahmanic Religion, Atman is the name given to an entity which was held to be abiding separate from the body, but living inside the body constantly existing from the moment of his birth.
13. Belief in the soul included other beliefs, connected with it.
14. The soul does not die with the body. It takes birth in another body when it comes into being.
15. The body serves as an external clothing for the soul.
16. Did the Buddha believe in the soul? No. He did not. His doctrine about the soul is called An-atta, no soul.
17. Given a disembodied soul various questions arise : What is the soul? Where did it come from? What becomes of it on the death of the body? Where does it go? In what form does it exist " hereafter."

How long does it remain there? These questions the Buddha tried to argue out with the upholders of the doctrine of the soul.

18. He first tried to show how vague was the
III idea about the soul by his usual method of cross-examination.

260 19. He asked those who believed in the existence of the soul, what the soul was like in size and in shape.

20. To Ananda he said the declarations concerning the soul are abounding. Some declare: "My soul has a form and it is minute." Others declare the soul to have form and to be boundless and minute. Others declare it to be formless and boundless.

21. "In so many ways, Ananda, are declarations made concerning the soul."

22. "How is the soul conceived by those who believe in the soul?" was another question raised by the Buddha. Some say, "My soul is feeling." Others say, "Nay, my soul is not feeling, my soul is not sentient"; or again: "Nay, my soul is not feeling, nor is it non-sentient; my soul has feeling, it has the property of sentience." Under such aspects as these is the soul conceived.

23. The Buddha next asked those who believed in the existence of the soul as to the condition of the soul after the death of the body.

24. He also raised the question whether the soul was visible after the death of the body.

25. He found infinite number of vague statements.

26. Does the soul keep its form after the death of the body? He found that there were eight different speculations.

27. Does the soul die with the body? There were innumerable speculations on this.

28. He also raised the question of the happiness or misery of the soul after the body is dead. Is the soul happy after the death of the body? On this also the Recluses and Brahmins differed. Some said it was altogether miserable. Some said it was happy. Some said it is both happy and miserable and some said it is neither happy nor miserable.

29. His answer to all these theories about the existence of the soul was the same which he gave to Cunda.

30. To Cunda he said : " Now, Cunda, to those
recluses and Brahmins, who believe and profess any III
one of these views, I go and say this : 'Is this so,
friends ?' And if they reply: 'Yes. This alone 261
is true, any other view is absurd.' I do not admit their claim. Why is this ? Because persons hold different opinions on such questions. Nor do I consider this (or that) view on a level with my own, let alone higher."

31. Now the more important question is what were the arguments of the Buddha against the existence of the soul.

32. The general arguments he advanced in support of his denial of the soul were the same as those which he advanced in support of his denial of the existence of God.

33. He argued that the discussion of the existence of the soul is as unprofitable as the discussion of the existence of God.

34. He argued that the belief in the existence of the soul is as much against the cultivation of *Samma Ditthi* as the belief in the existence of God.

35. He argued that the belief in the existence of the soul is as much a source of superstition as the belief in God is. Indeed in his opinion the belief in the existence of a soul is far more dangerous than the belief in God. For not only does it create a priesthood, not only is it the origin of all superstition but it gives the priesthood complete control over man from birth to death.

36. Because of these general arguments it is said that the Buddha did not express any definite opinion on the existence of the soul. Others have said that he did not repudiate the theory of the existence of the soul. Others have said that he was always dodging the issue.

37. These statements are quite incorrect. For to Mahali he did tell in most positive terms that there is

no such thing as a soul. That is why his theory of the soul is called Anatta, i.e., non-soul.

38. Apart from the general arguments against the existence of the soul, the Buddha had a special
III argument against the existence of the soul which he
262 regarded as fatal to the theory of the soul.

39. His theory against the existence of the soul as a separate entity is called Nama-Rupa.

40. The theory is the result of the application of the Vibhaja test, of sharp, rigorous analysis, of the constituent elements of Sentient Being otherwise called Human Personality.

41. Nama-Rupa is a collective name for a Sentient Being.

42. According to the Buddha's analysis, a Sentient Being is a compound thing consisting of certain physical elements and certain mental elements. They are called *Khandas.*

43. The Rupa Khanda primarily consists of the physical elements such as earth, water, fire and air. They constitute the Body or Rupa.

44. Besides Rupa Khanda, there is such a thing as Nama Khanda which goes to make up a Sentient Being.

45. This Nama Khanda is called Vinana, or consciousness. This Nama Khanda includes the three mental elements : Vedana (sensation springing from contact of the six senses with the world), Sanna (perception); Sankhara (states of mind). Chetana (consciousness) is sometimes spoken of along with the three other mental states as being one of them. A modern psychologist would say that consciousness is the mainspring from which other psychological phenomena arise. Vinana is the centre of a sentient being.

46. Consciousness is result of the combination of the four elements, Prithi, Apa, Tej and Vayu.

47. An objection is raised to this theory of consciousness propounded by the Buddha.

48. Those who object to this theory ask, " How is consciousness produced ? "

49. It is true that consciousness arises with birth and dies with death. All the same, can it be said that consciousness is the result of the combination of the four elements ?

50. The Buddha's answer was not that the co-existence or aggregation of the physical elements produces consciousness. What the Buddha said was that wherever there was rupa or kaya there was consciousness accompanying it.

51. To give an analogy from science, there is an electric field and wherever there is an electric field it is always accompanied by a magnetic field. No one knows how the magnetic field is created or how it arises. But it always exists along with the electric field.

52. Why should not the same relationship be said to exist between body and consciousness ?

53. The magnetic field in relation to the electric field is called an induced field. Why cannot consciousness be called an induced field in relation to Rupa-Kaya.

54. The Buddha's argument against the soul is not yet complete. He had further to say something of importance.

55. Once consciousness arises man becomes a sentient being. Consciousness is, therefore, the chief thing in man's life.

56. Consciousness is cognitive, emotional and volitional.

57. Consciousness is cognitive when it gives knowledge, information, as appreciating or apprehending, whether it be appreciation of internal facts or of external things and events.

58. Consciousness is emotional when it exists in certain subjective states, characterized by either pleasurable or painful tones, when emotional consciousness produces feeling.

59. Consciousness in its volitional stage makes a being exert himself for the attainment of some end. Volitional consciousness gives rise to what we call will or activity.

60. It is thus clear that all the functions of a sentient being are performed by the sentient being through and as a result of consciousness.

61. After this analysis the Buddha asked what
III are the functions which are left to be performed by the soul? All functions assigned to the soul are
264 performed by consciousness.

62. A soul without any function is an absurdity.

63. This is how the Buddha disproved the existence of the soul.

64. That is why the existence of the soul cannot be a part of Dhamma.

§ 5. *Belief in Sacrifices is Not—Dhamma*

(i)

1. The Brahmanic religion was based upon sacrifices.

2. Some sacrifices were classified as *Nittya* and other sacrifices were classified as *Naimitik*.

3. The Nittya sacrifices were obligations and had to be performed whether one got any fruit therefrom or not.

4. The Naimittitik sacrifices were performed when the performer wanted to gain something by way of worldly advantage.

5. The Brahmanic sacrifices involved drinking, killing animals and merry-making.

6. Yet these sacrifices were held as religious observances.

7. The Buddha declined to regard a religion based on sacrifices as worth having.

8. He has given his reasons to many a Brahmin who went to have a controversy with him as to why sacrifices were not part of religion.

9. It is reported that there were three Brahmins who had a controversy with him on the subject.

10. They were Kutadanta, Ujjaya and the third was Udayin.

11. Kutadanta the Brahmin requested the Blessed

One to tell him what he thought about the value of a sacrifice.

12. The Blessed One said : "Well then, O Brahmin, give ear and listen attentively and I will speak."

13. "Very well, sir," said Kutadanta in reply ; and the Blessed One spoke as follows :

14. "Long ago, O Brahmin, there was a king by name Maha Vigeta, mighty, with great wealth and large property; with stores of silver and gold, of aids to enjoyment, of goods and corn ; with his treasure-houses and his garners full.

15. "Now when King Maha Vigeta was once sitting alone in meditation he became anxious at the thought: 'I have in abundance all the good things a mortal can enjoy. The whole wide circle of the earth is mine by conquest to possess. It were well if I were to offer a great sacrifice that should ensure me weal and welfare for many days.'

16. "Thereupon the Brahmin who was chaplain said to the king : 'The king's country, sire, is harassed and harried. There are dacoits abroad who pillage the villages and townships and who make the roads unsafe. Were the king, so long as that is so, to levy a fresh tax, verily his majesty would be acting wrongly.

17. "'But perchance his majesty might think : 'I'll soon put a stop to these scoundrels' game by degradation and banishment, and fines and bonds and death !' But their licence cannot be satisfactorily put a stop to. The remnant left unpunished would still go on harassing the realm.

18. "'Now there is one method to adopt to put a thorough end to this order. Whosoever there be in the king's realm who devote themselves to keeping cattle and the farm, to them let His Majesty the King give food and seed-corn. Whosoever there be in the king's realm who devote themselves to trade, to them let His Majesty the King give capital. Whosoever there be in the king's realm who devote themselves to government service, to them let His Majesty the King give wages and food.

19. " 'Then those men, following each his own
business, will no longer harass the realm; the king's
revenue will go up; the country will be quiet and at
peace; and the populace, pleased one with another
III and happy, dancing their children in their arms, will
dwell with open doors without fear.'

266 20. "Then King Maha Vigeta, O Brahmin,
accepted the word of his chaplain, and did as he had
said. And those men, following each his business, harassed the realm no more. And the king's revenue went up. And the country became quiet and at peace. And the populace, pleased one with another and happy, dancing their children in their arms, dwelt with open doors.

21. "When peace and order was restored, King Maha Vigeta had his chaplain called again and said: 'The disorder is at an end. The country is at peace. I want to offer that great sacrifice—let the Venerable One instruct me how—for my weal and my welfare for many days.'

22. "The chaplain, replying to the king, said, 'Be it so. Let His Majesty the King send invitations to those in the town and the country in his realm who are Kshatriyas, vassals of his; who are ministers and officials of his or who are Brahmins of position, or who are householders of substance, saying: 'I intend to offer a great sacrifice. Let the Venerable Ones give their sanction to what will be to me for weal and welfare for many days.'

23. "Then the king, O Brahmin Kutadanta, accepted the word of his chaplain, and did as he had said. And they each—Kshatriya and Ministers and Brahmins and householders—made a like reply: 'Let His Majesty the King celebrate the sacrifice. The time is suitable, O King!'

24. "King Vigeta was wise and gifted in many ways. And his chaplain was equally wise and gifted.

25. "The chaplain, O Brahmin, before the sacrifice had begun, explained to the king what it would involve.

26. " 'Should His Majesty the King, before

starting on the great sacrifice or whilst he is offering the great sacrifice, or when the great sacrifice has been offered, feel any such regret as : 'Great alas, has been the portion of my wealth used up herein,' let not the king harbour such regret. III

27. "And further, O Brahmin, the chaplain,
before the sacrifice had begun, in order to prevent any 267
compunction that might afterwards arise as regards those who had taken part therein, said: 'Now there will come to your sacrifice, sire, men who destroy the life of living things, and men who refrain therefrom—men who take what has not been given, and men who refrain therefrom, men who act evilly in respect of lusts, and men who refrain therefrom, men who speak lies, and men who do not, men who slander, and men who do not, men who speak rudely, and men who do not, men who chatter vain things and men who refrain therefrom, men who covet, and men who covet not, men who harbour ill will and men who harbour it not, men whose views are wrong, and men whose views are right. Of each of these let them, who do evil, alone with their evil. For them who do well let Your Majesty offer, for them, sire, arrange the rites, them let the king gratify, in them shall your heart within find peace.'

28. "And further, O Brahmin, at that sacrifice neither were any oxen slain, neither goats, nor fowls, nor fatted pigs, nor were any kinds of living creatures put to death. No trees were cut down to be used as posts, no Dabbha grasses mown to strew around the sacrificial spot. And the slaves and messengers and workmen there employed were driven neither by rods nor fear, nor carried on their work weeping with tears upon their faces. Whoso chose to help, he worked whoso chose not to help, worked not. What each chose to do, he did; what they chose not to do, that was left undone. With ghee, and oil and butter, and milk and honey, and sugar only was that sacrifice accomplished.

29. "Let your sacrifice be such as that of King Vigeta if you at all wish to perform any sacrifice.

Sacrifices are a waste. Animal sacrifices are cruelties. Sacrifices cannot be part of religion. It is a worst form of religion which says you can go to heaven by killing an animal."

30. I was inclined to ask "Is there, O Gautama, any other sacrifice with more fruit and more advantage than killing animals ?"

31. "Yes, O Brahmin, there is."

32. "And what, O Gautama, may that be ?"

33. "When a man with trusting heart takes upon himself the precepts—abstinence from destroying life; abstinence from taking what has not been given; abstinence from evil conduct in respect of lusts; abstinence from lying words; abstinence from strong, intoxicating, maddening drinks, the root of carelessness that is a sacrifice better than open largesse, better than perpetual alms, better than the gift of dwelling places, better than accepting guidance."

34. And when he had thus spoken, Kutadanta the Brahmin said to the Blessed One: "Most excellent, O Gautama, are the words of thy mouth, most excellent."

(ii)

1. Now the Brahmin Ujjaya said this to the Exalted One :

2. "Pray does the worthy Gautama praise sacrifice ?"

3. "No Brahmin, I do not praise every sacrifice. Yet I would not withhold praise from every sacrifice. In whatever sacrifice, Brahmin, cows are slaughtered, goats and sheep are slaughtered, poultry and pigs are slaughtered and divers living creatures come to destruction—such sacrifice, Brahmin, which involves butchery, I do not praise." "Why so ?"

4. "To such a sacrifice, Brahmin, involving butchery, neither the worthy ones nor those who have entered on the worthy way draw near.

5. "But in whatever sacrifice, Brahmin, cows are not slaughtered—and living creatures come not to destruction, such sacrifice not involving butchery,

I do praise; such as, for instance, a long-established charity, an oblation for the welfare of the family."

6. "Why so?" "Because, Brahmin, the worthy ones, those who have entered on the worthy way, do draw near to such a sacrifice which involves not butchery."

(iii)

1. The Brahmin Udayin asked the same question to the Exalted One as was asked by the Brahmin Ujjaya:

2. "Pray, does the worthy Gautama praise sacrifice?" The Buddha gave the same answer which he gave to Ujjaya.

3. He said:

" *Fit sacrifice performed in season due*
And free from cruelty, to such draw near
Those well trained in the God-life, even those
Who have the veil rolled back while (yet on earth),
Who have transcended time and going. Such do the enlightened praise, those skilled in merit.

" *Whether in sacrifice or act of faith,*
Oblation fitly made with heart devout
To that good field of Merit,—those who live
The Good—life, sacrificed, conferred,—so given
Lavish the offering; devas therewith are pleased.
Thus offering, the thoughtful, thereby becoming wise,
Wins the blissful world from suffering free."

§ 6. *Belief Based on Speculation is Not—Dhamma*

(i)

1. It was usual to ask such questions as (1) Was I in ages past? (2) Was I not in ages past? (3) What was I then? (4) From what did I pass to what? (5) Shall I be in ages to come? (6) Shall I not

be in ages to come? (7) What shall I then be? (8) How shall I then be? (9) From what shall I pass to what? Or, again, it is Self today about which he is in doubt, asking himself—(1) Am I? (2) Am I not? (3) What
III am I? (4) How am I? (5) Whence came my being? (6) Whither will it pass?"

270 2. As regards the Universe various questions were raised. Some of them were as follows :—

3. "How was the Universe created? Is it everlasting?"

4. In answer to the first question some said everything was created by Brahma—others said it was created by Prajapati.

5. In answer to the second question some said it was everlasting. Others said it was not. Some said it was finite. Others said it was infinite.

6. These questions the Buddha refused to entertain. He said that they could only be asked and entertained by wrong-headed people.

7. To answer these questions required omniscience which nobody had.

8. He said that he was not omniscient enough to answer these questions. No one could claim to know all that is to be known nor what we wish to know at any time is known at the time. There is always something that is unknown.

9. It is for these reasons that the Buddha excluded such doctrines from his religion.

10. He regarded a religion which made such doctrines a part of it as a religion not worth having.

(ii)

1. The doctrines with which the contemporaries of the Buddha had made the basis of their religion were concerned with (1) Self; and (2) the origin of the Universe.

2. They raised certain questions about the self. They asked: "(1) Was I in ages past? (2) Was I not in ages past? (3) What was I then? (4) From what did I pass to what? (5) Shall I be in ages to come? (6) Shall I not be in ages to come? (7) What

shall I then be? (8) How shall I then be? (9) From what shall I pass to what? Or, again, it is Self today about which he is in doubt, asking himself—(1) Am I? (2) Am I not? (3) What am I, (4) How am I, (5) Whence came my being? (6) Whither will it pass?"

3. Others raised the question regarding the origin of the Universe.

4. Some said it was created by Brahma.

5. Others said it was created by Prajapati sacrificing himself.

6. Other teachers had other questions to raise: "The world is everlasting,—the world is not everlasting—the world is finite,—the world is infinite, the body is the life (jiva),—the body is the one thing and the life another,—truth-finder exists after death,—a truth-finder does not exist after death,—he both exists and does not exist after death,—he neither exists nor does not exist after death."

7. These were questions which the Buddha said could be asked by wrong-headed persons.

8. There were three reasons why the Buddha condemned these religious theories.

9. In the first place, there was no reason to make them part of religion.

10. In the second place, to answer these questions required omniscience which nobody had. He emphasised this in his addresses.

11. He said that at one and the same time, no one can know and see everything. Knowledge is never final. There is always something more to be known.

12. The third argument against these theories was that they were merely speculative. They are not verified nor are they verifiable.

13. They were the result of imagination let loose. There was no reality behind them.

14. Besides of what good were these speculative theories to man in his relation to men? None whatever.

15. The Buddha did not believe that the world was created. He believed that the world had evolved.

§ 7. *Reading Books of Dhamma is Not—Dhamma*

1. The Brahmins put all their emphasis upon
III knowledge. They taught that knowledge was the be-all and end-all of every thing. Nothing further
272 was to be considered.

2. The Buddha was on the other hand an upholder of education for all. Besides, he was more concerned with the use of knowledge a man is likely to make than with knowledge itself.

3. Consequently he was very particular to emphasize that he who has knowledge must have Sila (Virtue) and that knowledge without Sila (Virtue) was most dangerous.

4. The importance of Sila as against Prajna is well illustrated by what he told the Bhikku Patisena.

5. In olden times when Buddha was residing at Sravasti, there was an old mendicant called Patisena who being by nature cross and dull, could not learn so much as one Gatha by heart.

6. The Buddha accordingly ordered 500 Arahatas day by day to instruct him, but after three years he still was unable to remember even one Gatha.

7. Then all the peoples of the country (the four orders of people) knowing his ignorance, began to ridicule him, on which the Buddha, pitying his case, called him to his side, and gently repeated the following stanza : " He who guards his mouth, and restrains his thoughts, he who offends not with his body, the man who acts thus shall obtain deliverance."

8. Then Patisena, moved by a sense of the Master's goodness to him, felt his heart opened, and once he repeated the stanza.

9. The Buddha then addressed him further— " You now, an old man, can repeat a stanza only, and men know this, and they will still ridicule you, therefore, I will now explain the meaning of the verse to you, and do you on your part attentively listen."

10. Then the Buddha declared the three causes connected with the body, the four connected with the

mouth, and the three connected with the thoughts, by destroying which men might obtain deliverance, on which the mendicant, fully realizing the truth thus explained, obtained the condition of an Arahat.

11. Now, at this time, there were 500 Bhikkhu- III
nis dwelling in their Vihara, who sent one of their
number to the Buddha to request him to send them a 273
priest to instruct them in the Dhamma.

12. On hearing their request the Buddha desired the old mendicant Patisena to go to them for this purpose.

13. On knowing that this arrangement had been made, all the nuns began to laugh together, and agreed on the morrow, when he came, to say the Gatha wrong (backward), and so confuse the old man and put him to shame.

14. Then on the morrow when he came, all the Bhikkhunis, great and small, went forth to salute him and as they did so, they looked at one another and smiled.

15. Then sitting down, they offered him food. Having eaten and washed his hands, they then begged him to begin his sermon. On which the aged mendicant ascended the elevated seat, and sitting down, began :

16. " Sisters ! My talent is small, my learning is very little. I know only one Gatha, but I will repeat that and explain its meaning. Do you listen with attention and understand."

17. Then all the young nuns began to attempt to say the Gatha backwards; but lo! they could not open their mouths ; and filled with shame, they hung down their heads in sorrow.

18. Then Patisena having repeated the Gatha, began to explain it, as the Buddha instructed him.

19. Then all the Bhikkhunis hearing his words, were filled with surprise, and rejoicing to hear such instruction, with one heart they received it, and became Arahatas.

20. On the day after this, the King Prasenjit invited the Buddha and the whole congregation of

priests to assemble at his palace to partake of hospitality.

21. The Buddha therefore recognizing the superior and revered appearance of Patisena, desired him
III to bear his alms-dish and follow him as he went.

22. But when they came to the palace gate, the
274 porter, knowing his character (antecedents), would not let him go into the hall, saying : "We have no hospitality for a priest who knows but one Gatha ; there is no room for such common fellows as you—make place for your betters and begone."

23. Patisena accordingly sat down outside the door.

24. The Buddha now ascended the dais, after having washed his hands, and lo ! the arm of Patisena, with the alms-dish in its hand, entered the room.

25. Then the king, the ministers, and all the assembly seeing this sight, were filled with astonishment, and said, "Ah ! Who is this ?"

26. On which the Buddha replied, "It is Patisena, the mendicant. He has but just obtained enlightenment, and I desired him to bear my alms-dish behind me; but the porter has refused him admission."

27. On this he was admitted and entered the assembly.

28. Then Prasenjit, turning to Buddha, said : "I hear that this Patisena is a man of small ability, and knows only one Gatha, how, then, has he obtained the supreme wisdom ?"

29. To which Buddha replied : "Learning need not be much, conduct (Sila) is the first thing.

30. "This, Patisena, has allowed the secret virtue of the words of this one Gatha to penetrate his spirit ; his body, mouth, and thoughts have obtained perfect quietude; for though a man knows ever so much, if his knowledge reaches not to his life, to deliver him from the power which leads to destruction, what benefit can all his learning be ?"

31. Then the Buddha said :

32. "Although a man repeats a thousand stanzas (sections), but understands not the meaning of the

lines he repeats, his performance is not equal to the repetition of one sentence well understood, which is able when heard to control thought. To repeat a thousand words without understanding, what profit is there in this ? But to understand one truth, and hearing it, to act accordingly, this is to find deliverance.

33. "A man may be able to repeat many books but if he cannot explain them what profit is there in this ? But to explain one sentence of the law and to walk accordingly, this is the way to find supreme wisdom."

34. On hearing these words, the two hundred bhikkhus, the king and his ministers were filled with joy.

§ 8. *Belief in the Infallibility of Books of Dhamma is Not–Dhamma*

1. The Brahmins had declared that the Vedas were not only sacred but in point of authority they were final.

2. Not only were the Vedas declared by the Brahmins to be final but they were declared by them to be infallible.

3. The Buddha was totally opposed to the Brahmins on this point.

4. He denied that the Vedas were sacred. He denied that whatever the Vedas said was final. He denied that the Vedas were infallible.

5. There were many teachers who had taken the same position as he had done. However, later on they or their followers all gave in in order to win respect and goodwill from the Brahmins for their systems of philosophy. But the Buddha never yielded on this issue.

6. In the Tvijja Sutta the Buddha declared that the Vedas were a waterless desert, a pathless jungle, in fact perdition. No man with intellectual and moral thirst can go to the Vedas and hope to satisfy his thirst.

7. As to infallibility of the Vedas, he said nothing

is infallible, not even the Vedas. Everything, he said, must be subject to examination and re-examination.

8. This he made clear in his sermon to the Kalamas.

III 9. Once the Blessed One, while passing through
the land of the Kosalas accompanied by a large follow-
276 ing of disciples, came to the town of Kesaputta which
was inhabited by the Kalamas.

10. When the Kalamas came to know of his arrival they betook themselves thither where the Blessed One was and sat down on one side. So seated, the Kalamas of Kesaputta spoke thus to the Blessed One:

11. "There are, Lord, some ascetics and recluses who come to Kesaputta and who elucidate and exalt their own views, but they break up, crush down, revile and oppose the views of others. And there be other ascetics and recluses, Lord, who come to Kesaputta, and they too expound and magnify their own beliefs, but destroy, suppress, despise and set themselves against the beliefs of others.

12. "And so, Lord, we are in uncertainty and doubt, knowing not which among these venerable ascetics speaks truth and which falsehood."

13. "Good cause, indeed, have you Kalamas to be uncertain ; good cause have you to doubt," said the Blessed One. "Truly, upon just occasion has uncertainty and doubt arisen in you."

14. "Come, O you Kalamas," continued the Lord, "do not go merely by what you hear ; do not go merely by what has been handed down from one to another ; do not go by what is commonly reported ; do not go merely by what is found written in the scriptures ; do not go by subtleties of reasoning, do not go by subtleties of logic ; do not go merely by considerations based upon mere appearances ; do not go merely by agreeable beliefs and views ; do not go merely by what looks to be genuine ; do not go merely by word of some ascetic or superior."

15. "What, then, should we do? What test should we apply?" asked the Kalamas.

16. "The tests are these," replied the Blessed One; "ask yourselves, do we know whether: 'These things are insalutary; these things are blameworthy; these things are reprehended by the wise; these things being done or attempted lead to ill-being III
and to suffering.'

17. "Kalamas, you should go further and ask 277
whether the doctrine taught promotes craving, hatred, delusion, and violence.

18. "This is not enough, Kalamas, you should go further and see whether the doctrine is not likely to make a man captive of his passions, and is not likely to lead him to kill living creatures; take what has not been given to him; go after another's wife; utter falsehood, and cause others to practise like deeds?

19. "And finally you should ask: 'Whether all this does not tend to his ill-being and suffering.'

20. "Now, Kalamas, what think you?

21. "Do these things tend to man's ill-being or well-being?"

22. "To his ill-being, Lord," replied the Kalamas.

23. "What think you, Kalamas,—are these things salutary or insalutary?"

24. "They are insalutary, Lord."

25. "Are these things blameworthy?"

26. "Blameworthy, Lord," replied the Kalamas.

27. "Reprehended by the wise or approved by the wise?"

28. "Reprehended by the wise," replied the Kalamas.

29. "Being done or attempted, do they lead to ill-being and to suffering?"

30. "Done or attempted, Lord, they lead to ill-being and to suffering."

31. "A scripture which teaches this cannot be accepted as final or infallible?"

32. "No, Lord," said the Kalamas.

33. "But this, O Kalamas, is just what I have said. What I have said is "do not go merely by what you hear; do not go merely by what

has been handed down from one to another; do not go merely by subtleties of reasoning; do not go by subtleties of logic ; do not go by considerations based upon mere appearances ; do not go merely by
III agreeable beliefs and views ; do not go merely by the word of some ascetic or superior.

278 34. " Only when of yourselves you indeed know : ' These things are insalutary ; these things are blameworthy ; these things are reprehended by the wise ; these things being done or attempted lead to ill-being and to suffering '—then, Kalamas, you should put them away."

35. " Wonderful, Lord, most wonderful ! We go to Lord, the Blessed One, for refuge, and to his Teachings. As followers, Lord, may the Blessed One accept us, from this day henceforth long as life shall last, we take our refuge in you."

36. The substance of the argument is plain. Before you accept anybody's teachings as authoritative, do not go by the fact that it is contained in the scriptures, do not go by the subtleties of logic ; do not go by considerations based upon mere appearances ; do not go merely by the fact that beliefs and views preached are agreeable ; do not go merely because they look to be genuine; do not go merely by the fact that the beliefs and views are those of some ascetic or superior.

37. But consider whether the beliefs and views sought to be inculcated are salutary or insalutary, blameworthy or blameless, lead to well-being or ill-being.

38. It is only on these grounds that one can accept the teachings of anybody.

PART V

What is Saddhamma

Section I—*The Functions of Saddhamma.*

1. To cleanse the Mind of its impurities.
2. To make the world a Kingdom of Righteousness.

Section II—*Dhamma to be Saddhamma must promote Pradnya.*

1. Dhamma is Saddhamma when it makes learning open to all.

2. Dhamma is Saddhamma when it teaches that mere learning is not enough. It may lead to pedantry.

3. Dhamma is Saddhamma when it teaches that what is needed is Pradnya.

Section III—*Dhamma to be Saddhamma must promote Maitri.*

1. Dhamma is Saddhamma only when it teaches that mere Pradnya is not enough. It must be accompanied by Sila.

2. Dhamma is Saddhamma only when it teaches that besides Pradnya and Sila what is necessary is Karuna.

3. Dhamma is Saddhamma only when it teaches that more than Karuna what is necessary is Maitri.

Section IV—*Dhamma to be Saddhamma must pull down all social barriers.*

1. Dhamma to be Saddhamma must break down barriers between man and man.

2. Dhamma to be Saddhamma must teach that worth and not birth is the measure of man.

3. Dhamma to be Saddhamma must promote equality between man and man.

SECTION I

THE FUNCTIONS OF SADDHAMMA

§ *1. To Cleanse the Mind of its Impurities* III 281

1. Once when the Blessed Lord was residing at Shravasti, Prasenjit, the king of the Kosalas, came to the place where he was staying and descending from his chariot, approached the Teacher with the deepest reverence.

2. And invited him on the morrow to enter the city and partake of his hospitality, with a view to exhibit to the people the excellence of his person and doctrine, that they might believe in him.

3. The Buddha having consented, on the morrow entered the city with all his disciples, and having passed through the four cross streets of the town, he came to the place appointed and sat down.

4. After finishing the meal, he began, on the request of the king, to preach in the midst of the four highways, whilst his auditors were very many.

5. At this time there were two merchants listening to him.

6. One of them reflected, "What excellent wisdom on the part of the king to have such doctrines as these publicly preached ! How wide their application, how searching their character !"

7. The other reflected thus, "What folly is this on the part of the king, bringing this man here to preach !

8. "Like the calf that follows the cow, here and there, fastened to a vehicle she draws, bleating as it goes, so is this Buddha following the king." The two merchants having departed from the city came to an inn where they put up.

9. In taking some wine the good merchant was restrained and protected by the four guardian spirits that watch over the world.

10. The other, on the contrary, was incited by an

evil spirit to drink on, till he was overpowered by sleep, and lay down in the road near the inn.

11. Early in the morning, the merchants' wagons leaving the place, the drivers not perceiving the man
III lying in the road, crushed him to death by the wagon
282 wheels.

12. The other merchant, having come to a distant country, was selected by the genuflection of a sacred horse to succeed the king ; and he accordingly was appointed to the throne.

13. After this, considering the strange turn, events had taken, he returned and invited the Buddha to visit him, and preach to his people.

14. On which occasion the World-honoured One declared the reason of the death of the evil-minded merchant, and the prosperity of him who thought wisely, and then added these lines :

15. " *The mind is the origin of all this is ; the mind is the master, the mind is the cause.*

16. " *If in the midst of the mind there are evil thoughts, then the words are evil, the deeds are evil, and the sorrow which results from sin follows that man, as the chariot wheel follows him (or it) who draws it.*

17. " *The mind is the origin of all that is ; it is the mind that commands, it is the mind that contrives.*

18. " *If in the mind there are good thoughts, then the words are good and the deeds good, and the happiness which results from such conduct follows that man, as the shadow accompanies the substance.*"

19. On hearing these words, the king and his ministers, with countless others, were converted, and became disciples.

§ 2. *To Make the World a Kingdom of Righteousness*

1. What is the purpose of Religion ?

2. Different religions have given different answers.

3. To make man seek after God and to teach

him the importance of saving his soul is the commonest answer one gets to this question.

4. Most religions speak of three kingdoms.

5. One is called the kingdom of heaven. The second is called the kingdom of earth and the third is called the kingdom of hell.

6. This kingdom of heaven is said to be ruled by God. The kingdom of hell is described to be a place where the supremacy of the Evil One is undisputed. The kingdom of earth is a disputed field. It is not under the dominance of the Evil One. At the same time God's sovereignty does not extend to it. It is hoped that one day it will.

7. In some religions the kingdom of heaven is said to be a kingdom in which Righteousness prevails no doubt because it is directly ruled by God.

8. In other religions the kingdom of heaven is not on earth. It is another name for heaven. It can be reached by one who believes in God and his Prophet. When he reaches heaven all the carnal pleasures of life are placed within the reach of all those who are faithful.

9. All religions preach that to reach this kingdom of heaven should be the aim of man and how to reach it is the end of all.

10. To the question "What is the purpose of religion?" the Buddha's answer is very different.

11. He did not tell people that their aim in life should be to reach some imaginary heaven. The kingdom of righteousness lies on earth and is to be reached by man by righteous conduct.

12. What he did was to tell people that to remove their misery each one must learn to be righteous in his conduct in relation to others and thereby make the earth the kingdom of righteousness.

13. It is this which distinguishes his religion from all other religions.

14. His religion emphasizes Panch Sila, the Ashtanga Marga and the Paramitas.

15. Why did the Buddha make them the basis

of his religion ? Because they constitute a way of life which alone can make man righteous.

16. Man's misery is the result of man's inequity to man.

17. Only righteousness can remove this inequity and the resultant misery.

18. That is why he said that religion must not only preach but must inculcate upon the mind of man the supreme necessity for being righteous in his conduct.

19. For the purpose of inculcating righteousness religion, he said, had certain other functions to undertake.

20. Religion must teach man to know what is right and to follow what is right.

21. Religion must teach man to know what is wrong and not to follow what is wrong.

22. Besides these purposes of religion he emphasized two other purposes which he regarded as of supreme importance.

23. The first is training of man's instincts and dispositions as distinguished from offering prayers or performing observances or doing sacrifices.

24. This the Buddha has made clear in his exposition of Jainism in the Devadaha Sutta.

25. What Mahavira, the founder of Jainism, affirmed was that whatsoever the individual experiences—be it pleasant or unpleasant, all comes from acts done in former births.

26. That being so, by expiration and purge of former misdeeds and by not committing fresh misdeeds, nothing accrues for the future: as nothing accrues for the future, the misdeeds die away ; as misdeeds die away, misery dies away : as misery dies away, feelings die away : and as feelings die away, all misery will wear out and pass.

27. This is what Jainism affirmed.

28. On this the Buddha asked this question: "Do you know that, here and now, wrong dispositions have been got rid of and right dispositions acquired?"

29. The answer was " No."

30. " What is the use," asked the Buddha, " of a purge for former misdeeds, what is the use of not committing fresh misdeeds, if there is no training of the mind to turn bad disposition into good disposition."

31. This was in his opinion a very serious defect in religion. *A good disposition is the only permanent foundation of and guarantee of permanent goodness.*

32. That is why the Buddha gave the first place to the training of the mind which is the same as the training of a man's disposition.

33. The second thing to which he gave great importance is courage to stand by what is right even if one is alone.

34. In the Sallekha-Sutta the Buddha has emphasized this point.

35. This is what he has said :

36. " You are to expunge by resolving that, though others may be harmful, you will be harmless.

37. " That though others may kill, you will never kill.

38. " That though others may steal, you will not.

39. " That though others may not lead the higher life, you will.

40. " That though others may lie, traduce, denounce, or prattle, you will not.

41. " That though others may be covetous, you will covet not.

42. " That though others may be malignant, you will not be malignant.

43. " That though others may be given over to wrong views, wrong aims, wrong speech, wrong actions, and wrong concentration, you must follow (the Noble Eightfold Path in) right outlook, right aims, right speech, right actions, right mode of livelihood, right effort, right mindfulness and right concentration.

44. " That though others are wrong about the truth and wrong about Deliverance, you will be right about truth and right about Deliverance.

45. "That though others may be possessed by sloth and torpor, you will free yourselves therefrom.

46. "That though others may be puffed up, you will be humble-minded.

III 47. "That though others may be perplexed by doubts, you will be free from them.

286 48. "That though others may harbour wrath, malevolence, envy, jealousy, niggardliness, avarice, hypocrisy, deceit, imperviousness, arrogance, forwardness, association with bad friends, slackness, unbelief, shamelessness, unscrupulousness, lack of instruction, inertness, bewilderment, and unwisdom, you will be the reverse of all these things.

49. "That though others may clutch at and hug the temporal nor loose their hold thereon, you will clutch and hug the things that are not temporal, and will ensue Renunciation.

50. "I say it is the development of the will which is so efficacious for right states of consciousness, not to speak of act and speech. And therefore, Cunda, there must be developed the will to all the foregoing resolves I have detailed."

51. Such is the purpose of religion as conceived by the Buddha.

SECTION II

DHAMMA TO BE SADDHAMMA MUST PROMOTE PRADNYA

§ *1. Dhamma is Saddhamma when it Makes Learning Open to All*

1. The Brahminic doctrine was that acquisition of knowledge cannot be thrown open to all. It must necessarily be limited to a few.

2. They permitted acquisition of knowledge only to the Brahmins, Kshatriyas and Vaishyas. But it was only to the male sex of these three classes.

3. All women, no matter whether they belonged to the Brahmin, Kshatriya and Vaishyas, and all Shudras, both males and females, were prohibited from acquiring knowledge, even from acquiring literacy.

4. The Buddha raised a revolt against this atrocious doctrine of the Brahmins.

5. He preached that the road to knowledge must be open to all—to males as well as to females.

6. Many Brahmins tried to controvert his views. His controversy with the Brahmin Lohikka throws great light on his views.

7. The Exalted One, when once passing on a tour through the Kosala districts with a multitude of the members of the Order, arrived at Salavatika, a village surrounded by a row of sala trees.

8. Now at the time, Lohikka the Brahmin was living at Salavatika, a spot teeming with life, with much grassland and woodland and corn, on a royal domain granted him by King Pasenadi of Kosala, as a royal gift, with power over it as if he were the king.

9. Lohikka the Brahmin was of opinion that if a Samana or a Brahmana acquired knowledge, he should not communicate it to the women or to the Shudras.

10. Then the Brahmin Lohikka heard that the Blessed Lord was staying in Salavatika.

11. Having heard of this he said to Bhesika the barber : " Come now, good Bhesika, go where the

Samana Gotama is staying, and, on your arrival, ask in my name as to whether his sickness and indisposition has abated, as to his health and vigour and condition of ease ; and speak thus : "May the venerable
III Gotama, and with him the brethren of the Order, accept tomorrow's meal from Lohikka the Brahmin."

288 12. "Very well, sir," said the barber.

13. Acquiescing in the word of Lohikka the Brahmin, he did so even as he had been enjoined. And the Exalted One consented, by silence, to his request.

14. Early next morning, the Exalted One went robed, and carrying his bowl with him, with the brethren of the Order, towards Salavatika.

15. Bhesika, the barber, who had been sent by Lohikka to fetch the Blessed One, walked step by step, behind the Exalted One. On the way he told the Blessed One that Lohikka the Brahmin held the wicked opinion that a Samana or a Brahmana shall not communicate any knowledge or learning to women and the Shudras.

16. "That may well be, Bhesika, that may well be," replied the Blessed One.

17. And the Exalted One went on to the dwelling place of Lohikka the Brahmin, and sat down on the seat prepared for him.

18. And Lohikka the Brahmin served the Order, with the Buddha at its head, with his own hand, with sweet food both hard and soft, until they refused any more.

19. And when the Exalted One had finished his meal, and had cleansed the bowl and his hands, Lohikka the Brahmin, brought a low seat and sat down beside him.

20. And to him, thus seated, the Exalted One said : "Is it true, what they say, Lohikka, that you hold the view that a Samana or a Brahmana should not communicate any knowledge or learning to women and Shudras ?"

21. "That is so, Gotama," replied Lohikka.

22. "Now what think you, Lohikka? Are you

not established at Salavatika?" "Yes, that is so, Gotama."

23. "Then suppose, Lohikka, one were to speak thus: 'Lohikka the Brahmin has a domain at
Salavatika. Let him alone enjoy all the revenue and III
all the produce of Salavatika, allowing nothing to
anybody else!' Would the utterer of that speech 289
be a danger-maker as touching the men who live in dependence upon you or not?"

24. "He would be a danger-maker, Gotama."

25. "And making that danger, would he be regarded as a person who sympathised with their welfare?"

26. "No. He would not be considering their welfare, Gotama," replied Lohikka.

27. "And not considering their welfare, would his heart stand fast in love towards them or in enmity?"

28. "In enmity, Gotama."

29. "But when one's heart stands fast in enmity, is that unsound doctrine, or sound?"

30. "It is an unsound doctrine, Gotama."

31. "Now what think you, Lohikka? Is not King Pasenadi of Kosala in possession of Kasi and Kosala?"

32. "Yes, that is so, Gotama."

33. "Then suppose, Lohikka, one were to speak thus: 'King Pasenadi of Kosala is in possession of Kasi and Kosala. Let him enjoy all the revenue and all the produce of Kasi and Kosala, allowing nothing to anybody else.' Would the utterer of that speech be a danger-maker as touching the men who live in dependence on King Pasenadi of Kosala—both you yourself and others—or not?"

34. "He would be a danger-maker, Gotama."

35. "And making that danger, would he be a person who sympathised with their welfare?"

36. "He would not be considering their welfare, Gotama."

37. "And not considering their welfare, would his heart stand fast in love towards them, or in enmity?"

38. "In enmity, Gotama."

39. " But when one's heart stands fast in enmity, is that unsound doctrine, or sound ? "

40. " It is an unsound doctrine, Gotama."

41. " So then, Lohikka, you admit that he who
III should say that you, being in occupation of Salavatika,
should therefore yourself enjoy all the revenue and
290 produce thereof, bestowing nothing on anyone else ;
and he who should say that King Pasenadi of Kosala, being in power over Kasi and Kosala, should therefore himself enjoy all the produce thereof, bestowing nothing on anyone else, would be making danger for those living in dependence on you ; or for those, you and others, living in dependence upon the king. And that those who thus make danger for others, must be wanting in sympathy and have their hearts set fast in enmity. And that to have one's heart set fast in enmity is unsound doctrine.

42. " Then just so, Lohikka, is he who should say that a Samana or a Brahmin should not communicate his knowledge and learning to women and Shudras.

43. " Just so, he who should say thus, would be putting obstacles in the way of others and would be out of sympathy for their welfare.

44. " Being out of sympathy for their welfare his heart would become established in enmity ; and when one's heart is established in enmity, that is unsound doctrine."

§ 2. *Dhamma is Saddhamma when it Teaches that Mere Learning is Not Enough: it may Lead to Pedantry*

1. Once when the Buddha was residing in the country of Kausambi, in a certain Vihara called the " Beautiful Voice," preaching to the people assembled there was a certain Brahmacharin.

2. The Brahmacharin felt that he was unrivalled for knowledge of scriptures and being unable to find anyone equal to himself in argument, was accustomed to carry, wherever he went, a lighted torch in his hand.

3. One day a man in the market place of a certain town, seeing him thus, asked him the reason of his strange conduct, on which he replied :

4. " The world is so dark, and men so deluded, that I carry this torch to light it up so far as I can."

5. Seeing this the Buddha forthwith called out to the Brahmacharin, " What ho there ! What are you about with that Torch ? "

6. The Brahmacharin replied, " All men are so wrapped in ignorance and gloom, that I carry this torch to illumine them."

7. Then the Blessed Lord asked him again, " And are you so learned as to be acquainted with the four treatises (Vidyas) which occur in the midst of the Sacred Books, to wit, the treatise on ' Literature' (Sabdavidya) ; the treatise on the ' Heavenly Bodies and their Paths ' ; the treatise on ' Government' and the treatise on ' Military Art ' ? "

8. On the Brahmacharin being forced to confess he was unacquainted with these things, he flung away his torch, and the Buddha added these words :

9. " If any man, whether he be learned or not, considers himself so great as to despise other men he is like a blind man holding a candle—blind himself, he illumines others."

§ 3. *Dhamma is Saddhamma when it Teaches that what is Needed is Pradnya*

1. The Brahmins regarded Vidya (Knowledge, Learning) as in itself a thing of value. A man of mere learning and knowledge was to them an object of veneration irrespective of the question whether or not he was a man of virtue.

2. Indeed they said that a king is honoured in his own country but a man of learning is honoured all over the world, suggesting thereby that a man of learning is greater than the king.

3. The Buddha made a distinction between Vidya and Pradnya, i.e., between knowledge and insight.

4. It may be said that the Brahmins also made a distinction between Pradnya and Vidya.

5. That may be true. But there is a vast difference between the Pradnya of the Buddha and the Pradnya of the Brahmins.

6. This distinction has been well brought out by the Buddha in his sermon reported in Anguttara Nikaya.

7. On a certain occasion the Exalted One was staying near Rajagraha, in the bamboo grove at the squirrels' feeding ground.

8. Now on that occasion Vassakara the Brahmin, a great official of Magadha, came to visit the Exalted One, and on coming to him greeted him courteously, and after exchange of greetings and courtesies sat down at one side. As he sat thus Vassakara the Brahmin said this to the Exalted One :

9. " Master Gotama, we Brahmins proclaim a man, if he possesses four qualities, as one of great wisdom, as a great man. What are the four qualities ?

10. " Herein, Master Gotama, he is learned. Of whatsoever he hears he understands the meaning as soon as it is uttered, saying : 'This is the meaning of that saying !' Moreover, he has a good memory, he can remember and recall a thing done long ago, and said long ago.

11. " Again, in all the business of a householder he is skilled and diligent, and therein he is resourceful and capable of investigating what is proper to be done, what should be arranged.

12. " Now, master Gotama, if a man possesses these qualities, we proclaim him as one of great wisdom, as a great man. If the worthy Gotama thinks me worthy of commendation herein, let him commend me. On the contrary, if he thinks me blameworthy, let him blame me therefor."

13. " Well, Brahmin I neither commend you nor blame you herein. I myself proclaim a man to be one of great wisdom, if he possesses the following four qualities which are quite different from those mentioned by you.

14. "Herein, Brahmin, we have a man given to the welfare of many folk, to the happiness of many folk. By him are many folk established in the Ariyan Method, to wit: in what is of a lovely nature, in what is of a profitable nature. III

15. "To whatsoever train of thought he wishes
to apply himself, to that train of thought he applies 293
himself: to whatever train of thought he desires not to apply himself, to that train of thought he applies not himself.

16. "Whatever intention he wishes to intend, he does so or not if he so wishes. Thus is he master of the mind in the ways of thought.

17. "Also he is one who attains at will, without difficulty and without trouble the four musings which belong to the higher thought, which even in this very life are blissful to abide in.

18. "Also by destruction of the asavas (fetters) in this very life thoroughly comprehending it by himself, he realizes the heart's release, the release by wisdom, and attaining it abides therein.

19. "No Brahmin, I neither commend nor blame you herein, but I myself proclaim a man possessed of these four different qualities to be one of great wisdom, to be a great man."

20. "It is wonderful, Master Gotama! It is marvellous, Master Gotama, how well this has been said by the worthy Gotama!

21. "I myself do hold the worthy Gotama to be possessed of these same four qualities. Indeed, the worthy Gotama is given to the welfare of many folk, to the happiness of many folk. By him are many folk established in the Ariyan Method, to wit: in what is of a lovely nature, in what is of a profitable nature.

22. "Indeed, the worthy Gotama, to whatever train of thought he wishes to apply himself, to that train of thought applies himself . . Surely the worthy Gotama is master of the mind in the ways of thought.

23. "Surely the worthy Gotama is one who attains at will . . . the four musings . . . Surely the

worthy Gotama by destruction of the asavas . . . realizes the heart's release, the release by wisdom . . . and attaining it abides therein."

24. Herein is stated in the clearest terms the
III difference between Pradnya according to the Buddha
and Pradnya, according to the Brahmins.

294 25. Herein is set out his case why the Buddha regarded Pradnya as more important than *Vidya*.

SECTION III

DHAMMA TO BE SADDHAMMA MUST PROMOTE MAITRI

§ *1. Dhamma is Saddhamma only when* III
it Teaches that Mere Pradnya is Not 295
Enough: it must be accompanied by Sila

1. Pradnya is necessary. But Sila is more necessary. Pradnya without Sila is dangerous.

2. Mere Pradnya is dangerous.

3. Pradnya is like a sword in the hand of a man.

4. In the hand of a man with Sila it may be used for saving a man with danger.

5. But in the hand of a man without Sila it may be used for murder.

6. That is why Sila is more important than Pradnya.

7. Pradnya is Vichar Dhamma or thinking aright. Sila is Achar Dhamma, acting aright.

8. The Buddha prescribed five basic principles regarding Sila.

9. One relating to taking life.

10. Second relating to stealing.

11. Third relating to sexual immorality.

12. Fourth relating to telling a lie.

13. Fifth relating to drink.

14. On each of these the Blessed Lord directed the people not to kill; not to steal; nor to tell a lie; nor to indulge in sex immorality and not to indulge in drinking.

15. The reason why the Buddha gave greater importance to Sila than to knowledge is obvious.

16. The use of knowledge depends upon a man's Sila. Apart from Sila, knowledge has no value. This is what he said.

17. At another place, he said, " Sila is incomparable in this world.

18. " Sila is the beginning and the refuge, Sila is the mother of all good. It is the foremost of all good conditions. Therefore, purify your Sila."

§ 2. *Dhamma is Saddhamma only when it Teaches that besides Pradnya and Sila what is Necessary is Karuna*

III 1. There has been some difference of opinion on
296 the issue as to foundation of Buddha's Dhamma.

2. Is *Pradnya* alone the foundation of his religion? Is *Karuna* alone the foundation of his religion?

3. The controversy had divided the followers of the Buddha into two schools. One school held that Pradnya alone is the foundation of the Buddha's religion. The other school held that Karuna alone is the foundation of the Buddha's religion.

4. These two schools still remain divided.

5. Both the schools seem to be wrong if judged in the light of the Buddha's own words.

6. There is no difference of opinion that Pradnya is one of the two pillars of the Buddha's religion.

7. The dispute is whether Karuna is also a pillar of his religion.

8. That Karuna is a pillar of his religion is beyond dispute.

9. His own words can be quoted in support of it.

10. In days gone by there was a country called Gandhara, in which was a very old mendicant afflicted with a very loathsome disease, which caused him to pollute every place he occupied.

11. Being in a certain Vihara belonging to the place, no one would come near him or help him in his distress.

12. On this Buddha came with his 500 followers, and obtaining all sorts of necessary utensils and warm water, they together visited the place where the old mendicant lay.

13. The smell in the place was so offensive that all the Bhikkus were filled with contempt for the man; but the World-honoured, causing Sakra-deva to bring the warm water, then with his own hand began to

wash the body of the mendicant and attend to his maladies.

14. Then the earth shook, and the whole place was filled with a supernatural light, so that the king and the ministers, and all the heavenly host (Devas, Nagas, etc.) flocked to the place, and paid adoration to Buddha.

15. Having done so, they all addressed the World-honoured, and inquired how one so highly exalted could lower himself to such offices as these, on which Buddha explained the matter thus :

16. "The purpose of Tathagata in coming into the world is to befriend those poor and helpless and unprotected, to nourish those in bodily affliction, whether they be Samanas or men of any other religion—to help the impoverished, the orphan and the aged, and to persuade others so to do."

§ 3. *Dhamma is Saddhamma only when it Teaches that More than Karuna what is Necessary is Maitri*

1. The Buddha did not stop with teaching Karuna.

2. Karuna is only love for human beings. Buddha went beyond and taught Maitri. Maitri is love for living beings.

3. The Buddha wanted man not to stop with Karuna but to go beyond mankind and cultivate the spirit of Maitri for all living beings.

4. This he has well explained in a Sutta when the Blessed One was staying in Shravasti.

5. Speaking about Maitri, the Blessed Lord told the almsmen:

6. "Suppose a man comes to dig the earth. Does the earth resent?"

7. "No, Lord," the almsmen replied.

8. "Supposing a man comes with lac and colours to paint pictures in the air. Do you think he could do it?"

9. " No, Lord."

10. " Why ? " " Because there are no dark patches in the air, " said the Bhikkus.

11. " In the same way you must not have any dark patches in your mind which are the reflections of your evil passions."

12. " Suppose a man comes with a blazing wisp of bracken to set the River Ganges on fire. Could he do it ? "

13. " No, Lord."

14. " Why ? " " Because the Ganges has no combustibility in its water."

15. Concluding his address, the Blessed Lord said : " Just as the earth does not feel hurt and does not resent, just as the air does not lend to any action against it, just as the Ganges water goes on flowing without being disturbed by the fire so also you Bhikkus must bear all insults and injustices inflicted on you and continue to bear Maitri towards your offenders.

16. " So almsmen, Maitri must flow and flow for ever. Let it be your sacred obligation to keep your mind as firm as the earth, as clean as the air and as deep as the Ganges. If you do so your Maitri will not be easily disturbed, by an act however unpleasant. For all who do injury will soon be tired out.

17. " Let the ambit of your Maitri be as boundless as the world and let your thought be vast and beyond measure in which no hatred is thought of.

18. " According to my Dhamma, it is not enough to practise Karuna. It is necessary to practise Maitri."

19. In the course of the sermon the Blessed Lord told a story to the almsmen which is worth remembering.

20. " Once upon a time there lived in Shravasti a lady named Videshika, who was reputed gentle and meek, and mild. She had a maid servant named Darkie, a bright girl, an early riser and a good worker. ' I wonder,' thought Darkie, ' whether my mistress, who is so well spoken of, has really got a temper of her own which she does not show or whether she has got no temper at all ? Or do I do my work so well,

that though she has got a temper, she does not show it? I will try her.'

21. "So next morning she got up late. 'Darkie!
Darkie! cried the mistress.' 'Yes, madam,' answered
the girl. 'Why did you get up so late?' 'Oh, that's III
nothing, madam.' 'Nothing indeed, you naughty
girl!' thought the mistress, frowning with anger 299
and displeasure.

22. "'So she has got a temper, though she does not show it," thought the maid: 'It is because I do my work so well that she does not show it; I will try her further.' So she got up later next morning. 'Darkie! Darkie!' cried the mistress. 'Yes, madam,' answered the girl. 'Why did you get up so late?' 'Oh that's nothing, madam.' 'Nothing, indeed, you naughty girl!' exclaimed the mistress, giving vent in words to her anger and displeasure.

23. "'Yes,' thought the maid, 'she has got a temper though she does not show it because I do my work so well; I will try her yet further.' So next morning she got up later still. 'Darkie! Darkie! cried her mistress.' 'Yes, madam,' answered the girl. 'Why did you get up so late?' 'Oh, that's nothing, madam.'

24. "'Nothing indeed you naughty girl, to get up so late!' exclaimed the mistress and in her anger and displeasure she picked up the lynch-pin and struck the girl on the head with it, drawing blood.

25. "With her broken head streaming with blood, Darkie roused the neighbourhood with shrieks: 'See, lady, what the gentle one has done! See, lady, what the meek one has done! See, lady, what the mild one has done. What for? Just because her only maid got up late, she was so angry and displeased that she just jumped with the lynch-pin to strike her on the head and break it.'

26. "In the result the lady Videshika got the reputation of being violent, anything but meek and mild.

27. "In like manner an almsman may be gentle and meek, and mild enough so long as nothing

unpleasant is said against him. It is only when unpleasant things are said against him that you can test if he has Maitri—fellowship in him."

28. Then he added, " I do not call an almsman
III charged with the spirit of Maitri if he shows it only to
get clothes and food. Him only do I recognize as a
300 true almsman whose Maitri springs from the doctrine."

29. " None of the means employed to acquire religious merit, O Monks, has a sixteenth part of the value of loving kindness. Loving kindness, which is freedom of heart, absorbs them all ; it glows, it shines, it blazes forth.

30. " And in the same way, O Monks, as the light of all the stars has not a sixteenth part of the value of the moonlight, but the moonlight absorbs it and glows and shines and blazes forth ; in the same way, O Monks, none of the means employed to acquire religious merit has a sixteenth part of the value of loving kindness. Loving kindness, which is freedom of heart, absorbs them; it glows, it shines, it blazes forth.

31. " And in the same way, O Monks, as at the end of the rainy season, the sun, rising into the clear and cloudless sky, banishes all the dark spaces and glows and shines and blazes forth ; and in the same way again, as at night's end the morning star glows and shines and blazes forth ; so, O Monks, none of the means employed to acquire religious merit has a sixteenth part of the value of loving kindness. Loving kindness, which is freedom of heart, absorbs them ; it glows, it shines, it blazes forth."

SECTION IV

DHAMMA TO BE SADDHAMMA MUST PULL DOWN ALL SOCIAL BARRIERS

§ 1. *Dhamma to be Saddhamma must break down barriers between Man and Man* III 301

1. What is an ideal society? According to the Brahmins, the Vedas have defined what is an ideal society and the Vedas being infallible, that is the only ideal society which man can accept.

2. The ideal society prescribed by the Vedas is known by the name Chaturvarna.

3. Such a society, according to the Vedas, must satisfy three conditions.

4. It must be composed of four classes, Brahmins, Kshatriyas, Vaishyas and Shudras.

5. The interrelations of these classes must be regulated by the principle of graded inequality. In other words, all these classes are not to be on equal level but to be one above the other, in point of status, rights and privileges.

6. The Brahmins were placed at the top ; the Kshatriyas were placed below the Brahmins but above the Vaishyas ; the Vaishyas were placed below the Kshatriyas but above the Shudras and the Shudras were placed the lowest of all.

7. The third feature of Chaturvarna was that each class must engage itself in an occupation assigned to it. The Brahmins' occupation was to learn, teach and officiate at religious ceremonies. The Kshatriyas' occupation was to bear arms and to fight. The occupation of the Vaishyas was trade and business. The Shudras' occupation was to do menial service for all the three superior classes.

8. No class is to transgress and trench upon the occupation of the other classes.

9. This theory of an ideal society was upheld by the Brahmins and preached to the people.

10. The soul of this theory, it is obvious, is

inequality. This social inequality is not the result of historical growth. Inequality is the official doctrine of Brahminism.

11. The Buddha opposed it root and branch.

12. He was the strongest opponent of caste and the earliest and staunchest upholder of equality.

13. There is no argument in favour of caste and inequality which he did not refute.

14. There were many Brahmins who challenged Buddha on this issue. But he silenced them completely.

15. The story is told in the Assalayana-Sutta that once the Brahmins persuaded one of them, by name Assalayana, to go to the Buddha and controvert his views against caste and inequality.

16. Assalayana went to the Buddha and placed before him the case in favour of the superiority of the Brahmins.

17. He said, " Brahmins maintain, Gotama, that only Brahmins form the superior class, all other classes being inferior ; that only Brahmins form the white class, all other classes being black fellows ; that purity resides in Brahmins alone and not in non-Brahmins ; and that only Brahmins are Brahma's legitimate sons, born from his mouth, offspring of his, creations of his, and his heirs. What does Gotama say hereon ? "

18. The Buddha's answer simply pulverized Assalayana.

19. The Buddha said : " Assalayana, are not the Brahmin wives of Brahmins known to have their periods, and to conceive, and to lie and give birth ? Notwithstanding this do Brahmins really maintain all what you have said though they are themselves born of women like everybody else ? "

20. Assalayana gave no answer.

21. The Buddha went further and asked Assalayana another question.

22. " Suppose, Assalayana, a young noble consorts with a Brahmin maiden, what would be the issue ? Will it be an animal or human being ? "

23. Again Assalayana gave no answer.

24. "As to the possibility of moral development, is it only a Brahmin and not a man of the other three classes, who in this country, can develop in his heart the love that knows no hate or ill-will?"

25. "No. All four classes can do it," replied Assalayana.

26. "Assalayana! Have you ever heard," asked the Buddha, "that in the Yona and Kamboja countries and in other adjacent countries, there are only two classes, namely, masters and slaves, and that a master can become a slave and *vice versa*?"

27. "Yes, I have heard so," replied Assalayana.

28. "If your Chaturvarna is an ideal society, why is it not universal?"

29. On none of these points was Assalayana able to defend his theory of caste and inequality. He was completely silenced. He ended by becoming a disciple of the Buddha.

30. A Brahmin by name Vasettha had embraced the religion of the Blessed Lord. The Brahmins used to abuse him for his conversion.

31. One day he went to Buddha and disclosed to him what the Brahmins said of him.

32. Then Vasettha said: "The Brahmins, Lord, say thus: 'Only a Brahmin is of the best social grade; other grades are low. Only a Brahmin is of a clear complexion; other complexions are swarthy. Only Brahmins are of pure breed; not they that are not of the Brahmins. Only Brahmins are genuine children of Brahma, born of his mouth, offspring of Brahma, created by Brahma, heirs of Brahma.

33. "'As for you, you have renounced the best rank and have gone over to that low class, to the shaven recluses, to vulgar rich, to them of swarthy skins, to the foot-born descendants. Such a course is not good, such a course is not proper, even this, that you, having forsaken that upper class, should associate with an inferior class, to wit, with shavelings, fair folks, menials, swarthy of skin, the offspring of our kinsmen's heels.'

34. "In these terms, Lord, do the Brahmins blame and revile me with characteristic abuse, copious, not at all stinted."

35. "Surely, Vasettha," said the Buddha, "the
III Brahmins have quite forgotton the ancient lore when they say so. On the contrary, the wives of Brahmins,
304 like all women of other classes, are seen to be with child, bringing forth and nursing children. And yet it is these very womb-born Brahmins who say that Brahmins are genuine children of Brahma, born from his mouth ; his offspring ; his creation ; and his heirs ! By this they make a travesty of the nature of Brahma."

36. Once the Brahmin Esukari went to the Buddha to argue with him three questions.

37. The first question he raised related to the permanent division of occupations. In defence of the system he began by saying : "I have come to ask you a question. The Brahmins say they shall serve nobody because they stand above all. Everyone else is born to serve them.

38. "Service, Gotama, is divided into four—service of Brahmin, service of noble, service of a middle-class man, or by a peasant ; while a peasant may be served only by a peasant,—for who else could ?" What does the reverend Gotama say hereon ?"

39. The Buddha answered him by asking a question : "Is the whole world in accord with Brahmins in their fourfold division of service ?" asked the Lord.

40. "For myself, I neither assert that all service is to be rendered nor that all service is to be refused. If the service makes a man bad and not good, it should not be rendered; but if it makes him better and not bad, then it should be rendered.

41. "This is the guiding consideration which should decide the conduct alike of nobles, of Brahmins, of middle-class men and of peasants ; each individual should refuse service which makes him bad and should accept only the service which makes him a better man."

42. The next question raised was by Esukari.

" Why should ancestry and lineage not have a place in determining the status of a man ? "

43. To this question the Buddha replied thus : " As against pride of ancestry, the station into which
a man happens to be born determines only his desig- III
nation be it noble or Brahmin or middle-class or
peasant. Even as a fire is called after the material 305
out of which it is kindled, and may thus be called either a wood-fire, or a chip-fire, or a bracken-fire, or a cowdung fire, just in the same way the noble, transcendant doctrine, I aver, is the source of true wealth for every man, birth merely determining his designation in one of the four classes.

44. " Lineage does not enter into a man's being either good or bad : nor do good looks or wealth. For, you will find a man of noble birth who is a murderer, a thief, a fornicator, a liar, a slanderer, a man of bitter tongue, a tattler, a covetous person, a man of rancour or of wrong views, and therefore I assert that noble birth does not make a good man. Or again you will find a man of noble birth who is innocent of all these vices ; and, therefore, I assert that it is not lineage which makes a man bad."

45. The third question which Esukari raised was with regard to the ways of earning a living assigned to each class.

46. The Brahmin Esukari said to the Lord : " Brahmins give a fourfold assignment of income, from alms, for Brahmins ; from his bow and arrows, for the noble ; from ploughing and tending cattle, for the middle-class man ; and for the peasant, by the carriage of crops on the pole slung over his shoulder. If anyone of these deserts his vocation for something else, he does what he should not do, not less than a guardian who appropriates what is not his. What does the reverend Gotama say on this ? "

47. " Is the whole world in accord with this Brahmin classification ? " asked the Lord.

48. "No," replied Esukari.

49. To Vasettha he said : " What is important is high ideals and not noble birth.

50. " No caste ; no inequality ; no superiority ; no inferiority ; all are equal. This is what he stood for.

51. " Identify yourself with others. As they,
III so I. As I, so they," so said the Buddha.

306 § 2. *Dhamma to be Saddhamma must Teach that Worth and not Birth is the Measure of Man*

1. The theory of Chaturvarna, preached by the Brahmins, was based on birth.

2. One is a Brahmin because he is born of Brahmin parents. One is a Kshatriya because he is born of Kshatriya parents. One is a Vaishya because one is born of Vaishya parents. And one is a Shudra because one is born of Shudra parents.

3. The worth of a man according to the Brahmins was based on birth and on nothing else.

4. This theory was as repulsive to the Buddha as was the theory of Chaturvarna.

5. His doctrine was just the opposite of the doctrine of the Brahmins. It was his doctrine that worth and not birth was the measure of man.

6. The occasion on which the Buddha propounded his doctrine has its own peculiar interest.

7. Once the Blessed One was staying in Anathpindika's Asram. One day in the forenoon he took his begging bowl and entered Shravasti for alms.

8. At that time a sacrificial fire was burning and an offering was prepared. Then the Blessed One, going for alms from house to house in Shravasti, approached the house of the Brahmin Aggika.

9. The Brahmin, seeing the Blessed One coming at a distance, became angry and said : " Stay there, O Shaveling ! There, stay, ye wretched monk ! Stay there, ye miserable outcast."

10. When he spoke thus, the Blessed One addressed him as follows: " Do you know, O Brahmin, who an outcast is, or the things that make a person an outcast ? "

11. " No, Gotama, I do not know who an outcast is. Nor indeed do I know what things make a man an outcast."

12. The Lord pleaded that nothing would be lost
in knowing who is an outcast. " Now that you insist III
on my knowing it," the Brahmin Aggika said, " well
go on and explain." 307

13. The Brahmin having responded, the Blessed One spake as follows :

14. " The man who is irritable, rancorous, vicious, detractive, perverted in views, and deceitful—know ye that he is an outcast.

15. " Whosoever in this world harms living beings once-born or twice-born, in whom there is no compassion for living beings—know ye that he is an outcast.

16. " Whosoever destroys and besieges villages and hamlets, and is known as an oppressor—know ye that he is an outcast.

17. " Whether in the village or in the forest whosoever appropriates by theft what belongs to others, or what is not given—know ye that he is an outcast.

18. " Whosoever, having really taken a debt, flees, when pressed, saying, ' There is no debt to you,'—know ye that he is an outcast.

19. " Whosoever, desiring some trifle, kills a man going alone on the road, and pillages him—know ye that he is an outcast.

20. " Whosoever for his own sake, or for the sake of others, or for the sake of wealth, utters lies when asked as a witness—know ye that he is an outcast.

21. " Whosoever by force or with consent is seen transgressing with the wives of relatives or friends—know ye that he is an outcast.

22. " Whosoever, being rich, does not support aged mother and father who have passed their youth—know ye that he is an outcast.

23. " Whosoever, when questioned about what is good, counsels what is wrong and teaches in a concealing way—know ye that he is an outcast.

24. " No one is an outcast by birth—and no one is a Brahmin by birth."

25. Aggika, on hearing this, felt greatly ashamed for the abuse he had hurled against the Blessed Lord.

§ 3. *Dhamma to be Saddhamma must Promote Equality between Man and Man*

1. Men are born unequal.

2. Some are robust, others are weaklings.

3. Some have more intelligence, others have less or none.

4. Some have more capacity, others have less.

5. Some are well-to-do, others are poor.

6. All have to enter into what is called the struggle for existence.

7. In the struggle for existence if inequality be recognized as the rule of the game the weakest will always go to the wall.

8. Should this rule of inequality be allowed to be the rule of life?

9. Some answer in the affirmative on the ground that it results in the survival of the fittest.

10. The question, however, is : Is the fittest the best from the point of view of society.

11. No one can give a positive answer.

12. It is because of this doubt that religion preaches equality. For equality may help the best to survive even though the best may not be the fittest.

13. What society wants is the best and not the fittest.

14. It is, therefore, the primary reason why religion upholds equality.

15. This was the viewpoint of the Buddha and it was because of this that he argued that a religion which does not preach equality is not worth having.

16. Can you respect or believe in a religion which recommends actions that bring happiness to oneself by causing sorrow to others, or happiness to others

by causing sorrow to oneself or sorrow to both oneself and others ?

17. Is not that a better religion which promotes the happiness of others simultaneously with the happiness of oneself and tolerates no oppression. III

18. These were some of the most pertinent questions which he asked the Brahmins who opposed 309
Equality.

19. The religion of the Buddha is perfect justice springing from a man's own meritorious disposition.

BOOK IV

Religion and Dhamma

Part I—Religion and Dhamma.

Part II—How Similarities in Terminology Conceal Fundamental Difference.

Part III—The Buddhist Way of Life.

Part IV—His Sermons.

PART I

Religion and Dhamma

§ 1. *What is Religion?*

1. The word "religion" is an indefinite word with no fixed meaning.

2. It is one word with many meanings.

3. This is because religion has passed through IV
many stages. The concept at each stage is called 315
Religion though the concept at one stage has not had the same meaning which it had at the preceding stage or is likely to have at the succeeding stage.

4. The conception of religion was never fixed.

5. It has varied from time to time.

6. Because most of the phenomena such as lightning, rain and floods, the occurrence of which the primitive man could not explain, any weird performance done to control the phenomenon was called magic. Religion therefore came to be identified with magic.

7. Then came the second stage in the evolution of religion. In this stage religion came to be identified with beliefs, rituals, ceremonies, prayers and sacrifices.

8. But this conception of religion is derivative.

9. The pivotal point in religion starts with the belief that there exists some power which causes these phenomena which primitive man did not know and could not understand. Magic lost its place at this stage.

10. This power was originally malevolent. But later it was felt that it could also be benevolent.

11. Beliefs, rites, ceremonies and sacrifices were necessary both to propitiate a benevolent power and also to conciliate an angry power.

12. Later that power was called God or the Creator.

13. Then came the third stage that it is this God who created this world and also man.

14. This was followed by the belief that man has

a soul and the soul is eternal and is answerable to God for man's actions in the world.

15. This is, in short, the evolution of the concept of Religion.

16. This is what Religion has come to be and this is what it connotes—belief in God, belief in soul, worship of God, curing of the erring soul, propitiating God by prayers, ceremonies, sacrifices, etc.

§ 2. *How Dhamma Differs From Religion*

1. What the Buddha calls Dhamma differs fundamentally from what is called Religion.

2. What the Buddha calls Dhamma is analogous to what the European theologians call Religion.

3. But there is no greater affinity between the two. On the other hand, the differences between the two are very great.

4. On this account some European theologians refuse to recognize the Buddha's Dhamma as Religion.

5. There need be no regrets over this. The loss is theirs. It does no harm to the Buddha's Dhamma. Rather, it shows what is wanting in Religion.

6. Instead of entering into this controversy it is better to proceed to give an idea of Dhamma and show how it differs from Religion.

7. Religion, it is said, is personal and one must keep it to oneself. One must not let it play its part in public life.

8. Contrary to this, Dhamma is social. It is fundamentally and essentially so.

9. Dhamma is righteousness, which means right relations between man and man in all spheres of life.

10. From this it is evident that one man if he is alone does not need Dhamma.

11. But when there are two men living in relation to each other they must find a place for Dhamma whether they like it or not. Neither can escape it.

12. In other words, Society cannot do without Dhamma.

13. Society has to choose one of the three alternatives.

14. Society may choose not to have any Dhamma, as an instrument of Government. For Dhamma is nothing if it is not an instrument of Government.

15. This means Society chooses the road to anarchy.

16. Secondly, Society may choose the police, i.e., dictatorship as an instrument of Government.

17. Thirdly, Society may choose Dhamma plus the Magistrate wherever people fail to observe the Dhamma.

18. In anarchy and dictatorship liberty is lost.

19. Only in the third liberty survives.

20. Those who want liberty must therefore have Dhamma.

21. Now what is Dhamma ? and why is Dhamma necessary ? According to the Buddha, Dhamma consists of Prajna and Karuna.

22. What is Prajna ? And why Prajna ? Prajna is understanding. The Buddha made Prajna one of the two corner-stones of His Dhamma because he did not wish to leave any room for superstition.

23. What is Karuna ? And why Karuna ? Karuna is love. Because, without it Society can neither live nor grow, that is why the Buddha made it the second corner-stone of His Dhamma.

24. Such is the definition of the Buddha's Dhamma.

25. How different is this definition of Dhamma from that of Religion.

26. So ancient, yet so modern is the definition of Dhamma given by the Buddha.

27. So aboriginal yet so original.

28. Not borrowed from anyone, yet so true.

29. A unique amalgam of Pradnya and Karuna is the Dhamma of the Buddha.

30. Such is the difference between Religion and Dhamma.

§ 3. *The Purpose of Religion and the Purpose of Dhamma*

1. What is the purpose of Religion? What is
IV the purpose of Dhamma? Are they one and the same? Or are they different?

318 2. The answer to these questions are to be found in two dialogues—one between the Buddha and Sunakkhatta and the other between the Buddha and the Brahmin Potthapada.

3. The Exalted One was once staying among the Mallas at Anupiya, one of their towns.

4. Now the Exalted One having robed himself in the early morning, put on his cloak and took his bowl and entered the town for alms.

5. On the way he thought it was too early to go for alms. Therefore he went to the pleasance where Bhaggava the wanderer dwelt and called on him.

6. On seeing the Blessed One Bhaggava got up, saluted him and said, "May it please you, sire, to be seated; here is a seat made ready for you."

7. The Exalted One sat down thereon, and Bhaggava taking a certain low stool sat down beside him. So seated, Bhaggava, the wanderer, spake thus to the Exalted One:

8 "Some days ago, Lord, a good many days ago, Sunakkhatta of the Licchavis called on me and spake thus: 'I have now given up the Exalted One, Bhaggava. I am remaining no longer under him (as my teacher).' Is the fact really so, just as he said?"

9. "It is just so Bhaggava, as Sunakkhatta of the Licchavis said," replied the Blessed One.

10. "Some days ago, Bhaggava, a good many days ago, Sunakkhatta, the Licchavi, came to call on me, and spake thus: 'Sir, I now give up the Exalted One. I will henceforth remain no longer under him (as my teacher).' When he told me this, I said to him: 'But now, Sunakkhatta, have I ever said to you, Come, Sunakkhatta, live under me (as my pupil)?'

11. "'No, sir, you have not.'

12. " Or have you ever said to me: 'Sir, I would fain dwell under the Exalted One (as my teacher) ? '

13. " 'No, sir, I have not.'

14. " Then I asked him 'If I said not the one,
and you said not the other, what are you and what am IV
I that you talk of giving up ? See, foolish one, in 319
how far the fault here is your own.'

15. " 'Well, but, sir, the Exalted One works me no mystic wonders surpassing the power of ordinary men.'

16. " Why, now Sunakkhatta, have I ever said to you: 'Come, take me as your teacher, Sunakkhatta, and I will work for you mystic wonders surpassing the power of ordinary men ? '

17. " 'You have not, sir.'

18. " Or have you ever said to me: 'Sir, I would fain take the Exalted One as my teacher, for he will work for me mystic wonders beyond the powers of ordinary men ? '

19. " 'I have not, sir.'

20. " 'But if I said not the one, and you said not the other, what are you and what am I, foolish man, that you talk of giving up ? What think you, Sunakkhatta ? Whether mystic wonders beyond the power of ordinary man are wrought, or whether they are not is the object for which I teach the Dhamma: that it leads to the thorough destruction of ill for the doer thereof ? '

21. " 'Whether, sir, they are so wrought or not, that is indeed the object for which the Dhamma is taught by the Exalted One.'

22. " 'If then, Sunakkhatta, it matters not to that object whether mystic wonders are wrought or not, of what use to you would be the working of them ? See, foolish one, in how far the fault here is your own.'

23. " 'But, sir, the Exalted One does not reveal to me the beginning of things.'

24. " Why now, Sunakkhatta, have I ever said to you: 'Come, Sunakkhatta, be my disciple and I will reveal to you the beginning of things ? '

25. " ' Sir, you have not.'

26. "Or have you ever said to me: 'I will become the Exalted One's pupil, for he will reveal to me the beginning of things?'

27. "'Sir, I have not.'

IV 28. "'But if I have not said the one and you have not said the other, what are you and what am I, foolish
320 man, that you talk of giving up on that account? What think you, Sunakkhatta? Whether the beginning of things be revealed, or whether it be not, is the object for which I teach the Dhamma that it leads to the thorough destruction of ill for the doer thereof?'

29. "'Whether, sir, they are revealed or not, that is indeed the object for which the Dhamma is taught by the Exalted One.'

30. "'If then, Sunakkhatta, it matters not to that object whether the beginning of things be revealed, or whether it be not, of what use to you would it be to have the beginning of things revealed?'"

31. This illustrates that Religion is concerned with revealing the beginning of things and Dhamma is not.

(2)

The other differences between Religion and Dhamma are brought out in the discussion between the Blessed One and Potthapada.

1. The Blessed One was once staying at Shravasti in Anathapindika's pleasance of the Jeta's wood. Now at that time Potthapada, the wandering mendicant was dwelling in the hall put up in Queen Mallika's park for a debate on general systems of philosophical opinion.

2. There was with him a great following of mendicants; to wit, three hundred. A dialogue took place between the Blessed Lord and Potthapada. Potthapada asked:

3. "Then, sir, if that be so, tell me at least: 'Is the world eternal? Is this alone the truth, and any other view mere folly?'"

4. "That, Potthapada, is a matter on which I have expressed no opinion," replied the Blessed Lord.

5. Then, in the same terms, Potthapada asked each of the following questions :

(i) ‘ Is the world not eternal ? ’

(ii) ‘ Is the world finite ? ’

(iii) ‘ Is the world infinite ? ’ IV

(iv) ‘ Is the soul the same as the body ? ’

(v) ‘ Is the soul one thing, and the body another ? ’ 321

(vi) ‘ Does one who has gained the truth live again after death ? ’

(vii) ‘ Does he not live again after death ? ’

(viii) ‘ Does he both live again and not live again, after death ? ’

(ix) ‘ Does he neither live again, nor not live again, after death ? ’

6. And to each questions the Exalted One made the same reply :—

7. “ That too, Potthapada, is a matter on which I have expressed no opinion.”

8. “ But why has the Exalted One expressed no opinion on that ? ”

9. “ Because this question is not calculated to profit, it is not concerned with the Dhamma, it does not redound even to the elements of right conduct, nor to detachment, nor to purification from lusts, nor to quietude, nor to tranquillisation of heart, nor to real knowledge, nor to the insight (of the higher stages of the Path), nor to Nirvana. Therefore is it that I express no opinion upon it. ”

10. “ Then what is it that the Exalted One has determined ? ”

11. “ I have expounded, Potthapada, what Dukkha is ; I have expounded what is the origin of Dukkha ; I have expounded what is the cessation of Dukkha : I have expounded what is the method by which one may reach the cessation of Dukkha.”

12. “ And why has the Exalted One put forth a statement as to that ? ”

13. “ Because that question, Potthapada, is calculated to profit, is concerned with the Dhamma, redounds to the beginnings of right conduct, to detachment, to purification from lusts, to quietude, to tran-

quillisation of heart, to real knowledge, to the insight of the higher stages of the Path and to Nirvana. Therefore is it, Potthapada, that I have put forward a statement as to that."

14. In this dialogue it is clearly put forth what is the subject matter of Religion and what is not the subject matter of Dhamma. The two are poles apart.

15. The purpose of Religion is to explain the origin of the world. The purpose of Dhamma is to reconstruct the world.

§ 4. *Morality and Religion*

1. What is the place of morality in Religion ?
2. As a matter of truth morality has no place in Religion.
3. The content of religion consists of God, soul, prayers, worship, rituals, ceremonies and sacrifices.
4. Morality comes in only wherein man comes in relation to man.
5. Morality comes in into religion as a side wind to maintain peace and order.
6. Religion is a triangular piece.
7. Be good to your neighbour because you are both children of God.
8. That is the argument of religion.
9. Every religion preaches morality but morality is not the root of religion.
10. It is a wagon attached to it. It is attached and detached as the occasion requires.
11. The action of morality in the functioning of religion is therefore casual and occasional.
12. Morality in religion is therefore not effective.

§ 5. *Dhamma and Morality*

1. What is the place of morality in Dhamma ?
2. The simple answer is Morality is Dhamma and Dhamma is Morality.
3. In other words, in Dhamma morality takes the place of God although there is no God in Dhamma.

4. In Dhamma there is no place for prayers, pilgrimages, rituals, ceremonies or sacrifices.

5. Morality is the essence of Dhamma. Without it there is no Dhamma.

6. Morality in Dhamma arises from the direct necessity for man to love man.

7. It does not require the sanction of God. It is not to please God that man has to be moral. It is for his own good that man has to love man.

§ 6. *Mere Morality is not Enough. It must be Sacred and Universal*

1. When is a thing sacred? Why is a thing sacred?

2. In every human society, primitive or advanced, there are some things or beliefs which it regards as sacred and the rest as profane.

3. When a thing or belief has reached the stage of being sacred (pavitra) it means that it cannot be violated. Indeed it cannot be touched. It is taboo.

4. Contrary to this, a thing or a belief which is profane (apavitra), i.e., outside the field of the sacred, may be violated. It means one can act contrary to it, without feeling any fear or qualms of conscience.

5. The sacred is something holy. To transgress it is a sacrilege.

6. Why is a thing made sacred? To confine the scope of the question to the matter in hand, why morality should have been made sacred?

7. Three factors seem to have played their part in making morality sacred.

8. The first factor is the social need for protecting the best.

9. The background of this question lies imbedded in what is called the struggle of existence and the survival of the fittest.

10. This arises out of the theory of evolution. It is common knowledge that evolution takes place through a struggle for existence because the means of food supply in early times were so limited.

11. The struggle is bitter. Nature is said to be red in claw and tooth.

12. In this struggle which is bitter and bloody only the fittest survive.

13. Such is the original state of society.

14. In the course of ancient past someone must have raised the question, Is the fittest (the strongest) the best? Would not the weakest if protected be ultimately the best for advancing the ends and aims of society?

15. The then prevailing state of society seems to have given an answer in the affirmative.

16. Then comes the question what is the way to protect the weak?

17. Nothing less than to impose some restraints upon the fittest.

18. In this lies the origin and necessity for morality.

19. This morality had to be sacred because it was imposed originally on the fittest, i.e., the strongest.

20. This has very serious consequences.

21. First, does morality in becoming social become anti-social?

22. It is not that there is no morality among thieves. There is morality among businessmen. There is morality among fellow castemen and there is also morality among a gang of robbers.

23. But this morality is marked by isolation and exclusiveness. It is a morality to protect "group interest." It is therefore anti-social.

24. It is the isolation and exclusiveness of this kind of morality which throws its anti-social spirit in relief.

25. The same is true where a group observes morality because it has interests of its own to protect.

26. The results of this group organization of society are far-reaching.

27. If society continues to consist of anti-social groups, society will remain a disorganized and a factional society.

28. The danger of a disorganized and factional

state of society is that it sets up a number of different models and standards.

29. In the absence of common models and common standards society cannot be a harmonious whole.

30. With such different models and standards it is impossible for the individual to attain consistency of mind.

31. A society which rests upon the supremacy of one group over another irrespective of its rational or proportionate claims inevitably leads to conflict.

32. The only way to put a stop to conflict is to have common rules of morality which are sacred to all.

33. There is the third factor which requires morality to be made sacred and universal. It is to safeguard the growth of the individual.

34. Under the struggle for existence or under group rule the interests of the individuals are not safe.

35. The group set-up prevents an individual from acquiring consistency of mind which is possible only when society has common ideals, common models. His thoughts are led astray and this creates a mind whose seeing unity is forced and distorted.

36. Secondly the group set-up leads to discrimination and denial of justice.

37. The group set-up leads to stratification of classes. Those who are masters remain masters and those who are born in slavery remain slaves. Owners remain owners and workers remain workers. The privileged remain privileged and the serfs remain serfs.

38. This means that there can be liberty for some but not for all. This means that there can be equality for a few but none for the majority.

39. What is the remedy? The only remedy lies in making fraternity universally effective.

40. What is fraternity? It is nothing but another name for brotherhood of men which is another name for morality.

41. This is why the Buddha preached that Dhamma is morality and as Dhamma is sacred so is morality.

PART II

How Similarities in Terminology Conceal Fundamental Difference

Section I—*Rebirth*

1. Preliminary.
2. Rebirth of What ?
3. Rebirth of Whom ?

Section II—*Karma*

1. Is the Buddhist doctrine of Karma the same as the Brahminic doctrine ?

2. Did the Buddha believe in past Karma having effect on future life ?

3. Did the Buddha believe in past Karma having effect on future life ?—concluded.

Section III—*Ahimsa*

1. The different ways in which it is interpreted and followed.
2. The true meaning of Ahimsa.

Section IV—*Transmigration*

Section V—*Causes of his Misunderstandings*

SECTION I

REBIRTH

§ *1. Preliminary*

IV

1. What happens after death is a question often asked. 329

2. The contemporaries of the Buddha held two different views. One set was called Eternalist and the other was called Annihilationist.

3. The Eternalist said that the soul knows no death: therefore life is eternal. It is renewed by rebirth.

4. The thesis of the Annihilationists was summed up in one word, *Ucchedvad*, which meant that death is the end of everything. There is nothing left after death.

5. The Buddha was not an eternalist. For it involved a belief in the existence of a separate, immortal soul to which he was opposed.

6. Was the Buddha an annihilationist? With his belief in the non-existence of the soul, the Buddha would naturally be expected to be an annihilationist.

7. But in the Alagaddupamma-Sutta the Buddha complains that he is called an annihilationist when as a matter of fact he is not.

8. This is what he says: "Though this is what I affirm and what I preach yet some recluses and Brahmins, wrongly, erroneously and falsely charge me in defiance of facts, with being an annihilationist and with preaching the disintegration, destruction and extirpation of human beings.

9. "It is just what I am not, and what I do not affirm, that is wrongly, erroneously, and falsely charged against me by these good people who would make me out to be an annihilationist."

10. If this statement is a genuine one and is not an interpolation by those who wanted to foist a Brahmanic doctrine on Buddhism the statement raises a serious dilemma

11. How can the Buddha not believe in the existence of the soul and yet say that he is not an annihilationist?

12. This raises the question : Did the Buddha believe in rebirth ?

§ 2. *Rebirth of What?*

1. Did the Buddha believe in rebirth ?

2. The answer is in the affirmative.

3. It is better to split this question further into two parts : (1) Rebirth of What and (2) Rebirth of Whom.

4. It is better to take each one of these two questions separately.

5. Here we may consider the first, *Rebirth of What.*

6. This question is almost always ignored. It is because of the mixing of the two questions that so much confusion has arisen.

7. According to the Buddha there are four elements of Existence which go to compose the body. They are (1) Prithvi ; (2) Apa ; (3) Tej ; and (4) Vayu.

8. Question is when the human body dies what happens to these four elements? Do they also die along with dead body ? Some say that they do.

9. The Buddha said no. They join the mass of similar elements floating in (Akash) space.

10. When the four elements from this floating mass join together a new birth takes place.

11. This is what the Buddha meant by rebirth.

12. The elements need not and are not necessarily from the same body which is dead. They may be drawn from different dead bodies.

13. It must be noted that the body dies. But the elements are ever living.

14. This is the kind of rebirth in which the Buddha believed.

15. Great light is thrown upon the subject by Sariputta in his dialogue with Maha-Kotthita.

16. It is said that once when the Lord was staying at Shravasti in Jeta's Grove in Anathapindika's Aram, the Maha-Kotthita rising up at even-tide from his meditations, went to Sariputta and asked him to elucidate some of the questions which troubled him.

17. The following was one of them.

18. *Maha-Kotthita* asked : " How many factors has the first ecstasy (Dhyana) put from it and how many does it retain ? "

19. *Sariputta* replied : " Five of each. Gone IV
are lusts, malevolence, torpor, worry and doubt. Obser-
vation, reflection, zest, satisfaction and a focussed 331
heart persist."

20. *Maha-Kotthita* asked : " Take the five senses of sight, sound, smell, taste and touch,—each with its own particular province and range of function, separate and mutually distinct. What ultimate base have they ? Who enjoys all their five provinces and ranges ? "

21. *Sariputta* replied: " Mind (Mano). "

22. *Maha-Kotthita* asked : " On what do these five faculties of sense depend ? "

23. *Sariputta* replied : " On vitality."

24. *Maha-Kotthita* asked : " On what does vitality depend ?

25. *Sariputta* : " On heat."

26. *Maha-Kotthita* asked : " On what does heat depend ? "

27. *Sariputta* replied : " On vitality."

28. *Maha-Kotthita* asked : " You say that vitality depends on heat, you also say that heat depends on vitality ! What precisely is the meaning to be attached to this ? "

29. *Sariputta* replied : " I will give you an illustration. Just as in the case of a lamp, the light reveals the flame and the flame the light, so vitality depends upon heat and heat on vitality.

30. *Maha-Kotthita* asked : " How many things must quit the body before it is flung aside and cast away like a senseless log ? "

31. *Sariputta* answered : " Vitality, heat and consciousness."

32. *Maha-Kotthita* asked : " What is the difference between a lifeless corpse and an almsman in trance, in whom perception and feelings are stilled?"

33. *Sariputta* replied : " In the corpse not only

are the plastic forces of the body and speech and mind stilled and quiescent but also vitality is exhausted, heat is quenched and the faculties of sense broken up ; whereas in the almsman in trance vitality persists, heat abides, and the faculties are clear, although respiration, observation and perception are stilled and quiescent."

34. This probably is the best and most complete exposition of Death or Annihilation.

35. There is only one lacuna in this dialogue. Maha-Kotthita should have asked Sariputta one question. What is heat?

36. What answer Sariputta would have given it is not easy to imagine. But there can be no doubt that heat means energy.

37. Thus amplified, the real answer to the question : What happens when the body dies? is : The body ceases to produce energy.

38. But this is only a part of the answer. Because death also means that whatever energy that had escaped from the body joins the general mass of energy playing about in the Universe.

39. Annihilation has therefore a two-fold aspect. In one of its aspects it means cession of production of energy. In another aspect it means a new addition to the stock of general floating mass of energy.

40. It is probably because of this two-fold aspect of annihilation that the Buddha said that he was not an absolute annihilationist. He was an annihilationist so far as soul was concerned. He was not an annihilationist so far as matter was concerned.

41. So interpreted it is easy to understand why the Buddha said that he was not an annihilationist. He believed in the regeneration of matter and not in the rebirth of the soul.

42. So interpreted, the Buddha's view is in consonance with science.

43. It is only in this sense that the Buddha could be said to have believed in rebirth.

44. Energy is never lost. That is what science affirms. Annihilation in the sense that after death

nothing is left would be contrary to science. For it would mean that energy is not constant in volume.

45. This is the only way by which the dilemma could be solved.

§ 3. *Rebirth of Whom*?

1. The most difficult question is Rebirth of Whom.

2. Does the same dead person take a new birth?

3. Did the Buddha believe in this thesis? The answer is " Most improbable."

4. The answer depends upon the elements of existence of the dead man meeting together and forming a new body then the possibility of the Rebirth of the same Sentient being is possible.

5. If a new body is formed after a mixture or the different elements of the different men who are dead then there is rebirth but not the rebirth of the same sentient being.

6. This point has been well explained by sister Khema to King Pasenadi.

7. Once the Exalted One was staying near Savatthi at Jeta Grove in Anathapindika's Aram.

8. Now on that occasion the sister Khema, after going her rounds among the Kosalana, took up her quarters at Toranavatthu, between Shravasti and Saketa.

9. Now the Rajah Pasenadi of Kosala was journeying from Saketa to Shravasti, and midway between Saketa and Shravasti he put up for one night at Toranavatthu.

10. The Rajah Pasenadi of Kosala called a certain man and said : " Come thou, good fellow ! Find out some recluse or brahmin such that I can wait upon him today."

11. " Even so, your majesty," said that man in reply to the Rajah Pasenadi of Kosala, and after wandering through all Toranavatthu he saw not any one, either recluse or brahmin, on whom the Rajah Pasenadi might wait.

12. Then that man saw the sister Khema, who

had come to reside at Toranavatthu. And on seeing her he went back to the Rajah Pasenadi of Kosala, and said :—

13. “Your Majesty, there is no recluse or
IV brahmin in Toranavatthu such that your majesty can
wait upon him. But, your majesty, there is a sister
334 named Khema, a woman-disciple of that Exalted One. Now of this lady a lovely rumour has gone abroad, that she is sage, accomplished, shrewd, widely learned, a brilliant talker, of goodly ready wit. Let your majesty wait upon her.”

14. So the Rajah Pasenadi of Kosala went to visit the sister Khema, and on coming to her saluted and sat down at one side. So seated he said to her :—

15. “How say you, lady? Does the Tathagata exist after death?”

16. “That also, maharajah is not revealed by the Exalted One.”

17. “How then, lady? When asked ‘Does the Tathagata exist after death?’ you reply, “That is not revealed by the Exalted One,’ and, when I ask . . . the other questions, you make the same reply. Pray, lady, what is the reason, what is the cause, why this thing is not revealed by the Exalted One?”

18. “Now in this matter, maharajah, I will question you. Do you reply as you think fit. Now how say you, maharajah? Have you some accountant, some ready reckoner or calculator, able to count the sand in Ganges, thus : There are so many hundred grains, or so many thousand grains, or so many hundreds of thousands of grains of sand?”

19. “No, indeed, lady.”

20. “Then have you some accountant, ready reckoner or calculator able to reckon the water in the mighty ocean, thus : There are so many gallons of water, so many hundreds, so many thousands, so many hundreds of thousand gallons of water?”

21. “No, indeed, lady.”

22. “How is that?”

23. “Mighty is the ocean, lady, deep, boundless, unfathomable.”

24. " Even so, maharajah, if one should try to define the Tathagata by his bodily form, that bodily form of the Tathagata is abandoned, cut down at the root, made like a palm-tree stump, made some thing that is not, made of a nature not to spring up again in future time. Set free from reckoning as body, maharajah, is the Tathagata. He is deep, boundless, unfathomable, just like the mighty ocean. To say, ' The Tathagata exists after death ' does not apply. To say, ' The Tathagata exists not after death,' does not apply. To say, 'The Tathagata both exists and exists not, neither exists nor not exists after death,' does not apply.

25. " If one should try to define the Tathagata by feeling,—that feeling of the Tathagata is abandoned, cut down at the root . . . Yet free from reckoning as feeling is the Tathagata, maharajah, deep, boundless, unfathomable like the mighty ocean. To say, ' The Tathagata exists after death . . . exists not after death,' does not apply.

26. " So also if one should try to define the Tathagata by perception, by the activities, by consciousness . . . set free from reckoning by consciousness is the Tathagata, deep, boundless, unfathomable as the mighty ocean. To say, ' The Tathagata exists after death . . . exists not after death,' does not apply."

27. Then the Rajah Pasenadi of Kosala was delighted with the words of the sister Khema, and took pleasure therein. And he rose from his seat, saluted her by the right and went away.

28. Now on another occasion the Rajah went to visit the Exalted One, and on coming to him saluted him and sat down at one side. So seated he said to the Exalted One :

29. " Pray, Lord, does the Tathagata exist after death ? "

30. " Not revealed by me, maharajah, is this matter."

31. " Then Lord, the Tathagata does not exist after death."

32. " That also, maharajah, is not revealed by me."

33. He then asks the other questions and gets the same reply.

IV 34. " How then, Lord ? When I ask the question,
' Does the Tathagata exist ? . . . does he not exist
336 after death ? ' you reply, ' It is not revealed by me.'
Pray, Lord, what is the reason, what is the cause why this thing is not revealed by the Exalted One ? "

35. " Now, maharajah, I will question you. Do you reply as you think fit. Now what say you, maharajah ? Have you some accountant . . . (the rest is exactly as before).'

36. " Wonderful, Lord ! Strange it is, Lord, how the explanation both of Master and disciple, both in spirit and in letter, will agree, will harmonize, will not be inconsistent, that is, in any word about the highest.

37. " On a certain occasion, Lord, I went to visit the sister Khema, and asked her the meaning of this matter, and she gave me the meaning in the very words, in the very syllables used by the Exalted One. Wonderful, Lord ! Strange it is, Lord, how the explanation both of Master and disciple will agree, will harmonize, in spirit and in letter, how they will not be inconsistent,—that is, in any word about the highest.

38. " Well, Lord, now we must be going. We are busy folk. We have many things to do.

39. " Do now what you think it is time for, maharajah."

40. Thereupon the Rajah Pasenadi of Kosala was delighted with the words of the Exalted One and welcomed them. And he rose from his seat, saluted the Exalted One by the right and went away.

SECTION II

KARMA

§ *1. Is the Buddhist Doctrine of Karma the same as the Brahminic Doctrine?* IV

1. There is no doctrine in the Buddha's Dhamma which has created so much confusion as this doctrine of Karma. 337

2. What is its place in the Buddha's Dhamma and what is its significance which has already been told.

3. Ignorant Hindus out of sheer want of understanding say by comparing merely the similarity of words that Buddhism is the same as Brahmanism or Hinduism.

4. The educated and orthodox section of the Brahmins also do the same. They do so deliberately to mislead the ignorant masses.

5. The educated Brahmins know full well that the Buddhist Law of Karma is quite different from the Brahminic Law of Karma. Yet they keep on saying that Buddhism is the same as Brahmanism and Hinduism.

6. The similarity in terminology gives them an easy handle for their false and malicious propaganda.

7. It is, therefore, necessary to examine the position closely

8. The Buddha's Law of Karma, however much may be similarity of words cannot be the same in its connotation as the Brahminic Law of Karma.

9. The premises of the two are so widely different, indeed so widely opposed that the result of the two cannot be the same. They must be different.

10. The principles of the Hindu Law of Karma may be stated seriatim for convenience.

11. The Hindu Law of Karma is based on the soul. The Buddhist is not. In fact there is no soul in Buddhism.

12. The Brahminic Law of Karma is hereditary.

13. It goes on from life to life. This is so because of the transmigration of the soul.

14. This cannot be true of the Buddhist Law of Karma. This is also because there is no soul.

15. The Hindu Law of Karma is based on the existence of a soul which is distinct from the body. When the body dies the soul does not die. The soul flies away.

16. This is not true of the Buddhist Law of Karma.

17. According to the Hindu Law of Karma what happens when a man does a karma is this. His act produces two-fold results. It affects the doer and secondly it produces an impress upon his soul.

18. Each act he does produces an impress upon his soul.

19. When a man dies and when his soul escapes, the soul is full of such impressions.

20. It is these impressions which determine his birth and status in his future life.

21. This Hindu theory is inconsistent with the Buddhist theory of no-soul.

22. For these reasons the Buddhist doctrine of Karma cannot be and is not the same as the Hindu doctrine of Karma.

23. It is therefore simply foolish to talk about the Buddhist doctrine of Karma being the same as the Brahminic doctrine of Karma.

24. All that one can say is beware of this jugglery.

§ 2. *Did the Buddha believe in Past Karma having effect on Future Life?*

1. The Law of Karma was enunciated by the Buddha. He was the first to say : "Reap as you sow."

2. He was so emphatic about the Law of Karma that he maintained that there could be no moral order unless there was a stern observance of the Law of Karma.

3. The Buddha's Law of Karma applied only to Karma and its effect on present life.

4. There is, however, an extended doctrine of Karma. According to it Karma includes Karma done in past life or lives.

5. If a man is born in a poor family it is because of his past bad karma. If a man is born in a rich family it is because of his past good karma.

6. If a man is born with a congenital defect it is because of his past bad karma.

7. This is a very pernicious doctrine. For in this interpretation of karma there is no room left for human effort. Everything is predetermined for him by his past karma.

8. This extended doctrine is often found to be attributed to the Buddha.

9. Did the Buddha believe in such a doctrine?

10. To examine this extended doctrine properly it is better to change the language in which it is usually expressed.

11. Instead of saying that past karma is transmitted it should be better if it was said that past karma is inherited.

12. This change of language enables us to test it by the law of heredity. At the same time it does no harm to the doctrine either to its *de jure* or *de facto* connotation.

13. This restatement makes it possible to pose the two questions which could not otherwise be posed and without answering which the matter could not be made clear.

14. The first question is how is past karma inherited? What is the process?

15. The second question is what is the nature of past karma in terms of heredity? Is it an inherent characteristic or acquired characteristic?

16. What do we inherit from our parents?

17. Starting with science the new individual begins when a sperm enters the egg. Fertilization consists in fusion of the head of the sperm with the nucleus of the egg.

18. Each human being takes its origin from the union of two bits of living matter, an egg from the

mother which has been fertilized by a single sperm from the father.

19. That human birth is genetic is told by the Buddha to a Yakkha who came to discuss the matter with him.

20. The Exalted One was then staying near Rajagraha, on the hill called Indra's Peak.

21. Now that Yakkha drew near to the Exalted One and addressed him as follows :

> ' Material form is not the living soul '
> So says th' Enlightened One. Then how doth soul possess this body ?
> Whence to soul doth come
> Our bunch of bones and bowels ?
> How doth soul within the mother-cave suspended bide ?

22. To this the Exalted One replied:

> At first the *Kalala* takes birth, and thence the *abudde*.
> Therefrom the *pesi* grows,
> Developing as *ghana* in its turn.
> Now in the *ghana* doth appear the hair,
> The down, the nails.
> And whatsoever food and drink the mother of him takes, thereby the man in mother's womb doth live and grow.

23. But the Hindu doctrine differs.

24. It says that the body is genetic. But the soul is not. It is implanted into the body from outside—the doctrine is unable to specify the source.

25. Turning to the second question as to what is the nature of past karma, it must be determined whether it is an inherent characteristic or an acquired characteristic.

26. Unless an answer to this question is forthcoming it cannot be tested by the scientific theory of heredity.

27. But assuming there is an answer one way or the other to this question how is it possible to get any help from science whether it is a sensible theory or senseless theory.

28. According to science a child inherits the characteristics of his parents.

29. In the Hindu doctrine of karma a child inherits nothing from its parents except the body. The past karma in the Hindu doctrine is the inheritance of the child by the child and for the child.

30. The parents contributes nothing. The child brings everything.

31. Such a doctrine is nothing short of an absurdity.

32. As shown above the Buddha did not believe in such an absurdity.

33. " Yes, if it were not reborn; but if it were, no. "

34. " Give me an illustration. "

35. " Suppose, O king, a man were to steal another man's mangoes, would the thief deserve punishment ? "

36. " Yes."

37. " But he would not have stolen the mangoes the other set in the ground. Why would he deserve punishment ? "

38. " Because those he stole were the result of those that were planted."

39. " Just so, great king. this name-and-form commits deeds, either pure or impure, and by that karma another name-and-form is reborn. And therefore is it not set free from its evil deeds ? "

40. " Very good, Nagasena ! "

41. The king said : " When deeds are committed, Nagasena by one name-and-form, what becomes of those deeds ? "

42. " The deeds would follow it, O king, like a shadow that never leaves it."

43. " Can any one point out those deeds, saying: ' Here are those deeds or there ? '

44. " No. "

45. " Give me an illustration."

46. " Now what do you think, O king ? Can any one point out the fruits which a tree has not yet produced, saying :

47. ' Here they are, or there ? ' "

48. " Certainly not, sir,"

49. " Just so, great king, so long as the continuity of life is not cut off, it is impossible to point out the
IV deeds that are done."

50. " Very good, Nagasena."
342

§ 3. *Did the Buddha believe in Past Karma having effect on Future Life?* —concluded

1. The Buddha's doctrine of Past Karma is thus in keeping with science.

2. He did not believe in the inheritance of Past Karma.

3. How can he, having held to the view that birth is genetic and whatever inheritance comes to the child it comes through its parents ?

4. Apart from logic there is more direct evidence on the point contained in a sutta called the Cula—Dukkha—Khanda—Sutta which contains a dialogue between the Buddha and the Jains.

5. In this dialogue this is what the Buddha says :—" Niganthas, you have done evil in the past ; extirpate it by these severe austerities. Every present restraint on body, speech and mind will hereafter undo the evil doings of the past. Hence, by expelling through penance all past misdeeds, and by not committing fresh misdeeds, the future becomes cleared; with the future cleared, the past is wiped out ; with the past wiped out, Ill is no more ; with Ill no more (Painful) feelings are no more ; and, with painful feelings now no more, all Ill will be outworn.—This teaching commends and approves itself to us, and we rejoice in it."

6. Thereupon, I said to those Niganthas :— " Do you know, reverend sirs, whether you had an existence before this or you were not non-existent ?"

7. " No, Sir. "

8. " Do you know that, in a former existence, you were guilty, and not guiltless, of misdeeds ? "

9. " No. "

10. " Do you know that (in that former existence) you were guilty, and not guiltless, of this or that specific misdeed ? "

11. " No."

12. Secondly the Buddha asserts that the status of a man may be governed not so much by heredity as by his environment.

13. In the Devadaha—Sutta this is what the Buddha says : Some recluses and Brahmins there are who affirm and hold the view that, whatsoever the individual experiences—be it pleasant or unpleasant or neither—all comes from former actions. Hence, by expiation and purge of former misdeeds and by not committing fresh misdeeds, nothing accrues for the future, the misdeeds die away ; as misdeeds die away, Ill dies away ; as Ill dies away, feelings die away ; and as feelings die away, all Ill will wear out and pass. This is what the Niganthas affirm.

14. If it is because of their birth's environment that creatures experience pleasure and pain, the Niganthas are blameworthy, and they are also blameworthy, if environment is not the cause.

15. Now these statements of the Buddha are very relevant. How could the Buddha throw doubt on past karma if he believed in it ? How could the Buddha maintain pain and pleasure in present life being due to environment if he believed that it was due to past karma ?

16. The doctrine of past karma is a purely Brahminic doctrine. Past karma taking effect in present life is quite consistent with the Brahminic doctrine of soul, the effect of karma on soul. But it is quite inconsistent with the Buddhist doctrine of non-soul.

17. It has been bodily introduced into Buddhism by some one who wanted to make Buddhism akin to Hinduism or who did not know what the Buddhist doctrine was.

18. This is one reason why it must be held that the Buddha could not have preached such a doctrine.

19. There is another and a more general reason why it must be held that the Buddha could not have preached such a doctrine.

20. The basis of the Hindu doctrine of past
IV karma as the regulator of future life is an iniquitous doctrine. What could have been the purpose of
344 inventing such a doctrine?

21. The only purpose one can think of is to enable the state or the society to escape responsibility for the condition of the poor and the lowly.

22. Otherwise such an inhuman and absurd doctrine could never have been invented.

23. It is impossible to imagine that the Buddha who was known as the Maha Karunika could have supported such a doctrine.

SECTION III

AHIMSA

§ 1. *The different ways in which it was interpreted and followed* IV

1. Ahimsa or non-killing forms a very important part of the Buddha's teachings. 345

2. It is intimately connected with Karuna and Maitri.

3. The question has, however, been raised whether His Ahimsa was absolute in its obligation or only relative. Was it only a principle? Or was it a rule?

4. People who accept the Buddha's teachings find it difficult to accept Ahimsa as an absolute obligation. They say that such a definition of Ahimsa involves the sacrifice of good for evil, the sacrifice of virtue for vice.

5. This question requires to be clarified. There is no subject which is a matter of greater confusion than this subject of Ahimsa.

6. How have the people of Buddhist countries understood and practised Ahimsa?

7. This is an important question which must be taken into account.

8. The monks of Ceylon fought against and asked the people of Ceylon to fight against the foreign invaders.

9. On the other hand the monks of Burma refused to fight against the foreign invaders and asked the Burmese people not to fight.

10. The Burmese people eat eggs but not fish.

11. This is how Ahimsa is understood and followed.

12. Recently the German Buddhist Association passed a resolution by which they accepted all the Panch Silas except the first which deals with Ahimsa.

13. This is the position about the Doctrine of Ahimsa.

§ 2. *True Meaning of Ahimsa.*

1. What does Ahimsa mean?

2. The Buddha has nowhere given any definition of Ahimsa. In fact he has very seldom, if at all,
IV referred to the subject in specific terms.

346 3. One has, therefore to spell out his intention from circumstantial evidence.

4. The first circumstantial evidence on the point is that the Buddha had no objection to eating meat if it was offered to him as part of his alms.

5. The monk can eat meat offered to him provided he was not a party to the killing of it.

6. He resisted the opposition of Devadatta who insisted that the monks should be prohibited from eating meat given to them by way of alms.

7. The next piece of evidence on the point is that he was only opposed to the killing of animals in yajna (sacrifice). This he has himself said.

8. Ahimsa Permo Dharma is an extreme Doctrine. It is a Jain Doctrine. It is not a Buddhist Doctrine.

9. There is another piece of evidence which is more direct than circumstantial which almost amounts to a definition of Ahimsa. He has said: "Love all so that you may not wish to kill any." This is a positive way of stating the principle of Ahimsa.

10. From this it appears that the doctrine of Ahimsa does not say " Kill not. It says love all."

11. In the light of these statements it is quite easy to have a clear understanding of what the Buddha meant by Ahimsa.

12. It is quite clear that Buddha meant to make a distinction between will to kill and need to kill.

13. He did not ban killing where there was need to kill.

14. What he banned was killing where there was nothing but the will to kill.

15. So understood there is no confusion in the Buddhist doctrine of Ahimsa.

16. It is a perfectly sound or moral doctrine which everyone must respect.

17. No doubt he leaves it to every individual to decide whether the need to kill is there. But with whom else could it be left. Man has Pradnya and he must use it.

18. A moral man may be trusted to draw the line at the right point.

19. Brahminism has in it the will to kill.

20. Jainism has in it the will never to kill.

21. The Buddha's Ahimsa is quite in keeping with his middle path.

22. To put it differently the Buddha made a distinction between Principle and Rule. He did not make Ahimsa a matter of Rule. He enunciated it as a matter of Principle or way of life.

23. In this he no doubt acted very wisely.

24. A principle leaves you freedom to act. A rule does not. Rule either breaks you or you break the rule.

SECTION IV

TRANSMIGRATION

1. The Blessed Lord preached that there was
IV rebirth. But the Blessed Lord also preached that
there was no transmigration.

348 2. There were not wanting people who criticized the Lord for preaching what they regarded as two such contradictory doctrines.

3. How can there be rebirth unless there is transmigration ? asked the critics.

4. There is here a case of rebirth without transmigration, they said. Can this be ?

5. There is no contradiction. There can be rebirth although there is no transmigration.

6. This has been well explained by Nagasena in his replies to the questions of King Milinda.

7. Milinda, King of Bactria, asked Nagasena— " Did the Buddha believe in Rebirth (Transmigration) ?"

8. His reply was " Yes."

9. " Is this not a contradiction ?"

10. Nagasena replied, " No."

11. " Can there be rebirth without a soul ?"

12. Nagasena said, " Of course, yes, there can be."

13. " Explain how it can be."

14. The king said : " Where there is no transmigration, Nagasena, can there be rebirth ? "

15. " Yes, there can."

16. " But how can that be ? Give me an illustration."

17. " Suppose a man, O king, were to light a lamp from another lamp, can it be said that the one transmigrates from, or to, the other ? "

18. " Certainly not."

19. " Just so, great king, is rebirth without transmigration."

20. " Give me a further illustration."

21. " Do you recollect, great king, having learnt, when you were a boy, some verse or other from your teacher ? "

22. " Yes, I recollect that."

23. " Well then, did that verse transmigrate from your teacher ? "

24. " Certainly not."

25. " Just so, great king, is rebirth without transmigration." IV

26. " Very good, Nagasena ! "

27. The king said : " Is there such a thing, Nagasena, as the soul ? " 349

28. " In the highest sense, O king, there is no such thing."

29. " Very good, Nagasena ! "

SECTION V

CAUSES OF THIS MISUNDERSTANDING

1. What the Buddha preached was heard by his
IV audience, which largely consisted of the Bhikkus.

2. It is the Bhikkus who reported to the people
350 at large what the Buddha had said on any particular matter.

3. The art of writing had not yet developed. The Bhikkus had therefore to memorize what they had heard. Not every Bhikku cared to memorize what he heard. But there were some who had made it their profession to memorize. They were called Bhanakas.

4. The Buddhist canonical literature is as vast as ocean. To memorize all this was indeed a great feat.

5. In reporting the Buddha it has often been found that he has been misreported.

6. Many cases of misreporting had been brought to the knowledge of the Buddha while he was alive.

7. Reference may be made by way of illustration to five such cases. One is mentioned in the Alagaddupama Sutta and the other in the Maha-Kamma-Vibhanga Sutta, a third in the Kannakatthala Sutta, fourth in the Maha-Tanha-Sankhya Sutta and fifth in the Jivaka Sutta.

8. There were perhaps many more such cases of misreporting. For we find that even the Bhikkus going to the Buddha asking him to tell them what they should do in such contingencies.

9. The cases of misreporting are common with regard to karma and rebirth.

10. These doctrines have also a place in the Brahminic religion consequently it was easy for the Bhanakas to incorporate the Brahminic tenets into the Buddhist Religion.

11. One has therefore to be very careful in accepting what is said in the Buddhist canonical literature as being the word of the Buddha.

12. There is however one test which is available.

13. If there is anything which could be said with confidence it is : He was nothing if not rational,

if not logical. Anything therefore which is rational and logical, other things being equal, may be taken to be the word of the Buddha.

14. The second thing is that the Buddha never cared to enter into a discussion which was not profitable for man's welfare. Therefore anything attributed to the Buddha which did not relate to man's welfare cannot be accepted to be the word of the Buddha.

15. There is a third test. It is that the Buddha divided all matters into two classes. Those about which he was certain and those about which he was not certain. On matters which fell into class I, he has stated his views definitely and conclusively. On matters which fell into class II, he has expressed his views. But they are only tentative views.

16. In discussing the three questions about which there is doubt and difference it is necessary to bear these tests in mind before deciding what the view of the Buddha was thereon.

PART III

The Buddhist Way of Life

1. On good, evil and sin.
2. On craving and lust.
3. On hurt and ill-will.
4. On anger and enmity.
5. On man, mind and impurities.
6. On self and self-conquest.
7. On wisdom, justice and good company.
8. On thoughtfulness and mindfulness.
9. On vigilance, earnestness and boldness.
10. On sorrow and happiness; On Charity and Kindness.
11. On hypocrisy.
12. On following the Right Way.
13. Mix not true Dhamma with false Dhamma.

§ *1. On Good, Evil and Sin*

1. Do good. Be no party to evil. Commit no sin.

2. This is the Buddhist way of life.

3. If a man should do that which is good, let IV
him do it again and again, let him turn the desires of 355
his heart thereto. Happy is the heaping of good.

4. Think not casually of the good saying, " It will not come to me." Drop by drop is the water pot filled. By little added to little does good grow.

5. But well done is that deed which brings one no regrets, the fruit whereof is received with delight and satisfaction.

6. Well done is the deed which done brings no regrets, the fruit whereof is received with delight and satisfaction.

7. If a man does what is good, let him do it again ; let him delight in it; the accumulation of good is delightful.

8. Even a good man sees evil days so long as his good deed does not ripen; but when his good deed ripens, then does the good man see good things.

9. Let no man think lightly of good, saying in his heart, it will not come right unto me. Even by the falling of water drops a water-pot is filled—the wise man becomes full of good, even if he gathers it little by little.

10. Far surpassing the fragrance of sandal or incense or lotus or jasmine, is the fragrance of virtue.

11. Faint is this fragrance of incense and sandal, but the fragrance of virtue ascends to the highest place.

12. Treat not lightly of evil, saying it will not come to me. Drop by drop is the water pot filled. By little added to little evil accumulates.

13. It is not well to do a deed which done brings regrets, the fruit whereof is received with tears and lamentations.

14. If a man speaks or acts evil of mind, suffering follows him close as the wheel the hoof of the beast that draws the cart.

15. Follow not after things evil. Dwell not in negligence. Cherish not false ideas.

16. Hasten towards the excellent, suppress all evil thoughts. Who so is backward in doing good, his mind delights in evil.

IV
17. It is not well to do that deed which done
356 brings regrets, the fruit whereof is received with tears
and lamentations.

18. Even an evil-doer sees happiness so long as his evil deed does not ripen; but when his evil deed ripens, then does the evil-doer see evil.

19. Let no man think lightly of evil saying in his heart 'It will not come right unto me.' Even by the filling of water drops a water-pot is filled ; the fool becomes full of evil, even if he gathers it little by little.

20. A man should hasten towards the good, and should keep his thought away from evil; if a man does what is good slothfully, his mind delights in evil.

21. If a man commits a sin, let him not do it again, let him not delight in sin ; the accumulation of evil is painful.

22. Follow the law of virtue; do not follow that of sin. The virtuous rests in bliss in this world.

23. From lust is born sorrow, from lust is born fear. To him who is wholly free from lust there is neither sorrow nor fear.

24. Hunger is the worst of diseases (component), existence the worst of distress. This knowing in accordance with truth and fact, Nibbana becomes the highest happiness.

25. The evil done by oneself, self-begotten, self-bred, crushes the doer as a diamond breaks even a precious stone.

26. He whose wickedness is very great brings himself down to that state where his enemy wishes him to be, as a creeper does with the tree which it surrounds.

27. Bad deeds, and deeds hurtful to ourselves, are easy to do ; difficult to do what is beneficial and good.

§ 2. *On Craving and Lust*

1. Do not be possessed by Craving nor by Lust.

2. This is the Buddhist way of life.

3. Not in a rain of riches is satisfaction of desire
to be found. " Unsatisfying, grievous are desires," IV
so the wise man well knows. 357

4. Even in the pleasures of the heaven-worlds he takes no delight; his delight is in the ending of craving, he is the disciple of the Supremely Awakened One, the Buddha.

5. From craving is born sorrow, from craving is born fear. To him who is wholly free from craving there is neither sorrow nor fear.

6. From craving is born sorrow, from craving is born fear. To him who is wholly free from craving there is neither sorrow nor fear.

7. He who gives himself to vanity, forgetting (the real aim of life) and grasping at pleasure, will in time envy him who has exerted himself in meditation.

8. Let no man have attachment to anything; loss of it gives pain. Those who love nothing, and hate nothing have no fetters.

9. From pleasure comes grief, from pleasure comes fear; he who is free from pleasure knows neither grief nor fear.

10. From attachment comes grief, from attachment comes fear ; he who is free from attachment knows neither grief nor fear.

11. From lust comes grief, from lust comes fear ; he who is free from lust knows neither grief nor fear.

12. From greed comes grief, from greed comes fear; he who is free from greed knows neither grief nor fear.

13. He who possesses virtue and intelligence, who is just, speaks the truth, and does what is his own business, him the world will hold dear.

14. Kinsmen, friends and lovers salute a man who has been long away, and returns safe from afar.

15. In like manner his good works receive him

who has done good, and has gone from this world as kinsmen receive a friend on his return.

§ 3. *On Hurt and Ill-will*

IV

1. Cause no hurt ; Cherish no ill-will.

358 2. This is the Buddhist Way of Life.

3. Is there in all the world a man so blameless that he gives no occasion for reproach, as a spirited horse gives no occasion for the stroke of the lash ?

4. By confidence, by virtue, by energy, by meditation, by investigation into the Truth, by perfection in knowledge and conduct, by recollectedness, leave ye this great suffering behind.

5. The most excellent of ascetic practices is the practice of forbearance, of long suffering ; " most excellent of all is Nibbana " ; so says the Buddha. He is no ascetic who does hurt to others ; he is no disciple who works another's woe.

6. To speak no ill, to do no harm, to practise restraint in conformity with the discipline, this is the counsel of the Buddha.

7. Kill, nor cause slaughter.

8. He who seeking his own happiness does not punish or kill beings who also long for happiness, will find happiness.

9. If, like a shattered, metal plate (gong), thou utter nothing, then thou hast reached Nibbana ; anger is not known to thee.

10. He who inflicts pain on innocent and harmless person, will soon come to grief.

11. He who, dressed in fine apparel of tranquillity, is quiet, subdued, restrained, chaste, and has ceased to find fault with all other beings, he indeed is an ascetic (Samana), a friar (Bhikku).

12. Is there in this world any man so restrained by shame that he does not provoke reproof, as a noble horse the whip ?

13. If a man offend a harmless, pure, and innocent person, the evil falls back upon that fool, like light dust thrown up against the wind.

§ 4. *On Anger and Enmity*

1. Cherish no anger. Forget your enmities. Win your enemies by love.

2. This is the Buddhist Way of Life.

3. The fire of anger should be stilled.

4. One who harbours the thought : " He reviled me, maltreated me, overpowered me, robbed me," in him anger is never stilled."

5. He who harbours not such a thought, in him anger is stilled.

6. Enemy works evil to enemy, hater to hater, but whose is the evil.

7. Let a man overcome anger by love, let him overcome evil by good ; let him overcome the greedy by liberality, the liar by truth.

8. Speak the truth, do not yield to anger ; give, if thou art asked for little.

9. Let a man leave anger, let him forsake pride, let him overcome all bondage ; no sufferings befall the man who is not attached to name and form, and who calls nothing his own.

10. He who holds back rising anger like a rolling chariot, him I call a real driver, other people are but holding the reins.

11. Conquest begets enmity ; the conquered lie down in distress. The tranquillized lies down in happiness, dismissing alike victory and defeat.

12. There is no fire like lust, no ill-fortune like hatred. There is no misery like the constituents of existence, no happiness higher than the Peace of Nibbana.

13. For hatred does not cease by hatred at any time : hatred ceases by love, this is an old rule.

§ 5. *On Man, Mind and Impurities*

1. Man is what his mind makes him.

2. The training of the mind to seek the good, is the first step in the path of Righteousness.

3. This is the main teaching in the Buddhist Way of Life.

4. In everything the primal element is mind. Mind is pre-eminent.

5. If a man speaks or does evil suffering follows
him, close as the wheel of the hoof of the beast that
IV draws the cart.

6. If a man speaks or acts from uprightness of
360 mind, happiness follows him, close like his never-departing shadow.

7. This fickle, unsteady mind, difficult to guard, difficult to guide—the wise man makes it straight as the fletcher makes straight the arrow.

8. As quivers and throbs the water-dwelling fish, when thrown up out of the water on to the land, so quivers and throbs the mind forsaking the realm of Mara.

9. Hard to control, unstable is this mind, ever in quest of delight. Good is it to subdue the mind. A mind subdued brings happiness.

10. Make thyself an island, work hard, when thy impurities are blown away, and thou art free from guilt, thou wilt enter into the heavenly world of the elect.

11. Let a wise man blow off the impurities of himself, as a smith blows off the impurities of silver, one by one, little by little, and from time to time.

12. As the impurity which springs from the iron, when it springs from it, destroys it ; thus to a transgressor's own works lead him to the evil path.

13. But there is a taint worse than all taints. Ignorance is the greatest taint. O! mendicants, throw off that taint, and become taintless.

14. Life is easy to live for a man who is without shame, a crow here, a mischief maker, an insulting, bold and wretched fellow.

15. But life is hard to live for a modest man, who always looks for what is pure, who is disinterested, quiet, spotless and intelligent.

16. He who destroys life, who speaks untruth, who in the world takes what is not given him, who goes to another man's wife.

17. And the man who gives himself to drinking

intoxicating liquors, he even in this world, digs up his own grave.

18. O man, know this, that the unrestrained are in a bad state; take care that greediness and vice do not bring thee to grief for a long time.

19. The world gives according to its faith or according to its pleasure ; if a man frets about the food and the drink given to others, he will find no rest either by day or by night.

20. He in whom that feeling is destroyed, and taken out with the very root, finds rest by day and by night.

21. There is no fire like passion, there is no torrent like greed.

22. The fault of others is easily perceived, but that of oneself is difficult to perceive; a man winnows his neighbour's faults like chaff but his own faults he hides, as a cheat hides the bad dice from the player.

23. If a man looks after the faults of others, and is always inclined to be offended, his own passions will grow, and he is far from the destruction of passions.

24. Refrain from all evil; cultivate the good ; cleanse your own thoughts; this is the teaching of the Buddha.

§ 6. *On Self and Self-Conquest*

1. If one has self, let him practise self-conquest.

2. This is the Buddhist Way of Life.

3. Self is the lord of self, who else could be the lord ? With self well subdued, a man finds a lord such as few can find.

4. The foolish man who scorns the rule of the venerable (arahat), of the elect (ariya), of the virtuous and follows a false doctrine, he bears fruit to his own destruction, like the fruits of the Katthaka reed.

5. By oneself the evil is done, by oneself one suffers; by oneself evil is left undone, by oneself one is purified. The pure and the impure (stand and fall) by themselves, no one can purify another.

6. He who loves looking for pleasures only, his

senses uncontrolled, immoderate in his food, idle and weak, will certainly be overthrown by his own overdoing as the wind throws down a weak tree.

7. He who lives without looking for pleasures,
IV his senses well controlled, moderate in his food, faithful and strong, he will not be overthrown any more than
362 the wind throws down a rocky mountain.

8. If to himself a man is dear, let him keep close watch upon himself.

9. First establish thyself in the right then thou mayest counsel others. Let not the wise man give occasion for reproach.

10. Oneself, they say is hard to control. If one shapes oneself according as one counsels others, thus well controlled one will have control over others.

11. A man pays in himself for the evil he has done and in himself is purified. The good and evil are purified severally, no one purifies another.

12. Though one should conquer in battle thousands and thousands of men, whoso shall conquer himself, he is the greatest of warriors.

13. First establish thyself in the right, then thou mayest counsel others. Let not the wise man give occasion for reproach.

14. If one shapes oneself according as one counsels others, thus well controlled, one will have control over others. Oneself they say, is hard to control.

15. Verily oneself is the guardian of oneself. What other guardian should there be. Guarded by oneself, one gets a guardian the like of which is not likely gotten.

16. If to himself a man is dear, let him keep close watch upon himself.

17. A man pays in himself for the evil he has done, and in himself is purified. The good and evil are purified severally, no one purifies another.

18. Verily oneself is the guardian of oneself; what other guardian should there be? Guarded by oneself, one gets a guardian the like of which is not easily gotten.

§ 7. *On Wisdom, Justice and Good Company*

1. Be wise, be just and choose good company.

2. This is the Buddhist Way of Life. IV

3. If you see a man who shows you what is to be
avoided, who administers reproofs, and is intelligent, 363
follow that wise man as you would one who tells of hidden treasures ; it will be better, not worse, for him who follows him.

4. Let him admonish, let him teach, let him forbid what is improper—he will be beloved of the good, by the bad he will be hated.

5. Do not have evil-doers for friends, do not have low people for friends ; have virtuous people for friends, have for friends the best of men.

6. He who drinks in the Dhamma lives happily with a serene mind; the sage rejoices always in the Dhamma as preached by the elect.

7. Well-makers lead the water (wherever they like), fletchers bend the arrow ; carpenters bend a log of wood ; wise people fashion themselves.

8. As a solid rock is not shaken by the wind, the wise people falter not amidst blame and praise.

9. Wise people, after they have listened to the Dhamma become serene, like a deep, smooth and still lake.

10. Good men indeed walk (warily) under all circumstances; good men speak not out of a desire for sensual gratification; whether touched by happiness or sorrow wise people never appear elated or depressed.

11. It is sweet as honey, so thinks the fool, while as yet the evil has not ripened. But when the evil ripens the fool comes to grief.

12. A fool does not know when he commits his evil deeds ; but a wicked man burns by his own deeds, as if burnt by fire.

13. Long is the night to him who is awake ; long is a mile to him who is tired ; long is life to the foolish who do not know the true Dhamma.

14. If a traveller does not meet with one who

is his better, or his equal, let him firmly keep to his solitary journey; there is no companionship with a fool.

15. "These sons belong to me, and this wealth
IV belongs to me," with such thoughts a fool is tormented.
He himself does not belong to himself; how much
364 less sons and wealth?

16. The fool who knows his foolishness, is wise at least so far. But a fool who thinks himself wise, he is called a fool indeed.

17. If a fool be associated with a wise man even all his life, he will perceive the truth as little as a spoon perceives the taste of soup.

18. If an intelligent man be associated for one minute only with a wise man, he will soon perceive the truth, as the tongue perceives the taste of soup.

19. Fools of poor understanding have themselves for their greatest enemies, for they do evil deeds which bear bitter fruits.

20. That deed is not well done of which a man must repent and the reward of which he receives crying and with a tearful face.

21. Know, that deed is well done of which a man does not repent and the reward of which he receives gladly and cheerfully.

22. As long as the evil deed done does not bear fruit, the fool thinks it is like honey, but when it ripens, then the fool suffers grief.

23. And when the evil deed, after it has become known, turns to sorrow for the fool, then it destroys his bright lot, nay, it cleaves his head.

24. Let the fool wish for a false reputation, for precedence among the Bhikkus, for lordships in the convents, for worship among other people.

25. A man is not an elder because his head is grey; his age may be ripe, but he is called "old-and-vain."

26. He in whom there is truth, virtue, pity, restraint, moderation, he who is free from impurity and is wise, he is called an elder.

27. An envious, stingy, dishonest man does not

become respectable by means of much talking only, or by the beauty of his complexion.

28. He in whom all this is destroyed, and taken out with the very root, he when freed from hatred and
wise, is called respectable. IV
29. A man is not just if he carries a matter by
violence; no, he who distinguishes both right and 365
wrong, who is learned and guides others, not by violence, but by the same Dhamma, being a guardian of the Dhamma and intelligent, he is called just.

30. A man is not learned simply because he talks much; he who is patient, free from hatred and fear, is called learned.

31. A man is not a supporter of the Dhamma because he talks much; even if a man has learnt little, but sees the Dhamma bodily, he is supporter of the Dhamma, a man who never neglects the Dhamma.

32. If a man find a prudent companion who walks with him, is wise, and lives soberly, he may walk with him, overcoming all dangers, happy, but considerate.

33. If a man finds no prudent companion to walk with him, is wise, and lives soberly, let him walk alone, like a king who has left his conquered country behind, like an elephant in the forest.

34. It is better to live alone, there is no companionship with a fool; let a man walk alone, let him commit no sin, with few wishes, like an elephant in the forest.

35. If the occasion arises, friends are pleasant; enjoyment is pleasant, whatever be the cause; a good work is pleasant, whatever be the cause; a good work is pleasant in the hour of death; the giving up of all grief is pleasant.

36. Pleasant in the world is the state of a mother, pleasant the state of a father, pleasant the state of a Samana.

37. Pleasant is virtue lasting to old age, pleasant is a faith firmly rooted; pleasant is attainment of intelligence, pleasant is avoiding of sins.

38. He who walks in the company of fools suffers

a long way ; company with fools as with an enemy, is always painful ; company with the wise is pleasure, like meeting with kinsfolk.

39. Therefore, one ought to follow the wise, the
IV intelligent, the learned, the much enduring, the dutiful,
the elect, one ought to follow such a good and wise
366 man, as the moon follows the path of the stars.

40. Follow not after vanity, nor after the enjoyment of love and lust. He who is earnest obtains ample joy.

41. When the learned man drives away vanity by earnestness, he, the wise, climbing the terraced heights of wisdom, looks down upon the fools, free from sorrow he looks upon the sorrowing crowd, as one that stands on a mountain looks down upon them that stand upon the plain.

42. Earnest among the thoughtless, awake among the sleepers, the wise man advances like a richer, leaving behind the hack.

§ 8. *On Thoughtfulness and Mindfulness*

1. In everything be thoughtful; in everything be mindful ; in all things be earnest and bold.

2. This is the Buddhist Way of Life.

3. All that we are is the result of what we have thought ; it is founded on our thoughts, it is made up of your thoughts. If a man speaks or acts with an evil thought, pain follows him. If a man speaks or acts with a pure thought, happiness follows him. Therefore pure thoughts are important.

4. Be not thoughtless, watch your thought ! Draw yourself out of the evil way, like an elephant sunk in mud.

5. Let the wise man guard his thoughts, for they are difficult to perceive, very artful, and they rush whenever they list ; thoughts well-guarded bring happiness.

6. As rain breaks through an ill-thatched house, passion will break through an unreflecting mind.

7. As rain does not break through a well-thatched house, passion will not break through a well-reflecting mind.

8. This mind of mine went formerly wandering about as it liked, as it listed, as it pleased ; but I shall now hold it in thoroughly, as the Elder who holds the hook holds the furious elephant.

9. It is good to tame the mind, which is difficult to hold in and tightly, rushing wherever it listeth; a tamed mind brings happiness.

10. Those who bridle their mind which travels far, will be free from the bonds of temptation.

11. If a man's faith is unsteady, if he does not know the true Dhamma, if his peace of mind is troubled, his knowledge will never be perfect.

12. Whatever a hater may do to a hater, or an enemy to an enemy, a wrongly directed mind will do him greater mischief.

13. Not a mother, not a father will do so much, nor any other relatives as a well directed mind will do us.

§ 9. *On Vigilance, Earnestness and Boldness*

1. When, vigilant, the wise man puts from him negligence, ascending the tower of wisdom he looks down, free from sorrow, upon the sorrow-laden race of mankind. As from a mountain top, the wise man looks upon the fools in the valley.

2. Vigilant among the negligent, awake among those asleep, as a fleet courser leaves behind a sorry nag, so go the wise.

3. Give not yourselves unto negligence. Have naught to do with the lust of the flesh. The vigilant is given to meditation.

4. Earnestness leads to where death is not ; heedlessness is the way to death. Those who continue in earnestness do not die, but the heedless are as if already dead.

5. Fall not away from your purpose for the

sake of another, however great this latter may be. When once you have seen your goal, hold it firm and fast.

6. Be watchful! Have done with indolence! Travel the True Path! Whoso walks thereon happy he lives in the world.

7. Idleness is a disgrace; constant sloth is defilement. By strenuous striving and with the help of insight you should pull out the poisoned arrow of indolence.

8. Give not yourselves unto negligence. Have not to do with the lust of the flesh. The vigilant, the given to meditation, these attain an overflowing happiness.

9. If an earnest person has roused himself, if he is not forgetful, if his deeds are pure, if he acts with consideration, if he restrains himself, and lives according to Dhamma, his glory will increase.

§ *10. On Sorrow and Happiness; On Charity and Kindness*

1. Poverty gives rise to sorrow.

2. But removal of poverty does not necessarily give rise to happiness.

3. Not high standard of living but a high standard of culture is what gives happiness.

4. This is the Buddhist Way of Life.

5. Hunger is the worst of diseases.

6. Health is the greatest of gifts, contentedness the best riches; trust is the best of relationships, Nibbana the highest happiness.

7. We must learn to live happily indeed, not hating those who hate us!

8. We must learn to live happily indeed, free from ailments among the ailing men.

9. We must learn to live happily indeed, free from greed among the greedy.

10. Mankind is ruined by passion, just as fields are damaged by weeds: therefore charity done to the passionless brings great reward.

11. Mankind is damaged by vanity, just as fields are damaged by weeds. Therefore charity done to those who are free from vanity brings great reward.

12. Mankind is ruined by lust, just as fields are damaged by weeds. Therefore charity done to those IV
who are free from lust brings great reward.

13. Charity to Dhamma exceeds all gifts. The 369
sweetness of the Dhamma exceeds the Dhamma. The delight in the Dhamma exceeds all delights.

14. Victory breeds hatred, for the conquered is unhappy. He who has given up both victory and defeat, he, the contented, is happy.

15. There is no fire like passion ; there is no losing throw like hatred ; there is no pain like this body ; there is no happiness higher than the rest.

16. Fix not your gaze upon the ill-words and ill-deeds of others, upon what others do or leave undone. Look rather at what by yourself have done or left undone.

17. Hard always is life for the modest, the seeker after purity, the detached, the retiring, the cleanly of life, the discerning.

18. Is there in the world a man so blameless that he gives no occasion for reproach, as a spirited horse gives no occasion for the stroke of the lash ? Like a spirited horse that needs not the lash be fiery, be fleet.

19. Do not speak harshly to anybody : those who are spoken to will answer thee in the same way. Angry speech is painful, blows for blows will touch thee.

20. Liberty, courtesy, good-will and unselfishness—these are to the world what the lynch-pin to the Chariot.

21. This is the Buddhist Way of Life.

§ *11. On Hypocrisy*

1. Let not anyone speak falsely. Let not anyone lead another to speak falsely, nor yet approve of the action of one who speaks falsely. Let every kind of lying and false speech be put away from among you.

2. As the Perfect One speaks, so He acts. As

the Perfect One acts, so He speaks. And because He speaks as He Acts and acts as He speaks, therefore is He Called the Perfect One.

3. This is the Buddhist Way of Life.

§ *12. On following the Right Way*

1. Choose the Right Way. Depart not from it.

2. There are many paths ; not all lead to the Right Way.

3. The Right Path is for the happiness not of the few but of all.

4. It must be good at the beginning, good in the middle and good at the end.

5. To follow the right way is to lead the Buddhist Way of Life.

6. The best way is the eightfold way ; the best of truths the four words ; the best of virtues passionlessness; the best of men he who has eyes to see.

7. This is the way, there is no other that leads to the purifying of intelligence. Go on this path.

8. If you go on this way, you will make an end of pain ! The way was preached by me, when I had understood the removal of the thorns (in the flesh).

9. You yourself must make an effort. The Tathagatas are only preachers.

10. 'All created things perish,' he who knows and sees this becomes passive in pain.

11. 'All forms are unreal,' he who knows and sees this becomes passive in pain.

12. He who does not rouse himself when it is time to rise, who, though young and strong, is full of sloth, whose will and thought are weak, that lazy and idle man never finds the way to knowledge.

13. Watching his speech, well restrained in mind, let a man never commit any wrong with his body ! Let a man but keep these three roads of action clear, and he will achieve the way which is taught by the wise.

14. Through real knowledge is gotten, through lack of real knowledge is lost ; let a man who knows

this double path of gain and loss thus place himself that knowledge may grow.

15. Cut out the love of self, like an autumn lotus, with thy hand! Cherish the road of peace. Nirvana has been shown by the Sugata.

16. Do not follow the evil law! Do not live on in thoughtlessness! Do not follow false doctrine!

17. Rouse thyself! Do not be idle! Follow the law of virtue! The virtuous rests in bliss in this world.

18. He who formerly was reckless and afterwards became sober brightens up this world, like the moon when freed from clouds.

19. He whose evil deeds are covered by good deeds, brightens up this world, like the moon when freed from clouds.

20. If a man has transgressed the one law, and speaks lies, there is no evil he will not do.

21. Those who are ever watchful, who study day and night, and who strive after Nirvana, their passions will come to an end.

22. This is an old saying. 'They blame him who sits silent, they blame him who speaks much, they also blame him who says little'; there is no one on earth who is not blamed.

23. There never was, there never will be, nor is there now, a man who is always blamed, or a man who is always praised.

24. Beware of the anger of the tongue, and control thy tongue. Leave the sins of the mind, and practise virtue with thy mind.

25. Earnestness is the path of Nirvana, thoughtlessness the path of death. Those who are in earnest do not die, those who are thoughtless are as if dead already.

§ *13. Mix not True Dhamma with False Dhamma*

1. Those who mistake false for true and true for false, there abides wrong-mindedness—they arrive not at the truth.

2. Those who mistake false for true and true for false there abides wrong-mindfulness—they arrive not at the truth.

3. Those who know true as true and false as
IV false, there abides right-mindedness—these arrive at
the truth.

372 4. As rain gets into an ill-thatched house, so craving gets into an ill-trained mind.

5. As rain gets not into a well-thatched house, so craving gets not into a well-trained mind.

6. Arise! Be not negligent! Walk the Good Way of the Teaching! Who walks in the way of the teaching, happy is he in this and in all worlds.

7. Walk the Good Way of the teaching; walk not in ways that are evil. Who walks in the way of the teaching, happy he lives in this and in all worlds.

PART IV

His Sermons

Section 1—*Sermons for Householders.*

1. The Happy Householder.
2. Daughter may be better than a son.
3. Husband and wife.

Section 2—*Sermons on the need for maintaining character.*

1. What constitutes the downfall of man.
2. The wicked man.
3. The best man.
4. The enlightened man.
5. Man—just and good.
6. Need for doing good deeds.
7. Need for making good resolutions.

Section 3—*Sermons on Righteousness.*

1. What is Righteousness.
2. Need for Righteousness.
3. Righteousness and the claims of the world.
4. How to reach perfection in Righteous Conduct.
5. One need not wait for a companion to tread on the path of Righteousness.

Section 4—*Sermons on Nibbana.*

1. What is Nibbana.
2. The roots of Nibbana.

Section 5—*Sermons on Dhamma.*

1. Why right views rank first.
2. Why bother about life after death.
3. Prayers and invocations to God are a futility.
4. It is not what you eat that makes you holy.
5. Not food but evil actions that matter.
6. Not enough is outward washing.
7. What is holy life ?

Section 6—*Sermons on Socio-political questions.*

1. Do not depend on the favour of princes.
2. If the king is righteous his subjects will be righteous.
3. It is the social system on which depends political and military strength.
4. War is wrong.
5. The duties of a victor, who has won peace.

SECTION I

SERMONS FOR HOUSEHOLDERS

§ *1. The Happy Householder*

1. Once Anathapindika came to where the Exalted One was, made obeisance to the Exalted One and took a seat at one side. IV 375

2. Anathapindika was anxious to know wherein lay the happiness of a householder.

3. Accordingly Anathapindika asked the Lord to explain to him the secret of the householder's happiness.

4. The Lord said first is the happiness of possession. A householder is possessed of wealth, justly and righteously acquired by great industry, amassed by strength of the arm, and earned by sweat (of the brow). At the thought 'I am possessed of wealth justly gained' he gains happiness.

5. Second is the happiness of enjoyment. A householder is possessed of wealth justly and righteously acquired by great industry amassed by strength of the arm, and earned by sweat (of the brow), enjoys his wealth and performs acts of merit. Thus at the thought 'I am doing meritorious deeds with my wealth which was justly gained' and so forth he gains happiness.

6. Third is the happiness of freedom from debt. A householder, owes no one any debt great or small, thus he gains happiness, thus he at the thought of 'I owe no man anything' and so forth, gains happiness.

7. Fourth is the happiness of blamelessness. A householder, who is endowed with blameless action of body, blameless speech and blameless thinking, gains happiness of blamelessness.

8. Verily, Anathapindika, these four kinds of happiness are constantly obtainable by the householder, if he strives for them.

§ *2. Daughter may be better than a Son*

1. When the Exalted One was once at Shravasti, the king of the Kosalas, Pasendi, had come to visit him.

2. While the king was engaged in a conversation with the Blessed Lord a messenger from the Palace arrived and approaching the king, announced to his private ear that Queen Mallika had given birth to a
IV daughter.

3. The king appeared very sad and depressed.
376 The Blessed Lord asked the king the reason of his sadness.

4. The king replied that he had just received the sad news that Queen Mallika had given birth to a daughter.

5. Thereupon the Exalted One, discerning the matter said : 'A woman child, O lord of men, may prove even a better offspring than a male. For she may grow up wise and virtuous, her husband's mother reverencing true wife, a daughter.

6. The boy that she may bear may do great deeds and rule great realms, yea, such a son of a noble wife becomes his country's guide.

§ 3. *Husband and Wife*

1. At one time, the Exalted One had entered the high road between Madhura and Neranja. Also many householders and their wives had joined the high road between Madhura and Neranja.

2. Then the Exalted One having left the road took a seat under a certain tree, and these householders and their wives saw the Exalted One seated under it.

3. So seeing they came to where the Exalted One was. Having come they made obeisance to the Exalted One and sat at one side and asked the Blessed One the right relations between the husband and wife. To the householders and their wives so seated the Exalted One spake thus :

4. " Householders, there are four ways for a husband and wife, of living together. A vile man lives with a vile woman, a vile man lives with a goddess, a god lives with a vile woman and a god lives with a goddess.

5. " Householders ! a husband kills, steals ;

commits impurity, lies and indulges in fermented liquor, is wicked and sinful, with his heart possessed by avarice he lives the life of a householder and abuses and reviles virtuous people. Also his wife kills; steals, commits impurity, lies, and indulges in fermen- IV
ted liquor, is wicked and sinful, with her heart possessed
by avarice she lives the life of the family and abuses and 377
reviles virtuous people. Thus indeed, householders, a vile man lives with a vile woman.

6. "Householders! A husband kills, steals, commits impurity, lies and indulges in fermented liquor, is wicked and sinful, with his heart possessed by avarice, he lives the life of a householder and abuses and reviles virtuous people. But his wife abstains from killing, thieving, sexual impurity, lying and indulgence in fermented liquor. His wife is virtuous and of good behaviour; with her heart freed from the taint of avarice she lives the family life and abuses not nor reviles virtuous people. Thus indeed, householders, a vile man lives with a goddess.

7. "Householders! A husband abstains from killing, thieving, impurity, lying and indulgence in fermented liquor, is virtuous and of good behaviour; with his mind freed from the stains of avarice, he lives the family life and abuses not nor revile virtuous people. But his wife kills, steals, commits impurity, lies and indulges in fermented liquor, is wicked and sinful; with her heart possessed by avarice she lives the family life and abuses and reviles virtuous people. Thus indeed, householders, a god lives with a vile woman.

8. "Householders! Herein, a husband and a wife both abstain from killing, thieving, impurity, lying and indulgence in fermented liquor, are virtuous and of good behaviour, with mind freed from taints of avarice they live the family life and abuse not nor revile virtuous people. Thus indeed, householders, a god lives with a goddess.

9. "These, householders, are the four ways of living together."

SECTION II

SERMONS ON THE NEED FOR MAINTAINING CHARACTER.

IV

378

§ *1. What Constitutes the Downfall of Man*

1. On one occasion the Blessed One was dwelling in the monastery of Anathapindika, in the Jeta Grove, near Shravasti.

2. Now when the night was far spent a certain Deva whose splendour illuminated the whole Jeta Grove, came to the presence of the Blessed One, and, drawing near, respectfully saluted Him and stood at one side. Standing thus, he addressed the Blessed One in verse :

3. " Having come to interrogate the Blessed One, I ask thee, O Gotama, about the falling man. Pray, tell me the cause of one's downfall." The Blessed One consented to explain the causes of man's downfall.

4. " Easily known is the progressive one, easily known is the declining one. A lover of the Dhamma is the progressive one, a hater of the Dhamma is the declining one.

5. " The vicious are dear to him, in the virtuous he finds nothing pleasing; he favours the creeds of the vicious—this is the second cause of one's downfall.

6. " The man who is drowsy, fond of society, not industrious, indolent, and who manifests anger—this is the third cause of one's downfall.

7. " Whosoever, being rich, does not support his aged mother and father, who have passed their youth—this is the fourth cause of one's downfall.

8. " He who, by falsehood, deceives a Brahmana or an ascetic or any other medicant—this is the fifth cause of one's downfall.

9. " The man who owns much property, who has gold and food, but alone enjoys his delicacies—this is the sixth cause of one's downfall.

10. " The man who prides in birth or wealth

or clan, and despises his own kinsmen—this is the seventh cause of one's downfall.

11. "The man who is a debauchee, drunkard, a gambler, who squanders whatever he possesses—this is the eighth cause of one's downfall.

12. "Not contented with one's own wives, if one is seen amongst courtesans and the wives of others —this is the ninth cause of one's downfall.

13. "He who places in authority an intemperate spend-thrift woman, or a man of similar nature—this is the eleventh cause of one's downfall.

14. "He who, of slender means, but vast ambition, of warrior birth, aspires to sovereignty—this is the twelfth cause of one's downfall.

15. "Know these causes of downfall, ye noble Deva, and if ye succeed in overcoming them ye will be saved."

§ 2. *The Wicked Man*

1. The Blessed Lord while he was on journey gave as was his usual practice the following discourse to the Bhikkhus who were accompanying him.

2. Addressing the Bhikkhus the Lord said : "Do you know how to recognize a wicked man ?" "No, Lord" replied the Bhikkhus.

3. "I will tell you the characteristics of a wicked man.

4. "There is a man who shows up the faults of another even when unasked, not to say when asked. Being indeed asked and plied with questions, he speaks ill of another without suppressing or concealing, but with full details. Brethren, such a man is a wicked man.

5. "There is a man who, being asked, does not point out the good qualities of another, not to say when unasked. Being indeed asked and plied with questions, he speaks, well of another.

6. "There is a man who, being asked, does not disclose his own bad qualities, not to say when unasked. Being indeed asked and plied with questions, he points out his own bad qualities, but suppresses and conceals

them and does not give full details. Brethren, such a man is a wicked man.

7. " Then again, brethren, there is a man who, even unasked, discloses his good qualities, not to
IV say when asked. Brethren, being asked and plied with questions, he points out his own good qualities
380 without suppressing or concealing them and giving full details. Brethren, such a man is a wicked man."

§ 3. *The Best Man*

1. The Blessed One while he was on journey gave as was his practice the following discourse to the Bhikkhus who were accompanying him :

2. Addressing the Bhikkhus the Lord said : " There are four classes of persons, brethren, to be found in the world.

3. " He who has not striven for his own welfare nor that of others; he who has striven for others' welfare, but not his own; he who has striven for his own welfare but not others'; he who has striven for both his own welfare and that of others.

4. " One who has striven neither for his own welfare nor for that of others is like a torch from a funeral pyre, lit at both ends, and in the middle smeared with dung. He kindles no fuel either in village or in forest. He is useless to the world. And he is useless to himslef.

5. " One who has striven for the welfare of others at the cost of his own is both excellent and eminent of the two.

6. " Then again, brethren, in the case of the person who has striven both for his own welfare and for that of others—of these four persons this is best and chief, topmost and highest and supreme."

§ 4. *The Enlightened Man*

1. At one time, the Exalted One had reached the high road between (the two towns of) Ukkattha and Setabbya. Then the Brahmin named Dona had also reached the high road between Ukkattha and Setabbya.

2. Just then the Exalted One left the road and
sat down at the foot of a tree cross-legged. Then
Dona the Brahman, following the footsteps of the
Exalted One, saw Him seated at the foot of that tree
resplendent and of a comely appearance, with sense IV
controlled, with mind appeased, supremely tamed,
restrained and powerful. So seeing he approached 381
where the Exalted One was.

3. Having come he said thus to Him :

" Is not the Venerable One a Deva ? "

" Brahman, I am indeed not a Deva."

" Is not the Venerable One then a Gandhabba?"

" Brahman, I am indeed not a Gandhabba."

" Is not the Venerable One then a Yakkha ? "

" Brahman, I am indeed not a Yakkha."

" Is not the Venerable One then a man ? "

" Brahman, I am indeed not a man."

4. Having heard the Blessed One reply thus, the Brahman Dona said :

" When Thou art asked : Are ye a Deva ? Thou sayest : No.

When Thou art questioned : Are ye a Gandhabba ? Thou sayest : No.

When Thou art asked : Are ye a Yakkha ? Thou sayest : No.

When Thou art questioned : Are ye then a man ? Thou sayest : No.

Who then can the Venerable One be ? "

5. " Brahman, verily I was a Deva, a Gandhabba, Yakkha, a man, so long as I had not purged myself of the intoxicants. These very intoxicants have I now given up with roots cut out like unto a palm-tree, with its base destroyed and rendered unable to sprout again, so that in future they do not come into existence.

6. " Just as a lotus or a water-lily born of the water, grown in the water, risen out of the water, stands unstained by the water even so, Brahman, being born of the world, grown in the world, having overcome the world I abide unstained by the world.

7. " Therefore, O Brahman, consider me as the Enlightened One."

§ 5. *Man—Just and Good*

1. Addressing the Brethren, the Lord said, " There are four classes of persons whom you must
IV learn to distinguish if you wish to ascertain who are good and just.

382 2. " Brethren, there is a class of persons who strive for their own welfare but not that of others.

3. " Brethren, herein a certain person practises the extirpation of lust in himself, but does not urge the extirpation of lust in others : practises the extirpation of ill-will in himself but does not urge the extirpation of ill-will in others ; and also practises the extirpation of ignorance in himself but does not urge the extirpation of ignorance in others.

4. " Indeed, Brethren, this is the person who pursues his own welfare, but not the welfare of others.

5. " Brethren, there is a class of persons who have striven for others' welfare, but not their own.

6. " Brethren, herein a certain person does not practise the extirpation of lust, ill-will and ignorance in himself, but urges the extirpation of lust, ill-will and ignorance in others.

7. " Indeed, Brethren, this is the person who has striven for others' welfare, but not his own.

8. " Brethren, there is a class of persons who strive not, neither for their own welfare nor that of others.

9. " Brethren, herein a certain person practises not the extirpation of lust, ill-will and ignorance in himself nor urges the extirpation of lust, ill-will and ignorance in others.

10. " Brethren, this is the person that has not striven for his own welfare nor that of others.

11. " Brethren, there is a class of persons who strive for their own welfare as well as that of others.

12. " Brethren, herein a certain person both practises the extirpation of lust, ill-will and ignorance in himself and also urges the extirpation of lust, ill-will and ignorance in others.

13. " Brethren, this is the person who has striven for his own welfare as well as that of others.

14. " This last person is to be deemed just and good."

§ 6. *Need for Doing Good Deeds*

1. On one occasion, thus spake the Exalted One, to the Brethren.

2. " Be not afraid of good works, brethren. It is another name for happiness, for what is desired, beloved, dear and delightful, this word ' good works'. I myself brethren can bear witness to having reaped for many a long day the profit of good works a thing desired, beloved, dear and delightful.

3. " I often ask ' Of what deeds is all this the fruit ? Of what deed is it the ripening, in that I am now thus happy and contented.'

4. "The answer that comes to me is: 'Of three deeds this is the fruit. Of three deeds this is the ripening, the deeds of Charity, Self-taming, and Self-control.'

5. " Auspicious, festive, happy, blessed dawn ! Fair day, glad time is that when alms are given to worthy ones : when goodly acts, words, thoughts, right aspirations, bring auspicious gain to those that practise them.

6. " Happy are they that win such gain, and prosperous in the way ! So be ye also prosperous in the way free from disease and happy with your kin."

§ 7. *Need for Making Good Resolutions*

1. Once when he was at Shravasti in Jeta's Grove the Exalted One said to the Brethren :

2. " Brethren, there is a great need of good resolutions to be made and observed for a pure and happy life.

3. " I will tell you what your resolutions should be.

4. "Resolve that, 'all my life long may I support

my parents. May I respect the head of my clan. May I be of gentle speech. May I speak evil of none. Clearing my heart of the stain of selfishness, may I dwell at home generous pure-handed, delighting in
IV giving up, may I be a proper man to ask a boon of, delighting in sharing gifts with others.

384 5. "'All my life long, may I be angerless, and, if anger arise, may I quickly check it.'"

6. Such are the seven resolutions Brethren, by undertaking and performing which you will attain the state of happiness and purity.

SECTION III

SERMONS ON RIGHTEOUSNESS

§ 1. What is Righteousness

1. Once when the Lord was on an alms-pil- IV
grimage in Kosala, with a great train of almsmen, 385
he came to a Brahmin village of the Kosalans named Sala.

2. It came to the ears of the Brahmin heads of families in Sala that the Blessed Lord had come to their village in the course of an alms-pilgrimage in Kosala.

3. They felt it was good to go and visit him. So the Brahmins of Sala went to the Lord and, after exchanging civil greetings, took their seats on one side.

4. They asked the Blessed One if he would explain to them what he meant by righteousness.

5. So to the attentive Brahmins the Lord said : "There are three forms of unrighteousness and wickedness for the body ; four for speech ; and three for thoughts.

6. " As regards bodily unrighteousness, a man (*i*) may take life, as a hunter with hands bathed in blood, given to killing and slaying, merciless to living creatures ; or (*ii*) may take what is not his, by appropriating to himself in thievish fashion the belongings of other people in village and jungle ; or (*iii*) may be a fornicator, having intercourse with girls under the charge of mother or father or brother or sister or relations, yes, with girls affianced and plighted, and even wearing the very garlands of betrothal.

7. " As regards unrighteousness of speech a man (*i*) may be a liar; when cited to give testimony before assembly or village-meeting or family council or royal household or his guild, he may say that he knows when he does not know, or that he does not know when he does know, or that he saw when he did not see, or that he did not see when he did see, deliberately lying in the interests either of himself or of other people or for some trifling gain. Or (*ii*) he may

be a slanderer; repeating here what he has heard elsewhere so as to set one set of people by the ears, and repeating elsewhere what he has heard here so as to set another set of people by the ears; he is a dissolver of harmony and a fomenter of strife; discords prompts his utterances, discord being his pleasure, his joy, and his delight. Or (*iii*) he may be bitter of tongue; what he says is rough and harsh, hurtful and wounding to others, provocative of anger, and leading to distraction. Or (*iv*) he may be a tattler talking out of season, without heed to fact, always talking of the unprofitable, never of the Doctrine, never of the Rule, but ever of the trivial, of the ill-timed of the frivolous, of things leading nowhere, and unprofitable.

8. "As regards unrighteousness of thought, a man (*i*) may be covetous, coveting other people's gear with the yearning that it were all his own. Or (*ii*) he may be malevolent and wicked of heart,—wishing that creatures around him might be killed, destroyed, annihilated, or cease to be. Or (*iii*) he may be wrong in outlook and erroneous in his conceptions—holding that there are no such things as alms or sacrifice or oblations, that there is no such things as the fruit and harvest of deeds good and bad, that there is no such thing as this world or any other, that there are no such things as either parents or relations elsewhere, that there are no such things in the world as recluse and Brahmins who, having trodden the right path and walked aright, have, of and by themselves, comprehended and realized this and other worlds and made it all known to others too.

9. "Contrariwise, there are three forms of righteousness and goodness for the body; four for speech and three for thoughts.

10. "As regards bodily righteousness, a man (*i*) puts from him all killing and abstains from killing anything; laying aside cudgel and sword, he lives a life of innocence and mercy, full of kindliness and compassion for everything that lives. (*ii*) Theft he puts from him and eschews taking from others except what

is given to him by them, he lives an honest life.
(*iii*) Putting from him all sensual misconduct, he
abstains from fornication; he has no intercourse with
girls under the charge of mother or father or brother
or sister or relations, no intercourse with girls affianced IV
and plighted and with the garlands of betrothal upon 387
them.

11. "As regards righteousness in speech, (*i*) a man puts lying from him and abstains from lies; when cited to give testimony before assembly or village-meeting or family council or royal household or his guild he says that he does not know when he does not, and that he does know when he does, says that he did not see when he did not see and that he saw when he did see, never deliberately lying in the interests of himself or of other people or for some trifling gain. (*ii*) All slander he puts from him and from slandering he abstains; what he hears here he does not repeat elsewhere so to set one set of people by the ears, nor does he repeat here what he hears elsewhere so as to set another set of people by the ears, he is a promoter of harmony and a restorer of amity, for concord is his pleasure, his joy, and his delight. (*iii*) There is no bitterness in his tongue and he abstains from bitter speech; what he says is without gall, pleasant, friendly, hearty, urbane, agreeable, and welcome to all. (*iv*) No tattler, he abstains from tattle, speaking in season, according to fact, always of the profitable, of the Doctrine and Rule, in speech which is seasonable and memorable, illuminating, well-marshalled, and of great profit.

12. "As regards righteousness in thoughts, (*i*) a man is devoid of covetousness, never coveting other people's gear with the yearning that it were all his own. (*ii*) He harbours no malevolence or wickedness of thought; his wish is that creatures around him may live on in peace and happiness, safe, from all enmity and oppression. (*iii*) He is right in outlook and correct in his conceptions.

13. "This is what I mean by righteousness and unrighteousness."

§ 2. *Need for Righteousness*

1. Then the Exalted One addressed the lay brethren of Pataligama:

2. " There are losses, householders, which attend
IV the wicked and immoral man.

388 3. " The wicked, immoral man, as the result of sloth, comes to great loss of wealth.

4. " Then again, an evil report prevails about him which defames him in the eyes of the world.

5. " Whatever company he may enter, be it a company of the nobles, or the Brahmins, or the house-fathers, or a company of recluses, he enters shyly and confused in mind. He is not fearless. This is the third loss.

6. " Again, he has no peace of mind and is troubled in mind when he dies. This is the fourth loss.

7. " Such, householders, are the losses that attend the wicked and immoral man.

8. " Consider the profits which attend the righteous man who lives virtuously.

9. "The righteous man who lives virtuously comes by a great mass of wealth, due to his own exertions.

10. " Then, again, a good reputation prevails about him. He is honoured everywhere.

11. " Into whatsoever company he enters, be it of the nobles or the Brahmins or the housefathers or the recluses, he enters bold and confident.

12. " Again, he enjoys peace of mind and makes an end with mind untroubled.

13. " The fool in doing ill knows not his folly: His own deeds like a fire, the fool consume.

14. He who offends the harmless innocent soon reaches grievous disaster, or a mind distraught, loss of relations, loss of all his wealth.

§ 3. *Righteousness and the Claims of the World*

1. Once when the Lord was staying at Rajagraha in the Bamboo grove where the squirrels were fed, the

reverend Sariputta was making an alms pilgrimage with a great train of almsmen among the Southern Hills.

2. On his way he met an almsman who had spent the rainy season at Rajagraha. After interchange of greetings of friendliness and civility, Sariputta enquired IV
after the Master's health and was told he was well, as too was the Confraternity, and also the Brahmin 389
Dhananjani of Tandula-pala Gate in Rajagraha concerning whose health too Sariputta had made enquiries.

3. 'And is the Brahmin, Dhananjani, zealous and earnest?' asked Sariputta further of the Almsman.

4. 'How could earnest zeal possibly dwell in Dhananjani?' replied the Almsman. 'He uses the king to fleece the Brahmins and householders, and uses them to fleece the king. Also, his pious wife who came of a pious stock is dead now ; and he has taken to himself another wife who is not pious and comes of no pious stock.'

5. 'This is bad news, very bad news to hear of Dhananjani's lack of zeal,' said Sariputta. 'Perhaps, however, at some time and place I may meet him I should like to have a talk with him.'

6. After staying as long as he wanted in the Southern Hills, Sariputta proceeded on his alms pilgrimage till he reached Rajagraha, where he took up his abode in the Bamboo Grove.

7. Early in the morning, bowl in hand and duly robed, he went into Rajagraha for alms, at a time when the Brahmin Dhananjani was out of the city seeing his cows milked in the byre.

8. On his return after his round and meal, Sariputta sought out the Brahmin. Seeing him coming, the Brahmin came to meet him with the remark that they had time for a draught of milk before meal-time.

9. Not so, Brahmin, I have had my meal today, and shall be resting under the shade of a tree during the noontide. Come to me there.

10. Dhananjani agreed and after his own meal joined Sariputta seating himself by him after friendly greetings.

11. Said Sariputta: "May I rest assured, Dhanan-

jani, that zeal and earnestness and righteousness are yours?

12. "How can that be, when I have to support
my parents, my wife and family, and my slaves and
IV serving folk and have to entertain my acquaintances
and friends, my kith and kin, and guests, and have also
390 to provide for my kinsfolk dead and gone, and for the
deities, and for the king not to speak of supporting
myself in meat and drink?"

13. "What think you, Dhananjani? If we suppose a man who, for his parents' sake, has departed from righteousness and equity and is being hauled up would it avail him either to plead on his own behalf that it was for his parents' sake that he had departed from righteousness and equity and that therefore he should not be hauled up?"

14. "No; despite all appeals, the wardens would cast him into prison."

15. "Would it avail him either to plead on his own behalf, or to have his wife and family plead for him, that it was for their sake he had departed from righteousness and equity?"

16. "No."

17. "Would it avail him if his slaves and serving folk pleaded for him?"

18. "Not a whit."

19. "Or if his friends and acquaintances pleaded for him?"

20. "Not a whit."

21. "Or if his kith and kin, or his guests pleaded for him?"

22. "Not a whit."

23. "Or if his kinsfolk dead and gone, pleaded the claims of his deities, or his monarch's claims on him?"

24. "Not a whit."

25. "Would it avail him to plead on his own behalf or to have others pleading for him that it was to support himself in meat and drink that he departed from righteousness and equity?"

26. "No."

27. " What think you, Dhananjani ? Which is the better man ? He that for the sake of his parents departs from righteousness and equity or he that no matter what happens to them walks in righteousness and equity ? "

28. " The latter, " replied Dhananjani, " for to walk in righteousness and equity is better than to depart therefrom."

29. " Moreover, Dhananjani, there are other courses of action which are justified and righteous in themselves, whereby he can support his parents and yet avoid evildoing and walk uprightly. Now, does the same reasoning apply to the support of wife and family and everything else ?"

30. " It does, Sariputta."

31. " Hereupon the Brahmin rejoicing in what the reverend Sariputta had said, thanked him, rose up and went his way."

§ 4. *How to Reach Perfection in Righteous Conduct*

1. Once while the Lord was staying at Shravasti in Jeta's Grove there came to him five hundred lay-followers. One of them was Dhammika.

2. Dhammika asked the Lord : " What principles make your followers reach perfection in righteous conduct.

3. " I ask thee this question because thou art the most matchless judge of the weal of men.

4. " Trained Jains and Mendicants all failed to vanquish thee. Trained Brahmins, ripe in years—with others keen to air their point of view—are led to embrace thy saving truth. For, 'tis thy saving Truth,—subtle, but preached so well for which all yearn. Vouchsafe an answer, Lord, to us !

5. " Let the lay-followers learn from thy lips thy Lore immaculate ! "

6. The Blessed Lord in compassion for his lay-followers said : " Give me your ear. I will explain the principles of righteous conduct. Hear and follow them.

7. "Slay not, nor doom to death, nor sanction slaughter. Do no violence to aught that lives—strong or weak.

8. "No layman, wittingly, should thieve, or
IV order theft, or sanction any theft,—take but what others give.

392 9. "And shun incontinence as 'twere a pit of fire, or, failing continence, debauch no wedded wife.

10. "In conclaves, courts, or talk let him not lie; let him not prompt or sanction lies—let him renounce untruth.

11. "Layman, observe this law: Shun drink; make no man drink; sanction no drinking. Mark how drink to madness leads.

12. "Through drink fools sin, and egg lax brethren on to sin. So flee this maddening vice, this folly, bliss of fools.

13. "Slay not, nor steal, nor lie; from strong drink keep away; refrain from lechery; touch not wrong meals at night!

14. "Eschew both scents and wreaths; spread on the ground thy bed; so make thy sabbath vows as week succeeds to week, and keep with pious hearts this eightfold festival.

15. "At morn, these vows performed, with pious, thankful heart be wise and of thy means give Almsmen food and drink.

16. "Cherish thy parents well; follow a righteous trade. Thus shall the layman staunch reach realms of light above.

§ 5. *One Need Not Wait for a Companion to Tread on the Path of Righteousness*

1. An elephant in battle bears the arrow at him hurled, I must bear men's bitter tongues for every evil in the world.

2. Tamed, they lead him into battle; tamed, the king his back ascends; tamed, is he the best of beings when no bitter speech offends.

3. Good are well-tamed mules, and good are

Cindian steeds of lineage famed, good indeed the mighty tusker; best of all the men self-tamed.

4. Yet such mounts can naught avail us, cannot be Nibbana's guide. We can only reach the Path on the self-tamed self-ride. IV

5. Take delight in Earnestness ; watch thy
thoughts and never tire. Lift thee from the Path of 393
Evil, take the Tusker out of mire.

6. Hast thou found a fellow-traveller, upright, firm, intelligent? Leaving all thy cares behind thee, gladly walk with him intent.

7. Hast thou found no fellow-traveller, upright, intelligent? As a King deserts his borders, by the enemy pursued, like the tusker in the forest, so go thy way in solitude.

8. Better is the lonely life, for fools companions cannot be. Live alone and do no evil, live alone with scanty needs, lonely, as the mighty tusker in the forest lonely feeds.

9. Expunge all bad thoughts.

10. Here is the way to expunge.

11. You are to expunge by resolving that, though others may be harmful, you will be harmless.

12. That, though others may kill, you will never kill.

13. That, though others may steal, you will not.

14. That, though others may not lead the higher life, you will.

15. That, though others may lie, traduce, denounce, or prattle, you will not.

16. That, though others may be covetous, you will covet not.

17. That, though others may be malignant, you will be benignant.

18. That, though others may be given over to wrong views, wrong aims, wrong speech, actions, wrong modes of livelihood, wrong effort, wrong mindfulness and wrong concentration you must follow the Noble Eight-fold Path in right outlook, right aims, right speech, right actions, right mode of livelihood, right efforts, right mindfulness and right concentration.

19. That, though others are wrong about the truth and wrong about Deliverance, you will be right about truth and right about Deliverance.

20. That, though others may be possessed by
IV sloth and torpor, you will free yourself therefrom.

21. That, though others may be puffed up, you
394 will be humble-minded.

22. That, though others may be perplexed by doubts, you will be free from them.

23. That, though others may harbour wrath, malevolence, envy, jealousy, niggardliness, avarice, hypocrisy, deceit, imperviousness, arrogance, forwardness, unscrupulousness, lack of instruction, inertness, bewilderment, and unwisdom—you will be the reverse of all these things.

SECTION IV

SERMONS ON NIBBANA

§ *1. What is Nibbana*

1. Once the Blessed Lord was staying at IV
Shravasti in Anathapindika's Arama where Sariputta 395
was also staying.

2. The Lord addressing the Brethren said: " Almsmen, be ye partakers not of the world's goods but of my doctrine; in my compassion for you all I am anxious to ensure this."

3. Thus spoke the Lord, who thereupon rose and passed to his own cell.

4. Sariputta remained behind and the Brethren asked him to explain what is Nibbana.

5. Then Sariputta in reply to the Brethren said: " Brethren, know you that greed is vile, and vile is resentment.

6. " To shed this greed and this resentment, there is the Middle Way which gives us eyes to see and makes us know, leading us on to peace, insight, enlightenment and Nibbana.

7. " What is this Middle Way ? It is naught but the Noble Eight-fold Path of right outlook, right aims, right speech, right action, right means of livelihood, right effort, right mindfulness and right concentration; this, Almsmen is the Middle Way.

8. " Yes, sirs; anger is vile and malevolence is vile, envy and jealousy are vile, niggardliness and avarice are vile, hypocrisy and deceit and arrogance are vile, inflation is vile, and indolence is vile.

9. " For the shedding of inflation and indolence there is the Middle Way—giving us eyes to see, making us know, and leading us on to peace, insight, enlightenment.

10. " Nibbana which is naught but that Noble Eight-fold Path."

11. Thus spoke the reverend Sariputta—glad at heart, the Almsmen rejoiced at what he had said.

§ 2. *The Roots of Nibbana*

(i)

1. Once the venerable Radha came to the Exalted
IV One. Having done so he saluted the Exalted One and
sat down on one side. So seated the venerable Radha
396 thus addressed the Exalted One: " Pray, Lord, what
for is Nibbana."

2. " Nibbana means release from passion," replied the Lord.

3. " But Nibbana, Lord,—what is the aim of it ?"

4. " Rooted in Nibbana, Radha, the righteous life is lived. Nibbana is its goal. Nibbana is its end."

(ii)

1. Once the Exalted One was dwelling at Shravasti, in Jeta's Grove, at Anathapindika's Park. Then the Exalted One called the brethren, saying, 'Brethren.' ' Yes, Lord,' replied those brethren to the Exalted One. The Exalted One thus spake.

2. " Do ye bear in mind, brethren, the Five Fetters that bind to the lower world, as taught by me ?"

3. Whereupon the venerable Malunkyaputta said this to the Exalted One :

4. " I, Lord, bear in mind those Five Fetters."

5. " And how, Malunkyaputta, do you bear them in mind ?"

6. " I bear in mind, Lord, the view of bodyhood, as taught by the Exalted One, and wavering, and the moral taint of dependence on rite and ritual, the excitement of sensual delight, and malevolence, taught by the Exalted One as fetters that bind to the lower world. These are the Five Fetters that I bear in mind, Lord."

7. " As taught for whom, Malunkyaputta, do you bear in mind these Five Fetters ? Will not the wanderers of other views reproach you, using the parable of a tender baby for their reproach and saying thus :

8. " ' But, Malunkyaputta, there can be no bodyhood for a tender baby-boy, dull of wits and

lying on his back. How, then, can there arise in him any view of bodyhood? Yet there is indeed latent in him a tendency to the view of bodyhood.'

9. "'Likewise, Malunkyaputta, there can be
no mental conditions for a tender baby-boy, dull IV
of wits and lying on his back. How, then, can there
be in him any wavering of mental conditions? Yet 397
there is in him a latent tendency to wavering.'

10. "'So also, Malunkyaputta, he can have no moral practice. How, then, can there be in him any moral taint of dependence on rite and ritual? Yet he has a latent tendency thereto.'

11. "'Again, Malunkyaputta, that tender babe has no sensual passions. How, then, can be known the excitement of sensual delight? But the tendency is there.'

12. "'Lastly, Malunkyaputta, for that tender babe beings do not exist. How then can it harbour malevolence against beings? Yet the tendency thereto is in him.'

13. "Now, Malunkyaputta, will not those wanderers of other views thus reproach you, using for their reproach the parable of that tender baby-boy?"

14. When this was said, the venerable Ananda thus addressed the Exalted One: "Now is the time, Exalted One. O Wayfarer, now is the time for the Exalted One to set."

SECTION V

SERMONS ON DHAMMA

§ 1. *Why Right Views Rank First*

IV

1. Of the noble Eightfold path the noblest is
398, Right Outlook.

2. Right thinking is the preface and the key to every thing else in the higher life, and ignorance.

3. The lack of understanding is the root of all evil.

4. For developing right outlook one must see all phenomena of life as a process of causal law. To have right outlook is to recognise the law of cause and effect.

5. " Whatsoever individual, brethren, follows perverted views, perverted aim, perverted speech or acts or living, perverted effort, attention, and contemplation : whose knowledge and emancipation are perverted, for him every action of deed, word or thought, performed and achieved according to such perverted views ; every willed act, every aspiration, every resolve, all his activities, these things one and all conduce to what is distasteful, unpleasing, repulsive, unprofitable, and painful. And why so? Because of his evil view."

6. To be right is not enough. A baby may be right but that does not mean that a baby knows what is right. To be right one must know what is right.

7. " Anarda, who can be rightly described as an almsman? Only he who has mastered what is rationally possible and what is rationally impossible."

§ 2. *Why Bother About Life After Death*

1. On a certain occasion the venerable Kassapa the Great and the venerable Sariputta were staying near Benares at Isipatana in the Deer Park.

2. Then the venerable Sariputta rising up at eventide from solitude, went to the venerable Kassapa the Great and sat down on one side.

3. So seated, the venerable Sariputta said to the venerable Kassapa the Great. "How now friend Kassapa? Does the Tathagata exist beyond death?

4. "Undeclared is it, friend, by the Exalted One that the Tathagata exists beyond death.

5. "What then friend? Does the Tathagata both exist and not exist beyond death?

6. "This also, friend, is undeclared by the Exalted One.

7. "How then, friend? Does the Tathagata neither not exist beyond death? That also, friend, is not declared by the Exalted One.

8. "But why, friend, has it not been declared by the Exalted One?"

9. "This is a question not concerned with profit to humanity or with the first principles of holy life. It does not lead to perfect wisdom nor to Nibbana. That, friend, is why it is not declared by the Exalted One."

§ 3. *Prayers and Invocations to God are a Futility*

1. Once the Blessed Lord speaking to Vasettha said :

2. "If this river Achiravati were full of water even to the brim and overflowing, and a man with business to be done on the further bank of it should come up, and want to cross over :

3. "And standing on that bank, he should invoke the further bank and say : 'Come hither, O further bank ! Come over to this side !'

4. "Now what think you, Vasettha? Would the further bank of the river Achiravati, by that man's invoking and praying, and hoping, and praising, come over to this side?

5. "In just the same way, Vasettha, do the Brahmins, versed in the three Vedas, omitting the practice of those qualities which really make a man a Brahmin, and adopting the practice of those qualities which really make men non-Brahmins say thus :

6. " ' Indra we call upon, Brahma we call upon, Isana we call upon, Prajapati we call upon, Brahma, we call upon, we call, we call.'

7. " Verily, Vasettha, that these Brahmins, by
IV reason of their invoking and praying and hoping and
praising, should after death become united with
400 Brahma—verily such a condition of things can in
nowise be."

§ 4. *It is Not What You Eat that Makes You Holy*

1. A Brahmin happened to meet the Lord and raised the question of the effect of food on a man's character.

2. The Brahmin said : " The millet-grain, palm-nuts, pulse, bulbs, and wilding shoots—this diet rightly got, ever prompts the good life. 'Tis eating carrion that is bad."

3. The Blessed One replied : " Though you (Lord) say you touch no carrion, you eat choice dishes made with flesh of birds—I ask what you term 'carrion.'

4. " Killing and maiming, stripes, bonds, theft, lies, fraud, deceit, adultery—not meats, but these are carrion.

5. " Pursuit of pleasure, lust for guzzlings, life unclean, blatant dissent—not meats, but these are carrion.

6. " Backbiting, cruelty, betrayals, ruthless pride, mean stinginess—not meats, but these are carrion.

7. " Anger, conceit, revolt, guile, envy, bluster, pride, low company—not meats, but these are carrion.

8. " Base living, slander, fraud, cheating, the trickster's wiles, foul infamies—not meats, but these are carrion.

9. " This rage to slay and steal, these crimes, are fraught with doom and end in hell—not meats, but these are carrion.

10. " No abstinence from meat and fish, no nudity, no topknots, shaven crowns, or garb of pelt, no cult of sacred fire, no stark austerities to purchase

future bliss, no rinsing, burnt-offering, rites, can cleanse the man who doubts.

11. " Control thy sense, rule thy powers, hold to Truth, be kind. The saint who leaves all ties and
vanquishes all ills, is stained by naught he either sees IV
or hears."

12. Hearing the Lord preach these lofty, saving 401
truths, denouncing ' carrion ', and sweeping ills away, the Brahmin meekly knelt and asked to be enrolled as Almsman then and there.

§ 5. *Not Food But Evil Actions That Matter*

1. A Brahmin by name Amagandha was an ascetic who lived in the region of Himalayas with his pupils.

2. They ate neither fish nor flesh. Every year they came down from their hermitage in search of salt and acids. The inhabitants of the village received them with honour and gave them hospitality for four months.

3. Then the Blessed Lord with his monks visited the same village. The people on hearing the Lord preach his Dhamma became his followers.

4. That year even Amagandha and his disciples as usual went to the villagers but the villagers did not show the same enthusiasm.

5. Amagandha was disappointed to hear that the Lord did not forbid eating fish and flesh. Wishing to have the matter confirmed he went to Jeta Vana at Shravasti where the Blessed Lord was then staying and said :

6. " Millet, cingula-beans and peas, edible leaves and roots, the fruit of any creeper ; the righteous who eat these, obtained justly, do not tell lies for the sake of pleasures.

7. " Thou eatest whatever food is given by others, which is well prepared, nicely got up, pure and excellent. He who enjoys such food made of rice, he eats, Amagandha. You say that the charge of

Amagandha, does not apply to me, while eating rice with well prepared bird's flesh.

8. "I inquire the meaning of this from you, of what kind is your Amagandha ?"

9. The Lord replied : "Taking life, beating,
IV cutting, binding, stealing, lying, fraud, deceiving,
402 worthless knowledge, adultery ; this is Amagandha
and not the eating of flesh.

10. "In this world those individuals, who are unrestrained in sensual pleasures, who are greedy for sweet things, who are associated with impure actions, who are of Nihilistic views, crooked, difficult to follow ; this is Amagandha and not the eating of flesh.

11. "In this world those who are rude, harsh, backbiting, treacherous, unkind, excessively egoistic, ungenerous, and do not give anything to anybody ; this is Amagandha, and not the eating of flesh.

12. "Anger, pride, obstinacy, antagonism, deceit, envy, boasting, excessive egoism, association with the unrighteous ; this is Amagandha, and not eating of flesh.

13. "Those who are of bad morals, refuse to pay their debt, slanderers, deceitful in their dealings, pretenders, those who in this world being the vilest of men, commit such wrongdoings, this is Amagandha and not the eating of flesh.

14. "Those persons who, in this world, are uncontrolled towards living beings, who are bent on injuring others, having taken their belongings ; immoral, cruel, harsh, disrespectful ; this is Amagandha and not the eating of flesh.

15. "Those who attack these living beings either because of greed or of hostility, and always bent upon (evil), they go to darkness after death and fall into hell headlong ; this is Amagandha and not the eating of flesh.

16. "Abstaining from fish or flesh, nakedness, shaving of the head, matted hair, covering with ashes, wearing rough deer skins, attending the sacrificial fire, nor all these various penances in the world (performed) for immortality, neither incantations, oblations, sacri-

fices nor seasonal observances, purifies a person who has not overcome his doubt.

17. " He who lives with his senses guarded and conquered and is established in the Dhamma, delights in uprightness and gentleness, who has gone beyond attachments and has overcome all sorrows ; that wise man does not cling to what is seen and heard.

18. " It is evil actions which constitute Amagandha and not the eating of fish or flesh."

§ 6. *Not Enough Is Outward Washing*

1. Once the Exalted One was dwelling at Shravatsi. And the Brahmin Sangarava also dwelt there. Now he was a cleanser by water, and practised cleansing by water. Night and day he abode given to the habit of going down to bathe.

2. Now the venerable Ananda, robing himself at an early hour and taking outer robe and bowl, went forth to Shravatsi to beg. And when he had gone his rounds in Shravatsi and had eaten his meal, upon his return, he went to the Exalted One, saluted Him, and sat down on one side. So seated, the venerable Ananda said :

3. "Lord, there is here one Sangarava, a Brahmin, dwelling at Shravatsi, a cleanser by water, one who practises cleansing by water. Night and day does he abide given to the habit of going down to bathe. Well were it, Lord, if the Exalted One would pay a visit to the Brahmin Sangarava, out of compassion for him."

4. And the Exalted One consented by His silence.

5. So next day at an early hour, the Exalted One robed Himself and taking outer robe and bowl went to the dwelling of the Brahmin Sangarava, and when He got there He sat down on a seat made ready.

6. Then the Brahmin Sangarava came to the Exalted One and greeted Him, and after the exchange of mutual courtesies sat down on one side.

7. As he thus sat, the Exalted One said this to the Brahmin Sangarava : " Is it true, Brahmin, as they say, that thou art a cleanser by water, that thou dost

practise cleansing by water, abiding night and day given to the habit of going down to bathe ?"

8. "True it is, Master Gotama."

9. "Now, Brahmin, seeking what profit dost thou so practise the habit of going down to bathe, and so forth ?"

10. "It is in this way, Master Gotama. Whatsoever evil I do by day, I get it washed away that very evening by my bathing. Whatsoever evil I do by night I get it washed away next morning by my bathing. That is the profit I am looking for in being a cleanser by water and so forth."

11. Then said the Exalted One :

12. "The Norm is the pool. It is clear and undefiled."

13. "Hither when they have come to bathe, the masters of the lore, are cleansed in every limb, and pass unto the Further Shore."

14. Whereupon the Brahmin Sangarava said to the Exalted One : "Excellent it is, Master Gotama. May the Master Gotama accept me as His follower, from this day forth so long as life doth last, as one who has taken refuge in Him."

§ 7. *What is Holy Life*

1. Once while the Blessed Lord was on journey he gave, as was his practice, the following discourse to the Bhikkhus who were accompanying him.

2. Addressing the Bhikkhus the Lord said : "O brethren, this holy life is not practised with a view to deceive people, nor to seek their favour, nor for the purpose of gain, benefit, or fame, nor with the intention of getting out of difficulties in controversy, nor that one may be known as such and such by men. Indeed, brethren, this holy life is practised for the controlling (of body and speech), the cleansing (of corruptions) and the detachment (from) and cessation (of craving)."

SECTION VI

SERMONS ON SOCIO-POLITICAL QUESTIONS

§ *1. Do Not Depend on the Favour of Princes* IV 405

1. Once the Exalted One was staying at Rajagraha in the Bamboo Grove in the Squirrels' Feeding ground.

2. At that time Prince Ajatasatru was supporting Devadatta who had turned hostile to the Blessed Lord.

3. He was maintaining the supporters of Devadatta, late and early with five hundred carts, conveying therein food brought in five hundred cooking-pots.

4. Then a number of the brethren came before the Exalted One, saluted Him, and sat down on one side, and there sitting they told all of these things to the Exalted One.

5. Then the Blessed Lord addressing the brethren said : " Do ye not long for gains, favours and flattery from the kings. So long, brethren, as Prince Ajatasatru thus supports Devadatta late and early, with five hundred carts, conveying therein food brought in five hundred cooking-pots, it is ruin, brethren, that may be expected of Devadatta, and not growth in good conditions.

6. " Just as if, brethren, one were to crumble liver on a mad dog's nose, the dog would only get the madder, even so, brethren, so long as Prince Ajatasatru thus supports Devadatta it is ruin that may be expected of Devadatta, and not growth in good conditions. Thus terrible, brethren, are gains, favours, and flattery of the princes.

7. " They are a bitter, painful hindrance to the attainment of the sure peace that passeth all.

8. " Wherefore, brethren, thus must you train yourselves: 'When gains, favours and flattery befall us, we will reject them, and when they do befall us, they shall not lay hold of and be established in our hearts, and make us slaves of the prince.' "

§ 2. *If the King is Righteous His Subjects will be Righteous*

1. Once the Lord addressing the Almsmen said :

IV 2. " Brethren during such time as kings are
unrighteous their ministers and officers also become
406 unrighteous. The ministers and officers, brethren, being unrighteous, Brahmins and householders also become unrighteous. The Brahmins and householders, brethren, being unrighteous, the town-folk and villagers become unrighteous.

3. " But whenever, brethren, kings are righteous, then kings' ministers and officers also become righteous. Whenever kings' ministers and officers become righteous the Brahmins and householders also become righteous. Whenever Brahmins and householders become righteous, the town-folk and villagers also become righteous.

4. " When kine are crossing, if the old bull swerves, they all go swerving, following his lead. So among men, if he who is reckoned chief walks crookedly, the others crooked go.

5. " Similarly, the whole realm suffers when the king goes wrong. When kine are crossing, if the bull goes straight they all go straight because his course is straight. So among men, if he who's reckoned chief walks righteously, the others live aright. The whole realm lead happy lives when kings are good."

§ 3. *It is the Social System on which Depends Political and Military Strength*

1. The Blessed One was once dwelling in Rajagraha, on the hill called the Vultures' Peak.

2. Now at that time, Ajatasatru, the son of the queen consort of Videha origin, the king of Magadha, was desirous of attacking the Vajjins, and he said to himself, " I will root out these Vajjins, mighty and powerful though they be, I will destroy these Vajjins, I will bring these Vajjins to utter ruin ! "

3. So he spoke to the Brahmin Vasakara, the Prime Minister of Magadha, and said :

4. " Come now, O Brahmin, do you go to the Blessed One, and bow down in adoration at his feet on my behalf and enquire on my behalf whether he is free from illness and suffering and in the enjoyment of ease and comfort and vigorous health.

5. " Then tell him that Ajatasatru, son of Videhi, the King of Magadha, is eager to attack the Vajjins, mighty and powerful though they be, I will destroy these Vajjins, I will bring these Vajjins to utter ruin !

6. " And bear carefully in mind whatever the Blessed One may predict and repeat it to me. For the Buddha speaks nothing untrue."

7. Then the Brahmin Vasakara hearkened to the words of the king, saying, " Be it as you say." And ordering a number of magnificent carriages to be ready he went to the Vultures' Peak.

8. On arriving there he exchanged with the Blessed One the greetings and compliments and then delivered to him the message even as the king had commanded.

9. Now at that time the venerable Ananda was standing behind the Blessed One. And the Blessed One said to him: " Have you heard, Ananda, that the Vajjins hold full and frequent public assemblies?

10. " Lord, so I have heard," replied he.

11. " So long, Ananda," rejoined the Blessed One, " as the Vajjins hold these full and frequent public assemblies; so long may they be expected not to decline, but to prosper.

12. " So long, Ananda, as the Vajjins meet together in concord, and rise in concord, and carry out their undertakings in concord.

13. " So long as they enact nothing not already established, abrogate nothing that has been already enacted and act in accordance with the ancient institutions of the Vajjins as established in former days.

14. " So long as they honour and esteem and revere and support the Vajjin Elders, and make it a point of duty to hearken to their words.

15. " So long as no women or girls belonging to their clans are detained among them by force or abduction.

16. " So long as the Vajjins respect and follow
IV religion.

17. " So long, Ananda, the Vajjins may be ex-
408 pected not to decline but to prosper and no one can destroy them."

18. In short, the Blessed Lord declared that so long as the Vajjins believe in democracy and practise democracy there is no danger to their State.

19. Then the Blessed One addressed Vasakara and said :

20. " When I was once staying, O Brahmin, at Vaishali I taught the Vajjins these conditions of welfare.

21. " We may expect then," answered the Brahmin, " the welfare and not the decline of the Vajjins, so long as they observe these conditions. So, Gotama, the Vajjins cannot be overcome by the king of Magadha."

22. So Vasakara heard the words of the Blessed One, rose from his seat and went back to Rajagraha to inform the king of what the Lord had said.

§ 4. *War is Wrong*

1. It so happened that Ajatasatru, the king of Magadha, mustering an army of cavalry and infantry, invaded Kasi, a part of the kingdom of king Pasenadi. And Pasenadi, hearing of the expedition, also mustered a similar army and went to meet him.

2. The two fought with one another and Ajatasatru defeated the king Pasenadi, who retreated to his own capital Shravasti.

3. The Bhikkhus who were in Shravasti returning from their alms round came and told the Exalted One of the battle and the retreat.

4. " Almsmen, the king of Magadha, Ajatasatru, is a friend of whatever is evil. King Pasenadi is a

friend of whatever is good. For the present, Pasenadi will pass the night in misery, a defeated man.

5. "Conquest engenders hate; the conquered lives in misery. But whoso is at peace and passionless, happily doth he live; conquest hath he abandoned IV
and defeat."

6. Again it so happened these two kings met in 409
battle a second time. But in that battle the Kosala king Pasenadi defeated Ajatasatru and captured him alive. Then king Pasenadi thought: "Although this king injures me who was not injuring him, yet is he my nephew. What if I were now to confiscate his entire army, elephants, horses, chariots and infantry and leave him only his life?" And he did so.

7. And almsmen returning from their alms tour in Shravasti brought word of this to the Exalted One. Thereupon the Exalted One said: "A man may spoil another, just so far as it may serve his ends, but when he's spoiled by others, he, despoiled, spoils yet again.

8. "So long as evil's fruit is not matured, the fool doth fancy 'now's the hour, the chance!' But when the deed bears fruit, he fareth ill.

9. "The slayer gets a slayer in his turn; the conqueror gets one who conquers him; the abuser wins abuse from another.

10. "Thus by the evolution of the deed, a man who spoils is spoiled in his turn."

§ 5. *The Duty of the Victor Who Has Won Peace*

1. When the Victor in war has won the Peace he claims the right further to degrade the vanquished if not to enslave him. The Buddha had a totally different view on the matter. In His view if Peace had any meaning it means that the Victor has a duty to use his victory for the service of the vanquished. This is what he said to the Bhikkhus on this subject:

2. "When Peace is won, the adept in warfare needs to prove an able, upright man, of gracious speech,

kind mood, devoid of arrogance, an easy, grateful guest, no busybody wants but few sense-disciplined, quick-witted, bluster-free, never importunate; and let him never stoop to conduct mean or low, evoking
IV grave rebuke.

3. " May creatures all abound, in weal and peace ;
410 may all be blessed with peace always, all creatures weak or strong, all creatures great and small ; creatures unseen or seen dwelling afar or near, born or awaiting birth, may all be blessed with peace !

4. " Let none cajole or flout his fellows anywhere; let none wish others harm in dudgeon or in hate.

5. " Just as with her own life a mother shields from hurt her own, her only child, let all-embracing thoughts for all that lives be thine, an all-embracing love for all the universe in all its heights and depths and breadths, unstinted love, unmarred by hate within, not rousing enmity.

6. " So, as you stand or walk, or sit, or lie, reflect with all your might on this : ' 'Tis deemed a state divine.' "

BOOK V

The Sangh

Part I—The Sangh

Part II—The Bhikkhu—The Buddha's Conception of him.

Part III—The Duties of the Bhikkhu.

Part IV—The Bhikkhu and the Laity.

Part V—Vinaya for the Laity.

PART I

The Sangh

1. The Sangh and its Organization.
2. Admission to the Sangh.
3. The Bhikkhu and His Vows.
4. The Bhikkhu and Ecclesiastical Offences.
5. The Bhikkhu and Restraints.
6. The Bhikkhu and Good Conduct Rules.
7. The Bhikkhu and the Trial of Offences.
8. The Bhikkhu and Confession.

§ *1. The Sangh and Its Organization*

1. The followers of the Blessed Lord were divided into two classes: BHIKKHUS and Lay Followers called UPASAKAS.

2. The Bhikkhus were organized into a Sangh while the Upasakas were not.

3. The Buddhist Bhikkhu is primarily a Parivrajaka. This institution of Parivrajaka is older than that of the Buddhist Bhikkhu.

4. The old Parivrajakas were persons who had abandoned family life and were a mere floating body of wanderers.

5. They roamed about with a view to ascertain the truth by coming into contact with various teachers and philosophers, listening to their discourses, entering into discussion on matters of ethics, philosophy, nature, mysticism, etc.

6. Some of the old type of Parivrajakas lived under a teacher until they found another. Others lived singly without acknowledging any master.

7. Among these older type of Parivrajakas there were also women wanderers. The female Parivrajakas sometimes lived with men Parivrajakas ; sometimes they lived alone and by themselves.

8. These old type of Parivrajakas had no Sangh, had no rules of discipline and had no ideal to strive for.

9. It was for the first time that the Blessed Lord organized his followers into a Sangh or fraternity, and gave them rules of discipline and set before them an ideal to pursue and realize.

§ *2. Admission to the Sangh*

1. The Sangh was open to all.
2. There was no bar of caste.
3. There was no bar of sex.

4. There was no bar of status.

5. Caste had no place in the Sangh.

6. Social status had no place in the Sangh.

7. Inside the Sangh all were equal.

8. Inside the Sangh rank was regulated by worth and not by birth.

9. As the Blessed Lord said the Sangh was like the ocean and the Bhikkhus were like the rivers that fell into the ocean.

10. The river has its separate name and separate existence.

11. But once the river entered the ocean it lost its separate name and separate existence.

12. It becomes one with the rest.

13. Same is the case with the Sangh. When a Bhikkhu entered the Sangh he became one with the rest like the water of the ocean.

14. He lost his caste. He lost his status: so said the Lord.

15. The only distinction observed inside the Sangh was that of sex. The Bhikkhu Sangh was separate in its organization from the Bhikkhuni Sangh.

16. The entrants into the Sangh were divided into two classes: Shramaneras and Bhikkhus.

17. Anyone below twenty could become a Shramanera.

18. By taking the Trisaranas and by taking the ten precepts a boy becomes a Shramanera.

19. "I follow the Buddha; I follow the Dhamma; and I follow the Sangh"—are the Trisaranas.

20. "I shall abstain from killing; I shall not commit theft; I shall follow Brahmacharya; I shall not tell untruth; I shall abstain from drink."

21. "I shall abstain from taking food at an untimely hour; I shall abstain from indecent and immoral acts; I shall abstain from ornamenting and decorating myself; I shall abstain from luxuries; I shall abstain from the love of gold and silver."

22. These are the ten precepts.

23. A Shramanera can leave the Sangh at any time and become a layman. A Shramanera is attached

to a Bhikkhu and spends his time in the service of the Bhikkhu. He is not a person who has taken Parivraja.

24. The status of a Bhikkhu has to be reached in two stages. The first stage is called Parivraja and the second stage is called Upasampada. It is after Upasampada that he becomes a Bhikkhu.

25. A candidate who wishes to take Parivraja with a view ultimately to become a Bhikkhu has to seek a Bhikkhu who has the right to act as an Uppadhya. A Bhikkhu can become an Uppadhya only after he has spent at least 10 years as a Bhikkhu.

26. Such a candidate if accepted by the Uppadhya is called a Parivrajaka and has to remain in the service and tutelage of the Uppadhya.

27. After the period of tutelage ends it is his Uppadhya who has to propose the name of his student to a meeting of the Sangh specially called for the purpose for Upasampada and the student must request the Sangh for Upasampada.

28. The Sangh must be satisfied that he is a fit and a proper person to be made a Bhikkhu. For this purpose there is a set of questions which the candidate has to answer.

29. Only when the Sangh grants permission that Upasampada is granted and the person becomes a Bhikkhu.

30. The rules regulating entry into the Bhikkhuni Sangh are more or less the same as the rules regulating the entry into the Bhikkhu Sangh.

§ 3. *The Bhikkhu and His Vows*

1. A layman or a Shramanera takes precepts. His obligation is to follow them.

2. A Bhikkhu besides taking precepts takes them also as vows which he must not break. If he breaks them he becomes liable to punishment.

3. A Bhikkhu vows to remain celebate.

4. A Bhikkhu vows not to commit theft.

5. A Bhikkhu vows not to boast.

6. A Bhikkhu vows not to kill or take life.

7. A Bhikkhu vows not to own anything except what the rules allow.

8. No Bhikkhu is to possess more than the following eight articles:—

(1) Three pieces of cloth to cover his body:

(*i*) lower garment called Antarvaska.

(*ii*) upper garment called Uttarasang.

(*iii*) covering garment against cold called Sanghati.

(2) A girdle for the loins.

(3) An alms-bowl.

(4) A razor.

(5) A needle.

(6) A water-strainer.

9. A Bhikkhu takes the vow of poverty. He must beg for his food. He must live on alms. He must sustain himself only on one meal a day. Where there is no Vihar built for the Sangh, he must live under a tree.

10. A Bhikkhu does not take a vow of obedience. Outward respect and courtesy to his superiors is expected from the novice. His own salvation and his usefulness as a teacher depend on his self-culture. He is to obey not his superior but the Dhamma. His superior has no supernatural gift of wisdom or of absolution. He must stand or fall by himself. For that he must have freedom of thought.

11. Any breach of a vow taken by a Bhikkhu results in an offence of Parajika. The punishment for Parajika is expulsion from the Sangh.

§ 4. *The Bhikkhu and Ecclesiastical Offences*

1. Any breach of the vows taken by a Bhikkhu is an offence against the Dhamma.

2. In addition to these offences there were certain other offences to which he was also liable. They were called Sanghadisesa—ecclesiastical offences.

3. The list of such offences included in the Vinaya Pitaka are thirteen.

4. They are allied to the Parajika.

§ 5. *The Bhikkhu and Restraints*

1. Besides sailing clear of offences a Bhikkhu must observe certain restrictions and cannot be as free as others.

2. One set of such restrictions are called NISSAGIYA-PACITTIYA. It contains 26 restrictions to be observed by the Bhikkhu.

3. They relate to accepting gifts of robes, woollen mats, bowl and medical requisites.

4. They also relate to the acceptance of gold and silver. Engagement of a monk in buying and selling and appropriation of property given to the Sangh to himself.

5. The punishment for breach of these restrictions is restoration (nissagiya) and expression of repentance (pacittiya).

6. Besides these restrictions there are other restrictions which a Bhikkhu has to observe. They are called PACITTIYA. They number ninety-two.

§ 6. *The Bhikkhu and Good Conduct Rules*

1. A Bhikkhu must behave well. He should be a model person in his mode and manner of behaviour.

2. In order to secure this purpose the Blessed Lord framed a number of Good Conduct Rules.

3. These Good Conduct Rules were called Sekhiya Dhamma. They number seventy-five.

§ 7. *The Bhikkhu and the Trial of Offences*

1. The enactment of these acts and omissions were not a mere formality. They were legal in substance involving a definite charge, trial and punishment.

2. No Bhikkhu could be punished without a trial by a regularly constituted Court.

3. The Court was to be constituted by the Bhikkhus resident at the place where an offence had taken place.

4. No trial could take place without a proper number of Bhikkhus required to constitute a Court.

5. No trial would be legal without a definite charge.

V 6. No trial could be legal if it did not take place in the presence of the accused.

420 7. No trial could be legal if the accused had not been given the fullest opportunity to defend himself.

8. The following punishments could be awarded against a guilty Bhikkhu:

(i) Tarjaniya Karma (warn and discharge).

(ii) Niyasha Karma (declaring insane).

(iii) Pravrajniya Karma (expulsion from the Sangh).

(iv) Utskhepniya Karma (boycott).

(v) Parivasa Karma (expulsion from Vihar).

9. Expulsion may be followed by ABBANA KARMA. Abbana Karma means annulment of dismemberment. It may be followed after granting of Pardon granted by the Sangh after being satisfied with the proper performance of Parivasa Karma.

§ 8. *The Bhikkhu and Confession*

1. The most original and unique institution created by the Blessed Lord in connection with the organization of the Bhikkhus was the introduction of Confession, called UPOSATH.

2. The Blessed Lord realized that it was possible to enforce what he had laid down as offences. But he had laid down certain restrictions which were not offences. He said that the restrictions were most intimately connected with building up of character and maintaining character; and that there was equal necessity to see that they were observed.

3. But the Lord could find no effective way of enforcing them. He therefore thought of Confession in open as a means of organizing the Bhikkhu's conscience and making it act as a sentinel to guard him against taking a wrong or false step.

4. The Confession was confined to the transgressions of restrictions (which were called Patimokha).

5. For a Confession there was to be a meeting of the Bhikkhus of a given locality. There were to be three such meetings in a fortnight, one each on Chaturdashi, Panchadasi and Ashatami. On that day the Bhikkhus may fast. That is why the day is also called Uposath.

6. At the meeting a Bhikkhu reads the restrictions one by one contained in the Patimokha. After reading a restriction he says to the assembled Bhikkhus, "I take it that none of you have transgressed this Rule, that is why you are silent." He says this three times. Then deals with the next restriction.

7. A similar Confessional meeting is required of the Bhikhhuni Sangh.

8. On a Confession a charge and trial may follow.

9. On a failure to Confess, any Bhikkhu may report a transgression if he was a witness to it and then a charge and trial may follow.

PART II

The Bhikkhu—The Buddha's Conception of Him

1. Buddha's conception of what a Bhikkhu should be.
2. The Bhikkhu and the Ascetic.
3. The Bhikkhu and the Brahmin.
4. The Bhikkhu and the Upasaka.

§ 1. *Buddha's Conception of What a Bhikkhu Should Be*

1. The Buddha has himself told the Bhikkhus
what he expected of them as Bhikkhus. This is what V
he has said.

2. " He who wishes to put on the yellow dress 425
without having cleansed himself from sin, who disregards also temperance and truth, is unworthy of the yellow dress.

3. " But he who has cleansed himself from sin, is well grounded in all virtues, and endowed also with temperance and truth, he is indeed worthy of the yellow dress.

4. " A man is not a mendicant (Bhikkhu) simply because he asks others for alms; he who adopts the whole law is a Bhikkhu, not he who only begs.

5. " He who is above evil, who is chaste, who with care passes through the world, he indeed is called a Bhikkhu.

6. " Not only by discipline and vows, not only by much learning, not by entering into a trance not by sleeping alone, do I earn the happiness of release which no worldling can know. O Bhikkhu, he who has obtained the extinction of desires, has obtained confidence.

7. " The Bhikkhu who controls his mouth, who speaks wisely and calmly, who teaches the meaning of the law, his word is sweet.

8. " He who dwells in the law, delights in the law, meditates on the law, recollects the law, that Bhikkhu will never fall away from the true law.

9. " Let him not despise what he has received, nor ever envy others; a mendicant who envies others does not obtain peace of mind.

10. " A Bhikkhu who, though he receives little, does not despise what he has received, even the gods will praise him, if his life is pure, and if he is not slothful.

11. " He who never identifies himself with name

and form, and does not grieve over what is no more, he indeed is called a Bhikkhu.

12. "The Bhikkhu who behaves with kindness, who is happy in the doctrine of Buddha, will reach
v Nibbana—happiness arising from the cessation of natural inclinations.

426 13. "O Bhikkhu, empty this boat! If emptied, it will go quickly, having cut off passion and hatred, thou wilt go to Nibbana.

14. "Cut off the five (fetters), leave the five, rise above the five. A Bhikkhu who has escaped from the five fetters, he is called Oghatinna, 'saved from the flood.'

15. "Meditate, O Bhikkhu, and be not heedless! Do not direct thy thought to what gives pleasure.

16. "Without knowledge there is no meditation, without meditation there is no knowledge: he who has knowledge and meditation is near unto Nibbana.

17. "A Bhikkhu who has entered his empty house, and whose mind is tranquil, feels a more than human delight when he sees the Dhamma clearly.

18. "And this is the beginning here for a wise Bhikku; watchfulness over the senses, contentedness, restraint under the Dhamma; keep noble friends whose life is pure, and who are not slothful.

19. "Let him live on charity, let him be perfect in his duties; then in the fulness of delight he will make an end of suffering.

20. "Rouse thyself by thyself, examine thyself by thyself, thus self-protected and attentive wilt thou live happily, O Bhikkhu.

21. "For self is the lord of self, self is the refuge of self; therefore curb thyself as the merchant curbs a noble horse.

22. "A Bhikkhu (mendicant) who delights in earnestness, who looks with fear on thoughtlessness, moves about like fire, burning all his fetters, small or large.

23. "A Bhikkhu (mendicant) who delights in reflection, who looks with fear on thoughtlessness,

cannot fall away (from his perfect state)—he is close upon Nibbana."

24. The disciples of Gotama (Buddha) are always well awake, and their thoughts day and night are always set on Buddha.

25. The disciples of Gotama are always well awake and their thoughts day and night are always set on the church.

26. The disciples of Gotama are always well awake, and their thoughts day and night are always set on the Dhamma.

27. The disciples of Gotama are always well awake and their thoughts day and night are always set on their body.

28. The disciples of Gotama are always well awake, and their minds day and night always delight in compassion.

29. The disciples of Gotama are always well awake, and their minds day and night always delight in meditation.

30. It is hard to leave the world (to become a friar), it is hard to enjoy the world; hard is the monastery, painful are the houses; painful it is to dwell with equals (to share everything in common), and the itinerant mendicant is beset with pain.

31. A man full of faith, if endowed with virtue and glory, is respected, whatever place he may choose.

§ 2. *The Bhikkhu and the Ascetic*

1. Is the Bhikkhu an ascetic? The answer is in the negative.

2. This negative answer has been given by the Blessed Lord himself in a discussion with Nigrodha the wanderer.

3. The Exalted One was once staying near Rajagraha, on the Vulture's Peak. Now at that time there was sojourning in Queen Udumbarika's Park assigned to the wanderers, the wanderer Nigrodha, together with a great company of wanderers.

4. Now the Exalted One descending from the

Vulture's Peak came to the Peacock's Feeding-Ground on the bank of the Sumagadha and there walked to and fro in the open air. Then Nigrodha saw him thus walking, and on seeing him he called his company
V to order, saying: "Be still, sirs, and make no noise. The Samana Gotama is by the bank of the Sumagadha."
428 When he had said this the wanderers kept silence.

5. Then the Exalted One went up to Nigrodha the wanderer, and Nigrodha spake thus to him: "Let the Lord, the Exalted One, approach. Welcome is the Lord, the Exalted One! Long has the Lord, the Exalted One, taken ere deciding on this step of coming hither. May it please the Lord, the Exalted One, to take a seat. Here is one ready."

6. The Exalted One sat down on the seat made ready, and Nigrodha, taking a low seat, sat beside him.

7. Thereupon Nigrodha said to the Exalted One: "As the Samana Gotama has come to our assembly, we would like to ask him this question: 'What, Lord, is this religion of the Exalted One, wherein he trains his disciples, and which those disciples, so trained by the Exalted One as to win comfort, acknowledge to be their utmost support and the fundamental principles of righteousness?'"

8. "Difficult is it, Nigrodha, for one of another view, of another persuasion, of another confession, without practice and without teaching, to understand that wherein I train my disciples, and which they, so trained as to win comfort, acknowledge to be their utmost support and the fundamental principle of righteousness.

9. "But ask me, Nigrodha, a question about your own doctrine, about austere scrupulousness of life: in what does the fulfilment, in what does the non-fulfilment of these self-mortifications consist?"

10. Then Nigrodha spake thus to the Exalted One: "We, Lord, profess self-mortifying austerities; we hold them to be essential; we cleave to them. In what does the fulfilment, in what does the non-fulfilment of them consist?"

11. "Suppose, Nigrodha, that an ascetic goes

naked, is of certain loose habits, licks his hands,
respects no approach, sir, nor stop, sir; accepts nothing
expressly brought, nor expressly prepared, nor any
invitations. He accepts nothing taken from mouth
of cooking-pot, nor placed within the threshold, nor V
within a mortar, nor among sticks, nor within a quern;
nor anything from two eating together, nor from a 429
pregnant woman: nor from a nursing mother; nor
from a woman in intercourse with a man; nor food
collected in drought; nor from where a dog is; nor
from where flies are swarming; nor will he accept fish
or meat; nor drink strong drink, "nor intoxicants,
nor gruel. He is either a one-houser, a one-mouthful
man; or a two houser, a two-mouthful man; or a
seven-houser, a seven-mouthful man. He maintains
himself on one alms, on two, or on seven. He takes
food once a day, or once every two days, or once every
seven days. Thus does he dwell addicted to the
the practice of taking food according to rule, at
regular intervals, upto even half a month. He feeds
either on pot-herbs, or wild rice, or nivara seeds, or
leather parings, or on hata, or on the powder in rice
rusks, on rice-scum, on flour or oil-seeds, on grasses,
on cowdung, or fruits and roots from the wood or
on windfalls. He wears coarse hempen cloth, coarse
mixture cloth, discarded corps-cloths, discarded rags,
or tirita-bark cloth; or again he wears antelope-hide,
or strips of the same netted, or kusa fibre, or bark gar-
ments, or shale cloth, or a human-hair blanket, or a
horse-hair blanket, or an owl's-feather garment. He
is a hair-and-beard plucker, addicted to the practice of
plucking out both; a stander-up; a croucher on heels,
addicted to exerting himself (to move forward) when
thus squatting; a bed-of-thorns man, putting iron spikes
or thorns on his couch; he uses a plank-bed; sleeps on
the ground; sleeps only on one side; is a dust-and-dirt
wearer and an open-air man; a where-you-will sitter;
a filth-eater, addicted to the practice of eating such; a
non-drinker, addicted to the practice of drinking
(cold water); and even-for-third-time-man.

12. "After having done this, Nigrodha," the

Blessed Lord said, "What think you, Nigrodha? If these things be so, is the austerity of self-mortification carried out, or is it not?" "Truly, Lord, if these things be so, the austerity of self-mortification is carried out."

V 13. "Now I, Nigrodha, affirm that austerity by self-mortification thus carried out, involves blemish in
430 several ways."

14. "In what way, Lord, do you affirm that blemish is involved?"

15. "In case, Nigrodha, when an ascetic undertakes a course of austerity, he through that course, becomes self-complacent, his aim is satisfied. Now this, Nigrodha, becomes a blemish in the ascetic.

16. "And then again, Nigrodha, when an ascetic undertakes a course of austerity, he, through that undertaking exalts himself and despises others. This, too, becomes a blemish in the ascetic.

17. "And again, Nigrodha, when an ascetic undertakes a course of austerity, he, through that undertaking becomes inebriated and infatuated, and grows careless. This, too, becomes a blemish in the ascetic.

18. "And again, Nigrodha, when an ascetic undertakes a course of austerity, it procures for him gifts, attention and fame. Thereby he becomes complacent and his aim is satisfied. This, too, becomes a blemish in the ascetic.

19. "And again, Nigrodha, by the winning of gifts, attention and fame, the ascetic exalts himself and despises others. This, too, becomes a blemish in the ascetic.

20. "And again, Nigrodha, by the winning of gifts, attention and fame, he becomes inebriated and infatuated, and grows careless. This, too, becomes a blemish in the ascetic.

21. "And again, Nigrodha, when an ascetic undertakes a course of austerity, he comes to make a distinction in foods, saying: 'This suits me; this doesn't suit me. The latter kind he deliberately rejects. Over the former he waxes greedy and infatuated, and cleaves to them, seeing not the danger in them, discern-

ing them not as unsafe, and so enjoys them. This, too, becomes a blemish in the ascetic.

22. "And again, Nigrodha, because of his longing for gifts, attentions and fame, he thinks:
'Rajas will pay me attentions, and so will their officials; V
so too, will nobles, Brahmins, house-holders and
founders of schools.' This, too, becomes a blemish in 431
the ascetic.

23. "And again, Nigrodha, an asectic gets grumbling at some recluse or Brahmin, saying: 'That man lives on all sorts of things: things grown from tubers, or shoots, or berries, or joints, or fifthly, from seeds, munching them all up together with that wheel-less thunderbolt of a jawbone—and they call him a holy man!' This, too becomes a blemish in the ascetic.

24. "And again, Nigrodha, an ascetic sees a certain recluse or Brahmin receiving attentions, being revered, honoured and presented with offerings by the citizens. And seeing this he thinks: 'The citizens pay attention to this fellow who lives in luxury; they revere and honour him, and present him with offerings, while to me who, as ascetic, lives a really austere life, they pay no attentions, nor reverence, nor honour, nor offerings.' And so he cherishes envy and grudging at the citizens. This, too, becomes a blemish in the ascetic.

25. "And again, Nigrodha, the ascetic affects the mysterious. When asked: 'Do you approve of this?' He, not approving, says: 'I do,' or approving, says, 'I do not.' Thus he consciously tells untruths. This, too, becomes a blemish in the ascetic.

26. "And again, Nigrodha, the ascetic is liable to lose his temper and bear enmity. This, too, becomes a blemish in the ascetic.

27. "And again, Nigrodha, the ascetic is liable to be hypocritical and deceitful, as well as envious and grudging; he becomes cunning and crafty, hard-hearted and vain, he entertains evil wishes and becomes captive to them; he entertains false opinions, becomes possessed of metempirical dogma; misinterprets his experience; is avaricious and adverse from renunciation. This, too, becomes a blemish in the ascetic.

28. "What think you of this, Nigrodha? Are these things blemishes in the austerities of self-mortification, or are they not?"

29. "Verily, Lord, these things are blemishes in
V the austerities of self-mortification. It is possible, Lord, that an ascetic may be possessed even of all these
432 blemishes, much more by one or other of them."

30. The Bhikkhus are not to be guilty of these blemishes.

§ 3. *The Bhikkhu and the Brahmin*

1. Is the Bhikkhu the same as the Brahmin? The answer to this question is also in the negative.

2. The discussion of the subject has not been concentrated at any one place. It is scattered all over. But the points of distinction can be easily summed up.

3. A Brahmin is a priest. His main function is to perform certain ceremonies connected with birth, marriage and death.

4. These ceremonies become necessary because of the doctrines of original sin which requires ceremonies to wash it off, and because of the belief in God and in Soul.

5. For these ceremonies a priest is necessary. A Bhikkhu does not believe in original sin, in God and Soul. There are, therefore, no ceremonies to be performed. He is, therefore, not a priest.

6. A Brahmin is born. A Bhikkhu is made.

7. A Brahmin has a caste. A Bhikkhu has no caste.

8. Once a Brahmin always a Brahmin. No sin, no crime can unmake a Brahmin.

9. But once a Bhikkhu is not always a Bhikkhu. A Bhikkhu is made. So he can be unmade if by his conduct he makes himself unworthy of remaining a Bhikkhu.

10. No mental or moral training is necessary for being a Brahmin. All that is expected (only expected) of him is to know his religious lore.

11. Quite different is the case of the Bhikkhu, mental and moral training is his life-blood.

12. A Brahmin is free to acquire unlimited amount of property for himself. A Bhikkhu on the other hand cannot.

13. This is no small difference. Property is the severest limitation upon the mental and moral independence of man both in respect of thought and action. It produces a conflict between the two. That is why the Brahmin is always opposed to change. For, to him a change means loss of power and loss of pelf.

14. A Bhikkhu having no property is mentally and morally free. In his case there are no personal interests which can stand in the way of honesty and integrity.

15. They are Brahmins. None the less each Brahmin is an individual by himself. There is no religious organization to which he is subordinate. A Brahmin is a law unto himself. They are bound by common interests which are material.

16. A Bhikkhu on the other hand is always a member of the Sangh. It is inconceivable that there could be a Bhikkhu without his being a member of the Sangh. A Bhikkhu is not a law unto himself. He is subordinate to the Sangh. The Sangh is a spiritual organization.

§ 4. *The Bhikkhu and the Upasaka*

1. In the Dhamma there is a marked distinction between the Dhamma of the Bhikku and the Dhamma of the Upasaka or the layman.

2. The Bhikkhu is bound to celibacy. Not so the Upasaka. He can marry.

3. The Bhikkhu can have no home. He can have no family. Not so the Upasaka. The Upasaka can have a home and can have a family.

4. The Bhikkhu is not to have any property. But an Upasaka can have property.

5. The Bhikkhu is forbidden from taking life. Not so the Upasaka. He may.

6. The Panchasilas are common to both. But to the Bhikkhu they are vows. He cannot break them without incurring penalty. To the Upasaka they are precepts to be followed.

7. The Bhikkhu's observance of the Panchasilas is compulsory. Their observance by the Upasakas is voluntary.

8. Why did the Blessed Lord make such a distinction? There must be some good reason for it. For the Blessed Lord would not do anything unless there was some good reason for it.

9. The reason for this distinction is nowhere explicitly stated by the Blessed Lord. It is left to be inferred. All the same it is necessary to know the reason for this distinction.

10. There is no doubt that the Blessed Lord wanted through his Dhamma to lay the foundation of a kingdom of righteousness on earth. That is why he preached his Dhamma to all without distinction, to Bhikkus as well as to laymen.

11. But the Blessed Lord also knew that merely preaching the Dhamma to the common men would not result in the creation of that ideal society based on righteousness.

12. An ideal must be practical and must be shown to be practicable. Then and then only people strive after it and try to realize it.

13. To create this striving it is necessary to have a picture of a society working on the basis of the ideal and thereby proving to the common man that the ideal was not impracticable but on the other hand realizable.

14. The Sangh is a model of a society realizing the Dhamma preached by the Blessed Lord.

15. This is the reason why the Blessed Lord made this distinction between the Bhikkhu and the Upasaka. The Bhikkhu was the torch-bearer of the Buddha's ideal society and the Upasaka was to follow the Bhikkhu as closely as he could.

16. There is also another question that requires an answer. What is the function of the Bhikkhu?

17. Is the Bhikkhu to devote himself to self-culture or is he to serve the people and guide them ?

18. He must discharge both the functions.

19. Without self-culture he is not fit to guide. Therefore he must himself be a perfect, best man, righteous man and an enlightened man. For this he must practice self-culture.

20. A Bhikkhu leaves his home. But he does not retire from the world. He leaves home so that he may have the freedom and the opportunity to serve those who are attached to their homes but whose life is full of sorrow, misery and unhappiness and who cannot help themselves.

21. Compassion which is the essence of the Dhamma requires that every one shall love and serve and the Bhikkhu is not exempt from it.

22. A Bhikkhu who is indifferent to the woes of mankind, however perfect in self-culture, is not at all a Bhikkhu. He may be something else but he is not a Bhikkhu.

PART III

The Duties of the Bhikkhu

1. The Bhikkhu's Duty to Convert.
2. Conversion Not to be by Miracles.
3. Conversion Not to be by Force.
4. A Bhikkhu Must Fight to Spread Virtue (Dhamma).

§ *1. The Bhikkhu's Duty to Convert*

1. The news of the conversion of Yasa and his four friends to the Dhamma spread far and wide. The result was that lay persons belonging to the highest families in the country and to those next to the highest came to be instructed in the doctrine of the Blessed One and to take refuge in Him and in His Dhamma.

2. Many people were coming to Him to receive instruction in the Dhamma. The Lord knew that it was difficult for Him personally to give instruction to each one. He also felt the necessity of organizing Parivrajakas whose number was swelling every day into a religious order which He called the Sangh.

3. He accordingly made the Parivrajakas the members of the Sangh and framed rules of discipline called VINAYA and made them binding upon the members of the Sangh.

4. The Blessed Lord later on laid down two stages to be undergone by a disciple before he became a Bhikkhu. First a disciple became a Parivrajaka and remained a Parivrajaka for a certain number of years attached to a Bhikkhu and remaining in training under him. After his training period was over he was allowed to take Upasampada if he satisfied a body of examiners that he was fit for it. It is only then that he was allowed to become a Bhikkhu and a member of the Sangh.

5. There was no time in the early stages of the Dhamma to make such arrangements. The Lord, therefore, made them Bhikkhus and sent them out as Missionaries to spread His religion to anywhere and everywhere.

6. And before sending them out the Blessed One said to the Bhikkhus: "I am delivered, O Bhikkhus, from all fetters, human and divine. You, O Bhikkhus, from all fetters, human and divine. Go ye now, and wander for the gain of the many, for the welfare of the many, out of compassion for the world; for the good, for the gain and for the welfare of gods and men.

7. "Let not two of you go the same way.

Preach, Bhikkhus, the doctrine which is glorious in the beginning, glorious in the middle, glorious at the end, in the spirit and in the letter; proclaim a consummate, perfect and pure life of holiness.

V 8. " Go then through every country, convert
those not yet converted; throughout the world that
440 lies burnt up with sorrow, teach everywhere: (instruct)
those lacking right instruction;

9. " Go where there are great Rishis, royal Rishis, Brahman Rishis too, these all dwell there, influencing men according to their schools;

10. " Go, therefore, each one travelling by himself; filled with compassion, go! rescue and receive."

11. The Blessed Lord also told them:

12. " That the gift of the Dhamma exceeds all gifts; the sweetness of the Dhamma exceeds all sweetness; the delight in the Dhamma exceeds all delights;

13. "The fields are damaged by weeds, mankind is damaged by passion: therefore a gift of Dhamma brings great reward.

14. "The fields are damaged by weeds, mankind is damaged by hatred: therefore a gift of Dhamma brings great reward.

15. "The fields are damaged by weeds; mankind is damaged by vanity: therefore the gift of Dhamma brings great reward.

16. "The fields are damaged by weeds, mankind is damaged by lust: therefore a gift of Dhamma brings great reward."

17. Then the sixty Bhikkhus receiving orders to carry on the mission to propagate the Dhamma went through every land.

18. The Lord gave them further instruction in the matter of conversions.

§ 2. *Conversion Not to be by Miracles*

1. The Exalted One was once staying among the Mallas, at Anapiya, one of their towns.

2. Now the Exalted One, having robed himself, put on his cloak, and took his bowl, and entered the town for alms.

3. The Blessed One thought: "It is too early for me now to go through Anapiya for alms. I might go to the pleasance where Bhaggava, the wanderer dwells, and call upon him."

4. So the Exalted One went to the pleasance and to the place where Bhaggava, the wanderer was.

5. Then Bhaggava spake thus to the Exalted One: "Let my Lord, the Exalted One come near. Welcome to the Exalted One! It is long since the Exalted One has taken the opportunity to come our way. May it please You, Sir, to be seated; here is a seat made ready."

6. The Exalted One sat down thereon, and Bhaggava taking a certain low stool, sat down beside him. So seated, Bhaggava, the wanderer spake thus to the Exalted One:

7. "Some days ago, Lord, Sunakkhatta of the Licchavis called on me and spake thus: 'I have now given up the Exalted One, Bhaggava. I am remaining no longer under him as my teacher.' Is the fact really so?"

8. "It is just so, Bhaggava, as Sunakkhatta of the Licchavis said.

9. "Some days ago, Bhaggava, a good many days ago, Sunakkhatta, the Licchavi, came to call on me, and spake thus: 'Sir, I now give up the Exalted One, I will henceforth remain no longer under him as my teacher.' When he told me this, I said to him: 'But, now, Sunakkhatta, have I ever said to you: 'Come Sunakkhatta, live under me as my pupil?'

10. "'No, Sir, you have not,' replied Sunakkhatta.

11. "Or have you ever said to me: 'Sir, I would fain dwell under the Exalted One (as my teacher)?'

12. "'No, Sir, I have not,' said Sunakkhatta.

13. "'But if I said not the one, and you said not the other, what are you and what am I that you talk of giving up?'

14. "'Well, but, Sir, the Exalted One works me

no mystic wonders surpassing the power of ordinary men.'

15. "Why, now, Sunakkhatta, have I ever said to you 'Come, take me as your teacher, Sunakkhatta,
V and I will work for you mystic wonders surpassing the power of ordinary men?'

442 16. "'You have not, Sir.'

17. "Or have you ever said to me: 'Sir, I would fain take the Exalted One as my teacher for he will work for me mystic wonders beyond the powers of ordinary men?'

18. "'I have not, Sir.'

19. "'But if I said not the one, and you said not the other, what are you and what am I, foolish man, that you talk of giving up? What think you, Sunakkhatta?'

20. "Whether mystic wonders beyond the power of ordinary men are wrought, or whether they are not, is not the object for which I teach the Dhamma this: that it leads to the thorough destruction of ill for the doer thereof?'

21. "'Whether, Sir, they are wrought or not, that is indeed the object for which the Norm is taught by the Exalted One.'

22. "But Bhaggava, Sunakkhatta went on saying to me, 'Sir, the Exalted One does not reveal to me the beginning of things.'

23. "Why now, Sunakkhatta, have I ever said to you: 'Come, Sunakkhatta, be my disciple and I will reveal to you the beginning of things?'

24. "'Sir, you have not.'

25. "Or have you ever said to me: 'I will become the Exalted One's pupil, for he will reveal to me the beginning of things?'

26. "'Sir, I have not.'

27. "'But if I have not said the one and you have not said the other, what are you and what am I, foolish man, that you talk of giving up on that account? What you, Sunakkhatta? Whether the beginning of things be revealed, or whether it be not, is the object for which I teach the Dhamma this: that it leads to

the thorough destruction of ill for the doer thereof ?'

28. "'Whether, Sir, they are revealed or not, that is indeed the object for which the Dhamma is taught by the Exalted One.'

29. "'If then, Sunakkhatta, it matters not to that object whether the beginning of things be revealed, or whether it be not, of what use to you would it be to have the beginning of things revealed ?'

30. "'In many ways have you, Sunakkhatta, spoken my praises among the Vajjins.'

31. "'In many ways have you, Sunakkhatta, spoken the praises of the Dhamma among the Vajjins.'

32. "'In many ways have you, Sunakkhatta, spoken the praises of the Order among the Vajjins.'

33. "I tell you, Sunakkhatta, I make known to you, that there will be those that shall say concerning you thus: 'Sunakkhatta of the Licchavis was not able to live the holy life under Gotama the recluse. And he, not being able to adhere to it, hath renounced the discipline and turned to lower things.'

34. "Thus, Bhaggava, did Sunakkhatta of the Licchavis, addressed by me, depart from this Doctrine and Discipline, as one doomed to disaster."

35. And soon after, leaving the Doctrine and Discipline of the Buddha, Sunakkhatta started telling people that there was nothing superhuman about the Buddha's ennobling gifts of knowledge and insight; that it was his own reasoning which had hammered out a doctrine of his own evolving and of his personal invention, such that whoso hears it preached for his good has only to act up to it to be guided to the utter ending of ill.

36. Although, Sunakkhatta was slandering the Buddha, what he was telling people was true. For, the Buddha never resorted to the superhuman or the miraculous in propagating his Doctrine.

§ 3. *Conversion Not to be by Force*

1. The Blessed One was once going along the high road between Rajagraha and Nalanda with a great

company of the brethren,—with about five hundred brethren. And Suppiya the mendicant, too, was going along the high road between Rajagraha and Nalanda with his disciple, the youth Brahmadatta.

V 2. Now, just then, Suppiya the mendicant was
speaking in many ways in dispraise of the Buddha, in
444 dispraise of the Doctrine, in dispraise of the Order.
But young Brahmadatta, his pupil, gave utterance, in many ways, to praise of the Buddha, to praise of the Doctrine, to praise of the Order.

3. Thus they two, teacher and pupil, holding opinions in direct contradiction one to the other, were following, step by step, after the Blessed One and the company of the brethren.

4. Now the Blessed One put up at the royal rest-house in the Ambalatthika pleasance to pass the night, and with him the company of the brethren. And so also did Suppiya the mendicant, and with him his young disciple Brahmadatta. And there, at the rest-house, these two carried on the same discussion as before.

5. And in the early dawn a number of the brethren, assembled, as they rose up, in the pavilion; and the subject of the talk that sprang up among them was the conversation between Suppiya and Bramhadatta.

6. Now the Blessed One, on realising what was the drift of their talk, went to the pavilion, and took his seat on the mat spread out for him. And when he had sat down he said: "What is the talk on which you are engaged sitting here, and what is the subject of the conversation between you?" And they told him all. And he said:

7. "Brethren, if outsiders should speak against me or against the Doctrine, or against the Order, you should not on that account either bear malice, or suffer heart-burning, or feel ill-will.

8. "If you, on that account, should be angry and hurt, that would stand in the way of your own self-conquest. If, when others speak against us, you feel angry at that, and displeased, would you then be able

to judge how far that speech of their's is well said or ill ? "

9. " That would not be so, Sir."

10. " But when outsiders speak in dispraise of me, or of the Doctrine, or of the Order, you should unravel what is false and point it out as wrong, saying: ' For this or that reason this is not the fact, that is not so, such a thing is not found among us, is not in us.'

11. " But also, brethren, outsiders may speak in praise of me, in praise of the Doctrine, in praise of the Order. What are the things when they would say praising me you would say ?

12. " He may say ' Putting away the killing of living things, Gotama the recluse holds aloof from the destruction of life. He has laid the cudgel and the sword aside, and ashamed of roughness, and full of mercy, he dwells compassionate and kind to all creatures that have life.' It is thus that the unconverted man, when speaking in praise of the Tathagata, might speak.

13. " Or he might say: ' Putting away the taking of what has not been given, Gotama the recluse lived aloof from grasping what is not his own. He takes only what is given, and expecting that gifts will come. He passes his life in honesty and purity of heart.'

14. " Or he might say: ' Putting away unchastity, Gotama the recluse is chaste. He holds himself aloof, far off, from the vulgar practice, from the sexual act.'

15. " Or he might say: ' Putting away lying words, Gotama the recluse holds himself aloof from falsehood. He speaks truth, from the truth he never swerves; faithful and trustworthy, he breaks not his word to the world."

16. " Or he might say: ' Putting away slander, Gotama the recluse holds himself aloof from calumny. What he hears here he repeats not elsewhere to raise a quarrel against the people here; what he hears elsewhere he repeats not here to raise a quarrel against the people there. Thus does he live as a binder together of those who are divided, an encourager of those who are

friends, a peacemaker, a lover of peace, impassioned for peace, a speaker of words that make for peace.'

17. "Or he might say: 'Putting away rudeness of speech, Gotama the recluse holds himself aloof
V from harsh language. Whatsoever word is blameless,
pleasant to the ear, lovely, reaching to the heart,
446 urbane, pleasing to the people, beloved of the people—
such are words he speaks.'

18. "Or he might say: 'Putting away frivolous talk, Gotama the recluse holds himself aloof from vain conversation. In season he speaks, in accordance with the facts, words full of meaning, on religion, on the discipline of the Order. He speaks, and at the right time, words worthy to be laid up in one's heart, fitly illustrated, clearly divided, to the point.'

19. "Or he might say: 'Gotama the recluse holds himself aloof from causing injury to seeds or plants.

'He takes but one meal a day, no eating at night, refraining from food after hours (after midday).

'He refrains from being a spectator at shows, at fairs, with nautch dances, singing, and music.

'He abstains from wearing, adorning or ornamenting himself, with garlands, scents, and unguents.

'He abstains from the use of large and lofty beds.

'He abstains from accepting silver or gold.

'He abstains from accepting uncooked grain.

'He abstains from accepting women or girls.

'He abstains from accepting bond-men or bond-women.

'He abstains from accepting sheep or goats.

'He abstains from accepting fowls or swine.

'He abstains from accepting elephants, cattle, horses and mares.

'He abstains from accepting cultivated fields or waste.

'He abstains from acting as a go-between or messenger.

'He abstains from buying and selling.

'He abstains from cheating with scales or bronzes or measures.

'He abstains from the crooked ways of bribery, cheating and fraud.

'He abstains from maiming, murder, putting in bonds, highway robbery, dacoity and violence.'

20. "Such are the things, brethren, which an unconverted man, when speaking in praise of the Tathagata, might say. But you should not even on that account, be filled with pleasure or gladness, or be lifted up in heart. Were you to be so, that also would stand in the way of your self-conquest. When outsiders speak in praise of me, or of the Doctrine, or of the Order, you should acknowledge what is right to be the fact, saying: 'For this or that reason this is the fact, that is so, such a thing is found among us, is in us.'"

§ 4. *A Bhikkhu Must Fight to Spread Virtue (Dhamma)*

1. Addressing the Bhikkhus the Lord once said:

2. "It is not I,O disciples, that quarrel with the world," said the Lord, "but the world that quarrels with me. A teacher of the truth does not quarrel with anyone in the world."

3. "Warriors, warriors, Lord, we call ourselves. In what way then are we warriors?"

4. "We wage war, O disciples, therefore we are called warriors."

5. "Wherefore, Lord, do we wage war?"

6. "For lofty virtues, for high endeavour, for sublime wisdom—for these things do we wage war: therefore we are called warriors."

7. Where virtue is in danger do not avoid fighting, do not be mealy-mouthed.

PART IV

The Bhikkhu and the Laity

1. The Bond of Alms.
2. Mutual Influence.
3. Dhamma of the Bhikkhu and the Dhamma of the Upasaka.

§ 1. *The Bond of Alms*

1. The Sangh was an organized body the membership of which was not open to all.

2. To be a mere Parivrajaka was not enough to give the Parivrajaka a membership of the Sangh.

3. It is only after the Parivrajaka had obtained Upasampada that he could become a member of the Sangh.

4. The Sangh was an independent body. It was independent even of its founder.

5. It was autonomous. It could admit anyone it liked to its membership. It could dismember any member provided it acted in accordance with the rules of the Vinaya Pitaka.

6. The only cord which bound the Bhikkhu to the Laity was alms.

7. The Bhikkhu depended upon alms and it is the laity who gave alms.

8. The laity was not organized.

9. There was a Sangha-Diksha or a ceremony for marking the initiation of a person in the Sangh.

10. Sangha-Diksha included both initiation into the Sangh as well as into the Dhamma.

11. But there was no separate Dhamma-Diksha for those who wanted to be initiated into the Dhamma but did not wish to become members of the Sangh, one of the consequences of which was to go from home into homelessness.

12. This was a grave omission. It was one of the causes which ultimately led to the downfall of Buddhism in India.

13. For, this absence of the initiation ceremony left the laity free to wander from one religion to another and, worse still, follow at one and the same time.

§ 2. *Mutual Influence*

1. However, the bond of alms was enough for a Bhikkhu to reform an erring member of the laity.

2. In this connection the following rules mentioned in the Anguttara Nikaya are worthy of attention.

3. In addition to these prescriptions, the laity had a general right to complain against a Bhikkhu to other Bhikkhus, against any mischief or misconduct.

4. The moment the complaint reached the Buddha and he had verified it, the relevant rule in the Vinaya Pithaka was amended to make the repetition of such a conduct, an offence against the Sangh.

5. The Vinaya Pithaka is nothing but redress of the complaints of the laity.

6. Such was the relation between the Bhikkhu and the Laity.

§ 3. *Dhamma of the Bhikkhu and the Dhamma of the Upasaka*

1. Some critics of Buddhism allege that Buddhism is not a religion.

2. No attention should be paid to such criticism. But if any reply is to be given, it is that Buddhism is the only real religion and those who do not accept this must revise their definition of Religion.

3. Other critics do not go so far as this. What they say is that Buddhism as a religion is concerned only with the Bhikkhu. It does not concern itself with the common man. Buddhism kept the common man outside its pale.

4. The references to the Bhikkhu occur so often in the dialogues of the Buddha that they go to strengthen the criticism.

5. It, therefore, becomes necessary to make the matter clear.

6. Was the Dhamma common to both? Or is there any part of the Dhamma which is binding on the Bhikkhu but not so on the laity?

7. Merely because the sermons were addressed to the gathering of the Bhikkhus it must not be supposed that what was preached was intended to apply to them only. What was preached applied to both.

8. That the Buddha had the laity in mind when he preached: (1) The Panchasila, (2) The Ashtanga

Marga, and (3) The Paramitas, is quite clear from the very nature of things and no argument, really speaking, is necessary.

9. It is those who have not left their homes and who are engaged in active life that Panchasila, Ashtanga Marga, and Paramitas are essential. It is they who are likely to transgress them and not the Bhikkhu who has left home, who is not engaged in active life and who is not likely to transgress them.

10. When the Buddha, therefore, started preaching his Dhamma it must be principally for the laity.

11. It is not, however, necessary to rely merely on inference. There is direct evidence to disprove the criticism.

12. Reference may be made to the following sermon.

13. Once while the Lord was staying at Shravasti in Jeta's Grove in Anathapindika's pleasance, there came to him the lay follower Dhammika, with other five hundred lay followers, who after due salutations, took his seat to one side and addressed the Lord as follows :

14. "What conduct, Oh Lord, perfects, both those that are Bhikkhus and those that are only Upasakas, i.e., those who are homeless and those who are not.

15. "Let the almsmen seated round with these lay followers learn the saving truth."

16. The Blessed Lord said: "Give ear, almsmen. Hear, and keep the rules prescribed.

17. "Go not thy round when noon is past; betime seek alms. Snares greet the untimely guest.

18. "Before thou seek thy meal, clear thou thy mind of zest for forms, sounds, odours, taste and luck.

19. "Thine alms received, return alone, to sit apart and think, with fixed mind that never stays abroad.

20. "In talk with pious folk, almsmen, let thy theme be the Doctrine.

21. "Treat alms, cell, bed, water and rinsings just as means and nothing more.

22. "Such reasoned use will leave an almsman

as unstained as lotus leaf whereon no drop of water rests.

23. " I now pass to the conduct which perfects the lay followers. To them I say :

V 24. " Slay not, nor doom to death, nor sanction
slaughter. Do no violence to aught that lives, strong
454 or weak. Love all living beings.

25. " No layman wittingly should thieve or order theft ; take but what others give.

26. " Shun incontinence as it were a pit of fire, on failing continence, debauch no wedded wife.

27. " In conclaves, courts, let him not be, let him not prompt or sanction lies; let him renounce untruth.

28. " Observe this law : Shun drink, make no man drink ; sanction no drinking. Mark how drink to madness leads.

29. " Through drink, fools sin, and egg lax brethren on to sin. So flee this maddening vice, this folly, bliss of fools.

30. " Slay not, steal not, lie not ; from strong drink keep away ; refrain from lechery.

31. " So make thy sabbath vows as week succeeds week, and keep with pious hearts this eight-fold festival.

32. " At morn, these vows performed, with pious, thankful heart, be wise and of thy means give almsmen food and drink.

33. "Cherish thy parents well; follow a righteous trade.

34. " Thus shall the layman, staunch, reach realms of light above."

35. It will thus be seen that the Dhamma was the same for both.

36. There are of course differences in the call made upon the two.

37. A Bhikkhu must take five vows.

38. He must take the vow that he shall not kill.

39. He must take the vow that he shall not appropriate to himself property of another which has not been given to him.

40. He must take the vow that he shall never tell a lie.

41. He must take the vow that he shall not try to have carnal knowledge of a woman.

42. He must take the vow that he shall never drink any intoxicating drink.

43. All these rules are binding also upon the layman.

44. The only difference lies in this. With the Bhikkhu they are vows which are not to be transgressed, with the layman they are moral obligations to be voluntarily honoured.

45. Besides, there are two other differences which are noteworthy.

46. A Bhikkhu cannot have private property. A layman can have.

47. A Bhikkhu is free to enter parnibban. Nibbana is enough for a layman.

48. These are the similarities and differences between a Bhikkhu and the layman.

49. Dhamma, however, is the same for both.

PART V

Vinaya for the Laity

1. Vinaya for the Wealthy.
2. Vinaya for the Householder.
3. Vinaya for Children.
4. Vinaya for Pupil.
5. Vinaya for Husband and Wife.
6. Vinaya for Master and Servant.
7. Conclusions.
8. Vinaya for Girls.

§ 1. *Vinaya for the Wealthy*

(i)

1. The Blessed Lord did not elevate poverty by calling it a blessed state of life.

2. Nor did he tell the poor that they may remain content for they will inherit the earth.

3. On the contrary, he said riches are welcome. What he insisted upon is that the acquisition of riches must be subject to Vinaya.

(ii)

1. Once Anathapindika came to where the Exalted One was. Having come, he made obeisance to the Exalted One and took a seat at one side and asked, " Will the Enlightened One tell what things are welcome, pleasant, agreeable, to the householder but which are hard to gain."

2. The Enlightened One having heard the question put to him said,—" Of such things the first is to acquire wealth lawfully.

3. " The second is to see that your relations also get their wealth lawfully.

4. " The third is to live long and reach great age.

5. "For a true householder for the attainment of these three things, which in the world are welcome, pleasant, agreeable but hard to gain, there are also four conditions precedent. They are the blessing of faith, the blessing of virtuous conduct, the blessing of liberality and the blessing of wisdom.

6. " The blessing of faith and belief consist in the supreme knowledge of the Tathagata which teaches 'This is He, the Exalted One, the Holy One, the Supremely Awakened One, the perfect in Knowledge and in Conduct, the Auspicious, the Knower of all the worlds, the Incomparable Trainer of men, the Teacher of Devas and men.'

7. " The blessing of virtuous conduct which abstains from taking life, thieving, unchastity, lying and partaking of fermented liquor.

8. " The blessing of liberality consists in the

householder living with mind freed from the taint of avarice, generous, open-handed, delighting in gifts, a good one to be asked and devoted to the distribution of gifts.

V 9. "Wherein consists the blessing of Wisdom? Ye know that a householder who dwells with mind
460 overcome by greed, avarice, ill-will, sloth, drowsiness, distraction and flurry, commits wrongful deeds and neglects that which ought to be done, and by so doing is deprived of happiness and honour.

10. "Greed, avarice, ill-will, sloth and drowsiness, distraction and flurry and doubt are stains of the mind. A householder who gets rid of such stains of the mind acquires great wisdom, abundant wisdom, clear vision and perfect wisdom.

11. Thus, to acquire wealth legitimately and justly, earned by great industry, amassed by strength of the arm and gained by sweat (of the brow) is a great blessing. The householder makes himself happy and cheerful and preserves himself full of happiness; also make parents, wife and children, servants and labourers, friends and companions happy and cheerful, and preserves them full of happiness."

§ 2. *Vinaya for the Householder*

On this matter the Buddha's thoughts are embodied in his discourse with Sigala.

1. At one time the Exalted One was in the Squirrels' Feeding-ground in Velu Vana in Rajagraha.

2. Now at this time young Sigala, a householder's son, rising betimes, went forth from Rajagraha, and with wet hair and wet garments and clasped hands uplifted, paid worship to the several quarters of earth and sky—to the east, south, west and north, to the nadir and the zenith.

3. And the Exalted One early that morning dressed himself, took his bowl and robe and entered Rajagraha seeking alms. He saw young Sigala worshipping and asked him, "Why do you worship the several quarters of earth and sky?"

4. " My father, when he was dying, said to me : 'Dear son, you should worship the quarters of earth and sky. So I, sir, honouring my father's word worship in this wise.' "

5. " But how can this be the true religion of a man of the world " asked the Blessed One. " What else can be the religion of man," replied Sigala. " If there is, it would be an excellent thing if the Exalted One would tell me what it is."

6. " Hear then young householder, give ear to my words and I will tell you what it is." " So be it, Sir," responded young Sigala. And the Exalted One said :

7. " A religion to be a religion of man must teach him to shun bad conduct. The destruction of life, the taking of what is not given, licentiousness and lying speech are the four vices of conduct which he must avoid.

8. " Know ye, Sigala, evil deeds are done from motives of partiality, enmity, stupidity and fear. If he is not led away by these motives, he will do no evil deed.

9. " A religion to be religion of man must teach him not to dissipate his wealth. Dissipation of wealth results from being addicted to intoxicating liquors, frequenting the streets at unseemly hours, haunting fairs, being infatuated by gambling, associating with evil companions, the habit of idleness.

10. " There are, Sigala, six dangers which follow from being addicted to intoxicating liquors, actual loss of wealth, increase of quarrels, susceptibility to disease, loss of good character, indecent exposure, impaired intelligence.

11. " Six are the perils from frequenting the streets at unseemly hours : he himself is without guard or protection and so also are his wife and children, so also is his property, he, moreover, becomes suspected as the doer of undiscovered crimes, and false rumours fix on him, and many are the troubles he goes out to meet.

12. " Six are the perils from the haunting of fairs :

he is ever thinking where is there dancing? Where is there singing? where is there music? where is recitation? where are the cymbals? where the tam-tams?

13. "Six are the perils for him who is infatuated
V with gambling: as winner he begets hatred, when
beaten he mourns his lost wealth, his actual substance
462 is wasted, his word has no weight in a court of law,
he is despised by friends and officials, he is not sought
after by those who would give or take in marriage, for
they would say that a man who is a gambler cannot
afford to keep a wife.

14. "Six are the perils from associating with evil companions: any gambler, any libertine, any tippler, any cheat, any swindler, any man of violence is his friend and companion.

15. "Six are the perils of the habit of idleness: he says it is too cold and does no work, he says it is too hot and does no work, he says it is too early or too late and does no work, he says I am too hungry and does no work, he says I am too full and does no work. And while all that he should do remains undone, new wealth he does not get, and such wealth as he has dwindles away.

16. "A religion to be a religion of man must teach him to know who is a true friend.

17. "Four are they who should be reckoned as foes in the likeness of friends; to wit, a rapacious person, the man of words not deeds, the flatterer, and the fellow-waster.

18. "Of these the first is to be reckoned as a foe in the likeness of a friend: for, he is rapacious, he gives little and asks much; he does his duty out of fear, he pursues his own interests.

19. "A man of words who is not a man of deeds is to be reckoned as a foe in the likeness of a friend: For, he makes a friendly profession as regards the past, he makes friendly profession as regards the future, he tries to gain your favour by empty sayings, when the opportunity for service has arisen he avows his disability.

20. "The flatterer is to be reckoned as a foe

in the likeness of a friend: for, he both consents to do wrong, and dissents from doing right ; he praises to your face ; he speaks ill of you to others.

21. " So also the fellow-waster companion is to be reckoned as a foe in the likeness of a friend ; for, he is your companion when you frequent the streets at untimely hours, he is your companion when you haunt shows and fairs, he is your companion when you are infatuated with gambling.

22. " Four are the friends who should be reckoned as sound at heart: the helper ; the friend who is the same in happiness and adversity ; the friend of good counsel ; the friend who sympathises.

23. " The friend who is a helper is to be reckoned as sound at heart : because, he guards you when you are off your guard, he guards your property when you are off your guard, he is a refuge to you when you are afraid, when you have tasks to perform he provides a double supply of what you may need.

24. " The friend who is the same in happiness and adversity is to be reckoned as sound of heart : because, he tells you his secrets, he keeps secret your secrets, in your troubles he does not foresake you, he lays down even his life for your sake.

25. " The friend who declares what you need to do is sound of heart; because, he restrains you from doing wrong, he enjoins you to do what is right, he informs you of what you had not heard before, he reveals to you the way of heaven.

26. " The friend who sympathises is to be reckoned as sound at heart; because, he does not rejoice over your misfortunes, he rejoices over your prosperity, he restrains anyone who is speaking ill of you, he commends anyone who is praising you." Thus speaks the Exalted One.

27. " Instead of teaching him to worship the six quarters, a religion which is a religion of man must teach him to respect and revere his parents, his teachers, his wife and children, his friends and companions, his servants and workmen and his religious teachers."

§ 3. *Vinaya for Children*

1. "A child should minister to his parents saying: 'Once supported by them I will now be their support, I will perform duties incumbent on
V them; I will keep up the lineage and tradition of my
464 family, I will make myself worthy of my heritage.' For, the parents show their love for him, they restrain him from vice, they exhort him to virtue, they train him to a profession, they contract a suitable marriage for him, and in due time they hand over his inheritance."

§ 4. *Vinaya for Pupil*

1. "A pupil should minister to his teachers by rising from his seat, in salutation by waiting upon them, by eagerness to learn, by personal service, and by attention when receiving their teaching. For, teachers love their pupil, they train him in that wherein he has been well trained, they make him hold fast that which is well held, they thoroughly instruct him in the lore of every art, they speak well of him among his friends and companions. They provide for his safety in every quarter."

§ 5. *Vinaya for Husband and Wife*

1. "A husband should minister to his wife by showing respect, by courtesy, by faithfulness, by handing over authority to her, by providing her with adornment. For, the wife loves him, her duties are well performed, by hospitality to the kin of both, by faithfulness, by watching over the goods he brings, and by skill and industry in discharging all her business.

2. "A clansman should minister to his friends and companions by generosity, courtesy and benevolence, by treating them as he treats himself, and by being as good as his word. For, his friends and familiars love him, they protect him when he is off his guard, and on such occasion guard his property, they

become a refuge in danger, they do not forsake him in his trouble and they show consideration for his family."

§ 6. *Vinaya for Master and Servant* V

465
1. "A master should minister to his servants and employees by assigning them work according to their strength, by supplying them with food and wages, by tending them in sickness, by sharing with them unusual delicacies, by granting leave at times. For, servants and employees love their master, they rise before him, they lie down to rest after him, they are content with what is given to them, they do their work well, and they carry about his praise and good fame.

2. "A clansman should minister to religious teachers by affection in act and speech and mind, by keeping open house to them, by supplying their temporal needs. For, religious teachers restrain him from evil, they exhort him to good, they love him with kindly thoughts, they teach him what he had not heard, they correct and purify what he has heard."

§ 7. *Conclusions*

1. When the Exalted One had thus spoken Sigala, the young householder said this: "Beautiful, Lord, beautiful! As if one should set up again that which had been overthrown, or reveal that which had been hidden, or should disclose the road to one that was astray, or should carry a lamp into darkness, saying: They that have eyes will see! Even so hath the Truth been manifested by the Exalted One in many ways.

2. "And I, even I, do go to him as my refuge, and to the Truth and to the Order. May the Exalted One receive me as his lay-disciple, as one who has taken his refuge in him from this day forth as long as life endures."

§ 8. *Vinaya for Girls*

1. Once the Exalted One dwelt near Bhaddiya in Jatiya Wood; and there Uggaha, Mendaka's grandson,
V paid him a visit and, after saluting, sat down at one side. So seated, he said to the Exalted One:

466 2. " Lord let the Exalted One accept a meal at my house tomorrow, he as fourth (with us three)."

3. The Exalted One accepted by his silence.

4. Then Uggaha, seeing the Exalted One had accepted, rose from his seat, saluted, and took his leave, keeping the Exalted One on his right.

5. Now when the night was over, the Exalted One, robing himself in the morning, took his bowl and cloak and went to Uggaha's house, and there sat down on the seat made ready. And Uggaha served with his own hand and satisfied the Exalted One with plenty of food.

6. And when the Exalted One had removed his hand from his bowl, he sat down at one side. Thus seated, he said:

7. " Lord, these girls of mine will be going to their husbands' families; Lord, let the Exalted One counsel them, let the Exalted One advise them, for their good and happiness for many a day ! "

8. Then the Exalted One spoke to them and said: " Wherefor, girls, train yourselves in this way: ' To whatsoever husband our parents shall give us—wishing our weal, seeking our happiness, compassionate—because of compassion for him we will rise up early, be the last to retire, be willing workers, order all things sweetly and be gentle voiced. Train yourselves thus, girls.'

9. " And in this way also, girls: ' We will honour, revere, esteem and respect all who are our husband's relatives, whether mother or father, recluse or godly man, and on their arrival will offer them a seat and water. Train yourselves thus, girls.'

10. " And in this way also girls: ' We will be deft and nimble at our husband's home-crafts, whether they be of wool or cotton, making it our business to

understand the work so as to do and get it done. Train yourselves thus, girls.

11. "And in this way also, girls: 'Messengers and
workfolk we will know the work of each by what has
been done, their remissness, by what has not been done; V
we will know the strength and the weakness of the
sick; we will divide the hard and soft food, each 467
according to his share. Train yourselves thus, girls.'

12. "And in this way also, girls: 'The money, corn, silver and gold that our husband brings home, we will keep safe, watch and ward over it, and act as no robber, thief, carouser, wastrel therein. Train yourselves thus, girls.'"

13. On hearing this advice, the daughters of Uggaha felt exceedingly happy and were grateful to the Lord.

BOOK VI

He and His Contemporaries

Part I—His Benefactors.

Part II—His Enemies.

Part III—Critics of His Doctrines.

Part IV—Friends and Admirers.

PART I

His Benefactors

1. Gift from Bimbisara.
2. Gift from Anathapindika.
3. Gift from Jeevaka.
4. Gift from Ambrapali.
5. Munificence of Vishakha.

§ 1. *Gift from King Bimbisara*

1. King Bimbisara was not merely a follower of the Blessed Lord: he was also a great devotee and a great supporter of his Dhamma.

2. After his becoming a lay disciple Bimbisara VI
asked: "Might the Blessed Lord consent to take his 473
meal with me tomorrow together with the fraternity of the monks?"

3. The Blessed One expressed his consent by remaining silent.

4. Then King Bimbisara, when he understood that the Blessed One had accepted his invitation, rose from his seat, respectfully saluted the Blessed One, and, passing round him with his right side towards him, went away.

5. And when the night had elapsed, Bimbisara ordered excellent food to be prepared, and at time announced to the Blessed One in the words: "It is time, Lord, the meal is ready."

6. And in the forenoon the Blessed One, having put on his under-robe, took his alms-bowl, and with his robe on, entered the city of Rajagraha accompanied by monks who had all been Jatilas before.

7. And the Blessed One went to the palace of King Bimbisara. Having gone there, he sat down with the monks who followed him, on seats laid out for them. Then King Bimbisara with his own hands served the fraternity of monks with the Buddha at its head; and when the Blessed One had finished his meal and cleaned his bowl and his hands, he sat down near him.

8. Sitting near him King Bimbisara thought: "Where may I find a place for the Blessed One to live in, not too far from the village and not too near, suitable for going and coming, easily accessible for people who keep on seeking him, by day not too

crowded, where there is little sound, little noise by night, sequestered, hidden from men, well fitted for a retired life ?"

9. And King Bimbisara thought: "There is the Veluvana, my pleasure garden, which is not too far from the town and not too near, suitable for going and coming. What if I were to make an offering of the Veluvana pleasure garden to the fraternity of monks, with the Buddha at its head ?"

10. And King Bimbisara took a golden vessel with water in it, to be poured over the Buddha's hand; and made a gift to the Blessed One, saying, "I give this Veluvana pleasure garden, Lord, to the fraternity of monks with the Buddha at its head." The Blessed One accepted the park.

11. Then the Blessed One, after having taught, incited, animated, and gladdened King Bimbisara by religious discourse, rose from his seat and went away.

12. And in consequence of this event the Blessed One, after having delivered a religious discourse, addressed the monks: 'I allow you monks, to receive this donation of a park."

§ 2. *Gift from Anathapindika*

1. After his conversion Anathapindika once went to the Blessed Lord. Taking his seat on his right side, he said:

2. "The Lord knows that I dwell in Shravasti, a land rich in produce, and enjoying peace; Pasendi is the great king thereof.

3. "Now am I wishful to found a Vihar there, I pray you, of your tenderness come to Shravasti and accept it from me."

4. The Blessed Lord kept silent and thereby showed his willingness to accept the gift.

5. Anathapindika, the friend of the destitute and the supporter of orphans, having returned home, saw the garden of the heir-apparent, Jeta, with its green groves and limpid rivulets, and thought: "This is the place which will be most suitable as a Vihara for

the fraternity of the Blessed One." And he went to the prince and asked leave to buy the ground.

6. The prince was not inclined to sell the garden for he valued it highly. He at first refused but said at
last: "If you can cover it with gold, then, and for no VI
other price, shall you have it."

7. Anathapindika rejoiced and began to spread 475
his gold; but Jeta said: "Spare yourself trouble for I will not sell." But Anathapindika insisted. Thus they differed and contended until they resorted to the magistrate.

8. Meanwhile the people began to talk of the unwonted proceeding and the prince hearing more of the details, and knowing that Anathapindika was not only very wealthy, but also straightforward and sincere, inquired into his plans. On hearing the name of the Blessed One, the prince became anxious to share in the foundation and he accepted only one-half of the gold, saying: "Yours is the land but mine are the trees. I will give the trees as my share of the offering to the Lord."

9. Having made the foundation, they began to build the hall which rose loftily in due proportions according to the directions which the Blessed One had given; and it was beautifully decorated with appropriate carvings.

10. This Vihara was called Jetavana and the friend of the orphans invited the Lord to come to Shravasti and receive the gift. And the Blessed One left Kapilavastu and came to Shravasti.

11. While the Blessed One entered Jetavana, Anathapindika scattered flowers and burned incense, and as a sign of the gift he poured water from a golden dragon pitcher, saying, "This Jetavana Vihara I give for the use of the brotherhood throughout the world."

12. The Blessed One received the gift and replied: "May all evil influences be overcome; may the offering promote the kingdom of righteousness and be a permanent blessing to mankind in general and especially also to the giver."

13. Anathapindika was one of the eighty chief disciples who bore the title of Chief Almsgiver.

§ 3. *Gift from Jeevaka*

1. Jeevaka the physician visited the Blessed One twice a day whenever the Blessed One happened to be in Rajagraha.

2. Jeevaka found the Veluvana gifted away to the Blessed One by King Bimbisara too far away.

3. Jeevaka had his own park in Rajagraha, known as Ambavana, which was much nearer from his place.

4. He thought of building a Vihara with all its adjuncts and present the Ambavana and the Vihara to the Blessed One.

5. With this idea in his mind he approached the Blessed One and requested him to let him fulfil his wishes.

6. The Blessed Lord showed his acceptance by remaining silent.

§ 4. *Gift from Ambrapali*

1. Now the Exalted One was staying at Nadika and was wishing for a change. He addressed Ananda, and said: " Come, Ananda, let us go on to Vesali."

2. " So be it, Lord," said Ananda, in assent, to the Exalted One.

3. Then the Exalted One proceeded, with a great company of the brethren, to Vesali, and there at Vesali, the Exalted One stayed at Ambrapali's grove.

4. Now the courtesan Ambrapali heard that the Exalted One had arrived at Vesali and was staying there at her mango grove. And ordering a number of state vehicles to be made ready, she mounted one of them, and went forth with her train from Vesali towards her garden. She went in the carriage as far as the ground was passable for carriages; there she alighted and she proceeded on foot to the place where the Exalted One was, and took her seat respectfully on one side. And when she was thus seated the

Exalted One instructed her with religious discourse.

5. Then she addressed the Exalted One, and said: "May the Exalted One do me the honour of taking his meal, together with the brethren, at my house tomorrow?" VI

6. And the Exalted One gave, by silence, his consent. 477 Then when Ambrapali the courtesan saw that the Exalted One had consented, she rose from her seat and bowed down before him, and keeping him on her right hand as she passed him, she departed thence.

7. Now the Licchavis of Vesali heard that the Exalted One had arrived at Vesali, and was staying at Ambrapali's grove. They too wanted to invite the Buddha to their place for a meal. And ordering a number of state carriages to be made ready, they each mounted one of them and went forth with their train from Vesali.

8. They and Ambrapali crossed on the way.

9. And Ambrapali drove up against the young Licchavis, axle to axle, wheel to wheel, and yoke to yoke, and the Licchavis said to Ambrapali the courtesan, "How is it, Ambrapali, that thou drivest up against us thus?"

10. "My Lords, I have just invited the Exalted One and his brethren for their morrow's meal," said Ambrapali.

11. "Ambrapali, sell this honour to us for a hundred thousand," said they.

12. "My Lords, were you to offer all Vesali with its subject territory, I would not give it up."

13. The Licchavis cast up their hands, exclaiming: "We are outdone by this mango girl. We are out-reached by this mango girl," and they went on to Ambrapali's grove.

14. Knowing that they were outdone they still thought of approaching the Blessed One in the hope that he might reconsider and give their invitation first preference. So they went on to Ambrapali's grove.

15. When the Exalted One saw the Licchavis approaching in the distance, he addressed the brethren

and said: "Brethren, let those of the brethren who have never seen the devas, gaze upon this company of the Licchavis, behold this company of the Licchavis, compare this company of the Licchavis—for they are
VI even a company of next-world devas."

16. And when they had ridden as far as the
478 ground was passable for carriages the Licchavis alighted there, and then went on foot to the place where the Exalted One was, and took their seats respectfully by his side.

17. Then they addressed the Exalted One, and said : " May the Exalted One do us the honour of taking his meal, together with the brethren, at our house tomorrow ? "

18. " I have promised, Licchavis, to dine to-morrow with Ambrapali," was the reply.

19. Then the Licchavis knew that they had failed. And after expressing their thanks and approval of the words of the Exalted One, they rose from their seats and bowed down before the Exalted One, and keeping him on their right hand as they passed him, departed thence.

20. And at the end of the night Ambrapali the courtesan made ready in her mansion sweet rice and cakes, and announced the time to the Exalted One, saying: " The hour, Lord, has come, and the meal is ready."

21. And the Exalted One who had dressed himself early in the morning, took his bowl, and his robe and went with the brethren to the place where Ambrapali's mansion was ; and when he had come there he seated himself on the seat prepared for him. And Ambrapali, the courtesan, set the sweet rice and cakes before the order, with the Buddha at their head, and waited upon them till they refused any more.

22. And when the Blessed One had quite finished his meal and had cleansed the bowl and his hands, the courtesan had a low stool brought, and sat down at his side, and addressed the Exalted One, and said :

23. " Lord, I present my pleasance to you and to the order." And the Exalted One accepted the gift ; and

after giving a religious discourse he rose from his seat and took her leave.

§ 5. *Munificence of Vishakha* VI

1. Vishakha was a wealthy woman of Shravasti. 479
She had many children and grandchildren.

2. When the Blessed One stayed at Shravasti, Vishakha went up to the place where the Blessed One was, and tendered Him an invitation to take his meal at her house, which the Blessed One accepted.

3. And heavy rain fell during the night and the next morning; and the bhikkhus doffed their robes to keep themselves dry and let the rain fall upon their bodies.

4. When the next day the Blessed One had finished his meal, she took her seat at his side and spoke thus; " Eight are the boons, Lord, which I beg of the Blessed One."

5. Then the Blessed One said: " The Tathagatas, O Vishakha, grant no boons unless they know what they are."

6. Vishakha replied: " Proper, Lord, and unobjectionable are the boons I ask."

7. Having received permission to ask the boons, Vishakha said: " I desire, Lord, through all my life to bestow robes for the rainy season on the Sangha, and food for incoming bhikkhus, and food for outgoing bhikkhus and food for the sick, and food for those who wait upon the sick, and medicine for the sick, and a constant supply of rice-milk for the Sangha, and bathing robes for the bhikkhunis, the sisters."

8. " But," said the Lord, "What, O Vishakha, have you in view in asking these eight boons of the Tathagata ?"

9. And Vishakha replied: " I gave command, Lord, to my maid-servant, saying, ' Go thou and announce to the fraternity that the meal is ready,' and my maid went, but when she came to the vihara, she observed that the bhikkhus had doffed their robes, while it was raining, and she thought: ' These are not

bhikkhus, but naked ascetics letting the rain fall on them.' So she returned to me and reported accordingly and I had to send her a second time.

10. "Impure, Lord, is nakedness, and revolting. It was this circumstance, Lord, that I had in view in desiring to provide the Sangha throughout my life with special garments for use in the rainy season.

11. "As to my second wish, Lord, an incoming bhikku, not being able to take the direct roads, and not knowing the places where food can be procured, comes on his way wearied out by seeking for alms. It was this circumstance, Lord, that I had in view in desiring to provide the Sangha throughout my life with food for incoming bhikkhus.

12. "Thirdly, Lord, an outgoing bhikkhu, while seeking about for alms, may be left behind, or may arrive too late at the place whither he desires to go, and will set out on the road in weariness.

13. "Fourthly, Lord, if a sick bhikkhu does not obtain suitable food, his sickness may increase upon him, and he may die.

14. "Fifthy, Lord, a bhikkhu who is waiting upon the sick will lose his opportunity of going out to seek food for himself.

15. "Sixthly, Lord, if a sick bhikkhu does not obtain suitable medicines, his sickness may increase upon him, and he may die.

16. "Seventhly, Lord, I have heard that the Blessed One has praised rice-milk, because it gives readiness of mind, dispels hunger and thirst; it is wholesome nourishment for the healthy and for the sick as a medicine. Therefore I desire to provide the Sangha throughout my life with constant supply of rice-milk.

17. "Finally, Lord, the bhikkhunis are in the habit of bathing in the river Archiravati with the courtesans, at the same landing-place, and naked. And the courtesans, Lord, ridicule the bhikkhunis, saying, 'What is the good, ladies, of your maintaining chastity when you are young? When you are old, maintain chastity then; thus will you be obtainers of

both ends.' Impure, Lord, is nakedness for a woman, disgusting, and revolting.

18. "These are the circumstances, Lord, that I had in view."

19. The Blessed One said: "But what was the advantage you had in view for yourself, O Vishakha, in asking these eight boons of the Tathagatha?"

20. Vishakha replied: "Bhikkhus who have spent the rainy season in various places will come, Lord, to Shravasti to visit the Blessed One. And on coming to the Blessed One they will ask, saying: 'Such and such a bhikkhu, Lord, has died. What, now, is his destiny?' Then will the Blessed One explain that he has attained the fruits of conversion; that he has entered Nirvana or attained arhantship, as the case may be.

21. "And I, going up to them, shall ask, 'Was that brother, sirs, one of those who had formerly been at Shravasti,' then shall I arrive at the conclusion, 'For a certainty did that brother enjoy either the robes for the rainy season, or the food for the incoming bhikkhus, or the food for the outgoing bhikkhus, or the food for the sick, or the food for those that wait upon the sick, or the medicine for the sick, or the constant supply of rice-milk.'

22. "Then will gladness spring up within me; thus gladdend joy will come to me; and so rejoicing all my frame will be at peace. Being thus at peace I shall experience a blissful feeling of content; and in that bliss my heart will be at rest. That will be to me an exercise of my moral powers, an exercise of the seven kinds of wisdom! This, Lord, was the advantage I had in view for myself in asking those eight boons of the Blessed One."

23. Then the Blessed One said: "It is well, it is well, Vishakha. Thou hast done well in asking these eight boons of the Tathagata with such advantage in view. Charity bestowed upon those who are worthy of it is like good seeds sown in good soil that yields an abundance of fruits. But alms given to those who are yet under the tyrannical yoke of the passions are like

a seed deposited in bad soil. The passions of the receiver of the alms choke, as it were, the growth of merits."

24. And the Blessed One gave thanks to Vishakha
VI in these verses ; " Whatsoever donation a woman
upright in life, a disciple of the Blessed One, may
482 bestow in gladness of heart and without stint, her gift
is heavenly, destructive of sorrow, and productive of bliss." " A blissful life does she attain entering upon the path that is from corruption and impurity." " Aiming at good, happy does she become; and she rejoices in her charitable actions."

25. Vishakha gave to the Order the Purva-Aram or Eastern Garden, and was the first to become a matron of the lay-sisters.

PART II

His Enemies

1. Charge of Conversion by Glamour.
2. Charge of being a Parasite!
3. Charge of Breaking Happy Households.
4. Jains and a False Charge of Murder.
5. Jains and a False Charge of Immorality.
6. Devadatta a Cousin and an Enemy.
7. Brahmins and the Buddha.

§ 1. *Charge of Conversion by Glamour*

1. Once the Exalted One dwelt at Vesali, in the Gable-roofed Hall in the Great Wood. Now Bhaddiya the Licchavi came to the Exalted One and said: " Lord ! VI
People say ' Gotama the recluse is a charmer and knows a trick of glamour, whereby he entices the followers 485
of other sects.'

2. " They who say this disclaim any desire to misrepresent the Exalted One. Indeed, Lord, we Licchavis do not believe in this charge. But we would like to know what the Exalted One has to say about it."

3. The Lord said: " Come now, Bhaddiya, accept not on hearsay, nor by tradition, nor by what people say. Accept not because it is in the scriptures, by mere logic, nor by inference, nor by consideration of appearances, nor because it accords with your view, nor because you think it must be right, nor out of respect, with the thought that ' One must revere a recluse.'

4. "But, Bhaddiya, if at any time you know of yourself by examination of facts that what is being done is sinful or wrongful, that it is reproached by the wise and the result is loss or injury, then, Bhaddiya, eschew them.

5. "Now as to your question, Bhaddiya, what think you; Are not those who accuse me of performing conversion by glamour ambitious persons ? " " They are, Lord," replied Bhaddiya.

6. " What think ye, Bhaddiya; Does not an ambitious person, overcome by avarice and with mind overpowered, tell lies or commit crime to achieve his ambition ? " " It is so, Lord," replied Bhaddiya.

7. " What think you, Bhaddiya, when thoughts of ill-will and vindictiveness arise in the mind of such a person, does he not instigate others to level accusations against those who come in the way of his ambition ? " " That is so Lord," said Bhaddiya.

8. " Now, Bhaddiya, all I do is to exhort my pupil thus: ' Come you, my dear man, dwell controlling

(thoughts of) avarice. So dwelling you will not commit acts born of avarice, either by body, work or thought. Dwell controlling ill-will and ignorance.'

9. "So, Bhaddiya, those recluses and Brahmins,
VI who wrongly reproach me with being a teacher and
proclaimer of such views, are false, empty liars, when
486 they say: 'The recluse Gautama is a charmer and
knows a trick of glamour, whereby He entices the
followers of other sects.' "

10. " A lucky thing indeed, O Lord—a fair find is this trick of glamour ! Lord would that my beloved blood-relations were enticed by this same trick of glamour ! It would indeed conduce to their advantage and happiness ! Lord, would that all the classes the Brahmins, the Khatiyas, the Vessas and the Suddas were enticed by this same trick of glamour, it would indeed conduce to their advantage and happiness for a long time."

11. " It is so, Bhaddiya ! It is so Bhaddiya ! If all the classes enticed by this trick of glamour, were to eschew sinful conditions, my trick would result in great advantage and happiness to the world."

§ 2. *Charge of Being a Parasite!*

1. The Blessed One was accused of being a parasite, living upon others and not earning his living by working for it. The accusation and the reply of the Blessed Lord is set out below :

2. Once the Lord was living among the Magadha folk at Dakkhina-giri in the Brahmin village of Eka-Nala, at a time when the Brahmin Kasi-Bharadvaja's five hundred ploughs were harnessed for the sowing.

3. In the morning early, duly robed and bowl in hand, the Lord went to where the Brahmin was busy, at an hour when a meal was brought forward; and stood there to one side.

4. Observing him standing there for alms, the Brahmin said: "Before I eat, I plough and sow, anchorite; and you too should plough and sow before you eat."

5. "I too Brahmin, do plough and do sow before I eat."

6. "I fail, however, to see the worthy Gautama's yoke, or plough, or ploughshare, or goad, or ox-team —albeit, he asserts that he ploughs and sows before he VI
eats.

7. "You claim to be a tiller, though we see none 487
of your tillage. Tell us how you till; for of your tilling we would fain hear more."

8. "My seed is faith; austerity of life my rain; wisdom my yoke and plough; my pole is fear to err; with thought to strap the yoke; and mindfulness for plough share and the goad," replied the Lord.

9. "Watchful o'er word and deed, and temperate in diet, I make in sight weed my crop, nor rest till final bliss is harvested. Effort is my stout ox, which turns not back at headlands;—straight to Peace he bears me on, to that last bourne where anguish is no more. Thus, I till with Deathlessness for crop. And who tills as I, is freed from ills."

10. Thereupon the Brahmin served up milk-rice on a great bronze dish and offered it to the Lord, saying: "Eat this, Gautama, a tiller indeed art thou, in that thou tillest a crop that is Deathless."

11. But the Lord said: "I take no chanter's fee. Seers countenance it not; the Enlighten'd scout such fees; and while this Doctrine lasts, this practice must hold good. Provided with other fare a sage of holy calm, consummate, cankerless; merit to reap,—sow there."

12. On hearing these words the Brahmin went over to the Lord, and, bowing his head at the Lord's feet, cried: "Wonderful, Gautama; quite wonderful. Just as a man might set upright again what had fallen down, or reveal what had been hidden away, or tell a man who had fallen down, or reveal what had been hidden away, or tell a man who had gone astray which was his way, or bring a lamp into darkness so that those with eyes to see might see the things about them,—even so, in many ways has Gautama made his Doctrine clear!

13. "To the reverend Gotama I come for refuge and to his Doctrine and to his community. Be it mine to receive admission and confirmation at the hands of the Lord!" So the Brahmin Kasi-Bharadvaja was
VI admitted and confirmed as an almsman of the Lord.

488 § 3. *Charge of Breaking Happy Households*

1. Seeing that many distinguished young Magadha noblemen had become the disciples of the Blessed One, people became annoyed and angry, saying: "The Samana Gautama causes parents to be childless; the Samana Gautama causes wives to become widows; the Samana Gautama causes the uprooting of families.

2. "Now he has ordained one thousand Jatilas, and he has ordained these two hundred and fifty wandering ascetics who were followers of Sanjaya, and these many distinguished young Magadha clansmen are now leading a holy life under the Samana Gautama. What will happen next? No one can say!"

3. And, moreover, when they saw the monks they chide them in the following terms: "The great Samana has come to Giribhaja (i.e., Ragagaha) of the Magadha people, leading with him all the followers of Sanjaya ; who will be the next to be led by him ?"

4. The monks heard this accusation and they reported it to the Blessed One.

5. The Blessed One replied: "This noise, monks, will not last long; it will last only seven days; after seven days it will be over.

6. "And if they chide you, monks, you should reply that it is truly by a good Dhamma that the great heroes, the Tathagatas, lead. Who will murmur at the wise, why grudge the wise leading men righteously? There is no compulsion in my Dhamma. One is free to leave home. One is free to remain attached to his home."

7. When the Bhikkhus replied to the revilers as the Blessed One had directed, then the people under-

stood : "It is by Dhamma, and not unrighteously that the Sakyaputtiya Samana leads men"; and ceased to accuse the Blessed One.

§ 4. *Jains and a False Charge of Murder* VI 489

1. The Tirthikas were beginning to feel that the people no longer respected them with the appearance of Samana Gautama and that even some people did not know of their existence.

2. So, "let us see whether with the connivance of somebody, we can lower his prestige," thought the Tirthikas. "Perhaps with Sundari's help we might succeed."

3. And they approached Sundari and said to her: "Sister, you are extremely beautiful and charming. If you spread a scandal about Samana Gautama, the people might believe it, and it would lower his influence."

4. Sundari used to go every evening towards the Jetavana with garlands, camphor, and sweet scents when the people used to return to the city; and if anybody asked her, "Sundari, where are you going?" she used to answer, "I am going to Samana Gautama to stay with in the garden house (Gandha Kutir)."

5. And staying the night in some gardens of the Tirthikas, she used to return in the morning, and if anybody asked her where she had spent the night, she would say that she had spent the night with Gautama.

6. After a few days the Tirthikas hired a few assassins and told them: "Kill Sundari and throw her body on the rubbish heap near Gautama's Gandha Kutir." This the assassins did.

7. Then the Tirthikas brought it to the notice of the officers of peace and justice that Sundari used to frequent Jetavana and she was missing.

8. So with the assistance of the officers they found Sundari's body on the rubbish heap.

9. And the Tirthikas accused the disciples of

Gautama to have killed Sundari in order to hide the shame of their leader.

10. But the assassins began to quarrel amongst themselves in a liquor shop about the distribution of the prize money for having killed Sundari.

11. The officers at once arrested them and they admitted their guilt and implicated the Tirthikas at whose instigation they had committed the crime.

12. Thus the Tirthikas lost whatever influence was left for them.

§ 5. *Jains and a False Charge of Immorality*

1. As with the sunrise the glow-worms vanish, so miserable became the situation of the Tirthikas. The people ceased to pay them respects or presents.

2. Standing on the public streets they used to harangue : "If Samana Gautama is enlightened (Buddha), we are also. If you acquire virtue by showering presents on the Buddha, you will get the same by giving us presents. Therefore make gift to us."

3. But the public paid no heed to it. So they conspired in secret how by spreading scandal on the character of Samana Gautama, they could discredit the Sangha.

4. At that time there used to live in Shravasti a Brahmani Parivrajaka, known as Chincha. In bodily formation and physical charms she was a seductive beauty. She used to radiate voluptuous grace with her bodily movements.

5. One of the crafty schemers among the Tirthikas said that with the help of Chincha it would be easy to spread a scandal about Gautama, and thereby discredit him, to which other Tirthikas gave their consent.

6. Then, one day Chincha came to the park of the Tirthikas and saluting them, sat near them. But nobody talked with her.

7. Surprised at this she said : "How have I

offended you? I have saluted you thrice though you do not say a single word to me."

8. "Sister," the Tirthikas said, "Don't you know that Samana Gautama is causing us harm and loss by his popularity." "I do not know that. And have I got any duty to perform toward its solution?"

9. "Sister, if you mean to do us good, then by your own efforts, spread scandals about Gautama, and thus make him unpopular." "All right; be content; and depend that on me," saying thus she left the place.

10. Chincha was an expert in feminine charms and coquetry. When the citizens of Shravasti used to return from the religious discussions at Jetavana, Chincha wearing a red garment and with perfumes and garlands in her hands used to go towards it.

11. If anybody asked her: "Where are you going now?" "That's none of your business," she used to answer. Spending the night at the rest house of the Itinerants (Tirthikarama) near Jetavana, she used to return to the city in the morning, when the citizens used to go to the Jetavana to pay respect to the Buddha.

12. If anybody asked her, "Where did you spend the night?" she used to say, "That is none of your business. I spent the night with Samana Gautama in his garden house (Gandha Kutir) at Jetavana." The remark used to create doubts in the minds of some.

13. After four months she used to increase the size of her belly by wrapping round it some old rags, and say that she became pregnant through Samana Gautama. Some began to believe it.

14. In the ninth month, she suspending a wooden protuberance round her belly and having arms swollen through insect bites, appeared before the Buddha when he was making a religious discourse before monks and laymen and said: "Great teacher, you give many people religious lessons. Your voice is sweet, and your lips are very tender. Through cohabitation with you I have been pregnant, and my delivery time is near.

15. "You have not fixed any delivery place for me,

nor I do see any medicine for that emergency. If you cannot do that yourself, why don't you appoint one of your disciples, the king of Kosala, Anathpindika or Visakha for that purpose.

16. "It seems you know well how to seduce a girl, but you do not know how to take care of the new-born baby that is born out of the seduction." The assembly remained silent.

17. The Buddha, breaking the continuity of his lecture, answered her with reserved dignity. "Sister, whatever you have said, whether true or false, is only known to us both."

18. Chincha coughing loudly, said. "Yes, O Teacher, such a thing can be known to us only."

19. With her coughing the knot with which the wooden protuberance was tied round her belly slackened, and it fell on her feet to her discomfiture.

20. And she was turned away with stones and sticks.

§ 6. *Devadatta a Cousin and an Enemy*

1. Devadatta was a cousin of the Buddha. But from the beginning he was jealous of the Buddha and disliked him intensely.

2. When the Buddha had left his home, Devadatta tried to make love to Yeshodhara.

3. Once when Yeshodhara was about to retire, he without being intercepted by anybody entered into her chamber in the guise of a monk. She asked him, "Bhikkhu, what do you want? Have you got any message for me from my husband?"

4. "Your husband, he cares a damn for you. In your house of happiness he cruelly and wickedly abandoned you," said Devadatta.

5. "But he did it for the good of many," replied Yeshodhara.

6. "Whatever that be, now take revenge on his disdainful cruelty to you," suggested Devadatta.

7. "Stop it, O Monk : your words and thoughts are impure," countered Yeshodhara.

8. " Don't you recognize me, Yeshodhara ? I am Devadatta who loves you."

9. " Devadatta, I knew you to be false and vile. I thought you would make a bad monk, but did not suspect you to be so mean-minded."

10. " Yeshodhara, Yeshodhara, I love you" pleaded Devadatta. " And your husband shows you nothing but contempt. He has been cruel to you. Love me and revenge his cruelty."

11. Yeshodhara's pale and emaciated face became tinged with a purple hue. Tears rolled down her cheeks.

12. "Devadatta, it is you who are cruel to me. Even if your love were sincere, it would have been an insult to me. You are simply lying when you say you love me.

13. "When I was young and pretty you hardly looked at me. Now I am old, broken down by sorrow and anguish, you have come at night to declare your treacherous and guilty love. You are a base coward."

14. And she shouted: " Devadatta, get out from the place," and Devadatta left the place.

15. Devadatta was very angry with the Buddha who did not make him the chief in the Sangh and instead made Sariputta and Mogallana the chief men in the Sangh. Devadatta made three attempts on the Buddha's life, but did not succeed in any of them.

16. At one time the Blessed One was walking up and down in the shade below the hill called the Vultures Peak (Girdhra Kuta).

17. Devadatta climbed it up and hurled down a large stone with the intention of depriving the Blessed One of his life, but it fell upon another rock and there it was entombed; only a splinter falling from it made the foot of the Blessed One to bleed.

18. A second time he made an attempt to take the life of the Buddha.

19. This time Devadatta went to Prince Ajatasatru and said: " Give me some men." And Ajatasatru, the prince gave orders to his men : " Whatsoever the worthy Devadatta tells you, do that."

20. Then to one man Devadatta gave command: " Go, my friend ; the Samana Gautama is staying at such a place. Kill him." And the man returned and said to him : " I cannot deprive the Blessed One of his life.

21. He made a third attempt on the life of the Buddha.

22. This time there was at Rajgraha an elephant named Nalagiri, fierce and a man-slayer.

23. And Devadatta went into Rajgraha and to the elephant stables, and said to the elephant keepers : " I, my friends, am a relative of the raja, and am able to advance a man occupying a low position to a high position, and to order an increase of his rations or of his pay."

24. Therefore, my friends, when Samana Gautama shall have arrived at this carriage road, then loose the elephant Nalagiri and let him go down the road.

25. Devadatta engaged archers to kill the Buddha. He had also let loose on his way the mad elephant Nalagiri.

26. But he did not succeed. When these attempts became known, Devadatta lost all the public endowments given to him. And even the king (Ajatasatru) stopped giving him interview.

27. For living he had to beg from house to house. Devadatta received many favours from Ajatasatru, which he could not retain long. Devadatta lost all his influence after the Nalagiri incident.

28. By his acts, Devadatta becoming very unpopular in Magadha left it for Kosala, thinking that Prasenjit might receive him cordially. But he was contemptuously driven out by Prasenjit.

§ 7. *Brahmins and the Buddha*

(i)

1. Once when the Blessed One was travelling about in the Kosala country with a large company of the monks, he went down to a Brahmin village named Thuna.

2. The Brahmin householders of Thuna heard the news, "The Samana Gautama, they say, has arrived in the field of our village."

3. Now the Brahmin householders were non-believers, holding wrong views and avaricious by nature.

4. They said, "If the Samana Gautama should enter this village and stay two or three days, he would convert all these people. Then the Brahmin religion would have no support. We must, therefore, prevent his entry in our village.

5. To reach the village a river had to be crossed and the Brahmins, in order to prevent the Blessed One from entering the village, took the boats away from the landing places, and made the bridges and causeways unusable.

6. They filled all the wells except one with weeds and the like and concealed the watering-places, rest-houses and sheds.

7. The Blessed One learned of their misdeeds and having compassion on them, crossed the river with his company of monks, went on, and in due course of time reached the Brahmin village of Thuna.

8. He left the road and sat down at the foot of a tree. At that moment many women were passing by near the Blessed One carrying water.

9. And in that village an agreement had been made, "If the Samana Gautama comes there, there is to be no welcome or the like made for him and when he comes to a house, neither to him nor to his disciples is any food or water to be given."

10. Then a certain Brahmin's slave girl, going along with a jar of water, saw the Blessed One and the monks, realized that they were weary and thirsty, and being of devout heart, wanted to give them water.

11. "Even and though the people of this village have resolved that nothing at all is to be given to the Samana Gautama and not even a show of respect is to be made," she said to herself, "yet if after I have found these supreme fields of merit and worthy

recipients of meritorious giving, I do not lay the foundation for my salvation by a mere giving of water, when hereafter shall I be released from woe ?"

12. " So be it, my masters ! Let every one who
VI lives in the village beat or bind me, still I will give a gift of water to a field of merit such as this."

496 13. When she had made this resolve, though the other women carrying water tried to stop her, without regard for her life, she lifted down the water jar from her head, placed it on one side, approached the Blessed One, and gave him water; he washed his hands and feet and drank the water.

14. Her master, the Brahmin, heard of her giving water to the Blessed One. " She has broken the rule of the village and I am blamed," he said, and burning with rage and grinding his teeth he hurled her to the ground and beat her with hands and feet. Because of that she died.

(ii)

1. Now Brahmin Dona visited the Exalted One and greeted him; and after exchanging the customary words of greetings, sat down at one side. So seated, Brahmin Dona said to the Exalted One :

2. "I have heard it said, Master Gotama, that Master Gotama does not salute aged, venerable Brahmins, well stricken in years, long on life's road, grown old—nor rise up for them, nor offer them a seat.

3. "Master Gotama, it is just so; Master Gotama does none of these things . . . to aged, venerable Brahmins . . . This is not right, Master Gotama."

4. "Do you not profess to be a brahmin, Dona ?"

5. " If of anyone, Master Gotama, in speaking rightly it should be said: ' The brahmin is well born on both sides, pure in descent as far back as seven generations, both of mother and father, unchallenged and without reproach in point of birth; studious, carrying the mantras in mind, a past master in the three Vedas with the indices and ritual, in phonology too, and in the legends; an expert in verse and grammar, skilled in reading the marks of a great man, in

speculation on the universe' to be sure of me, Master Gotama, in speaking rightly that thing should be said; for I, Master Gotama, am so born . . . so skilled . . . "

6. "Dona, those Brahmin-sages of old, mantra- VI
makers, mantra-sayers, whose ancient collection of
mantra verses, hymns and sayings, Brahmins know 497
every hymn, every say, every word the word, ever have the sayings said to wit: Atthaka, Vamaka, Vamadeva. Vassamitta, Yamadaggi, Angirasa, Bharadvaja, have declared: the Brahma-like, the deva-like, the bounded, the breaker of bounds, and fifthly, the Brahmin outcast, which of them, Dona, are you?"

7. "We know not of these five Brahmins, Master Gotama; yet we know that we are Brahmins. It were well for me if Master Gotama would teach me Dhamma so that I may know of them five."

8. "Then listen, Brahma, give heed and I will speak!"

9. "Yes sir," replied he; and the Exalted One said:

10. "And how, Dona, becomes a Brahmin Brahma-like?"

11. "Take the case, Dona, of a Brahmin who is well born on both sides, pure in descent as far back as seven generations, both of mother and father, unchallenged and without reproach in point of birth—he for eight and forty years leads to the Brahma-life of virginity, applying himself to the teacher's fee for teaching according to Dhamma, not non-Dhamma.

12. "And what there is Dhamma, Dona? Never as ploughman nor trader nor cowherd nor bowman nor rajah's man nor by any craft (to get his living), but solely by going about for alms, despising not the beggar's bowl.

13. "And he hands over the teacher's fee for teaching, has his hair-beard shaved off, dons the yellow robe and goes forth from the home to the homeless life.

14. "And thus gone forth, he abides in mind pervading with amity one world quarter, so a second,

a third, a fourth; then above, below, athwart, everywhere, the whole wide world he pervades with thoughts of amity, far-reaching, expansive, measureless, without hatred or ill-will.

VI 15. "He abides in mind pervading with pity . . .
sympathy . . . poise, one world quarter, so a second,
498 a third, a fourth; then above, below, athwart, every-
where, the whole wide world he pervades with thoughts of pity, sympathy and poise, far-reaching, expansive, measureless, without hatred or ill-will.

16. "And having made these four Brahma-abidings become, on the breaking up of the body after death, he arises in the well-faring Brahma world. Thus, Dona, Brahmin becomes Brahma-like.

17. "And how, Dona, becomes a Brahmin deva-like?

18. "Take the case, Dona, of a Brahmin of similar birth and conduct . . . . He does not get a living by ploughing and so forth, but by going about for alms . . . . He hands over the teacher's fee for teaching and seeks a wife according to Dhamma, not non-Dhamma.

19. "And what then is Dhamma? Not with one bought or sold, but only with a Brahmani on whom water has been poured. And he goes only to a Brahmani, not to the daughter of an outcast, hunter, bamboo-worker, cart-maker, or aboriginal, nor goes to a woman with child, nor to one giving suck, nor to one not in her season.

20. "And wherefore, Dona, goes not a Brahmin to one with child? If he go, the boy or girl will surely be foully born, therefore he goes not. And wherefore goes he not to one giving suck? If he go, the boy or girl will surely be an unclean suckling, therefore he goes not.

21. "And wherefore goes he not to one not in her season? If, Dona, a Brahmin go to one not in her season, never for him does the Brahmani become a means for lust, for sport, for pleasure; the Brahmani is for the Brahmin just as a means to beget offspring.

22. "And when in wedlock he has begotten (a child), he has his hair-beard shaved off . . . and goes forth . . . .

23. "And being thus gone forth, aloof from sensuous appetites . . . he enters and àbides in the first VI
(to the) fourth musing . . . he enters and abides in
the first (to the) fourth musing. 499

24. "And having made these four musings become, on the breaking up of the body after death, he arises in the well-faring heaven world.

25. "Thus, Dona, a Brahmin becomes deva-like.

26. "And how, Dona, becomes a Brahmin Brahmin bounded?

27. "Take the case, Dona of a Brahmin of similar birth and conduct . . . who weds in like manner. . . .

28. "And when in wedlock he has begotten a child, the fondness for children obsesses him and he settles on the family estate, and does not go forth from the home to the homeless life.

29. "In the bounds of the Brahmin of old he stays nor transgresses them; and it is said: 'Within bounds he keeps and transgresses not.' And therefore the Brahmin is called bounded.

30. "Thus, Dona, the Brahmin becomes bounded.

31. "And how, Dona, becomes a Brahmin a breaker of bounds?

32. "Take the case, Dona, of a Brahmin of similar birth and conduct. . . . He hands over the teacher's fee and seeks a wife either according to Dhamma or non-Dhamma: one bought or sold or Brahmani on whom the water-pouring ceremony has been performed.

33. "He goes to a Brahmani or to the daughter of a noble or a low-caste man or a serf; to the daughter of an outcast or a hunter or a bamboo-worker or a cart-maker or an aboriginal; he goes to a woman with child, to one giving suck, to one in her season, to one not in her season; and for him the Brahmani

becomes just a means for lust, for sport and for pleasure or to beget offspring.

34. "And he keeps not within the ancient Brahmin
bounds, but transgresses them; and it is said: 'He
VI keeps not within bounds but transgresses,' and there-
fore he is called a breaker of bounds.

500 35. "Thus, Dona, the Brahmin becomes a breaker of bounds.

36. "And how, Dona, becomes a Brahmin a Brahmin outcast?

37. "Take the case, Dona, of a Brahmin of similar birth, he for eight and forty years leads the Brahma-life of virginity, applying himself to the mantras; then, completing that course, he seeks the teaching fee for teaching; (he gets his living according to Dhamma or non-Dhamma) as ploughman, trader, cowherd, bowman, rajah's man or by some craft or, despising not the beggar's bowl, just by going about for alms.

38. "On handing back the teacher's fee, he seeks a wife according to Dhamma or non-Dhamma; one bought or sold, or a Brahmani on whom water has been poured. He goes to a Brahmani or any other woman . . . one with child, giving suck and so forth . . . and she is for him a means for lust . . . or to beget offspring. He leads a life doing all these things.

39. "Then the Brahmans say thus of him: 'How is it that an honourable Brahmin leads this sort of life?'

40. "And to this he replies: 'Just as fire burns clean things or unclean, but not by that is the fire defiled; even so, good sirs, if a Brahmin lead a life doing all these things, not by that is a Brahmin defiled.'

41. And it is said: 'He leads a life doing all these things,' and therefore he is called a Brahmin outcast.

42. "Thus, Dona, a Brahmin becomes a Brahmin outcast.

43. "Verily, Dona, those Brahmin sages of old,

mantra-makers, mantra-sayers, whose ancient collection hymn, say, word each rest . . . these five Brahmins declared; the Brahma-like, the deva-like, the bounded, the breaker of bounds and, fifthly, the Brahmin outcast. VI

44. " Which of them Dona, are you ? " 501

45. " If such there are, Master Gotama, we at least do not fulfil (the ways) of the Brahmin-outcast ?

46. " But it is marvellous what you say, Master Gotama . . . let Master Gotama take me as a lay-disciple, gone to his refuge, henceforth as long as life lasts."

PART III

Critics of His Doctrines

1. Critics of Open Admission to the Sangh.
2. Critics of The Rule of Vows.
3. Critics of the Doctrine of Ahimsa.
4. Charge of Preaching Virtue and Creating Gloom.
5. Critics of the Theory of Soul and Rebirth.
6. Charge of being an Annihilationist.

§ *1.* *Critics of Open Admission to the Sangh*

1. It was open for the Sangh to admit a layman who was merely a disciple.

2. There were persons who criticised the Lord for making the Sangh a wide open temple for anybody to enter.

3. They argued that under such a scheme it may well happen that after they have been admitted into the Order they give it up, and return again to the lower state and by their back-sliding the people are led to say : " Vain must be this religion of Samana Gotama, which these men have given up."

4. The criticism was not well founded and had altogether missed the intention of the Blessed Lord in making such a scheme.

5. The Blessed Lord replied that in establishing his religion he had constructed a bathing tank full of the excellent waters of emancipation—the bath of good law.

6. It was the Lord's desire that whosoever is polluted with stains of sin, he, bathing in it, can wash away all his sins.

7. And if anyone, having gone to the bathing tank of good law, should not bathe in it, but turn back polluted as before and return again to the lower state, it is he who is to be blamed and not the religion.

8. "Or could I," said the Blessed Lord, "after constructing this bathing tank for enabling people to wash away their sins, say : 'Let no one who is dirty go down into this tank ! Let only those whose dust and dirt have been washed away, who are purified and stainless go down into the tank.'

9. "On such terms what good would have been my religion ? "

10. The critics forgot that the Blessed Lord did not wish to confine the benefit only to a few. He wanted to keep it open to all, to be tried by all.

§ 2. *Critics of the Rule of Vows*

1. Why are the five precepts not enough ? Why vows are felt necessary? These were the questions that were often raised.

2. It was argued that if diseases would abate without medicine, what could be the advantage of weakening the body by emetics, by purges, and other like remedies?

3. Just so, if laymen, living at home and enjoying the pleasures of the senses, can realize in themselves the conditions of peace, the Supreme Good, Nibbana, by taking precepts, what is the need of the bhikkhu taking upon himself these vows?

4. The Blessed Lord devised the vows because of the virtues inherent in them.

5. A life conditioned by vows is certain to bring with it growth in goodness, it is itself a protection against a fall.

6. Those who take vows and keep them as self-dependents, are emancipated.

7. The keeping of vows is the restriction of lust, and of malice, of pride, the cutting of evil thoughts.

8. Those who take vows and keep them, well guarded are they indeed and altogether pure are they in manners and in mind.

9. Not so with mere taking of precepts.

10. In the case of the precepts there is no protection against moral decline as there is in the case of vows.

11. A life of vows is very difficult and a life of precepts not so. It is necessary for mankind to have some who live the life of vows. So the Blessed Lord prescribed both.

§ 3. *Critics of the Doctrine of Ahimsa*

1. There were persons who objected to the doctrine of Ahimsa. They said that it involved surrender or non-resistance to evil.

2. This is a complete misrepresentation of what the Blessed Lord taught by his doctrine of Ahimsa.

3. The Blessed Lord has made his position clear on various occasions so as to leave no room for ambiguity or misunderstanding.

4. The first such occasion to which reference should be made is the occasion when he made a rule regarding the entry of a soldier in the Sangh.

5. At one time the border provinces of the kingdom of Magadha were agitated. Then the Magadha king Seniya Bimbisara gave order to the Commander of the army: 'Well now, go and ask your officers to search through the border provinces for the offenders, punish them and restore peace." The Commander acted accordingly.

6. On hearing the orders of the Commander the officers found themselves placed in a dilemma. They knew that the Tathagatha taught that those who go to war and find delight in fighting, do evil and produce great demerit. On the other hand, here was the king's order to capture the offenders and to kill them. Now what shall we do, asked the officers to themselves.

7. Then these officers thought: "If we could enter the order of the Buddha we would be able to escape from the dilemma."

8. Thus these officers went to the bhikkhus and asked them for ordination; the bhikkhus conferred on them the pabbajja and upasampada ordinations and the officers disappeared from the army.

9. The Commander of the army finding that the officers were not to be seen, asked the soldiers: "Why, how is it that the officers are nowhere to be seen?" "The officers, lord, have embraced religious life of the bhikkhus," replied the soldiers.

10. Then the Commander of the army was annoyed, and became very angry: "How can the bhikkhus ordain persons in the royal army?"

11. The Commander of the army informed the king of what had happened. And the king asked the

officers of justice: "Tell me, my good sirs, what punishment does he deserve who ordains a person in the royal service?"

12. "The Upagghaya, Your Majesty, should be
VI beheaded; to him who recites (the Kammavaka), the
tongue should be torn out; to those who form the
508 chapter, half of their ribs should be broken."

13. Then the king went to the place where the Blessed One was; and after obeisance informed him of what had happened.

14. "The Lord well knows that there are kings who are against the Dhamma. These hostile kings are ever ready to harass the bhikkhus even for trifling reasons. It is impossible to imagine the lengths to which they might go in their ill-treatment of the bhikkhus if they find that the bhikkhus are seducing the soldiers to leave the army and join the Sangh. Pray Lord to do the needful to avert the disaster."

15. The Lord replied: "It was never my intention to allow soldiers under the cloak of Ahimsa or in the name of Ahimsa to abandon their duty to the king or to their country."

16. Accordingly the Blessed One made a rule against the admission of persons in royal service to the Sangh and proclaimed it to the bhikkhus, saying: "Let no one, O Bhikkhus, who is in the royal service, receive the Pabbajja ordination. He who confers the Pabbajja ordination on such a person will be guilty of a dukkata offence."

17. A second time the Blessed One was cross-examined on the subject of Ahimsa by Sinha, a General in the army, and who was a follower of Mahavir.

18. Sinha asked: "One doubt still lurks in my mind concerning the doctrine of the Blessed One. Will the Blessed One consent to clear the cloud away so that I may understand the Dhamma as the Blessed One teaches it."

19. The Tathagata having given his consent, Sinha said: "I am a soldier, O Blessed One, and am appointed by the king to enforce his laws

and to wage his wars. Does the Tathagata, who teaches kindness without end and compassion with all sufferers, permit the punishment of the criminal? And further, does the Tathagata declare that it is wrong to go to war for the protection of our homes, our wives, our children, and our property? Does the Tathagata teach the doctrine of a complete self-surrender, so that I should suffer the evil-doer to do what he pleases and yield submissively to him who threatens to take by violence what is my own? Does the Tathagata maintain that all strifes, including such warfare as is waged for a righteous cause, should be forbidden?"

20. The Lord replied : "The Tathagata says: 'He who deserves punishment must be punished, and he who is worthy of favour must be favoured. Yet at the same time he teaches to do no injury to any living being but to be full of love and kindness. These injunctions are not contradictory, for whosoever must be punished for the crimes which he has committed suffers his injury not through the ill-will of the judge but on account of his evil-doing. His own acts have brought upon him the injury that the executor of the law inflicts. When a magistrate punishes, let him not harbour hatred in his breast, yet a murderer, when put to death, should consider that this is the fruit of his own act. As soon as he will understand that the punishment will purify his soul, he will no longer lament his fate but rejoice at it.'"

21. A proper understanding of these instances would show that the Ahimsa taught by the Blessed Lord was fundamental. But it was not absolute.

22. He taught that evil should be cured by the return of good. But he never preached that evil should be allowed to overpower good.

23. He stood for Ahimsa. He denounced Himsa. But he did not deny that Himsa may be the last resort to save good being destroyed by evil.

24. Thus it is not that the Blessed Lord taught a dangerous doctrine. It is the critics who failed to understand its significance and its scope.

§ 4. *Charge of Preaching Virtue and Creating Gloom*

(1)

VI *Dukkha as the Cause of Gloom*

510 1. Dukkha in its original sense given to it by Kapila means unrest, commotion.

2. Initially it had a metaphysical meaning.

3. Later on it acquired the meaning of suffering and sorrow.

4. The two senses were not far detached. They were very close.

5. Unrest brings sorrow and suffering.

6. Soon it acquired the meaning of sorrow and suffering from social and economic causes.

7. In what sense did the Buddha use the word sorrow and suffering?

8. There is a sermon on record from which it is clear that the Buddha was very much aware that poverty was a cause of sorrow.

9. In that sermon he says—" Monks, is poverty a woeful thing for a worldly wanton?"

10. " Surely, Lord."

11. " And when a man is poor, needy, in straits, he gets into debt, and is that woeful too?"

12. " Surely, Lord."

13. " And when he gets into debt, he borrows, and is that woeful too?"

14. " Surely, Lord."

15. " And when the bill falls due, he pays not and they press him; is that woeful too?"

16. " Surely, Lord."

17. " And when pressed, he pays not and they beset him; is that woeful too?"

18. " Surely, Lord."

19. " And when beset, he pays not and they bind him; is that woeful too?"

20. " Surely, Lord."

21. " Thus, monks, poverty, debt, borrowing,

being pressed, beset and bound are all woes for the worldly wanton.

22. "Woeful in the world is poverty and debt."

23. Thus the Buddha's conception of Dukkha is material. VI

(2) 511

Impermanence as the Cause of Gloom

1. Another ground for this accusation arises from the doctrine that everything which is compound is impermanent.

2. Nobody questions the truth of the doctrine.

3. Everything is impermanent is admitted by all.

4. The doctrine, if it is true, must be told just as truth must be told however unpleasant it may be.

5. But why draw a pessimistic conclusion?

6. If life is short it is short and one need not be gloomy about it.

7. It is just a matter of interpretation.

8. The Burmese interpretation is very much different.

9. The Burmese celebrate the event of death in a family as though it was an event of joy.

10. On the day of death the householder gives a public feast and the people remove the dead body to the graveyard dancing. Nobody minds the death for it was to come.

11. If impermanence is pessimistic it is only because permanence was assumed to be true although it was a false one.

12. Buddha's preaching cannot, therefore, be charged as spreading gloom.

(3)

Is Buddhism Pessimistic ?

1. The Buddha's Dhamma has been accused of creating pessimism.

2. The accusation arises from the first Aryan Truth which says that there is Dukkha (sorrow-misery) in the world.

3. It is rather surprising that a reference to Dukkha should give cause to such an accusation.

4. Karl Marx also said that there is exploitation in the world and the rich are being made richer and the poor are being made poorer.

5. And yet nobody has said that Karl Marx's doctrine is pessimism.

6. Why then should a different attitude be shown to the Buddha's doctrine?

7. It may be because the Buddha is reported to have said in his first sermon, Birth is sorrowful, old age is sorrowful, death is sorrowful, that a deeper pessimistic colouring has been given to his Dhamma.

8. But those who know rhetoric know that this is an artifice of exaggeration and that it is practised by skilled literary hands to produce effect.

9. That birth is sorrowful is an exaggeration by the Buddha can be proved by reference to a sermon of his in which he has preached that birth as a human being is a very precious thing.

10. Again, if the Buddha had merely referred to Dukkha such an accusation could be sustainable.

11. But the Buddha's second Aryan Truth emphasizes that this Dukkha must be removed. In order to emphasize the duty of removal of Dukkha he spoke of the existence of Dukkha.

12. To the removal of Dukkha the Buddha attached great importance. It is because he found that Kapila merely stated that there was Dukkha and said nothing more about it that he felt dissatisfied and left the Ashram of Muni Alara Kalam.

13. How can this Dhamma be called pessimistic?

14. Surely a teacher who is anxious to remove Dukkha cannot be charged with pessimism.

§ 5. *Critics of the Theory of Soul and Rebirth*

1. The Blessed Lord preached that there was no Soul. The Blessed Lord also affirmed that there was rebirth.

2. There were not wanting people who criticised the Lord for preaching what they regarded as two such contradictory doctrines.

3. How can there be rebirth if there is no Soul, they asked.

4. There is no contradiction. There can be rebirth even though there is no Soul.

5. There is a mango stone. The stone gives rise to a mango tree. The mango tree produces mangoes.

6. Here is rebirth of a mango.

7. But there is no Soul.

8. So there can be rebirth although there is no Soul.

§ 6. *Charge of Being an Annihilationist*

1. Once when the Lord was staying at Shravasti in Jeta's grove it was reported to him that a certain bhikkhu by name Arittha had come to certain views about the doctrines taught by the Lord, as the views of the Lord although they were not the views of the Lord.

2. One of the doctrines about which Arittha was misrepresenting the Lord was whether he was an annihilationist.

3. The Blessed Lord sent for Arittha. Arittha came. On being questioned he sat silent and glum.

4. The Lord then said to him : " Some recluses and Brahmins—wrongly, erroneously and falsely—charge me in defiance of facts, with being an annihilationist and with preaching disintegration, and extirpation of existing creatures.

5. It is just what I am not and what I do not affirm.

6. What I have consistently preached both in the past and today is the existence of ill and the ending of ill.

PART IV

Friends and Admirers

1. Devotion of Dhananjanani—a Brahmini.
2. The Abiding Faith of Visakha.
3. The Devotion of Mallika.
4. The ardent Wish of a Pregnant Mother.
5. Keniya's Welcome.
6. Pasendi in Praise of the Master.

§ 1. Devotion of Dhananjanani—a Brahmini

1. The Blessed Lord had many friends and admirers. Among them was Dhananjanani.

2. She was the wife of a Bharadvaja Brahmin. Her husband hated the Lord. But Dhananjanani was a devotee of the Lord. Her devotion is worthy of mention.

3. The Exalted One was once staying near Rajagraha in the bamboo grove at the Vihara known as the squirrels' feeding ground.

4. Now at that time Dhananjanani, a Brahmini, the wife of a certain Brahmin of the Bharadvaja family, was living with her husband in Rajagraha.

5. While her husband was a great opponent of the Buddha, Dhananjanani was a fervent believer in the Buddha, the Dhamma and the Order. She was in the habit of praising the triple gem. Whenever she broke out in this way in praise, her husband used to close his ears.

6. On the eve of his giving a great banquet to many fellow-Brahmins, he begged her to do what she liked, provided she did not offend his guests by her praises of the Buddha.

7. Dhananjanani would give no such undertaking and he threatened to slice her like a plantain with his dagger. She declared herself ready to suffer, so she retained her freedom of speech and proceeded to pour forth five hundred verses on her theme, so that he surrendered unconditionally.

8. Bowl and golden spoon were laid down and the guests sat down for food. While serving the guests the dominant impulse arose. In the midst she turned towards the bamboo grove and uttered the praises of the triple gem.

9. The scandalized guests hurried away, spitting out the food defiled by the presence of a heretic and the husband scolded her amid the ruins of his feast.

10. And she, while serving the Bharadvaja with his dinner, came before him and praised the gem.

Glory to that Exalted One, the Arahant, the Buddha Supreme! Glory to the Norm! Glory to the Order!

11. And when she had so said the Bharadvaja
Brahmin grew angry and exclaimed: "There now!
VI You wretch! Must you be singing the praises of that
518 shaveling friar at any and every opportunity? Now,
wretch, will I give that teacher of thine a piece of
my mind!"

12. "O Brahmin," replied Dhananjanani, "I know of no one throughout the world of gods, Maras, or Brahmas, recluses or brahmins, no one human or divine, who could so admonish that Exalted One, Arahant, Buddha Supreme. Nevertheless, go thou, Brahmin, and then thou wilt know."

13. Then the Bharadvaja, vexed and displeased, went to find the Exalted One; and coming into his presence, exchanged with him greetings and compliments, friendly and courteous, and sat down at one side.

14. So seated, he asked the Exalted One the following questions: "What must we slay if we would happy live? What must we slay if we could weep no more? What is above all other things, whereof the slaughter thou approvest, Gotama?"

15. The Exalted One replied as follows: "Wrath must ye slay if ye would happy live; Wrath must ye slay if ye would weep no more. Of anger, Brahmin, with its poisoned source, and fevered climax, murderously sweet. That is the slaughter by the Ariyans praised. That must ye slay in sooth, to weep no more."

16. Realizing the excellence of the reply given by the Exalted One, the Bharadvaja Brahmin said to him: "Most excellent, Lord, most excellent! Just as if a man were to set up that which had been thrown down, or were to reveal that which was hidden away, or were to point out the right road to him who had gone astray, or were to bring a lamp into the darkness so that those who had eyes could see external objects—even so, Lord, has the Lord Gotama shown me his doctrine in various ways. I, even I, Lord, betake myself to the

Exalted One as my refuge to the Norm and to the Order. I would leave the world under the rule of Gotama; I would take orders."

17. So Dhananjanani was not only a devotee of the Buddha, she made her husband also a devotee of the Buddha.

§ 2. *The Abiding Faith of Visakha*

1. Visakha was born in the city of Bhadiya in the Anga country.

2. Her father was Dhananjaya and her mother's name was Sumana.

3. Once the Buddha visited Bhadiya with a large company of monks at the invitation of the Brahmin Sela. Visakha his granddaughter was then seven years old.

4. Visakha though only seven expressed to her grandfather Mendaka her desire to see the Buddha. Mendaka allowed her to do so and gave her five hundred companions, five hundred slaves, and five hundred chariots, that she might visit the Buddha.

5. She stopped the chariot some distance away and approached the Buddha on foot.

6. He preached to her the Dhamma and she became his lay disciple.

7. For the next fortnight Mendaka invited the Buddha and his followers daily to his house, where he fed them.

8. Later, when at Pasendi's request, Bimbisara sent Dhananjaya to live in Kosala, Visakha accompanied her parents and lived in Saketa.

9. Migara, a wealthy citizen of Shravasti, wanted to get his son Punnavadhana married. He had sent a few people to find a suitable bride.

10. The party in search of a bride happened to come to Shravasti. They saw Visakha on her way to the lake to bathe on a feast day.

11. At that moment there was a great shower. Visakha's companions ran for shelter. But Visakha

did not. She walked at her usual pace and reached the spot where the messengers were.

12. They asked her why she did not run for shelter and so preserve her clothes. She answered that she had plenty of clothes, but that if she ran she might damage a limb which she could not replace. " Unmarried girls," she said, " are like goods awaiting sale, they must not be disfigured."

13. The party which was already struck by her beauty was greatly impressed by her intelligence. The party offered her a bouquet of flowers which she accepted as a proposal of marriage.

14. After Visakha returned home the marriage party followed her and laid Punnavadhana's suit before Dhananjaya. The proposal was accepted and confirmed by an exchange of letters.

15. When Pasendi heard of it, he offered to accompany Punnavadhana to Saketa, as a mark of signal honour. Dhananjaya welcomed the king and his retinue, Migara, Punnavadhana and their followers with all regard, attending personally to all the details of hospitality.

16. Five hundred goldsmiths were engaged to make ornaments for the bride. Dhananjaya gave his daughter, as dowry, five hundred carts full of money, five hundred with vessels of gold and cattle, etc.

17. When the time came for Visakha to leave, Dhananjaya gave her ten admonitions, which Migara overheard from the next room. These admonitions were: Not to give fire from the house outside: not to take into the house fire from without; to give only to those who gave in return, not to give to those who did not give in return, to give him that gives and to him that gives not; to seat, eat and eat happily; and to tend the fire and to honour the household deities.

18. On the following day Dhananjaya appointed eight householders to be sponsors to his daughter and inquire into any charges that might be brought against her.

19. Migara wanted that his daughter-in-law should be seen by the public of Shravasti. Visakha

entered Shravasti standing in her chariot with the public lining the road on both sides. The public showered gifts on her, but these she distributed among the people.

20. Migara was a follower of the Niganthas and soon after Visakha's arrival in his house, he sent for them and told her to minister to them. But Visakha repulsed by their nudity, refused to pay them homage.

21. The Niganthas urged that she should be sent away, but Migara bided his time.

22. One day as Migara was eating, while Visakha stood fanning him, a monk was seen standing outside the house. Visakha stood aside that Migara might see him. But Migara continued to eat without noticing the monk.

23. Seeing this Visakha said to the monk, "Pass on, sir, my father-in-law eats stale fare." Migara was angry and threatened to send her away, but at her request the matter was referred to her sponsors.

24. They inquired into the several charges brought against her and adjudged her not guilty.

25. Visakha then gave orders that preparations be made for her return to her parents. Both Migara and his wife begged for forgiveness which she granted, on condition that he would invite to the house the Buddha and his monks.

26. This he did, but, owing to the influence o the Niganthas, he left Visakha to entertain them, and only consented to hear the Buddha's sermon at the end of the meal from behind a curtain.

27. He was, however, so convinced by the sermon that he became a convert.

28. His gratitude towards Visakha was boundless. Henceforth he considered her to be his mother deserving all the honours due to a mother. From this time onward she was called Migarmata.

29. Such was the abiding faith of Visakha.

§ 3. *The Devotion of Mallika*

1. Once while the Lord was staying at Shravasti in Jeta's grove the darling son of a certain house-

holder died, and the loss made the father neglect his business and his meals.

2. He was always going to the charnel ground and wailing aloud saying, "Where are you, my son, where are you?"

3. The bereaved father came to the Blessed Lord and after due salutations sat on one side.

4. Seeing that his mind was absolutely vacant showing no interest in anything, not telling the purpose for which he had come, the Blessed Lord, noticing his condition, said "You are not yourself; your mind is all awry."

5. "How could my mind not be awry, sir, when I have lost my darling and only son?"

6. "Yes, householder; our dear ones bring sorrow and lamentation, pain, suffering and tribulation?"

7. "Who sir can entertain such a view?", said the angry householder, "Nay, our dear ones are a joy and happiness to us."

8. And with these words the householder, rejecting the Lord's pronouncement, indignantly got up and departed.

9. Hard by, there were a number of gamblers having a game with dice; and to them came the householder with his story of how he had related his sorrows to the recluse Gotama, how he had been received and how he had indignantly departed.

10. You were quite right, said the gamblers, for our dear ones are a source of joy and happiness to us. So the householder felt he had got the gamblers on his side.

11. Now all this, in due course, penetrated to the private apartments of the palace where the king told Queen Mallika that her recluse Gotama had stated that dear ones bring sorrow and lamentation, pain, suffering and tribulation.

12. "Well, sir, if the Lord said so, so it is."

13. "Just as a pupil accepts all his master tells him, saying, 'So it is, sir; so it is'—just in the same way Mallika, you accept all the recluse Gotama says with

your 'If the Lord said so, so it is'; away with you and begone!"

14. Then the queen told the Brahmin Nali Dhyan to go to the Lord and in her name, to bow his head at the Lord's feet and, after asking after his health, to enquire whether he had really said what was attributed to him.

15. "And be careful," she added, "to tell me exactly what the Lord answers."

16. In obedience to the queen's commands the Brahmin went off and duly asked the Lord whether he had really said so.

17. "Yes, Brahmin; our dear ones do bring sorrow and lamentation, pain, suffering, and tribulation. Here is the proof.

18. "Once, here in Shravasti, a woman's mother died and the daughter, crazed and beside herself, went about from street to street, from cross-road to cross-road, saying: 'Have you seen my mother? Have you seen my mother?'

19. "Another proof is a woman of Shravasti who lost her father—a brother—a sister—a son—a daughter—a husband. Crazed and beside herself, the woman went about from street to street and from cross-road to cross-road, asking if anyone had seen the dear ones she had lost.

20. "Another proof is a man of Shravasti who lost his mother—his father—a brother—a sister—a son—a daughter—a wife, crazed and beside himself, the man went about from street to street and from cross-road to cross-road, asking if anyone had seen the dear ones he had lost.

21. "Another proof is the woman of Shravasti who visited her people's home; and they wanted to take her from her husband and marry her to someone else whom she did not like.

22. "She told her husband about it, whereupon he cut her into two and then killed himself, so that they might both die together.

23. "All this the Brahmin Nali Dhyan duly reported to the queen.

24. "The queen then went to the king and asked: 'Are you fond, sir, of your only daughter, the princess Vajira.' 'Yes, I am,' replied the king.

25. "'If anything happened to your Vajira would you feel sorry or not?' 'If anything happened to her, it would make a great difference to my life.'"

26. "'Are you fond, sir, of me,' asked Mallika. 'Yes, I am.'

27. "'If anything happened to me would you feel sorry or would you not?' 'If anything happened to you it would make a great difference to my life.'

28. "'Are you fond, sir, of the people of Kasi and Kosala?' 'Yes,' replied the king. 'If anything happened to them would you be sorry or not?'

29. "'If anything happened to them, it would make great difference—how could it be otherwise?'

30. "'Did the Blessed Lord say anything different?' 'No Mallika,' said the king in repentance."

§ 4. *The Ardent Wish of a Pregnant Mother*

1. Once when the Lord was staying in the Bhagga country at Sumsumara-gira in the Bhesakala grove, in the deer-park there, Prince Bodhi's palace, called the Lotus, had just been finished but had not as yet been inhabited by recluse, Brahmin or any other person.

2. Said the prince to a young Brahmin named Sankika-putta: "Go to the Lord and in my name bow your head at his feet, ask after his health and invite him to be so good as to take his meal with me tomorrow and to bring his confraternity with him."

3. The message was delivered to the Lord who, by silence, signified acceptance—as was duly reported to the prince.

4. When night had passed, the prince, having ordered an excellent meal to be got ready in his palace and a carpeting of white cloth to be laid to the foot of the stairs of the Lotus palace, told the young Brahmin to announce to the Lord that all was ready.

5. This was done; and early that day the Lord, duly robed and bowl in hand, came to the palace where the prince was awaiting him, outside the portals.

6. Seeing the Lord approaching, the prince advanced and saluted him and moved in his train towards the palace.

7. At the foot of the stairs the Lord stood still. Said the prince: "I beg the Lord to step up on the carpeting; I beg the Blessed One to do this,—to my abiding weal and welfare." But the Lord kept silent.

8. A second time did the prince appeal, and still the Lord kept silent. A third time he appealed, and now the Lord looked towards Ananda.

9. Ananda understood what the trouble was and asked that the carpeting should be rolled up and removed for the Lord would not tread upon it as he is looking to those that shall follow hereafter.

10. So the prince ordered the carpeting to be rolled up and removed, after which he ordered seats to be set out upstairs in the palace.

11. The Lord then proceeding upstairs, sat down on the seat set for him, with the confraternity.

12. The prince with his own hand served that excellent meal without stint to the Lord and the confraternity.

13. The Lord's meal over and done, Prince Bodhi, seating himself on a low seat to one side, said to the Lord: "My view, sir, is that true weal must be sought not through things pleasant but through things unpleasant."

14. "In days gone by, Prince," said the Blessed One, "I too held the same view in the days before my enlightenment. Time was when being quite young—with a wealth of coal-black hair and in all the beauty of my early prime—despite the wishes of my parents who wept and lamented, I cut off hair and beard, donned the yellow robes and went forth from home to homelessness as a pilgrim. A pilgrim now, in quest of the Good and in search for the road to that utter peace which is beyond all compare.

15. "Now I hold a different view. If a man knows the Doctrine he will find the destruction of all ills."

16. Said the prince to the Lord: "What a doctrine! What an exposition of doctrine ! It is so easy to
VI understand."

17. Here the young Brahmin Sankika-putta
526 observed to the prince that, though he had testified thus, yet he had not gone on to say that he sought as a refuge the Lord and his doctrine and his confraternity as he should have.

18. "Say not so, my friend; say not so" said the Prince: "for, I have heard from the lips of my lady mother, how, when once the Lord was staying at Kosambi in the Ghosita pleasance, she, being then pregnant, came to the Lord, saluted him and took a seat to one side, saying: 'Be it a boy or be it a girl that I carry in my womb, my child unborn seeks refuge with the Lord and his doctrine and his confraternity; and I ask the Lord to accept the child as a follower who has found an abiding refuge from this time forth while life lasts.'

19. "Another time, when the Lord was staying here in this Bhagga country at Sumsumara-gira, in the Bhesakala grove, in the deer park there, my nurse carried me to the Lord, and standing before him, said: 'Here is Prince Bodhi who seeks refuge with the Lord and his doctrine and his confraternity.'

20. Now, in person, for the third time I seek such refuge and ask the Lord to accept me as a follower who has found an abiding refuge while life lasts."

§ 5. *Keniya's Welcome*

1. There was living at Apanath a Brahmin, Sela, who was versed in all three Vedas, was accomplished in ritual with the glosses thereon, in phonology, and in etymology, with chronicles as a fifth branch; he knew exegesis, and was learned in casuistry and in the signs that mark a superman; he had three hundred young brahmins to whom he taught the runes.

2. Keniya the fire-worshipper was an adherent

of this Brahmin Sela. Accompanied by his three hundred pupils, Sela went and saw all the fire-worshippers there busy with their several tasks, with Keniya himself marking off the reserved circles.

3. At the sight of this the Brahmin said to Keniya: "What is all this? Is it a wedding feast? Or is there a great sacrifice afoot? Or have you invited to a repast tomorrow Seniya Bimbisara, king of Magadha, with all his host?"

4. "It is no wedding feast, Sela, nor is the king coming with all his host. But I have got a great sacrifice afoot. For, the recluse Gotama has arrived at Apana, in the course of an alms-pilgrimage, with twelve hundred and fifty alms-men in his train.

5. "Now, such, according to report, is the high repute of this Gotama that he is deemed to be the Lord of Enlightenment.

6. "It is he whom I have invited to tomorrow's meal here, together with his confraternity. The feast that is being prepared is for him."

7. "Did you attribute to him Enlightenment, Keniya," asked Sela. "Yes, I did," replied Keniya. "Did you?" "Yes I did."

§ 6. *Pasendi In Praise of the Master*

1. Once the Exalted One was staying near Shravasti, at Jeta's grove, in Anathapindika's park.

2. Now at that time the rajah of Kosala, Pasendi, had just returned from a sham-fight, in which he was victorious, having carried out his object. And on reaching the park he turned in that way. So far as the cart-road went he rode in his chariot, and then got down and went on foot through the park.

3. On that occasion a number of the brethren were walking up and down in the open air. Then Pasendi, the rajah of Kosala, went up to those brethren and thus accosted them: "Reverend sirs, where now is the Exalted One staying, that Arahant, Buddha Supreme: for I long to behold Him?"

4. "Yonder, Maharajah, is his lodging, and the

door is shut. Do you go up quietly, without nervousness, enter the verandah, cough, and rattle the door-bar. The Exalted One will open the door to you."

5. So Pasendi, the rajah of Kosala, went up to
VI the lodging as he was told, coughed and rattled the
door-bar. And the Exalted One opened the door.
528 6. Then Pasendi entered the lodging, fell with his head at the feet of the Exalted One, kissed His feet and stroked them with his hands, and announced his name, saying, " Lord, I am Pasendi, the rajah of Kosala."

7. "But, Maharajah, seeing what significance therein, do you show me this profound humanity and pay such affectionate obeisance to this body," said the Lord !

BOOK VII

The Wanderer's Last Journey

PART I

The Meeting of Those Near and Dear

1. The Centres of His Preachings.
2. The Places He Visited.
3. Last Meeting between Mother and Son and between Wife and Husband.
4. Last Meeting between Father and Son.
5. Last Meeting between the Buddha and Sariputta.

§ 1. *The Centres of His Preachings*

1. It is not that after the appointment of the missionaries the Lord sat at one place. He too continued to be his own missionary.

2. The Lord seems to have made certain places chief centres of his missionary work.

3. Of such centres, the chief were Shravasti and Rajagraha.

4. He visited Shravasti about 75 times and Rajagraha about 24 times.

5. Certain other places were made minor centres.

6. They were Kapilavastu, which he visited 6 times, Vesali which he visited 6 times, and Kamassadhamma, 4 times.

§ 2. *The Places He Visited*

1. Besides these main and minor centres the Blessed Lord visited many other places during the course of his missionary tour.

2. He visited Ukkatha, Nadika, Sal, Assapura, Ghoshitaram, Nalanda, Appana, Etuma.

3. He visited Opasad, Iccha-naukal, Chandal Kuppa, Kushinara.

4. He visited Devadaha, Pava, Ambasanda, Setavya, Anupiya and Ugunma.

5. The names of the places he visited show that he travelled over the Sakya Desa, the Kuru Desa and Anga Desa.

6. Roughly speaking, he travelled over the whole of Northern India.

7. These appear to be a few places. But what distance do they cover? Rajagraha from Lumbini is not less than 250 miles. This just gives an idea of distances.

8. These distances the Lord walked on foot. He did not even use a bullock-cart.

9. In his wanderings he had no place to stay until later on when his lay disciples built Viharas and resting places which he and his Bhikkhus used as halts on their journeys. Most often he lived under the shade of wayside trees.

10. He went from place to place, sometimes from village to village, resolving the doubts and difficulties of those who were willing to accept his message, controverting the arguments of those who were his opponents and preaching his gospel to those who like children came to him for guidance.

11. The Blessed Lord knew that all those who came to listen to him were not all of them intelligent, not all of them came with an open and a free mind.

12. He had even warned the brethren that there were three sorts of listeners.

13. The empty-head, the fool who cannot see,—though oft and oft, unto the brethren going, he hears their talk, beginning, middle, end,—but can never grasp it. Wisdom is not his.

14. Better than he the man of scattered brains, who oft and oft, unto the brethren going, hears all their talk, beginning, middle, end, and seated there can grasp the very words, yet, rising, nought retains. Blank is his mind.

15. Better than these the man of wisdom wide. He, oft and oft unto the brethren going, hears all their talk, beginning, middle, end, and seated there, can grasp the very words, bears all in mind, steadfast, unwavering, skilled in the Norm and what conforms thereto.

16. Notwithstanding this, the Lord was never tired of going from place to place preaching his gospel.

17. As a bhikkhu the Lord never had more than three pieces of clothes. He lived on one meal a day and he begged his food from door to door every morning.

18. His mission was the hardest task assigned to any human being. He discharged it so cheerfully.

§ 3. *Last Meeting between Mother and Son and between Wife and Husband*

1. Before their death Mahaprajapati and Yeshodhara met the Blessed Lord.

2. It was probably their last meeting with him.

3. Mahaprajapati went and first worshipped him.

4. She thanked him for having given her the happiness of the good doctrine, for her having been spiritually born through him: for the doctrine having grown in her through him; for her having suckled him, drinking the Dhamma-milk of him; for her having plunged in and crossed over the ocean of becoming through him—what a glorious thing it has been to be known as the mother of the Buddha!

5. And then she uttered her plea:—

"I desire to die finally having put away this corpse. O sorrow-ender, permit me."

6. Yeshodhara, addressing the Blessed Lord, said that she was in her seventy-eighth year. The Blessed Lord replied that he was in his eighties.

7. She told him that she was to die that very night. Her tone was more self-reliant than that of Mahaprajapati. She did not ask his permission to die nor did she go to him to seek him as her refuge.

8. On the contrary, she said to him (*me saranam atthano*), "I am my own refuge."

9. She had conquered all the cankers in her life.

10. She came to thank him because it was he who had shown her the way and given her the power.

§ 4. *Last Meeting between Father and Son*

1. Once when the Lord was staying at Rajagraha in the bamboo grove Rahula was staying at Ambalathika.

2. The Blessed One arising towards eventide from his meditation went over to Rahula, who seeing the Lord some way off, set a seat for him and water to wash his feet.

3. Seating himself on the seat set for him, the Lord poured water over his feet while Rahula, after salutations, took his seat to one side.

4. Addressing Rahula, the Blessed Lord said—"He who does not shrink from deliberate lying has not—say I—left undone any evil thing which he could. Therefore, you must school yourself never to tell a lie even in jest.

5. "In the same way you must reflect and again in doing every act, in speaking every word and in thinking every thought.

6. "When you want to do anything you must reflect whether it would conduce to your or others' harm or to both, and so is a wrong act productive of woe and ripening into woe. If reflection tells you that this is the nature of that contemplated act, you should not do it.

7. "But if reflection assures you there is no harm but good in it, then you may do it.

8. "Grow in loving kindness; for as you do so malevolence will pass away.

9. "Grow in compassion; for as you do so vexation will pass away.

10. "Grow in gladness over others' welfare; for as you do so aversions will pass away.

11. "Grow in poised equanimity; for as you do so all repugnance will pass away.

12. "Grow in contemplation of the body's corruption; for as you do so passion will pass away.

13. "Grow in perception of the fleeting nature of things; for as you do so the pride of self will fall away."

14. Thus spoke the Lord. Glad at heart, Rahula rejoiced in what the Lord had said.

§ 5. *Last Meeting between the Buddha and Sariputta*

1. The Blessed Lord was staying in Shravasti in the Jetavana in the Gaudhakuti Vihar.

2. Sariputta arrived there with a company of five hundred brethren.

3. After saluting the Blessed One Sariputta told
him that the last day of his life on earth had arrived.
Will the Blessed Lord be pleased to permit him to give VII
up his mortal coils?

4. The Blessed Lord asked Sariputta if he had 537
selected any place for his parinibbana.

5. Sariputta told the Blessed One, "I was born in the village Nalaka in Magadha. The house in which I was born still stands. I have chosen my home for my parinibbana."

6. The Lord replied, "Dear Sariputta! Do what pleases you."

7. Sariputta fell on the feet of the Blessed Lord and said, "I have practised the paramitas for one thousand Kalpas with only one wish, to have the honour of falling on your feet. I have achieved that end and there is no end to my happiness."

8. "We do not believe in rebirth. Therefore this is our last meeting. Let the Lord forgive me my faults. My last day has come."

9. "Sariputta! There is nothing to forgive," said the Lord.

10. When Sariputta rose to go, the Lord in his honour got up and stood up on the verandah of the Gaudhakuti Vihar.

11. Then Sariputta said to the Blessed Lord, "I was happy when I saw you first. I am happy to see you now. I know this is the last *darshan* of you I am having. I shall not have your *darshan* again."

12. Joining together the palms of his hand he walked away without showing his back to the Blessed Lord.

13. Then the Blessed Lord said to the assembled brethren—"Follow your Elder Brother," and the assembly for the first time left the Blessed Lord and went after Sariputta.

14. Sariputta on reaching his village died in his home in the very room in which he was born.

15. He was cremated and his ashes were taken to the Blessed Lord.

16. On receiving the ashes the Blessed Lord said
to the brethren—" He was the wisest, he had no
VII acquisitive instinct, he was energetic and industrious,
he hated sin, ye brethren see his ashes. He was as
538 strong as the earth in his forgiveness, he never allowed
anger to enter his mind, he was never controlled by
any desire, he had conquered all his passions, he was
full of sympathy, fellowship and love."

17. About that time Mahamogallan was then living in a solitary Vihar near Rajagraha. He was murdered by some assassins employed by the enemies of the Blessed Lord.

18. The sad news of his end was conveyed to the Blessed One. Sariputta and Mahamogallan were his two chief disciples. They were called Dharma-Senapati —Defenders of the Faith. The Blessed Lord depended upon them to continue the spread of his gospel.

19. The Blessed Lord was deeply affected by their death in his lifetime.

20. He did not like to stay in Shravasti and to relieve his mind he decided to move on.

PART II

Leaving Vaishali

1. Farewell to Vesali.
2. Halt at Pava.
3. Arrival at Kushinara.

§ 1. *Farewell to Vesali*

1. Before he set on his last journey the Blessed Lord was staying at Rajagraha on the Vulture's Peak.

2. After staying there for some time he said: "Come Ananda, let us go to Ambalathika."

3. "So be it Lord!" said Ananda in assent, and the Blessed One, with a large company of the brethren, proceeded to Ambalathika.

4. After staying at Ambalathika he moved on to Nalanda.

5. From Nalanda he went to Pataligama, the capital of Magadha.

6. From Pataligama he went to Kotigam and from Kotigam he went to Nadika.

7. At each of these places he stopped for a few days and delivered a religious discourse either to the brethren or the householders.

8. From Nadika he went to Vesali.

9. Vesali was the birth-place of Mahavira and consequently a stronghold of his faith.

10. But the Blessed Lord soon succeeded in converting the people of Vesali to his own faith.

11. It is said that owing to drought, a famine ravaged the city of Vesali to such an extent that people died in large numbers.

12. The people of Vesali complained of it in a general assembly convoked by them.

13. The assembly after much discussion decided to invite the Blessed Lord to the city.

14. A Lichchavi by name Mahali, a friend of King Bimbisara and son of the chaplain of Vesali, was sent to offer the invitation.

15. The Blessed Lord accepted the invitation and started with five hundred Bhikkhus. As soon as he entered the territory of the Vajjins there was a thunder-storm, rain fell in torrents and famine disappeared.

16. This is the origin of the welcome which the people of Vesali gave to the Blessed Lord.

17. Having won their hearts it was natural that the people of Vesali should give him a warm response.

18. Then came *vasa*. The Blessed Lord went to Beluna for his *vasa* and asked the brethren to make their *vasa* in Vesali.

19. After finishing his *vasa* the Lord came to Vesali with a mind to leave Vesali and move on his journey.

20. So the Blessed Lord early one morning robed himself, and taking his bowl, entered Vesali for alms; and when he had passed through Vesali and eaten his meal he gazed at Vesali with an elephant's look and addressed the venerable Ananda and said: "This will be the last time Ananda that the Tathagatha will behold Vesali."

21. Thus saying he bade farewell to the people of Vesali.

22. He gave to the Lichchavis, when they took leave of him at the old city on their northern frontier, his alms-bowl as a memento.

23. It was his last visit to Vesali. He did not live to return to it again.

§ 2. *Halt at Pava*

1. From Vesali the Blessed Lord went to Bhandagam.

2. From Bhandagam he went to Hatthi-gam to Bhoga-Nagara.

3. And from Bhoga-Nagara he went to Pava.

4. At Pava the Blessed One stayed at the mango grove of one blacksmith by name Chunda.

5. Now Chunda heard that the Blessed One had come to Pava and was staying in his mango grove.

6. Chunda went to the mango grove and sat near the Blessed One, who gave him a religious discourse.

7. Gladdened by it Chunda addressed the Blessed One and said: "May the Blessed One do me the honour of taking his meal together with the brethren, at my house tomorrow."

8. And the Blessed One signified, by silence, his

consent. Seeing that the Blessed One had consented, Chunda departed thence.

9. Next day Chunda made ready in his dwelling-place sweet rice and cakes and some preparation of *Sukara-Madhava*. And he announced the hour to the Blessed One, saying: "The hour, Lord, has come, and the meal is ready."

10. And the Blessed One robed himself and taking his bowl went with the brethren to the dwelling-place of Chunda and partook of the food prepared by him.

11. Again after the meal the Blessed One gave a discourse on religion to Chunda, then rose from his seat and departed thence.

12. The food offered by Chunda did not agree with the Blessed One. There fell upon him a dire sickness, the disease of dysentery, and sharp and shooting pain came upon him even unto death.

13. But the Blessed One, mindful and self-possessed, bore it without complaint.

14. Returning to the mango grove and after nature was relieved, the Blessed One told Ananda: "Come let us go to Kushinara" and the party moved from Pava.

§ 3. *Arrival at Kushinara*

1. The Blessed Lord walked for part of the way. He soon felt the need for some rest.

2. On the way the Blessed One went aside from the path to the foot of a certain tree and said to Ananda: "Fold, I pray you, Ananda, the robe; and spread it out for me. I am weary, Ananda, and must rest awhile!"

3. "Even so, Lord!" said the venerable Ananda, in assent, to the Blessed One, and spread out the robe folded fourfold.

4. And the Blessed One seated himself on the seat prepared for him.

5. And when he was seated, the Blessed One addressed the venerable Ananda, and said: "Fetch me,

I pray you, Ananda, some water. I am thirsty, Ananda, and would drink."

6. Ananda replied: "This river Kakuttha is not far off, is clear and pleasant, cool and transparent, easy to get down into and delightful. There the Blessed One may both drink the water and cool his limbs. The water of this stream is foul and turbid."

7. The Blessed One was too weak to walk down to the river. He preferred to have the water of the nearby stream.

8. Ananda brought the water and the Blessed One drank it.

9. After resting for a while the Blessed One with the company of the brethren went on to the river Kakuttha; and when he had come there, he went down into the water, and bathed, and drank. And coming out again on the other side he went on to the mango grove.

10. And when he came there he again asked his robe to be spread out, saying: "I am weary and would lie down." The robe was accordingly spread out and the Blessed One laid himself down on it.

11. After resting for a while the Blessed One got up and said to Ananda: "Let us go on to the Sala grove of the Mallas, the Upavana of Kushinara on the further side of the river Hiranyavatti."

12. On reaching the place in the company of Ananda, he again asked Ananda to spread his robe between the twin Sala trees. "I am weary and would lie down."

13. Ananda spread the robe and the Blessed One laid himself down on it.

PART III

His End

1. The Appointment of a Successor.
2. The Last Convert.
3. Last Words.
4. Ananda in Grief.
5. The Lament of the Mallas and the Joy of a Bhikkhu.
6. The Last Rites.
7. Quarrel Over Ashes.
8. Loyalty to the Buddha.

§ 1. *The Appointment of a Successor*

1. The Exalted One was at one time sojourning
among the Sakyans in the mango grove of the Sakyan
family named the archers. VII

2. Now at that time Nataputta the Nigantha had
just died at Pava. And at his death the Niganthas 547
became disunited and divided into two parties, in
mutual strife and conflict, quarrelling and wounding
each other with wordy weapons.

3. Now Chunda, the novice, having passed the rainy season at Pava, came to see the venerable Ananda and said: " Nataputta, sir, the Nigantha had just died at Pava. And he being dead the Niganthas have become disunited and divided and are quarrelling and wounding one another. This is because they are without a protector."

4. Then said the venerable Ananda, " Friend Chunda, this is a worthy subject to bring before the Exalted One. Let us go to him, and tell him about it."

5. " Very good, sir," replied Chunda.

6. So the venerable Ananda and Chunda, the novice, sought out the Exalted One and saluting him, told him about the Niganthas and pleaded the necessity of appointing a successor.

7. The Blessed Lord on hearing what Chunda had said, replied: " But consider Chunda, where a teacher hath arisen in the world, Arahat, supremely enlightened: where a doctrine hath been well set forth, well imparted, effectual for guidance, conducive to peace; but where his disciples have not become proficient in good Norm, nor has it been made a thing of saving grace to them, well proclaimed among men when their teacher passes away.

8. "Now for such a teacher to die, Chunda, is a great affliction for his disciples and a great danger to his Dhamma.

9. " But consider, Chunda, where a teacher has appeared in the world who is all-enlightened; where the Norm has been well set forth, well imparted, effec-

tual for guidance, conducive to peace, and where the disciples have become proficient in the good Norm, and where the full scope of the higher life has become manifest to them when that teacher passes away.

10. " Now for such a teacher, Chunda, to die is not an affliction for his disciples. Why then have a successor ? "

11. When Ananda raised the same question on another occasion the Blessed Lord said: " What think you Ananda ? Do you observe even a couple of almsmen at variance about what I have taught ? "

12. " No. But those who are about the Lord might after his death, stir up quarrel in the confraternity respecting the regimen or of the code and such quarrels would make for general grief. "

13. " Of little concern, Ananda, are quarrels respecting rigours of regimen or of the code ; it is possible quarrels in the confraternity about the path which really matter," said the Blessed Lord.

14. " These disputes about the path cannot be settled by a dictator. What then a successor can do unless he acts as a dictator.

15. " The controversies regarding the path cannot be settled by a dictator.

16. "The decision of a controversy should be reached by the fraternity. The whole conjoint body should assemble and thrash out the matter till there is agreement and then to settle it conformably with such agreement.

17. " Majority agreements is the way to settle the disputes and not the appointment of a successor."

§ 2. *The Last Convert*

1. Now at that time Subhadda the Wanderer was staying at Kusinara. And Subhadda the Wanderer heard the rumour, " This very day, it is said, in the last watch of the night will be the final passing away of Gotama the recluse." Then this thought came to Subhadda the Wanderer.

2. "Thus have I heard it said by other wanderers

who are old and far gone in years, both teachers and disciples; 'Rarely, rarely do Tathagatas arise in the world, they, who are Arahats, fully Enlightened Ones, And here tonight, in the last watch, will be the final passing away of Gotama, the recluse. Now a doubt has arisen in my mind and I am assured of Gotama, the recluse. Gotama, the recluse, can show me a teaching, so that I may dispel this doubting state of mine."

3. Then Subhadda the Wanderer went towards the branch road to the Sala grove of the Mallas, where the venerable Ananda was, and coming there he told the venerable Ananda what he had thought and he exclaimed: "O Master Ananda! If only I could get a sight of Gotama the recluse!"

4. At these words the venerable Ananda said to Subhadda the Wanderer: "Enough, friend Subhadda! Trouble not the Master! The Exalted One is wearied."

5. Then a second and yet a third time did Subhadda the Wanderer make the same request, and got the same reply.

6. Now the Exalted One overheard this talk between the venerable Ananda and Subhadda the Wanderer. And He called to the venerable Ananda, saying, "Enough, Ananda! prevent not Subhadda. Let Subhadda be permitted to see the Tathagata. Whatsoever Subhadda shall ask of me, he will ask it all from a desire to know, not from a desire to trouble me. And whatever I shall say in answer, that will be quickly understood."

7. So then the venerable Ananda said to Subhadda the Wanderer, "Go you in, friend Subhadda. The Exalted One gives you leave."

8. So Subhadda the Wanderer went in to the Exalted One, and coming to Him greeted Him pleasantly, and after the exchange of friendly compliments he sat down at one side. So seated, Subhadda the Wanderer thus addressed the Exalted One:

9. "Master Gotama, all those recluses and Brahmins who have followings and companies of listeners, who are teachers of companies, well known,

renowned founders of sects, esteemed as holy men by the multitude, men like Purana Kassapa, Makkhali of the Cow-pen, Ajita of hairshirt, Kacchayana of the Pakudha tree, Sanjaya, son of Belatthi, and Nigantha
VII of the Natha clan,—have all these, as they say, realised by their own knowledge the truth of things, or have
550 they not one and all so realised, or have some realised and others not realised it, by their own knowledge?"

10. "Let be, Subhadda! Trouble not yourself about such things, as to whether one and all or some have realised or not. I will show you the Norm, Subhadda. Do you listen carefully. Apply your mind. I will speak."

11. "Even so, Lord," said Subhadda the Wanderer and gave heed to the Exalted One. Then the Exalted One said this:

12. "In whatsoever Norm-discipline, Subhadda, the Ariyan Eightfold Path is not found, therein also no recluse is found. And in whatsoever Norm-discipline, Subhadda, the Ariyan Eightfold Path is found, therein also is found a recluse.

13. "Now in this Norm-discipline (of mine), Subhadda, the Ariyan Eightfold Path is found. Herein also is found a recluse of these four degrees. Void of recluses are the other sects of disputants. But if, Subhadda, in this one, brethren were to live the perfect life, the world would not be void of arahats.

14. "My age was nine and twenty years when I went forth to seek the Good.

15. "Now fifty years and more are gone, Subhadda, since I left the world to range the Norm of Righteousness."

16. And when he had thus spoken, Subhadda the Wanderer said to the Exalted One: "Most excellent are these words of thy mouth, most excellent.

17. "Just as if a man *were* to set up that which is thrown down, or were to reveal that which is hidden away, or were to point out the right road to him who has gone astray or were to bring a lamp into darkness, so that those who have eyes can see.

18. "Just even so, has the truth been made

known to me by the Exalted One. And I, even I betake myself to the Exalted One as my refuge, to the truth and to the Order."

19. "Whosoever, Subhadda, has formerly been a
follower of another doctrine and thereafter wishes to VII
enter the Order remains on probation for the space of 551
four months."

20. "If that is the rule I too will remain on probation."

21. But the Exalted One said, "I acknowledge the difference in persons." So saying he called the venerable Ananda and told Ananda, "As it is, Ananda, receive Subhadda into the Order."

22. "Even so, Lord!" said the venerable Ananda, in assent to the Exalted One.

23. And Subhadda the Wanderer said to the venerable Ananda: "Great is your gain, friend Ananda, great is your good fortune, friend Ananda, in that you all have been sprinkled with the sprinkling of discipleship in this brotherhood at the hands of the Master himself."

24. "The same is true of you, Subhadda," replied Ananda.

25. So Subhadda the Wanderer was received into the Order under the orders of the Exalted One. He was the last disciple whom the Exalted One himself converted.

§ 3. *Last Words*

1. Then said the Exalted One to the venerable Ananda:

2. "It may be, Ananda, that you will say: 'Gone is the word of the Master: we have no longer any Master now!' But you must not so regard it, Ananda; for the Norm and discipline taught and enjoyed by me, they shall be your teachers when I am gone.

3. "Now, Ananda, whereas the brethren have the habit of calling one another 'friend,'—when I am gone this habit must not be followed. By an elder

brother, Ananda, a brother who is a novice should be called by his name or clan name or by the word 'friend': but by a novice, Ananda, an elder brother should be addressed as 'Lord' or 'Your reverence.'

VII 4. "Again, Ananda, if the Order so desires, when I am gone, let it abolish the lesser and minor charges.

552 5. "You know, Ananda, the brother Channa. How obstinate, perverse and devoid of the sense of discipline he is.

6. "And to him, Ananda, let the extreme penalty be applied when I am gone."

7. "What, Lord, do you mean by 'the extreme penalty'?"

8. "The brother Channa, Ananda, whatever he may say, is not to be spoken to, not to be admonished, not to be instructed by the brethren. He should be left alone. It might improve him."

9. Then the Exalted One addressed the brethren:

10. "It may be, brothers, that in the mind of some one brother there is doubt or perplexity, either about the Buddha, or about the Norm, or the Order, or the Path, or the Way to the Path. If it be so, brothers, do ye ask now. Be not hereafter remorseful at the thought, 'Here was our Master face to face with us, and yet we had not the heart to question the Exalted One, though we were in His very presence.'"

11. At these words the brethren were silent.

12. Then a second time and yet a third time did the Exalted One address the brethren in the same words. And a third time the brethren were silent.

13. Then said the Exalted One: "May be, brethren, it is out of respect for the Master that ye ask not. Speak to me, then, as friend to friend, brethren."

14. Whereat those brethren were silent.

15. Then exclaimed the venerable Ananda to the Exalted One: "Strange it is, Lord! A marvel it is, Lord! Thus assured am I, Lord, of this Order of Brethren. There is not any one brother that has a single doubt or perplexity as to the Buddha, the Norm, the Order, or as to the Path, or the Way to the Path."

16. "You speak out of assurance, Ananda. But in the Tathagata there is knowledge of the fact. There is not in any one brother a single doubt or perplexity as to this. Of these five hundred brethren of mine, Ananda, even he who is the most backward is a stream-winner, one who is assured from the Downfall, assured of reaching the Supreme Wisdom."

17. Then said the Exalted One to the brethren :

18. "Come now, brethren, I do remind ye, 'Subject to decay are all compounded things.' Do ye abide in heedfulness."

19. Those were the last words of the Exalted One.

§ 4. *Ananda in Grief*

1. As age advanced the Blessed Lord required a personal attendant to look after him.

2. He first chose Nanda. After Nanda he chose Ananda who served as his personal attendant till his death.

3. Ananda was his constant and dearest companion, not merely an attendant.

4. When the Blessed One came to Kushinara and rested between the Sal trees, he saw that his end was coming near, and felt that it was time he took Ananda into confidence.

5. So he called Ananda and said: "And now this Ananda, at the third watch of the night, in the Uppavana of Kushinara, between the twin Sal trees, the utter passing away of the Tathagata will take place."

6. And when he had thus spoken the venerable Ananda addressed the Blessed One, and said: "Vouchsafe, Lord, to remain during the Kalpa, O Blessed One!, for the good and the happiness of the great multitudes, out of pity for the world, for the good and the gain and the weal of gods and men."

7. Three times did Ananda make his plea. "Enough now, Ananda, beseech not the Tathagata !" was the reply. "The time for making such request is past."

8. "I, Ananda, am now grown old, and full of

years, my journey is drawing to a close. I have reached my sum of days. I am turning eighty years of age; and just as a worn-out cart must give way some day, methinks, the same must happen to the body of the Tathagata." Hearing this, Ananda left.

9. Not seeing Ananda, the Blessed One called the brethren, and said: "Where then is Ananda?" "The venerable Ananda is gone and is weeping," said the brethren.

10. And the Blessed One called a certain brother and said: "Go now brother, and call Ananda in my name and say, 'Brother Ananda, the Master calls for thee'."

11. "Even so, Lord!" said that brother.

12. When Ananda came back he took his seat by the side of the Blessed One.

13. Then the Blessed One said to Ananda: "Enough, Ananda! Do not weep! Have I not already, on former occasions, told you that it is in the very nature of things most near and dear unto us that we must divide ourselves from them, leave them, sever ourselves from them?

14. "For a long time, Ananda, you have been very near to me by acts of love, kind and good, beyond all measure.

15. "You have done well, Ananda! Be earnest in effort and you too shall be free from the great evils—from sensuality, from individuality, from delusion, and from ignorance."

16. Then addressing the brethren about Ananda the Blessed One said: "He is a wise man, brethren, is Ananda.

17. "He knows when it is the right time to come and visit the Tathagata, and when it is the right time for brethren and sisters of the Order, for devout men and devout women, for a king, or for a king's ministers, for other teachers and disciples, to visit the Tathagata.

18. "Brethren, there are these four special things about Ananda.

19. "All are happy to visit Ananda. They are

filled with joy on beholding him; they are happy to hear him. They are ill at ease when Ananda is silent."

20. After this Ananda again returned to the subject of the passing away of the Tathagata. Addressing the Blessed One, he said: "Let not the Blessed One die in this wattled and daub town in the midst of the jungle. For Lord there are great cities, such as Champa, Rajagraha, Savathi, Saketa, Kosambi and Benares. Let the Blessed One die in one of them."

21. "Say not so, Ananda! Say not so, Ananda. This Kushinara, Ananda, was the capital of king Maha-Sudassana under the name of Keshavati."

22. Thereafter the Blessed One gave Ananda two errands.

23. He told Ananda to see that belief does not spread that the Blessed One died as a result of the food given to Him by Chunda. He feared that Chunda might suffer. He asked Ananda to disabuse the mind of the public on this score.

24. The second thing he told Ananda was to inform the Mallas of Kushinara that the Blessed One had arrived there and would pass away in the last watch of the night.

25. "Give no occasion to reproach yourself. The Mallas may say: 'In our own village the death of our Tathagata took place and we did not know and had no opportunity of seeing him in his last hours.'"

26. Thereafter the venerable Anurudha and the venerable Ananda spent the rest of the night in religious discourse.

27. And in the third part of the night, as previously announced, the Blessed One breathed his last.

28. When the Blessed One died, the brethren and Ananda stretched out their arms and wept, and some even fell headlong on the ground, rolling to and fro in anguish, saying: "Too soon has the Blessed One died! Too soon has the Happy One passed away from existence! Too soon has the Light gone out of the world!"

29. It was at midnight on Vaishakha Paurnima

that the Blessed Lord breathed his last. The year of his death was 483 B.C.

30. As the Pali text truly says:

Diva tapati addicco
Ratin abhati candima;
Sannaddho khathio tapati
Jhayi tapati brahamano;
Atha Sabbain ahorattain
Buddho tapati tejasa.

31. "The sun shines only in the day and the moon makes bright the night. The warrior shines when he is in his armour. And the Brahmin when he is meditating. But the Buddha shines over all by day as well as by night by his own glory.

32. "He was beyond question the light of the world."

§ 5. *The Lament of the Mallas and the Joy of a Bhikkhu*

1. As desired by the Blessed One, Ananda went and informed the Mallas of the event.

2. And when they heard of this the Mallas, their wives, their young men and maidens were grieved and sad and afflicted at heart.

3. Some of them wept, dishevelling their hair, and stretched forth their arms and fell prostrate on the ground.

4. Then the Mallas, with their young men and maidens and their wives, went to the Sala grove in the Upavaana to have the last look of the Blessed One.

5. Then the venerable Ananda thought: "If I allow the Mallas of Kushinara one by one it will take a long time for them to pay homage to the dead body of the Blessed One."

6. So he decided to arrange them in groups, family by family. Each family then bowed humbly at the feet of the Blessed One and parted.

7. Now at the time the venerable Maha Kassapa was journeying along the high road from Pava to Kushinara with a great company of the brethren.

8. Just at the time a certain naked ascetic was coming along the high road to Pava.

9. And the venerable Maha Kassapa saw the naked ascetic coming in the distance; and when he had seen him he said to the naked ascetic: "O friend! Surely thou knowest our Master?"

10. "Yes, friend! I know him." "This day the Samana Gotama has been dead a week!"

11. Immediately on hearing the news the brethren were overcome with grief and started weeping.

12. Now at that time a brother named Subhadda, who had been received into the Sangh in his old age, was seated in their company.

13. And this Subhadda addressed the brethren and said: "Enough brethren! Weep not, neither lament! We are well rid of the great Samana. We used to be annoyed by being told, 'This beseems you, this beseems you not.' But now we shall be able to do whatever we like: and what we do not like, that we shall not have to do! Isn't it good he is dead? Why weep, why lament? It is a matter of joy."

14. So great and harsh a disciplinarian the Blessed One was.

§ 6. *The Last Rites*

1. Then the Mallas of Kushinara said to the venerable Ananda: "What should be done with the remains of the Tathagata?"

2. "As men treat the remains of a king of kings, so should you treat the remains of the Tathagata" replied Ananda.

3. "And how do they treat the remains of a king of kings?"

4. Ananda told them: "They wrap the body of a king of kings in a new cloth. When that is done they wrap it in cotton-wool. When that is done they wrap it in a new cloth and so on till they have wrapped the body in five hundred successive layers of both kinds. Then they place the body in an oil vessel of iron and cover that close up with another oil vessel of iron.

They then build a funeral pile of all kinds. This is the way in which they treat the remains of a king of kings."

5. " So be it," said the Mallas.

6. Then the Mallas of Kushinara said: " It is
VII much too late to burn the body of the Blessed One today. Let us now perform the cremation tomorrow."

558 7. And the Mallas of Kushinara gave orders to their attendants, saying: "Make preparations for the funeral of the Tathagata and gather perfumes and garlands and the musicians of Kushinara."

8. But in paying honour, reverence, respect, and homage to the remains of the Tathagata with dancing, and hymns and music and with garlands and perfumes; and in making canopies of their garments, and preparing decoration wreath to hand thereon, they passed the second day too, and then the third day, and the fourth and fifth and the sixth day also.

9. Then on the seventh day the Mallas of Kushinara thought: "Let us carry the body of the Blessed One and let us perform the cremation ceremony."

10. And thereupon eight chieftains among the Mallas bathed their heads, and clad themselves in new garments with the intention of acting as pall-bearers carrying the body of the Blessed One.

11. They carried the dead body to the Shrine of the Mallas, called Makuta-bandhana; to the east of the city and there they laid down the body of the Blessed One and set fire to it.

12. After some time the mortal remains of the Blessed One were reduced to ashes.

§ 7. *Quarrel Over Ashes*

1. After the body of the Blessed One had been consumed by fire, the Mallas of Kushinara collected the ashes and the bones of the Blessed One and placed them in their Council Hall with a lattice work of spears and with a rampart of bows; and guarded them against anybody stealing them or any part of them.

2. For seven days the Mallas paid honour and

reverence and respect and homage to them with dance and song and music and with garlands and perfumes.

3. Now the King of Magadha, Ajatasatru, heard the news that the Blessed One had died at Kushinara.

4. He, therefore, sent a messenger to the Mallas with a request for a portion of the relics of the Blessed One.

5. Similarly messengers came from the Licchavis of Vaishali, from the Sakyas of Kapilavastu, from the Bulis of Attakappa, from the Koliyas of Ramagama and from the Mallas of Pava.

6. Among the claimants for ashes there was also a Brahmin of Vethadipa.

7. When they heard these claims, the Mallas of Kushinara said: "The Blessed One died in our village. We will not give away any part of the remains of the Blessed One. They belong to us."

8. Seeing that the situation was tense a Brahmin by name Drona intervened and said: "Hear, reverend sirs, one single word from me."

9. Said Drona: "Forbearance was our Buddha to teach; unseemly is it that over the division of the remains of him who was the best of beings, strife should arise, and wounds and war!

10. "Let us all, sirs, with one accord unite in friendly harmony to make eight portions. Widespread let stupas arise in every land that the Enlightened One from all parts be reverenced."

11. The Mallas of Kushinara agreed and said: "Do thou then, O Brahmin, thyself, divide the remains equally into eight parts, with fair division."

12. "Be it so, sir!" said Drona in assent.

13. And he divided the remains of the Blessed One equally into eight parts.

14. After making the division Drona said to them: "Give me, sirs, this vessel. I will set up over it a stupa."

15. And they agreed to give the vessel to him.

16. Thus the ashes of the Blessed One were shared and the quarrel was settled peacefully and amicably.

§ 8. *Loyalty to the Buddha*

1. Shravasti was the occasion (of these events)....

2. Now on that occasion a number of monks were
VII busied with making a robe for the Exalted One, with
this idea : When the robe is finished, in three months'
560 time, the Exalted One will go forth on his rounds.

3. Now at that time Isidatta and Purana, the chamberlains, were staying at Sadhuka on some business or other. Then they heard the news : "They say that a number of monks are busied with making a robe for the Exalted One with this idea : When the robe is finished, in three months' time, the Exalted One will go forth upon his rounds."

4. So Isidatta and Purana, the chamberlains, stationed a man on the high-road (thus instructing him): "Now, good fellow, as soon as you see that Exalted One, that Arahat, that perfectly Enlightened One coming along, do you come and inform us."

5. So after standing there two or three days that man saw the Exalted One coming along, while yet some distance off, and he went to inform the chamberlains, Isidatta and Purana, saying: " Here comes my lord, the Exalted One, that Arahat, that perfectly Enlightened One ! Now's the time for you to do what you want !"

6. So Isidatta and Purana, the chamberlains, went towards the Exalted One, and on coming to him, saluted him, and followed behind the Exalted One step for step.

7. Then the Exalted One turned aside from the high road and went to the foot of a certain tree and there sat down on a seat made ready. And Isidatta and Purana, the chamberlains, saluting the Exalted One, also sat down at one side. As they thus sat, they said this to the Exalted One :

8. "Lord, when we heard of the Exalted One that he would go forth on his rounds among the Kosalans, at that time we were disappointed and depressed at the thought : the Exalted One will be far from us.

9. "And when, Lord, we learned that the Exalted

One was starting out from Shravasti on his rounds among the Kosalans, again we were disappointed and depressed at the thought: The Exalted One will be far from us.

10. "Again, lord, when we learned that the Exalt- VII
ed One would leave the Kosalans and go on his rounds
among the Mallas . . . that he was actually doing 561
so . . . we were disappointed and depressed.

11. "On hearing that the Exalted One would leave the Mallas and go on his rounds among the Vajji . . . that he was actually doing so . . . that he would leave the Vajji for Kasi . . . that he was doing so . . . that he would leave the folk of Kasi and go on his rounds in Magadha . . . that he was actually doing so . . . again we were disappointed and depressed . . . .

12. "But, Lord, when we heard that the Exalted One would leave the Magadhas for Kasi and was doing so, then we were delighted and elated at the thought: The Exalted One will be quite near us.

13. "And when we heard that he was actually going his rounds in Kasi among the Magadhas, we were likewise delighted and elated.

14. (They continue to trace the Master's steps from Kasi to the Vajji . . . from the Vajji to the Mallas . . . from the Mallas to the Kosalans in like terms.)

15. "But, Lord, when we heard that the Exalted One would be going on his rounds from the Kosalans to Savatthi, we were delighted and elated at the thought: Now the Exalted One will be quite near us!

16. "Then, when we heard: 'The Exalted One is staying at Shravasti, at Jeta grove, in Anathapindika's Park.' Then, Lord, boundless was our delight and boundless our elation at the thought: The Exalted One is near us!"

BOOK VIII

The Man who was Siddharth Gautama

Part I—His Personality.

Part II—His Humanity.

Part III—His Likes and Dislikes.

EPILOGUE.

PART I

His Personality

1. His Personal Appearance.
2. The Testimony of Eye-witnesses.
3. His Capacity to Lead.

§ 1. *His Personal Appearance*

1. From all accounts the Blessed Lord was a handsome person.

2. His form was like the peak of a golden mountain. He was tall and well built; with a pleasing appearance.

3. His long arms and lion gait, his bull-like eyes, and his beauty, bright like gold, his broad chest, attracted everyone to him.

4. His brows, his forehead, his mouth or his eyes, his body, his hands, his feet or his gait—whatever part of him anyone beheld that at once riveted his eyes.

5. Whoever saw him could not help being struck with his majesty and his strength, his splendid beauty, surpassing all other men.

6. On seeing him, he who was going elsewhere stood still and whoever was standing followed him: he who was walking gently and gravely, ran quickly, and he who was sitting at once sprang up.

7. Of those who met him some reverenced him with their hands, others in worship saluted him with their heads, some addressed him with affectionate words,—not one went on without paying him homage.

8. He was loved and respected by all.

9. Men as well as women were ever ready to hear him.

10. His voice was singularly sweet and deep as a drum, lovely, vibrant and eloquent. It made his speech as though it was heavenly music.

11. His very tones convinced the hearer, and his looks inspired awe..

12. His personality alone sufficed to make him not only a leader but a god to the hearts of his fellows.

13. When he spoke he obtained hearers.

14. It mattered little what he said. He influenced

the emotions and bent whoever listened to his will.

15. He could create in the minds of his hearers that what he taught was not only a verity, but the very hope of their salvation.

16. His hearers could recognize in his words the truth that makes of slaves free men.

17. When he talked with men and women his serene look inspired them with awe and reverence and his lovely voice struck them with rapture and amazement.

18. Who could have converted the robber Augulimala or the Cannibal of Atavi? Who could have reconciled King Pasenjit to his queen Mallika by a single word. To have come under his spell is to be his for ever. So charming was his personality.

§ 2. *The Testimony of Eye-witnesses*

1. This traditional view is supported by the testimony of eye-witnesses who saw him and met him while he was alive.

2. One such eye-witness is a Brahmin by name Sale. After seeing the Blessed One face to face he uttered the following sentiments in praise of him.

3. Arrived in the Lord's presence, the Brahmin, seating himself after greetings, scanned the Lord's body for the two and thirty marks of a Superman, and in time observed them.

4. Quite sure now about the presence of the two and thirty marks, Sale still did not know whether or not he had enlightenment. But he remembered hearing from old and aged Brahmins, teachers of teachers, that those who became Arahats, all enlightened, reveal themselves when their praises are sung, and so he made up his mind to extol the Lord to his face in the following lines of eulogy:

5. "Perfect of body, goodly, Lord, art thou, well grown, well liking, golden-hued, with teeth which gleam lustre; vigour fills the frame; the body's full

perfection manifests each single sign that marks a Superman.

6. "Clear-eyed and handsome, tall, upright art thou, effulgent as a sun among thy train, so debonair, so golden-hued; why waste thy beauty's prime as homeless anchorite.

7. "As world-wide monarch thou shouldst ride in State; and indeed from sea to sea should own thy sway. Proud princes shall thy village headmen be; rule thou mankind, as sovereign king of kings."

8. Ananda describes the colour of his body as exceedingly clear and bright so much so that the pair of cloth of gold when placed on the body of the Blessed One appears to have lost its splendour.

9. No wonder he was called by his opponents a glamour boy.

§ 3. *His Capacity to Lead*

1. The Sangh had no official head. The Blessed One had no authority over the Sangh. The Sangh was a self-governing body.

2. What was, however, the position of the Blessed One over the Sangh and its members?

3. In this we have the evidence of Sakuldai and Udai, contemporaries of the Blessed One.

4. Once the Lord was staying at Rajagraha in the bamboo grove.

5. One morning the Lord went into Rajagraha for alms; but, deeming the hour too early, he thought of going to Sakuldai in Wanderers' Pleasance; and thither he repaired.

6. At the time, Sakuldai was sitting with a great company of Wanderers, who were making a great noise about being and not being.

7. When from some way off, Sakuldai saw the Lord coming, he hushed his company by saying: "Be quiet, sirs; do not make a noise; here comes the recluse Gotama, who is a lover of silence."

8. So they became silent and the Lord came up. Said Sakuldai: "I pray the Lord to join us; he is truly

welcome; it is a long time since he last managed to come. Pray, be seated; here is a seat for the Lord."

9. The Lord sat down accordingly, asking Sakuldai what had been their theme and what was the
VIII discussion which had been interrupted.

10. "Let that pass for the moment," answered
570 Sakuldai; "you can easily gather that later on."

11. Of late, when recluses and Brahmins of other creeds met together in the Discussion Hall, the topic was mooted, what a good thing, what a very good thing, for the Magdha people in Anga, that such recluses and Brahmins—all at the head of confraternities or followings, all well known and famous teachers, all founders of saving creeds, held in high repute by many people should have come to spend the rainy season at Rajagraha.

12. There was Purana Kassappa, Makhali Ghosala, Ajit Kesakambal, Pakudha Kacchayana, Sanjaya Belaiputta, and Nata-putta the Nigantha, all men of distinction and all of them here for the rains; and among them there is also the recluse Gotama here, at the head of his confraternity and following, a well-known and famous teacher, a founder of a saving creed, who is held in high repute by many.

13. Now, which of these lords, which of these recluses and Brahmins of such eminence as teachers, is esteemed, respected, venerated and adored by his disciples? And on what terms of esteem and respect do they live with him?

14. Said some: "Purana Kassappa gets no esteem or respect; no veneration or adoration, from his disciples; they live with him on no terms of esteem and respect."

15. Time was when, as he was preaching his doctrine to some hundreds of his following, a disciple broke in with—"Don't question Purana Kassappa, who does not know about it; ask me who do; I will explain everything to your reverences."

16. With arms outstretched Purana Kassappa tearfully remonstrated, saying: "Do be quiet, sirs; do not make a noise."

PART II

His Humanity

1. His Compassion—The Maha Karunik.
2. Healing of the Stricken.
3. His Concern for the Sick.
4. His Tolerance of the Intolerant.
5. His Sense of Equality and Equal Treatment.

§ *1. His Compassion—The Maha Karunik*

1. When once the Blessed Lord was staying in Shravasti the almsmen came and informed him that they were constantly harassed by the Deva who disturbed them in their meditations.

2. After hearing their stories of harassment the Blessed Lord gave them the following instructions:—

3. "He, who is skilled in his godness, who wishes to attain that calm state, should act thus: he should be able, upright, near perfectly upright, of noble speech, gentle and humble.

4. "Contented, easily supportable, with few duties, of light livelihood, controlled in senses, discreet, not impudent, not greedily attached to families.

5. "He should not pursue anything trifling such that other wise men might censure him. He should wish, 'May all beings be happy and secure; may their hearts be wholesome.'

6. "Whatever living beings there be—feeble or strong, tall, stout and medium, short, small or large, without exception;

7. "Seen or unseen, those dwelling far or near, those who are born, or who are to be born, may all beings be happy.

8. "Let none deceive another, nor despise any person whatsoever in any place, let him not wish any harm to another, out of anger or ill-will.

9. "Just as a mother would protect her only child at the risk of her own life, even so let him cultivate a boundless heart towards all beings.

10. "Let his thoughts of boundless love pervade the whole world, above, below and across without any obstruction, without any enmity.

11. "Whether he stands, walks, sits, lies down, as long as he is awake, he should develop this mindfulness, this they say is the noblest living here.

12. "Not falling into error (self-illusion), being virtuous and endowed with insight, by discarding

attachment to sense desires never does he come again for conception in a womb."

13. In short, he told them "Love your enemies."

§ 2. *Healing of the Stricken*

A Consummate Healer of Sorrow.

(i)

Consoling Visakha

1. Visakha was an upasika. It was her routine to give alms to the bhikkhus.

2. One day her grand-daughter, Suddata, who lived with her, fell ill and died.

3. Visakha was unable to bear the grief.

4. After cremation she went to the Buddha and sat on one side sad with tearful eyes.

5. "O Visakha," asked the Blessed One, "wherefore dost thou sit, sad and mournful, shedding tears ?"

6. She told him of her grand-daughter's death, saying, " she was a dutiful girl, and I cannot find her like."

7. " How many young girls, say, are there dwelling in Shravasti, O Visakha ?"

8. "Lord, men say there are several kotis (several millions)."

9. " If all these were like thy grand-daughter, wouldst thou not love them ?"

10. " Verily, Lord," replied Visakha.

11. " And how many die daily in Shravasti ?"

12. " Many, Lord."

13. " Then there is never a moment when thou wouldst not be grieving for someone ?"

14. " True, Lord."

15. " Wouldst thou then spend thy life weeping day and night ?"

16. " I understand Lord ; it is well said !"

17. " Grieve then, no more."

(ii)

Comforting Kisa Gotami

1. Kisa Gotami was married to the son of a merchant of Shravasti. VIII

2. Soon after marriage a son was born to her.

3. Unfortunately her child died of a snake-bite 575 before it could walk.

4. She could not believe that her child was really dead as she had not seen death before.

5. The little spot red from the bite of a snake, did not look as if it could be the cause of the child's death.

6. She, therefore, took her dead child and wandered about from house to house, in such a wild state of mind that people believed that she had gone out of her senses.

7. At last one old man advised her to go and seek out Gotama who happened at the time to be in Shravasti.

8. So she came to the Blessed One and asked him for some medicine for her dead child.

9. The Blessed One listened to her story and to her lamentations.

10. Then the Blessed One told her, "Go enter the town, and at any house where yet there has been no death, thence bring a little mustard seed and with that I will revive your child."

11. She thought this was easy and with the dead body of her child she entered the town.

12. But she soon found that she had failed as every house she visited had suffered loss in the death of some member.

13. As one householder told her, "the living are few and the dead are many."

14. So she returned to the Blessed Lord disappointed and empty-handed.

15. The Blessed Lord then asked her if she did not then realize that death was the common lot of all and whether she should grieve as though it was her special misfortune.

16. She then went and cremated the child, saying: " All is impermanent; this is the law."

§ 3. *His Concern for the Sick*

VIII (i)

576 1. Now at one time a certain brother was suffering from dysentery and lay where he had fallen down in his own excreta.

2. And the Exalted One going on his rounds of the lodgings, with the venerable Ananda in attendance, came to the lodging of that brother.

3. Now the Exalted One saw that brother lying where he had fallen in his own excreta and seeing him he went towards him, and said: "Brother, what ails you ? "

4. " I have dysentery, Lord."

5. " But is there anyone taking care of you, brother ? "

6. " No, Lord."

7. " Why is it, brother, that the brethren do not take care of you ? "

8. " I am useless to the brethren, Lord, therefore the brethren do not care for me."

9. Then the Exalted One said to the venerable Ananda: "Go you, Ananda, and fetch water. I will wash this brother."

10. " Yes, Lord," replied the venerable Ananda to the Exalted One. When he had fetched the water, the Exalted One poured it out, while the venerable Ananda washed that brother all over. Then the Exalted One, taking him by the head and the venerable Ananda taking him by the feet, together they laid him on the bed.

11. Then the Exalted One, in this connection and on this occasion, gathered the Order of Brethren together, and questioned the brethren, saying:

12. " Brethren, is there in such and such a lodging a brother who is sick ? "

13. " There is, Lord."

14. " And what ails that brother ? "

15. " Lord, that brother has dysentery."

16. " But, brethren, is there anyone taking care of him ? "

17. " No, Lord."

18. " Why not ? Why do not the brethren take care of him ?" VIII

19. " The brother is useless to the brethren, 577
Lord. That is why the brethren do not take care of him."

20. " Brethren, ye have no mother and father to take care of you. If ye will not take care of each other, who else, I ask, will do so ? Brethren, he who would wait on me, let him wait on the sick.

21. " If he have a teacher, let his teacher take care of him so long as he is alive, and wait for his recovery. If he have a tutor or a lodger, a disciple or a fellow lodger or a fellow disciple, such should take care of him and await his recovery. If no one takes care of him, it shall be reckoned an offence."

(ii)

1. Once the Exalted One was staying near Rajagraha in the great grove, at the squirrels feeding ground.

2. On that occasion the venerable Vakkali was staying in the potter's shed, being sick, afflicted, stricken with a sore disease.

3. Now the venerable Vakkali called to his attendants, saying : " Come hither, friends ! Go ye to the Exalted One and, in my name worshipping at the feet of the Exalted One, say unto Him : 'Lord, the brother Vakkali is sick, afflicted, stricken with a sore disease. He worships at the feet of the Exalted One.' And thus do you say : ' Well, were it, Lord, if the Exalted One would visit brother Vakkali, out of compassion for him.' "

4. The Exalted One consented by His silence. Thereupon the Exalted One robed himself, and, taking bowl and robe, went to visit the venerable Vakkali.

5. Now the venerable Vakkali saw the Exalted

One coming while he was yet far off, and on seeing him he stirred upon his bed.

6. Then said the Exalted One to the venerable
Vakkali: " Enough, Vakkali ! Stir not on your bed !
VIII There are these seats made ready. I will sit there."
And he sat down on a seat made ready. So the
578 Exalted One sat down and said to the venerable
Vakkali:

7. " Well, Vakkali, I hope you are bearing up. I hope you are enduring. Do your pains abate and not increase? Are there signs of their abating and not increasing?"

8. "No, Lord, I am not bearing up. I am not enduring. Strong pains come upon me. They do not abate. There is no sign of their abating but of their increasing."

9. " Have you any doubt, Vakkali ? Have you any remorse."

10. "Indeed, Lord, I have no doubt. I have no remorse."

11. "Have you not anything, Vakkali, wherein you reproach yourself as to morals?"

12. " Nay, Lord, there is nothing wherein I reproach myself as to morals."

13. "Then, Vakkali, if that is so, you must have some worry, you must have something you regret."

14. "For a long time, Lord, I have been longing to set eyes on the Exalted One, but I had not strength enough in this body to come to see the Exalted One."

15. "Hush, Vakkali; what is there in seeing this vile body of mine ? He who seeth the Norm, he seeth me: he who seeth, Vakkali, seeth the Norm. Verily, seeing the Norm, Vakkali, one seeth me : seeing me, one seeth the Norm."

(iii)

1. Thus have I heard: The Exalted One was once staying among the Bhaggi, at crocodile haunt in Bhesakala grove in the deer-park. Then the house-father, Nakulapita, came to the Exalted One, saluted Him, and sat down at one side.

2. As he sat there, the housefather, Nakulapita, addressed the Exalted One, saying: " Master, I am a broken-down old man, aged, far gone in years, I have reached life's end, I am sick and always ailing. Moreover, Master, I am one to whom rarely comes the sight of the Exalted One and the worshipful brethren. Let the Exalted One cheer and comfort me, so that it be a profit and a blessing unto me for many a long day."

3. " True it is, true it is, housefather, that your body is weak and cumbered ! For one carrying this body about, housefather, to claim but a moment's health would be sheer foolishness. Wherefore, housefather, thus should you train yourself : 'Though my body is sick, my mind shall not be sick.' Thus, housefather, must you train yourself."

4. Then Nakulapita, the housefather, welcomed and gladly heard the words of the Exalted One, and rising from his seat he saluted the Exalted One by the right, and departed.

(iv)

1. Once the Exalted One was staying among the Sakyans at Kapilavastu, in the fig-tree park.

2. Then on that occasion a number of brethren were busy with making robes for the Exalted One, "For," said they, " when the three months are over, the Exalted One, his robes being complete, will go forth on his rounds."

3. Now Mahanama, the Sakyan, heard it said, "A number of brethren are busy with making robes, and so forth". . . and he went to the Exalted One, saluted him, and sat down at one side. So seated, Mahanama, the Sakyan, said :

4. "I hear it said, Lord, that a number of the brethren are busy with making robes for the Exalted One, saying, 'when the robes are complete, at the end of the three months, the Exalted One will go forth on his rounds.' Now, Lord, we have never heard from the Exalted One's own lips how a discreet layman who is sick, in pain, grievously afflicted, should be cheered by another discreet lay-brother."

5. " A discreet lay-brother, Mahanama, who is
sick . . . should be cheered by another discreet lay-
brother with the Four Comfortable Assurances, thus:
'Take comfort, good sir, in the Norm, and in the
VIII Order of Brethren: likewise in the virtues dear to the
Norm kept unbroken and unsoiled which tend to
580 balance of mind.'

6. " Then, Mahanama, when a discreet lay-brother who is sick has thus been cheered with the Four Comfortable Assurances by another lay-brother, such should be the words of that other:

7. " Suppose the sick man should have a longing for his parents. Then if the sick man says, 'I have a longing for my parents,' the other should reply, 'My dear good man, you are subject to death. Whether you have longing for your parents or not you will die. 'Twere just as well for you to abandon all longing for your parents.'

8. "And suppose the sick man says, 'That longing for my parents is now abandoned,' then the other should say, 'Yet my good sir, you still have a longing for your children. As you must die in any case, 'twere just as well for you to abandon longing for your children.'

9. "And so also should he speak in respect of the five pleasures of the senses. Suppose the sick man says, 'I have a longing for the five pleasures of sense,' the other should say, 'My friend, heavenly delights are more excellent than the five pleasures of sense, and more choice. 'Twere well for you to remove your mind from human joys and fix it on the joys of the Four Great Deva Kings.'

10. "Again, if the sick man say, 'My mind is so fixed,' let the other say, 'Better to fix your mind on the Brahma world,' And then if the sick man's mind is so fixed, let the other say :

11. " 'My good sir, even the Brahma world is impermanent, not lasting, subject to personality. Well for you, dear sir, if you raise your mind above the Brahma world and concentrate on cessation from the personal.'

12. "And if the sick man says he has done so, then I declare Mahanama, that there is no difference between the lay-brother who can thus aver and the disciple whose mind is freed from the asavas: that is to say, so far as emancipation goes."

§ 4. *His Tolerance of the Intolerant*

1. Once the Blessed Lord was dwelling in the realm of the Yakkha Alavaka in the town of Alavi. Then the Yakkha Alavaka approached the Blessed Lord, and having approached him, said thus:

"Get out, O Monk!"

2. The Blessed Lord departed, saying: "Very well, friend."

3. The Yakkha then ordered "Enter, O Monk."

4. The Blessed Lord entered, saying: "Very well, friend."

5. For the second time also the Yakkha Alavaka told the Blessed Lord, "Get out, O Monk!"

6. The Lord departed, saying: "Very well, friend."

7. "Enter, O Monk!" said the Yakkha, the second time.

8. The Lord entered, saying: "Very well, friend."

9. For the third time also the Yakkha Alavaka told the Lord, "Get out, O Monk!"

10. The Lord departed, saying: "Very well, friend."

11. "Enter, O Monk!" said the Yakkha again.

12. The Lord entered, saying: "Very well, friend."

13. For the fourth time did the Yakkha tell the Lord, "Get out, O Monk!"

14. This time the Lord replied: "I shall not get out, friend, you may do what you like."

15. "I shall put a question to you; monk; if you do not answer my question, I will drive you out of your wits or I will tear your heart, or I will take you by the feet and throw you to the other side of the river," said the angry Yakkha.

16. " I do not see, friend, anyone in the world who could drive me out of my wits or tear out my heart, or take me by the feet and throw me across the river. Still, friend, you may put any question you like."

17. Then the Yakkha Alavaka asked the Lord the following questions :

18. " What is the noblest wealth for a man in this world ? What pure action brings happiness ? What is the sweetest of all tastes ? What manner of living is said to be the noblest living ? "

19. The Lord replied : " Faith is the noblest wealth for a man in this world. The Dhamma well observed brings happiness. Truth is the sweetest of all tastes. The living endowed with wisdom is said to be the noblest thing.

20. Yakkha Alavaka asked : " How does one cross the flood (rebirth) ? How does one cross the sea (existence) ? How does one overcome suffering ? "

21. The Lord replied : " One crosses the flood by Faith. One crosses the sea by Vigilance. One overcomes suffering by Exertion. One purifies oneself by wisdom.

22. Yakkha Alavaka asked : "How does one acquire knowledge? How does one obtain wealth? How does one attain fame ? How does one gain friends ? Passing from this world to the other world after death, how does one not repent ?"

23. The Lord replied : " Having faith in Arahats and in the Dhamma for the attainment of Nibbana, and by obedience, the diligent, attentive person acquires wisdom.

24. " One who does what is proper, one who is resolute, one who is awake, he acquires wealth. One who gives acquires friends.

25. " The faithful householder in whom truthfulness, righteousness, patience and generosity are found, he does not repent after death.

26. " Come on! Also consult other numerous monks and Brahmins, whether there are any other qualities higher than truth, self-control, charity and patience."

27. Yakkha Alavaka said: " Now, why should I çonsult various Brahmins and monks? Today I know the prosperity which belongs to my future good.

28. " Indeed ! the Buddha came to the dwelling of Alavi for my benefit. To-day I know, to whom when given, it returns the greatest fruit.

29. " From today I will wander from village to village, from town to town, paying my respect to the fully Enlightened One, and his perfect Doctrine."

§ 5. *His Sense of Equality and Equal Treatment*

1. Whatever rules the Blessed Lord had made for the members of the Sangh were voluntarily and willingly accepted by him to be binding on him also.

2. He never claimed any exemption or any special treatment on the ground that he was the acknowledged head of the fraternity and to whom any concession would have been most willingly made by the fraternity out of the boundless love and respect they bore for him.

3. The rule that the members of the Sangh could take only one meal a day was accepted and followed by the Blessed Lord as much as it was by the bhikkhu.

4. The rule that the members of the Sangh should have no private property was accepted and followed by the Blessed Lord as much as it was by the bhikkhu.

5. The rule that no member of the Sangh should have more than three pieces of cloths was accepted and followed by the Blessed Lord as much as it was by the bhikkhu.

6. Once, when the Lord was living in the Sakyan country at Kapilavastu in the banyan grove, Maha-Prajapati Gautami, the mother of the Blessed Lord, came to the Lord with two new lengths of cloth which she begged the Lord to be so good as to accept from her as it was the work of her own hands at the loom expressly for him.

7. To her the Lord made the answer, "Give it to the confraternity."

8. A second and a third time did Gautami repeat her request, only to receive the same reply.

9. Then Ananda intervened, saying, "Pray accept, sir, the cloth presented by Gautami. She was of great service to the Lord as nurse and foster-mother suckling her nephew when his own mother died." But the Blessed Lord insisted upon the cloth being given to the confraternity.

10. Originally it was the rule of the Sangh that the robes of the members should be made of rags picked up from dung heaps. This rule was made to prevent the wealthier classes from joining the Sangh.

11. Once Jivika prevailed upon the Blessed Lord to accept a robe of newly made cloth. When the Lord accepted it, he at the same time relaxed the original rule and allowed the bhikkhu the same privilege.

PART III

His Likes and Dislikes

1. His Dislike of Poverty.
2. His Dislike of the Acquisitive Instinct.
3. His Joy at the Beautiful.
4. His Love for the Lovely.

§ 1. *His Dislike of Poverty*

1. Once the Exalted One was dwelling near
Shravasti in Jeta's grove, at Anathapindika's park;
and there Anathapindika, the householder, came
and visited him and after saluting, sat down at one VIII
side. So seated, he asked the Exalted One to explain 587
why one should acquire riches.

2. "Since you ask me, I will explain.

3. "Take the case of Ariyan disciple with riches gotten by work and zeal, gathered by the strength of the arm, earned by the sweat of the brow; justly obtained in a lawful way he makes himself happy, glad, and keeps that great happiness; he makes his parents happy, glad, and keeps them so; so likewise his wife and children, his slaves, workfolk and men. This is the first reason for getting riches.

4. "When riches are thus gotten, he makes his friends and companions happy, glad, and keeps them so. This is the second reason.

5. "Again, when riches are thus gotten, ill-luck from fire and water, rajas and robbers, enemies and heirs is warded off, and he keeps his goods in safety. This is the third reason.

6. "Then, when riches are thus gotten, he makes the five oblations, that is to say, oblations to kin, guests, pitaras, rajas and devas. This is the fourth reason.

7. "Moreover, when riches are thus gotten, the householder institutes offerings, of lofty aim, celestial ripening to happiness, leading heavenward, for all those recluses and godly men who abstain from pride and indolence, who bear all things in patience and humility, each mastering self, each calming self, each perfecting self. This is the fifth reason for getting rich."

8. Anathapindika well understood that the Blessed Lord did not comfort the poor by praising their poverty nor did he sublimate poverty as a happy state for man to live in.

§ 2. *His Dislike of the Acquisitive Instinct*

1. The Exalted One was once staying in the town
VIII of Kammassadamma in the country of Kurus.

2. The venerable Ananda came to where the
588 Exalted One was, bowed in salutation before him and took a seat on one side.

3. And so seated he said, "Marvellous is this law of causation which has been taught by the Blessed One. It is so deep. To me it seems as clear as clear can be."

4. "Say not so, Ananda, say not so! Deep is this doctrine of events arising from causes. It is through not understanding this doctrine, through not penetrating it, that this generation has become a tangled skein, a matted ball of thread, unable to overpass the way of woe.

5. "I have said that craving is the cause of grasping. Where there is no craving of any sort or kind whatever by anyone for anything, would there be any arising of grasping?"

6. "There would not, Lord."

7. "Craving gives rise to pursuit of gain.

8. "Pursuit of gain gives rise to desire and passion.

9. "Desire and passion give rise to tenacity.

10. "Tenacity gives rise to possession.

11. "Possession gives rise to avarice and more possession.

12. "Possessions lead to keeping watch and ward over possessions.

13. "Many a bad and wicked state of things arise from keeping watch and ward over possession, such as blows and wounds, strife, quarrelling, slander and lies.

14. "This is the chain of causation, Ananda. If there was no craving, would there arise pursuit of gain? If there was no pursuit of gain, would there arise passion? If there was no passion, would there arise tenacity? If there would be no tenacity, would there

arise the love for private possessions? If there would be no possession, would there arise avarice for more possession?"

15. "There would not, Lord."

16. "If there would not be the love of private possession, would there not be peace?"

17. "There would be, Lord."

18. "I recognise the earth as earth. But I have no craving for it," said the Lord.

19. "Therefore it is, say I, that by extirpating all cravings, by not lusting after them, but by destroying and abandoning and renouncing them all that I acquired enlightenment.

20. "Seek to be partakers, brethren, not of the world's goods but of my doctrines. For craving brings about attachment and attachment enslaves the mind."

21. In these words did the Blessed Lord explain to Ananda and the brethren the evils of the acquisitive instinct.

§ 3. *His Joy at the Beautiful*

1. The Buddha was so fond of the beautiful that he might well bear an *alias* and be called Buddha, the Lover of the Beautiful.

2. So he preached to his followers: "Be in the company of the lovely."

3. Addressing the bhikkhus, he said:

4. "Monks, I know not of any other single thing of such power to cause the arising of good states if not yet arisen, or the waning of evil states already arisen, as friendship with the lovely.

5. "In one who is a friend of what is lovely, good states not arisen do arise and evil states already arisen wane. Evil states and devotion to evil states wanes, lack of devotion to good states disappears, good states and devotion thereto arise; lack of devotion to evil states increases.

6. "Monks, I know not of any other single thing of such power to prevent the arising of the limbs of

wisdom, if not yet arisen, or, if they have already arisen, to prevent their reaching fulfilment by cultivation thereof, as unsystematic attention.

7. "In him who practices unsystematic attention, monks, the limbs of wisdom if not yet arisen, arise not and if arisen they reach not fulfilment by cultivation thereof.

8. "Of slight account, monks, is the loss of such things as relatives. Miserable indeed among losses is the loss of wisdom.

9. "Of slight account, monks, is the increase of such things as relatives. Chief of all the increases is that of wisdom.

10. "Wherefore I say, monks, ye should train yourselves thus: 'We will increase in wisdom.' You must train yourselves to win that.

11. "Of slight account, monks, is the increase of such things as wealth. Chief of all the increases is that of wisdom. Wherefore I say, monks, thus, must ye train yourselves. 'We will increase in wisdom.' You must train yourselves to win that.

12. "Of slight account, monks, is the loss of such things as reputation. Miserable indeed is the loss of wisdom."

§ 4. *His Love for the Lovely*

1. Once the Exalted One was staying among the Sakyans at Sakkara, a Sakyan township.

2. Then the venerable Ananda came to the Exalted One, saluted him and sat down at one side. So seated, the venerable Ananda said this:

3. "The half of the holy life, Lord, is friendship with what is lovely, association with what is lovely, intimacy with what is lovely!"

4. "Say not so, Ananda! Say not so, Ananda! It is the whole, not the half, of the holy life,—this friendship, this association, this intimacy with what is lovely.

5. "Of a monk who is a friend, an associate, an intimate of what is lovely we may expect this,—that he

will develop the Ariyan eightfold way, that he will make much of the Ariyan eightfold way.

6. "And how, Ananda, does such a monk develop and make much of the Ariyan eightfold way?

7. "Herein, Ananda, he cultivates the right view, which is based on detachment, on dispassion, on cessation, which ends in self-surrender. He cultivates the right aim, which is so based and concerned: likewise right speech, right action, right living, right effort, right mindfulness and right concentration, which ends in self-surrender.

8. "That, Ananda, is how a monk who is a friend, an associate, an intimate of what is lovely, cultivates and makes much of the Ariyan eightfold way.

9. "This is the method, Ananda, by which you are to understand how the whole of this holy life consists in friendship, in association, in intimacy with what is lovely.

10. "Indeed, Ananda, beings liable to decay, liable to death, liable to grief, woe, lamentation and despair, are liberated therefrom because of their friendship with what is lovely.

11. "It is by this method, Ananda, that you are to understand how the whole of this holy life consists in friendship, in association, in intimacy with what is lovely."

EPILOGUE

1. Tributes to the Buddha's Greatness.
2. A Vow to Spread His Dhamma.
3. A Prayer for His Return to His Native Land.

§ 1. *Tributes to the Buddha's Greatness*

1. The Buddha was born 2500 years ago.

2. What do modern thinkers and scientists say of him and his Dhamma? An anthology of their thoughts on the subject will be useful.

3. Prof. S. S. Raghavachar says:

4. " The period immediately antecedent to the life of the Buddha was one of the darkest ages in the history of India.

5. " It was intellectually a backward age. The thought of the time was characterised by an implicit veneration for the authority of the scriptures.

6. " Morally it was a dark age.

7. " Morality meant for the believing Hindus the correct performance of rites and ceremonies enjoined in the holy texts.

8. " The really ethical ideas like self-sacrifice or purity of will did not find appropriate positions in the moral consciousness of the time."

9. Mr. R. J. Jackson says:

10. " The unique character of the Buddha's teaching is shown forth in the study of Indian Religious thought.

11. " In the hymns of the Rig-Veda we see man's thoughts turned outwards, away from himself, to the world of the gods.

12. " Buddhism directed man's search inwards to the potentiality hidden within himself.

13. " In the Vedas we find prayer, praise and worship.

14. " In Buddhism for the first time we find training of the mind to make it act righteously."

15. Winwood Reade says:

16. " It is when we open the book of nature, it is when we read the story of evolution through millions of years, written in blood and tears, it is when we study the laws regulating life, the laws productive of development, that we see plainly how illusive is the theory that God is love.

17. " In everything there is wicked profligate and abandoned waste. Of all animals that are born only a very small percentage survives.

18. " Eat and be eaten is the rule in the ocean, the air, the forest. Murder is the law of growth."

19. This is what Reade says in his " Martyrdom of Man." How different is the Dhamma of the Buddha.

20. This is what Dr. Ranjan Roy says:

21. " Throughout the second half of the nineteenth century the three laws of conservation held sway. Nobody challenged them.

22. " They were the laws of matter, mass and energy.

23. " They were the trump cards of those idealists who cherished the thought of their being indestructible.

24. " Nineteenth century scientists professed them as the governing factors of creation.

25. " Nineteenth century scientists professed them as constituting the fundamental nature of the Universe.

26. " They conceived that the Universe was filled with indestructible atoms.

27. " Just as the nineteenth century was drawing to a close, Sir J. J. Thompson and his followers began to hammer the atoms.

28. " Surprisingly enough the atoms began to break up into fragments.

29. " These fragments came to be called electrons, all similar and charged with negative electricity.

30. " Atoms hailed by Maxwell as imperishable foundation-stones of the Universe or Reality broke down.

31. " They got broken into tiny particles, protons and electrons charged with positive and negative electricity respectively.

32. " The concept of a fixed unalterable mass abandoned Science for good. In this century the Universal belief is that matter is being annihilated at every instant.

33. "The Buddha's doctrine of Anicca (transitoriness) is confirmed.

34. "Science has proved that the course of the Universe is a grouping and dissolution and regrouping.

35. "The trend of Modern Science is the trend of an ultimate reality, unity and diversity of ego.

36. "Modern Science is the echoing of the Buddhists doctrines of transitoriness (annica) and of egolessness (anatta)."

37. Mr. E. G. Taylor, in his "Buddhism and Modern Thought," says:

38. "Man has been ruled by external authority long enough. If he is to be truly civilized, he must learn to be ruled by his own principles. Buddhism is the earliest ethical system where man is called upon to have himself governed by himself.

39. "Therefore a progressive world needs Buddhism to teach it this supreme lesson."

40. The Reverend Leslie Bolton, unitarian minister, says:

41. "I see in the spiritual psychology of Buddhism its most powerful contribution.

42. "Unitarian Christians like Buddhists reject the external authority of church books or creeds and find in man himself the guiding lamp.

43. "Unitarians see in Jesus and Gautama noble exponents of the way of life."

44. Prof. Dwight Goddard says:

45. "Among the world's religious teachers, Buddha alone has the glory of having rightly judged the intrinsic greatness of man's capacity to work out his salvation without extraneous aid."

46. "If the worth of a truly great man consists in his raising the worth of all mankind, who is better entitled to be called truly great than the Blessed One.

47. "Who instead of degrading him by placing another being over him, has exalted him to the highest pinnacle of wisdom and love."

48. Mr. E. J. Mills, author of "Buddhism," says:

49. "In no other religion are the values of

knowledge and evil of ignorance so much insisted upon as they are in Buddhism."

50. " No other religion lays so much stress upon keeping one's eyes open.

51. " No other religion has formulated such deep laid plans for mental culture."

52. Prof. W. T. Stace says in his Buddhist ethics :

53. "The Buddhist moral ideal, the Arhat, had to be both morally and intellectually great.

54. " He had to be a philosopher, as well as a man of good conduct.

55. " Knowledge was always stressed by Buddhism as essential to Salvation, and ignorance as one of the two main causes of failure to attain it (craving or attachment being the other).

56. " On the contrary, knowledge has never been any part of the Christian ideal man."

57. " Owing to the unphilosophical character of its founder in the Christian Scheme of thought the moral side of man has been divorced from the intellectual side.

58. " Far more of the world's misery is caused by stupidity and blind faith than by wickedness.

59. " The Buddha did not allow this."

60. Enough unto this to show how great and how unique is the Buddha and his Dhamma.

61. Who would not say let such a one be our Master ?

§ 2. *A Vow to Spread His Dhamma*

1. " There are beings without limit,
   Let us take the vow to convey them all across.
2. There are depravities in us without number,
   Let us take the vow to extinguish them all.
3. There are truths without end,
   Let us take the vow to comprehend them all.
4. There is the Way of Buddha without comparison,
   Let us take the vow to accomplish it perfectly."

Encyclopædia of Religion & Ethics, Vol. X, p. 168.

§ 3. *A Prayer for His Return to His Native Land*

1. "O Exalted One! I trust myself wholeheartedly
To the Tathagata whose light pervades, VIII
Without any impediment, the regions in the ten quarters, 599
And express my earnest desire to be born in Thy Land.

2. In realizing in vision the appearance of Thy Land,
I know that it surpasses all realms in the threefold existence.

3. That it is like sky, embracing all,
Vast and spacious without boundaries.

4. Thy mercy and compassion in accordance with the righteous way,
Is an outgrowth of the stock of merits (accumulated by Thee), which are beyond all worldly good;

5. And Thy light permeates everywhere,
Like the mirrors of the Sun and the Moon.

6. Let me pray that all beings, having been born there,
Shall proclaim the Truth, like Buddha Thyself.

7. Herewith I write down this essay and utter these verses,
And pray that I could see Thee, O Buddha, face to face,

8. And that I could, together with all my fellow-beings,
Attain the birth in the Land of Bliss."

Encyclopædia of Religion & Ethics, Vol. X, p. 169.